To those who spoke unheard before us.

OUR VOICES
Essays in Culture, Ethnicity, and Communication

Third Edition

Alberto González
Bowling Green State University

Marsha Houston
University of Alabama, Tuscaloosa

Victoria Chen
San Francisco State University

Foreword by Orlando L. Taylor

Roxbury Publishing Company
Los Angeles, California

Library of Congress Cataloging-in-Publication Data

Our Voices: Essays in Culture, Ethnicity, and Communication [edited by] Alberto González, Marsha Houston, Victoria Chen; foreword by Orlando L. Taylor–3rd ed.
p. cm.
Includes bibliographical references and index.
ISBN 1-891487-35-3(pbk.)
1. Intercultural Communication. 2. Ethnology–United States. 3. United States–Ethnic Relations. I. González, Alberto, 1954– II. Houston, Marsha, III. Chen, Victoria. Our Voices.
GN345.6.0927 2000
303.48'2–dc21

99-37121
CIP

Our Voices: Essays in Culture, Ethnicity, and Communication (*Third Edition*)

Publisher: Claude Teweles
Managing Editor: Dawn VanDercreek
Production Editor: Joshua H. R. Levine
Copy Editor: Ann West
Typography: Joan M. Cochrane/Synergistic Data Systems
Cover Design: Marnie Kenney

Printed on acid-free paper in the United States of America. This book meets the standards for recycling of the Environmental Protection Agency.

ISBN 1-891487-35-3

Roxbury Publishing Company
P.O. Box 491044
Los Angeles, California 90049-9044
Tel.: (310) 473-3312 • Fax: (310) 473-4490
Email: roxbury@crl.com
Website: www.roxbury.net

Contents

Acknowledgments xi

Foreword xii
Orlando L. Taylor

Introduction xiii
Alberto González, Marsha Houston, and Victoria Chen

Part I: Naming Ourselves

1. (De)hyphenated Identity: The Double Voice in
   The Woman Warrior 3

   Victoria Chen
   The double voice in Kingston's *The Woman Warrior* is
   explored in the context of Chinese American women's
   hyphenated identity.

2. Dis/orienting Identities: Asian Americans, History,
   and Intercultural Communication 13

   Thomas Nakayama
   Nakayama argues for the centrality of the Japanese
   American experience in the making of American culture
   and history.

3. How I Came to Know 'In Self Realization
   There Is Truth' 19

   Sidney A. Ribeau
   Ribeau examines the importance of the articulation of
   the African American experience.

4. Names, Narratives, and the Evolution of
   Ethnic Identity 25

   Dolores V. Tanno
   Tanno describes how each ethnic self-reference communicates a story and how multiple stories provide significance to an American identity.

Part II: Negotiating Sexuality and Gender

5. Jewish and/or Woman: Identity and
   Communicative Style 31

   Sheryl Perlmutter Bowen
   Perlmutter Bowen explores the particular intersection
   of her Jewish upbringing and the feminism she
   adopted as an adult.

6. Remembering Selena 37

Alberto González
Jennifer L. Willis-Rivera
The "borderland" metaphor is used to explore the discourses surrounding the late tejana singer.

7. When Miss America Was Always White.................. 42

Navita Cummings James
James reflects on the meaning of blackness and black womanhood through family stories and personal experiences.

8. Illusive Reflections: African American Women on Primetime Television 47

Bishetta D. Merritt
Images of African American women on primetime television are critically examined.

9. Black Queer Identity, Imaginative Rationality, and the Language of Home.................................. 54

Charles I. Nero
The meaning of home and community for African American gay men is explored through poetry and song lyrics, as well as feminist and gay/lesbian theory.

Part III: Representing Cultural Knowledge in Interpersonal and Mass Media Contexts

10. Negotiating Cyberspace/Negotiating RL 63

Radhika Gajjala
Gajjala discusses virtual life as created through information communication technologies and the (im)possibilities for empowerment and cross-cultural dialogue.

11. The Rhetoric of *La Familia* Among Mexican Americans 72

Margarita Gangotena
Gangotena uses the concept of *la familia* to explore Mexican American family communication.

12. When Mississippi Chinese Talk......................... 84

Gwendolyn Gong
Gong describes speech strategies used by Chinese from the Mississippi Delta.

13. The Reason Why We Sing: Understanding Traditional African American Worship 92

Janice D. Hamlet
Hamlet explores how the rhetorical style of preachers in traditional black churches preserves the cultural identity of black communities.

14. When Black Women Talk With White Women: Why the
    Dialogues Are Difficult 98
    Marsha Houston
    Houston explores ways to build satisfying conversa-
    tions between black and white women.

15. Latina/o Experiences With Mediated Communication 105
    Diana I. Ríos
    Ríos discusses the dual functions of mass media in
    Mexican American communities in Texas.

16. Native American Culture and Communication Through
    Humor 113
    Charmaine Shutiva
    Shutiva challenges some of the stereotypes about Na-
    tive Americans and discusses the role that humor plays
    in their culture.

Part IV: Celebrating Cultures

17. Capturing the Spirit of *Kwanzaa* 121
    Detine L. Bowers
    Bowers describes *Kwanzaa* as a ritual that invites a
    spiritual connection to African heritage.

18. A House as Symbol, a House as Family: Mamaw and
    Her Oklahoma Cherokee Family 125
    Lynda Dee Dixon
    Dixon reflects on a Cherokee matriarch who insured
    family unity by providing a home for family reunions
    and remembrance.

19. Communicating Good Luck During the
    Chinese New Year 129
    Mary Fong
    Fong discusses good luck expressed through speech
    and gift-giving practices that display good will and af-
    fection.

20. Hybrid Revivals: Defining Asian Indian Ethnicity
    Through Celebration 133
    Radha S. Hegde
    Hedge describes how Hindu festivals inspire their par-
    ticipants despite outside efforts to limit "foreign" cul-
    tural gatherings.

Part V: Valuing and Contesting Languages

21. Identity and Struggle in Jamaican Talk 141

    Dexter B. Gordon
    Gordon describes the creative "survival mechanisms"
    in Jamaican talk that privilege the local and counter the
    colonial.

22. The Power of *Wastah* in Lebanese Speech 150

    Mahboub Hashem
    Hashem examines *wastah* as an effective Lebanese
    method of mediating conflicts and relationships.

23. *Wa-Zha-Zhe I-E*: Notions on a Dying
    Ancestral Language 155

    Steven B. Pratt
    Merry C. Buchanan
    Pratt and Buchanan foresee the end of the Osage lan-
    guage, and they describe the immense responsibility
    that comes with trying to save a culture's way of speak-
    ing.

24. Broadening the View of Black Language Use: Toward a
    Better Understanding of Words and Worlds 164

    Karla D. Scott
    Scott examines misconceptions about black language
    use and explains how local ways of speaking are mark-
    ers of identity and solidarity.

25. Confessions of a Thirty-Something Hip-Hop (Old) Head 171

    Eric King Watts
    Watts interprets the tensions that arise when popular
    culture takes the "N-word" from private in-house dia-
    logues and distributes it in easy-to-open packages of
    hip.

Part VI: Living in Bicultural Relationships

26. Sapphire and Sappho: Allies in Authenticity 179

    Brenda J. Allen
    Allen describes her interracial friendship with a les-
    bian woman and how the two overcame sanctions
    against such a relationship.

27. 'I Know It Was the Blood': Defining the Biracial Self in a
    Euro-American Society 184

    Tina M. Harris
    In exploring the biracial identities of her students, Har-
    ris comes to appreciate her own biracial heritage.

28. Being *Hapa*: A Choice for Cultural Empowerment 190

   Diane M. Kimoto
   Kimoto reflects on her Japanese and Mexican heritage
   and the role of culture in raising her child.

29. Living In/Between 195

   Richard Morris
   Morris describes a life caught between two discourses,
   one that valorizes a Mescalero worldview and another
   that negates it.

Part VII: Traversing Cultural Paths

30. Women Writing Borders, Borders Writing Women:
    Immigration, Assimilation, and the Politics of Speaking 207

   Aimee M. Carillo Rowe
   Carrillo Rowe deconstructs immigration politics as she
   examines her family's migratory history.

31. How We Know What We Know About Americans:
    Chinese Sojourners Account for Their Experiences 220

   Ling Chen
   Chen uses conversational episodes to examine assump-
   tions and misunderstandings between Chinese and
   Americans in the United States.

32. The Cultural Experience of Space and Body: A Reading of
    Latin American and Anglo American Comportment in Public . . 228
    Lozano discusses assumptions about "public space" in
    Anglo American and Latin American cultures.
   Elizabeth Lozano

33. Regionalism and Communication: Exploring Chinese
    Immigrant Perspectives 235

   Casey Man Kong Lum
   Lum discusses regional differences among Chinese
   communities in New York City and how ethnic identity
   is maintained.

34. Traversing Disparate Cultures in a Transnational
    World: A Bicultural/Hybrid Experience 242

   Maria Rogers-Pascual
   Drawing from her Mexican and U.S. cultural experiences, Rogers-Pascual elaborates notions of hybridity
   and Fourth World orientation.

Appendices

Suggested Questions for Discussion 255
Supplementary Readings 258
About the Contributors 263

Acknowledgments

We wish to acknowledge that this volume represents the efforts of more than the editors, contributors, and publication staff. We thank Claude Teweles and Josh Levine at Roxbury Publishing Company for their patience, support, and editorial suggestions. Our thanks also to the many adopters of the Second Edition; the comments from these instructors and their students were essential to the new edition of this anthology. We are grateful for their insights and encouragement. Finally, our deep thanks to the following individuals for their various contributions, often on very short notice: J.B. González and Rosalinda Cantú. ◆

Foreword

Orlando L. Taylor
Howard University

One of my favorite stories involves a little boy who loved to hear his mother read tales to him about lions. The boy was simply fascinated with the lion, king of the jungle. A regal and most beautiful animal who never, absolutely never, lost in battle when in combat with another animal.

But one thing was most perplexing to the little boy about these stories. It was the fact that the lion always lost battles in which the opponent was a man.

How could it be, the boy wondered, that this most powerful animal warrior, who never lost a battle when in combat with other animals, would invariably lose when in combat with a man?

One day, the boy asked his mother about this. In all of the stories she read to him, why did the lion always manage to lose against man?

With a slight smile, his mother replied, "Son, that's an easy question to answer. You see, as long as men write the books in which these stories appear, the lion will always lose!"

The book you are about to read, *Our Voices* (Third Edition), reminds me so much of this tale. As long as the story of human communication—whether presented in journal articles, books, or monographs— is written largely from a selective, traditionally privileged viewpoint, those people without such privilege always lose because of limited opportunities for contributing stories in their own voices. All of us who study communication also lose the chance to encounter this multitude of human communicative experiences in our literature.

Since the First Edition's publication in 1994, *Our Voices* has offered publishing access for scholars from groups traditionally unrepresented or marginalized in communication studies. Here, these individuals have the opportunity to tell cultural communication stories from their particular cultural perspectives. Providing such a forum is critical to all of us who desire a deeper and more concrete understanding of cultural diversity and, thereby, of the human condition.

As an African American male born before World War II, I feel enlightened and empowered when I encounter the visions of the gendered, generational, and cultural groups represented in *Our Voices*. The stories, critiques, ideas, and emotions shared by these authors illumine both our common humanity and the immensely diverse range of human cultural communicative experiences. In this latest edition, *Our Voices* remains an important forum through which cultural voices that were muted for far too long are brought to light and celebrated as we begin our journey into a new millennium. ✦

Introduction

We began this project in April, 1991, during a panel titled Cultural Diversity and Communication: Exploring the Curriculum at the Southern States Speech Communication Association Convention. Because the organizers were sensitive to the ways in which speech communication had previously silenced or marginalized the perspectives of ethnic minority scholars, we often found ourselves speaking as the "minority voices" on conference panels. During one panel, a note made its way down the table from Marsha Houston to Alberto González and Victoria Chen. It proposed that we compile our voices and those of others we knew who were not being sufficiently heard—and develop a single book of essays. The book would offer the views of minority groups different from those in volumes already written from the cultural majority perspective. It would also serve as a point of departure for those interested in exploring how the theoretically grounded telling of experience constructs and informs about a culture and its participants. The result was the birth of the first edition of *Our Voices* in 1994.

Since then we have used this book in our classes, consulted instructors who have adopted it for their students, and heard from various people who generously shared their thoughts and comments with us. Some have told us that our work has provided a refreshing, challenging, and useful perspective for studying intercultural communication, and others have suggested different topics for inclusion. We were further delighted and deeply honored that the book won the 1994 Distinguished Scholarship Book Award given by the International and Intercultural Communication Division of the Speech Communication Association. Nothing gratifies us more than knowing that the contributors' and our ideas have been so recognized and valued in our own discipline. Moreover, it has also come to our attention that the perspectives we encouraged in this volume have found their way into other scholars' works. We believe that we have made a difference in how people study and understand intercultural communication.

In the Second Edition, we expanded the range of marginalized cultural voices by adding two new sections: Celebrating Cultures and Living in Bicultural Relationships. The concepts behind these sections stem from the comments of those who read and used the First Edition. The section titled Celebrating Cultures extends beyond those voices critical of the discrimination and injustice experienced by minority groups to emphasize that every culture is something to celebrate. The essays here invite readers to participate in the celebratory activities that are vividly described. The cultural significance of these celebrations changes over time within evolving social and political contexts, transforming and recreating the meaning of communication through their cultural practice. The section titled Living in Bicultural Relationships highlights the complex process of the social and political construction of "race." The authors discuss the possibilities for genuine interracial friendship and the struggles of mixed-race individuals who endeavor to construct and enact coherent cultural identities. Some authors' biracial backgrounds provide them with a unique challenge, especially in a society where there is an ongoing and paradoxical conflict between the value of diversity and the promotion of homogeneity.

In this Third Edition, we have added another new section: Valuing and Contesting Languages. The four new essays in this section recognize the political, emotional, and pragmatic dimensions of language. Three new essays are also included in Part III and Part VII. In Part III, the new essay deals with cultural experiences in cyberspace. The first new essay in Part VII addresses immigration politics, and the second new essay critically examines the hybrid experiences in a transnational world.

Spurred by the emerging debate on immigration policies and the intensifying interracial conflict in the United States during the late 1990s, the direction of definitions of race and culture is shifting. Some despair over the flux of new immigrants and the heightened visibility of minority groups, but others find cultural diversity emancipating and a unique strength in America, celebrating such changes toward a more colorful and polyphonic society. Because these issues require insightful and passionate interpretation, we have added two new chapters about immigration: Chapter 33, "Traversing Disparate Cultures in a Transnational World: A Bicultural/Hybrid Experience," and Chapter 34, "Women Writing Borders, Borders Writing Women: Immigration, Assimilation, and the Politics of Speaking." Our task for future editions remains challenging. We now feel a sense of responsibility and urgency to provide more space to diverse cultural voices and perspectives.

In this Third Edition, we maintain the same theoretical view that race, culture, gender, class, and ethnicity are not "external" variables but rather inherent features in an ongoing process of constructing how collectively we understand and participate in the larger social, cultural, and political discourse. This in turn continues to shape the way individuals perceive these issues and acknowledge the multiple and historically conflicting narratives that create and recreate what we call American society.

Purposes and Goals of This Anthology

Beginning in the 1960s and continuing well into the 1980s, the mission of intercultural studies was largely to prepare students for travel abroad, which usually meant Europe. Studies of cultural communities in the United States were considered "intracultural," just as America was thought to represent one culture. At best, non-mainstream cultures, like radioactive elements, were assumed to possess a diminishing half-life due to the process of assimilation. At worst, such cultures were deemed non-standard, irrelevant, and inferior.

But today, a different reality challenges the presumption that a passport is required for intercultural experience. A continuous flow of immigration extends to the United States, especially from Asian and Latin American countries; demographic trends indicate that ethnic populations are increasing more rapidly than Euro-American populations; accessible air travel allows first- and second-generation U.S. citizens to visit their ancestral lands with relative ease; racial and ethnic populations, unlike their European predecessors, are reluctant to relinquish cultural origins; and increasingly interdependent and volatile global economies and politics bring awareness of the world's people into our everyday lives. The metaphor of the melting pot has been challenged by a social movement that not only celebrates cultural pluralism but also engages a critique of the assimilationist tradition. *Our Voices* was inspired by this dynamic reality. It is intended as a resource for exploring the relationships between culture and communication.

The resulting essays examine communication in a variety of settings and from a variety of cultural perspectives. *Our Voices* signifies that each contributor is writing from the perspective of his or her cultural experience instead of writing to accommodate the voice that is culturally desirable by the mainstream Anglo standard. This collected work offers an alternative for those interested in learning something about culture, ethnicity, and communication from the viewpoint of ethnic scholars. Our premise is that communication has much to do with specific individuals' perspectives in social interaction, and that one person's unique descriptions and interpretations of his or her experience will contribute to a better understanding of that person's cultural group as a whole.

One purpose of this book is to provide a discussion of the communication styles and practices of cultural groups from these writers' points of view. Currently in American intercultural studies, writers from the dominant culture and some ethnic writers who represent and reproduce the interests of the dominant culture often "speak for" cultural communities to which they are unrelated. Through the privileged form of scientific inquiry, these scholars often display unfamiliarity with the specific practices that lend significance to the general cultural categories or dimensions that are created. Furthermore, we rarely hear any single cultural participant's voice in the abundant intercultural work that has been produced by various researchers. Surely, research by the cultural outsider is legitimate and can be useful, but the literature does not yet reflect a *balance* between the voices of the dominant perspective and our voices—the voices in this volume.

Many of the contributors to this book teach courses in intercultural communication. They report that students and instructors alike complain of one ironic fact: the lack of a truly intercultural perspective in intercultural literature. In a field that has traditionally adopted a Eurocentric theoretical and methodological approach, this book offers the first collection of works by so-called "minority" scholars' who address cultural and intercultural issues in what we hope are accessible, helpful, and intriguing essays.

A second purpose of this volume is to maintain a consistent focus on communication and culture. Each essay applies concepts and ideas from areas of the communication field (such as rhetoric, mass communication, and interpersonal communication) that examine how culture influences the creation and sharing of meaning and how various meanings and symbols constitute what we call cultural reality. Our goal then is to place communication practices within specific cultural contexts. Each essay addresses the question "What is a cultural explanation and interpretation for this communication phenomenon from the ethnic scholar's perspective?"

A third purpose is to invite *experience* into our understanding and studying of cultural communication. Shuter (1990) noted that most intercultural research is essentially directed toward "theory validation" and fails to describe how people actually live and interact. He argued, "The challenge for intercultural communication in the 1990s. . . is to develop a research direction and teaching agenda that returns culture to preeminence . . ." (238). The notion that theory is developed solely through the traditionally defined scientific paradigm is ethnocentric. As Christian (1988) observed, "People of color have always theorized—but in forms quite different from the Western form of abstract logic. . . [O]ur theorizing (and I intentionally use the verb rather than the noun) is often in narrative forms, in the stories we create, in riddle and proverbs, in the play with language, because dynamic rather than fixed ideas seem more to our liking" (68). What Marsha Houston wrote of feminist research also applies to intercultural research. She stated that as students of human communication we should be open to "research methods that free communication scholars to emphasize the experiential rather than the experimental, the specific case as much as the general tendency" (Stanback 1989, 190).

Some readers may not recognize this anthology as a product of "typical" intercultural research. It is one of our goals to expand and recreate the notion and scope of "scholarly work," providing an alternative form to learn about cultural practices and to engage in intellectual conversations. We take the anthropologists' idea of "experience-near understanding" very seriously, believing that one can be better enlightened by the rich stories and experiences told and lived by real people than by scientific findings reported by researchers. We also view this experience-driven approach as a complement to theory-driven approaches in intercultural communication research. Part of being human is our capacity to tell stories and to actively interpret social activities and cultural experiences. As Rabinow and Sullivan (1987) stated, "This interpretive turn refocuses attention on the concrete varieties of cultural meaning, in their particularity and complex texture . . ." (5–6).

A fourth purpose of this anthology is to demonstrate the vast cultural diversity within any given racial, ethnic, and national category. In much of the intercultural literature, studies of African American, Asian, Asian American, Native American, and Latino/a communication tend to treat these cultures monolithically; that is, they reduce each category to one type. Our premise is that there is not "one" style of any particular ethnic group any more than there is one style of Anglo American communication. Collectively, our essays explore the rich variety of communication practices within a broad cultural spectrum.

Approaching Cultural Intersections: Our Influences

On the whole, we do not turn to the academic world for intellectual emancipation. After centuries of exclusion from and misrepresentation in academic literature, we derive our warrants from sources that we trust and appreciate, knowing that they are perhaps unfamiliar or may not be credible to mainstream interculturalists.

The pressure is great to put aside our cultural selves in order to gain scholarly credibility. We are led to think that the two cannot coexist. In *Talking Back: Thinking Feminist, Thinking Black,* bell hooks recounts her experience as a graduate student in English. She concludes that "The academic setting, the academic discourse I work in, is not a known site for truthtelling" (1989, 29). Her professors and peers, women and men alike, required of hooks a transformation out of her cultural self and into someone they recognized. With such recognition came the possibility of control. "Within the educational institutions," she continues, "where we learn to develop and strengthen our writing and analytical skills, we also learn to think, write, and talk in a manner that shifts attention away from personal experience" (77).

Like hooks, many authors in this volume know all too well the struggle to avoid control and the determination to allow the personal experience of culture to inform the study of communication. This is particularly challenging because a number of communication departments in the United States may not even acknowledge what we do as research, given the traditionally privileged form of scholarship.

Inventing Landmarks

Our influences are interdisciplinary, contradictory, and often contentious. They are noted in the supplementary reading lists following each unit in this volume. We do not include them for any purpose other than to indicate those sources that resonate with our own experiences as members of cultural groups. In the field of communication, we invent and celebrate our own landmarks. The early work of Turner (1949), for example, remains a point of reference that exemplifies the merging of scholarship and the exploration of one's own cultural present.

Landmarks also include studies that assume and represent the "naturalness" of our everyday interaction and issues that concern us. Ramos and Ramos (1979) wrote that "the more I read and do research, the more I realize that there is a contradiction between my own self-image and what others have written about how I am supposed to be" (49–50). Therefore, the publication of articles by scholars, such as Sedano (1980), Garner (1983), and Nakagawa (1990), and of such books as *Talkin' and Testifyin': The Language of Black America* (Smitherman 1977) and The Afrocentric Idea (Asante 1987) is important because the analyses of communication grew out of a social context we could recognize. What had always been vital and visible to us suddenly became visible to the field of communication as well. The ordinary and extraordinary communicative practices and patterns of meaning among people of color began to inform the field's understanding of human communication.

Thus, the theoretical position of this anthology is couched within a broad social constructionist and interpretive framework. As Berger and Luckmann (1967) stated, "[T]he sociology of knowledge must concern itself with whatever passes for 'knowledge' in a society, regardless of the ultimate validity or invalidity (by whatever criteria) of such 'knowledge.' And . . . the sociology of knowledge must seek to understand the processes by which this is done in such a way that the taken-for-granted 'reality' congeals for the [hu]man in the street" (3). Within this social constructionist approach we see both culture and communication as human creations and as ongoing processes of making history and meanings. The strength of this perspective is that it takes communication to be the primary social process by which we create meanings and engage in cultural practices. We recognize and welcome the reflexive connection between social structure and an individual's action, between communication and culture (Cronen, Chen, and Pearce 1988). Furthermore, the social constructionist approach also highlights the fluid nature of studying communication and culture. It draws our attention to the specificity, uniqueness, and richness of individual cases.

An interpretive framework allows the introduction of the ethnography of communication in our field, which we consider to be akin to our approach to understanding cultural communication. More than two decades ago, Philipsen (1975) concluded his study of the cultural talk of a Chicago neighborhood by stating, "We have barely any information on what groups in the United States view speaking as an effective means of social influence and what alternatives they envision. Such a deficit in the fund of information should be remedied by descriptive and comparative studies of American speech communities" (22). More recently, Carbaugh's (1988a, 1990) work examined various forms of cultural talking with the assumption that communication must be studied in a specifically situated cultural setting. Whereas the ethnography of communication examines shared cultural meanings and rules that render the individual's action intelligible, this book explores personal voices that contribute to shared cultural meanings.

Playing With Conceptualization

A brief introduction of our conceptualization of culture and intercultural communication may be useful to the reader. First, we want to emphasize the importance of regarding culture as a dynamic, communication-based idea. Humans are organizing beings, and culture is an organizing term. Culture is an idea for recognizing and understanding how groups create communities and participate in social activities. Geertz (1973) insisted that "culture is public because meaning is" (12) and noted that "[i]t is through the flow of behavior—or more precisely, social action—that cultural forms find articulation" (17). As an ordering term, *culture* renders coherent the values held and the actions performed in a community. At the same time, cultural participants engage in communication that constantly defines and redefines the community.

We are concerned with the production of cultural knowledge. As Geertz (1983) pointed out in *Local Knowledge*, we often treat our cultural knowledge as common sense, as something "natural" beyond question. We take our acculturation for granted without realizing that our experience is accumulative and always historically based. In the study of cultures, we attempt to learn as much as we can about this natural side to the patterns of everyday life. Culture then can be said to refer to a community of meaning and a shared body of local knowledge rather than a region or a nation. Charmaine Shutiva for example, is Native American, but this does not describe her culturally. Her cultural community is the Acoma of New Mexico. Gwendolyn Gong is Chinese American, and her cultural community is the Chinese of the Mississippi Delta. Both are American citizens, yet their dialogue is intercultural.

Second, we see culture as an idea that is creating and being recreated symbolically. For example, one day, Alberto González had a meeting with Charmaine Shutiva. When the meeting was over, both had to walk to a classroom in a nearby building. During the walk, a thunderstorm began. González offered his umbrella to Shutiva, but she declined. "We pray for rain in the desert," she said, laughing in the storm. "It's against my teachings to shield myself from something so sacred." As the two walked on, González ignored the glares of passersby who judged him selfish for not sharing his umbrella. Shutiva then turned to him and said, "But that doesn't mean we can't run!"

Langer (1942) wrote that language transforms experience. For the Acoma, the desire for rain in the desert was transformed into solemn prayer. Moving beyond language, for Shutiva the prayer's meaning was transformed into a nonverbal act (i.e., refusing the umbrella and exposing herself to rain). In this episode one cultural belief of the Acomas was enacted and reconstructed through verbal and nonverbal symbols. Access to symbols becomes access to the shared meanings of a people. For Geertz (1973), cultural analysis is "sorting out the structures of signification" (9). And as Carbaugh (1988b) stated, "[I]f one wants to understand the action persons do, from their point of view, one should listen for the terms they use to discuss it" (217). Both statements suggest that cultural meanings are constructed through people's use of symbols, both verbal and nonverbal. Communication then is an ongoing process of reconstructing the meanings of the symbols through social interaction.

Our experience-driven view of intercultural communication allows a reevaluation of previous literature. For example, Hall (1976) wrote, "[T]he natural act of thinking is greatly modified by culture . . . [t]here are many different and legitimate ways of thinking; we in the West value one of these ways above all others—the one we call 'logic,' a linear system that has been with us since Socrates" (9). From our perspective, Hall is only partially right. Western societies *have* privileged logical demonstration and scientific reasoning as "ways of knowing." "The West," however, is not one culture. Hall could not contemplate that various cultural communities exist *within* the West that privilege epistemologies other than logic and linear reasoning. Furthermore, in Hall's influential work, we miss the voices of real cultural participants who narrate their personal stories and cultural experiences to shed light on the ways of knowing as described by the scholar.

A useful conception of culture allows a critique of power in society. We believe communication and social power to be interdependent. Kramerae, Schulz, and O'Barr (1984) noted that "Speech functions in different ways for different cultures as well as for different individuals and groups within a culture" (13). In a hierarchically stratified society, the communication styles and practices of every individual are not accorded equal prestige. Members of privileged social groups have the material resources and social position to define their ways of speaking and acting as "standard" and to define other groups as "deviant," "incompetent," or "powerless."

Yet, as individuals and groups negotiate their relationships with one another, ways of speaking are redefined or recoded according to culture-specific criteria. For example, Marsha Houston remembers an African American woman who had been a top debater at a predominately white high school. During her first year at a traditionally black women's college, this student ran for class president. Her campaign speech, a model of the low-keyed Anglo American rhetorical style taught in her high school public-speaking class, was greeted by her classmates with polite applause. Her opponent's speech, enlivened by the high-keyed Afrocentric delivery style characteristic of such African American orators as Jesse Jackson, received an enthusiastic ovation. The student later confided, "When I heard the audience reaction to my opponent, I knew I'd lost."

The contributors to this volume demonstrate how socially privileged speakers use communication to diminish the voices of those less privileged and how cultural communities are empowered by a recreation and reinvention of historical-traditional communication forms, styles, and strategies. Admittedly, in a North American society that tends to value the universal over the particular, attention to cultural community can be both emancipating and awkward.

Yet if human experiences are indeed characterized by storytelling and the creation of meanings, we offer this volume as an invitation to a form of intercultural communication inquiry in which ethnic scholars create their own research agenda and contribute to a truly polyphonic cultural melody.

The Essays in This Book

Each essay represents what each contributor feels is most significant to share about his or her culture. Some contributors respond to what they perceive as gaps in the knowledge we possess about their cultures. Others acknowledge "the central role that narrative structure plays in the formation of the self and in the construction, transmission, and transformation of cultures" (Witherell and Noddings 1991, 3) and employ narrative to express their cultural knowledge.

As editors, we organized the essays not by approach but by overlapping concerns centering around: (1) examining of the language of self-identification and construction of "others"; (2) exploring the intersection of culture, sexuality, and gender; (3) describing the cultural knowledge imbedded in various communication contexts; (4) relating the affirmation available in cultural celebrations; (5) interpreting the fluid and negotiated uses of language; (6) addressing the complexity of living a biracial identity; and (7) suggesting the experience of crossing in and through multiple cultural systems of meaning.

Part I: Naming Ourselves

Victoria Chen's essay begins with the assumption that the autobiographies of ethnic Americans provide the most captivating and useful sources for learning about the construction of cultural experience. By examining one Chinese American woman's writing, Chen explores the double voice in Maxine Hong Kingston's *The Woman Warrior*. She argues that the hyphen commonly used to designate ethnic Americans marginalizes their position.

Thomas Nakayama's essay poses the question: What does being an American mean? As a fourth-generation Japanese American who has never visited Japan, Nakayama is still constructed as the "other" because of his Asian heritage and physical characteristics. He tells us what it is like to be a "perpetual foreigner" in one's native country and asks the reader to redefine Japanese American experience as central, instead of peripheral, to the making of American culture and history.

Sidney A. Ribeau recounts his struggle to unite his personal and intellectual identities as an African American and a communications scholar. He highlights the importance of the articulation of African American experience and its conspicuous absence in intercultural literature. Ribeau uses Afrocentricity as an example of how historically marginalized Americans and ethnic scholars can recreate their identity through communication.

Dolores V. Tanno, echoing Victoria Chen's discussion of double vision for Chinese Americans, provides a response to the central concern of this section: What do we call ourselves as ethnic Americans? She argues that each ethnic self-reference is a rhetorical device insofar as it communicates a particular story. Tanno then offers the possibility of multiple names that allow the historical and cultural continuity of identity.

Part II: Negotiating Sexuality and Gender

Sheryl Perlmutter Bowen reflects on the particular intersection of her Jewish upbringing and the feminism she has adopted as an adult. Yet even her Judaism is specific to her position as a woman because "Jewish women and men have traditionally lived in different worlds." Perlmutter Bowen describes how cultural roles are open to transformation in traditional ways and reinterpreted on the basis of new values and perspectives.

Alberto González and Jennifer L. Willis-Rivera offer a tribute to Selena Quintanilla Perez, the "fallen star" of Tejano music. They use remembrances of the singer's career and their own journey through her hometown as an interpretive framework to understand how Selena's death began a discourse that revealed a cultural divide between some Mexican Americans and Euro-Americans.

In two separate essays, Navita Cummings James and Charles I. Nero offer meditations on their personal and gendered communicative lives. James traces her own meanings for blackness and black womanhood, as a "baby boomer, middle-class African American woman who grew up in the integrated North," to the personal narratives of her extended family. Nero charts key moments in his life by interweaving poetry, popular song lyrics, feminist and gay-lesbian theory, and personal experience to probe the meanings of home, family, and community for African American gay men.

Bishetta D. Merritt discusses the persistent illusions beneath the apparent changes in African American female characters on primetime television. She argues that television's portrayal of black women has not advanced far beyond traditional images of "the oversized, sexless mammy [and] the yellow gal of unbridled passion."

Part III: Representing Cultural Knowledge in Interpersonal and Mass Media Contexts

Computer mediated communication is becoming increasingly popular. People may shop online, download music from their favorite performers, view solar eclipses and meteor showers that are continents away, and even listen to politicians who answer questions from internet subscribers. But do these online interactions provide new opportunities for intercultural dialogue and critique, or do they merely reproduce familiar preferences of power elites? Radhika Gajjala probes the ambivalences and paradoxes that pervade information communication technologies (ICTs). How do real life (RL) and virtual life (VL) blend into one another? How do ICTs render her at once a victor and a victim in the struggle to resist domination? How do ICTs allow her to disguise her identity as an Indian woman of the diaspora, and still proclaim that identity? Her essay addresses these issues as she describes her own efforts to establish open discussion websites.

Margarita Gangotena describes Mexican American family communication. Through a review of several critiques of previous social science research on Mexican Americans, she states that research on la familia has been biased, leaning toward an assimilationist agenda. That is, a family is assessed as "normal" only if it conforms to Eurocentric models of family structure and communication. Gangotena argues that the distinctive rhetorical devices Mexican Americans use to show family affiliation should not be seen as rejections of Eurocentric values but as enactments of values informed by Mexican heritage.

Gwendolyn Gong writes about the conversational strategies of the Chinese from the Mississippi Delta, on the basis of her experience growing up in that part of the United States. She presents a unique combination of Chinese Confucianism and Southern Genteelism that influences Mississippi Chinese when they talk. In a personal narrative, Gong provides us with insightful analyses of how these conversational features play out in communication practices. Like Nakayama, she also experienced others' construction of her Chineseness.

Concentrating on the traditional black church, the central institution in most African American communities, Janice D. Hamlet analyzes traditional black preaching as "the careful orchestration of the biblical scriptures interpreted in view of the people's history and experiences." Her study reinforces the notion that, in addition to worshipping, the rhetorical action of preachers powerfully preserves the cultural identity of black communities.

Marsha Houston explores some of the barriers African American women perceive as preventing them from having satisfying conversations with white women. The communication climate is such that "blacks can never take for granted that whites will respect them, treat them with courtesy, judge them fairly, or take them seriously." Houston concludes by describing attributes of a positive communication environment.

Diana I. Ríos discusses how mass communication functions in two seemingly contradictory ways. Among Mexican Americans in Texas, Ríos argues, media messages serve to acculturate audiences to mainstream values and to preserve and strengthen ethnic identity. Interestingly, the latter is not achieved simply by the existence of Mexican American-owned media outlets or through Spanish language messages. These forms of communication quite often serve the goal of assimilation. Ríos suggests that media outlets open to audience involvement in the development of media content are more directly connected to the function of cultural self-preservation.

Charmaine Shutiva contradicts a popular notion that Native Americans are a "stoic, quiet people." She argues that, as an element of interpersonal talk, humor often functions pedagogically as it is used to maintain traditional values of respect for nature, humility, and care for the group.

Part IV: Celebrating Cultures

Detine L. Bowers describes how her participation in a *Kwanzaa* celebration in Milwaukee reconnected her with her heritage and provided her with a powerful spiritual awareness. As she states, "*Kwanzaa*, a Swahili term for the first fruits of harvest, represents a time. . . to encourage healing through the common bonds that nurture community." Through her rich descriptions of the ceremonies, Bowers invites the reader to share her recollections of the past in the praise of ancestors.

Lynda Dee Dixon relates how her Oklahoma Cherokee family celebrates the memory of Mamaw, their eldest matriarch. Mamaw encouraged her extended family to remain united by willing her house to the family and stipulating that it be used by consensus for reunions and as a safe refuge. Shaver describes how the family's care for the house came to represent Mamaw's care for each member of the family.

Mary Fong's essay focuses on the Cantonese dialect's use of words during the Chinese New Year's celebration. She describes various cultural practices that bring good luck throughout the new year, such as giving red envelopes of money to children or young people. Fong also explores various types of speaking rituals that offer good fortune during this most important Chinese holiday.

Radha S. Hegde writes about Asian Indian celebrations that fortify a sense of affirmation for immigrants and provide an important way to assert a cultural distinctiveness in a pluralistic American society. She argues that ethnicity and identity are not static and that through celebrations a hybridization of cultural form is created and recreated in the Asian Indian community. As Hegde writes, the present becomes "an eclectic production of the past."

Part V: Valuing and Contesting Languages

Dexter B. Gordon argues that through everyday talk, Jamaicans "demonstrate their particular brand of struggle and survival." Through language use, the speaker reveals a knowledge of the colonial presence and an opposition to that presence. Gordon charts the cultural significance of Jamaican Patios.

Mahboub Hashem's essay analyzes the various interpretations of *wastah* (translated as 'mediation'), a culturally significant term in Lebanon. He explains how *wastah* is used with different meanings in various contexts such as religion, kinship, and political leadership. Hashem's discussion emphasizes that the meaning of communication is always in use and that the significance of any cultural term is embedded in the way we use language in our social relationships and practices.

Steven B. Pratt and Merry C. Buchanan describe a language on the verge of extinction. Although the loss of tribal languages is widespread among native peoples, the Osage Nation faces the challenge of recuperating its language among the young. The authors report that tribal governments either are not aware of the centrality of language to cultural vitality, or understandably choose economic development over cultural development. Pratt and Buchanan conclude by describing a language and culture restoration program that, unfortunately, did not gain approval from the Osage tribal government.

Karla D. Scott's discussion of black English, like Dexter B. Gordon's discussion of Jamaican Patios, argues that judgments about Ebonics, or black English, as a defective form of Standard English are misinformed and culturally biased. Scott describes the efforts to equate black English with stupidity and slang as consistent with a power majority that feels threatened by blackness. Scott concludes by explaining the dangers of language rejection, and the advantages of language-switching, among speakers of black English.

Eric King Watts focuses on a particular language device—use of the *N-word*—in hip-hop culture. Watts locates himself between generational understandings of the term. From this location, he knows that the term can be taken as a "racial slur" that should never be uttered. But, as a hip-hop head, he also takes the term to signify "close friendship, cultural awareness, or fearlessness." Watts argues that the "controversy over the *N-word* is normal and necessary." For Watts, the use of the term is a spoken, sonic summary of "the troubles of living in community with (white and black) others."

Part VI: Living in Bicultural Relationships

Brenda J. Allen, an African American teacher, describes her close friendship with her professional colleague, a white lesbian woman named Anna. Sharing similar experiences as members of traditionally marginalized groups, Brenda and Anna illustrate the possibility for an interracial friendship that is founded on respect, caring, understanding, and reciprocity.

Tina M. Harris celebrates diversity in the complex and often difficult process of constructing a coherent biracial identity. She explores the experiences of biracial individuals and the process by which they search for cultural identity. Harris argues for a fusion of biracial identity rather than the forced dichotomy that is imposed on those with biracial parentage.

Diane M. Kimoto reflects on the role that adoption continues to play in the shaping of her cultural identity, stressing that one's identity makes sense only in relation to others' identities. With her multiracial biological and adoptive background, Kimoto relates to herself as "a living example of the United Nations." Being *hapa* (i.e., from a mixed Asian American background) affirms her power to self-identify in different social contexts.

Richard Morris offers a critical look at the consequences of forcing Native Americans to assimilate into mainstream American society. He argues that requiring "the other" to cast off cultural identity leads to a culturally divided self for Native Americans and that cultural differences cannot be cultivated by creating a unity of singularity.

Part VII: Traversing Cultural Paths

Aimee M. Carrillo Rowe advances "alternative ways of thinking about contemporary immigration. . . ." By taking a "spatial view of cultural politics," Carrillo Rowe addresses the following issues: What are the legitimized and delegitimized histories of movement and mobility? Who moves from here to there (and from there to there), and in what ways? Who has access to, or occupies, particular spaces and what do those spaces mean? How are spaces rewritten? Carrillo Rowe uses cases from migrant labor as well as her own personal history to rethink immigration.

On the assumption that making sense and creating meaning are inherent features of communication, Ling Chen's essay offers a detailed description of how Chinese students in the United States interpret the various facets of American culture. The value of Chen's work lies in the specific, detailed accounts given by native Chinese at different stages of their acculturation into American society. As she points out, things can "go wrong" in intercultural communication if we impose our own cultural knowledge when trying to make sense of interaction that has a totally different logic from another cultural perspective.

Elizabeth Lozano describes "the particular tensions and differences that appear when the posited 'standard' voice—the Anglo-Saxon American—confronts a 'marginal' voice—such as the Latino— with the consequent noise and mutual inflection of accents." She shows how an entire range of perceptions and behaviors reveals contrasting Latin American and Anglo cultural concepts of "public space." As a bicultural participant observer, Lozano articulates an insider's assumptions in both Anglo and Latin American settings.

Casey Man Kong Lum's essay begins with an anecdote highlighting the fact that various dialects and practices exist and can create confusion and difficulties when two Chinese persons communicate. He examines three dominant groups of Chinese immigrants in New York City and discusses how they maintain their own ethnicity through specific forms of interaction.

Finally, Maria Rogers-Pascual describes her changing relationships to her birth culture (English) and her spirit culture (Spanish). She states: "Learning to operate in both cultural systems at such a young age was the key to my emotional survival." The immigrant, she argues, often adopts a bicultural identity strategically. That is, the creative blend of cultural elements, hybridity, generates a new space for both subversion and resistance to domination. Rogers-Pascual explores this hybrid identity through her work in a multinational non-profit organization.

* * *

Even with the addition of seven new essays in this Third Edition, *Our Voices* only scratches the surface of the social and cultural knowledge that informs one's symbolic creations of and responses to the experience of living in the United States. We hope to emphasize that various cultural worlds are outgrowths of a complex history that has indeed incorporated multiple cultural voices. And we hope that this new edition continues to inspire the reader to explore further and become part of the ongoing conversation about cultural experiences.

As we conclude this introduction, we survey still more sites of cultural conflict: demonstrators in Virginia wave confederate flags in opposition to a statue honoring the late tennis star, Arthur Ashe; the FBI and Egyptian authorities are locked in disagreement over the meaning of a pilot's prayer spoken in Arabic as EgyptAir Flight 990 plunged into the Atlantic; in Hudson, Ohio, a school board rejects teachers' recommendations for a history text because it emphasizes the accomplishments of women and people of color in the United States; a tax assessor in Huntsville, Alabama, refuses to give standard tax exemptions to those who do not speak English very well and is ordered by a court to end this practice.

These events and others ignite rather than perplex us. The struggle to dominate others is as old as society. Understanding domination is an intellectual project, but we are immersed in this project in very real ways. When one of us walks into a restaurant and overhears someone say, "What's *that* doing in here?" We cannot help but respond emotionally as well as intellectually. Yet people often ask us, "Why are you so angry?" To them, we ask our own question. . .

'Why Aren't *You* Angry?'

One of the reactions some students have to the essays in *Our Voices* is to ask, "Why is the author so angry?" or "Why are they (i.e., the members of the ethnic group written about in the essay) so angry?" Struggling to comprehend this response, we keep in mind that most students, regardless of their gender or ethnicity, are unaccustomed to reading texts in which scholars speak frankly about their cultural communicative experiences. We usually respond by saying, "You are mistaking the earnest and sincere tone of the essay for an 'angry' one." Since we know a central belief of the white Western tradition dominating education in the U.S. is that anger is typically unproductive, irrational venting of emotion, we do not want students to mistake the thoughtful, carefully reasoned, reflective scholarship in this volume for mere "angry" diatribes.

Yet, in our hearts, we know that our usual response to questioning students is not totally honest. We know that a sense of outrage as well as a desire for positive change motivate us to write about the long-standing problems of intercultural and interracial communication. We suspect that many other intercultural scholars (especially those from non-dominant groups) are similarly motivated. We keep in mind Audre Lorde's distinction between *anger* and *hatred*.

Anger can be productive if channeled into a critique of or challenge to injustice; such critical anger can lead one to develop incisive analyses of the social order and to discover means for creating a more just society and for encouraging individual change. Hatred, directed to individuals and groups, is unproductive and results in perpetuating or exacerbating injustice. Lorde's contrast confirms what most of us know intuitively: the Western response has something to learn about anger; much positive personal and social change is the result of righteous indignation about abuse and injustice.

If students think they hear hatred, maybe even hatred directed toward them as members of privileged social groups (e.g., whites or men or heterosexuals) that certainly would be a misperception—a misreading—of the essays. To discourage such a misreading, the next time we encounter the question, "Why are they so angry?" we will respond differently. We might answer with: "One of the author's goals is to raise our awareness of the communicative problems caused by an unjust social order that perpetuates inequitable relationships and bigoted and discriminatory behaviors." I don't know whether the author is angry or not, but I do know that injustice, bigotry, and discrimination are things that all of us should be angry about. We can be justifiably incensed about these things without hating the people who practice them (hate the deed but not the doer). Our anger can lead us to change ourselves and to work toward eliminating injustice, bigotry, and discrimination from the social order. So, after reading the essay, why aren't you angry?

References

Asante, M.K. (1987). *The Afrocentric Idea*. Philadelphia, PA: Temple University Press.

Berger, P.L. and Luckmann, T. (1967). *The Social Construction of Reality: A Treatise in the Sociology of Knowledge*. New York: Doubleday Anchor.

Carbaugh, D. (1988a). *Talking American: Cultural Discourses on 'Donahue.'* Norwood, NJ: Ablex.

Carbaugh, D. (1988b). Cultural Terms and Tensions in the Speech at a Television Station. *The Western Journal of Speech Communication, 52*, 216–237.

Carbaugh, D. (Ed.). (1990). *Cultural Communication and Intercultural Contact*. Hillsdale, NJ: Erlbaum.

Christian, B. (1988). The Race for Theory. *Feminist Studies, 14*, 67–79.

Cronen V.E., Chen, V. and Pearce, W.B. (1988). Coordinated Management of Meaning: A Critical Theory. In Kim, Y.Y. and Gudykunst, W.B. (Eds.), *International and Intercultural Communication Annual, XII: Theories in Intercultural Communication* (66–98). Newbury Park, CA: Sage.

Garner, T. (1983). Playing the Dozens: Folklore as Strategies for Living. *The Quarterly Journal of Speech, 69*, 47–57.

Geertz, C. (1973). *The Interpretation of Cultures*. New York: Basic.

Geertz, C. (1983). *Local Knowledge*. New York: Basic.

Hall, E.T. (1976). *Beyond Culture*. New York: Anchor.

hooks, b. (1989). *Talking Back: Thinking Feminist, Thinking Black*. Boston: South End.

Kramerae, C., Schulz, M. and O'Barr, W. (1984). *Language and Power*. Beverly Hills: Sage.

Langer, S.K. (1942). *Philosophy in a New Key: A Study in the Symbolism of Reason, Rrite, and Art* (3rd ed.). Cambridge, MA: Harvard University Press.

Nakagawa, G. (1990). 'What Are We Doing Here With All These Japanese?': Subject-Constitution and Strategies of Discursive Closure Represented in Stories of Japanese American Internment. *Communication Quarterly, 38*, 388–402.

Philipsen, G. (1975). Speaking 'Like a Man' in Teamsterville: Culture Patterns of Role Enactment in an Urban Neighborhood. *The Quarterly Journal of Speech, 61,* 13–22.

Rabinow, P. and Sullivan, W.M. (Eds.). (1987). *Interpretive Social Science: A Second Look.* Berkeley: University of California Press.

Ramos, R. and Ramos, M. (1979). The Mexican American: Am I Who They Say I Am? In Trejo, A.D. (Ed.), *The Chicanos: As We See Ourselves* (49–66). Tucson: University of Arizona Press.

Sedano, M.V. (1980). Chicanismo: A Rhetorical Analysis of Themes and Images of Selected Poetry from the Chicano Movement. *The Western Journal of Speech Communication, 44,* 170–190.

Shuter, R. (1990). The Centrality of Culture. *The Southern Communication Journal, 55,* 237–249.

Smitherman, G. (1977). *Talkin' and Testifyin': The Language of Black America.* Boston: Houghton Mifflin. Reissued, Detroit, MI: Wayne State University, 1986.

Stanback, M.H. (1988–89). Feminist Theory and Black Women's Talk. *The Howard Journal of Communications, 1,* 187–194.

Turner, L.D. (1949). *Africanisms in the Gullah Dialect.* Chicago, IL: University of Chicago Press.

Witherell, C. and Noddings, N. (Eds.). (1991). *Stories Lives Tell: Narrative and Dialogue in Education.* New York: Teachers College Press. ✦

Part I

Naming Ourselves

1

(De)hyphenated Identity

The Double Voice in *The Woman Warrior*

Victoria Chen
San Francisco State University

> *It's difficult to hear the songs of more than one world at any one time. And yet sometimes it's necessary to forget the songs of one world and learn the songs of another, especially if you're a Chinese American.*
>
> —Laurence Yep

Maxine Hong Kingston's (1976) *The Woman Warrior: Memoirs of a Girlhood Among Ghosts* tells the story of an American-born Chinese woman. In her nostalgic and yet critical voice, Kingston narrates her experience of growing up in Stockton, California, in the late 1940s as a second-generation Chinese American daughter. In her dramatic autobiographical style, she describes the ambiguity of living on the interface between two cultural traditions, the pain of defying some elements of her Chinese heritage, and the struggle to find a legitimate private and public voice in American society. In the process of trying to maintain a bittersweet relationship with her cultural heritage and with her Chinese mother, the champion storyteller, Kingston has herself become a powerful storyteller and one of America's most prominent writers. *The Woman Warrior* is one of the most widely studied works in American literature on college campuses.

I have chosen to write on the issue of bicultural identity using Kingston's autobiography. I was first introduced to this book when I was sitting in an Asian American literature class at University of California, Berkeley, in the mid 80s. I remember being totally enthralled by Kingston's magical storytelling. I could not put down the book and was captivated by the intricate and playful descriptions of her Chinese American experience that resonated with my own. Even though there are significant differences between the time, places, and families that we grew up with, Kingston's book introduced me to a world in which I could think, talk, and even write about my own bicultural experience, having lived in Canada, Asia, and the States. When I finally had the opportunity to meet Kingston some years ago, I felt an immediate connection with the storyteller's warrior spirit that runs throughout *The Woman Warrior*. Reading Kingston's book and writing this essay about it provide me with a framework for hope, strength, and vision. I hope that through my interpretation and discussion of her "talk-stories," readers will gain a new critical insight into understanding and appreciating the dual cultural enmeshment that so many Americans experience.

There has been little work done in intercultural communication that has emphasized the importance of learning from literature produced by ethnic Americans. Although mainstream research has by and large adopted a "scientific" approach to comparing different cultures within a quantitative framework, we rarely learn how bicultural participants make sense of their experiences in their own words.

I begin with the assumption that ethnic American literature provides us with valuable knowledge of and insights into culture and communication from the point of view of those who have lived the experience. Writings by these Americans illuminate us with fresh, different perspectives and interpretations of their cultural experience within the broader cultural milieu. Autobiographies are particularly enlightening about how authors construct their own cultural identities in response to changing family structures, traditional narratives, and social and historical contexts. As Fischer (1986) discussed, an autobiography is predicated on a vibrant yet

3

ambiguous relation between a sense of self and community: "Thus what seems initially to be individualistic autobiographical searchings turn out to be revelations of traditions, recollections of disseminated identities and of the divine sparks from the breaking of the vessel" (198). Fischer also interpreted *The Woman Warrior* as "an archetypical text for displaying ethnicity processes analogous to translations of dreams" (208).

Autobiographical works such as *The Woman Warrior* present both intrigue and confusion to the reader. Kingston had to cross the boundaries of both ethnicity and gender to reach a mainstream audience. We can learn about a writer's work from the response that it generates. A look at some of the critiques of Kingston's widely celebrated book helps us to focus on the issues of cultural identity and bicultural voices. In this essay I use *The Woman Warrior* as my primary source of data to explore the marginalization of Chinese Americans and the possibilities of transcending hyphenated identity. I will first outline three critical views of Kingston's work, from "general" Americans, from Chinese, and from Chinese Americans. I will then discuss the notion of hyphenated identity and explain why I believe the expression "Chinese American" should be dehyphenated as a means to empower a double vision for individuals who are simultaneously enmeshed in disparate cultural traditions.

Critiques of *The Woman Warrior*

Three broad critical viewpoints of *The Woman Warrior* can be identified. The first comes from the "general" American audience, readers who are not familiar with Chinese or Chinese American culture, as well as those who hope to find the "truth" about Kingston's life and cultural heritage. A typical response from these readers has been that the book is interesting but confusing: Kingston does not write clearly, and it is difficult to tell where her fantasies end and reality begins. While praising the charming, exotic myths and customs described in the work, these critics insist that clarity and certainty are the most important criteria by

which to judge the quality of Kingston's autobiography. Furthermore, they feel that the real contribution of Kingston's work lies in how she reveals Chinese culture through her and her mother's storytelling.

One response to these comments would be that writing is a symbolic activity. It is not necessarily intended to reflect the *truth*, even in the genre of autobiography. There are multiple ways to be an ethnic American, as Fischer (1986) stated: "Being Chinese American exists only as an exploratory project, a matter of finding a voice and style" (210). Kingston found a new way to construct her life stories with a bicultural voice that is imbued with her imagination and dreams. The fictionalization of her autobiography conveys the idea that all cultural discourse is made up, fabricated, and reconstructed, always engaging the reader in an ongoing dialogue.

If these critics would be willing to suspend their disbeliefs long enough to fathom Kingston's talk-story, they might discover that Kingston herself, in her double voice, could not sort out which part of her childhood consisted of stories, which part was dreams, and which part was the real historical events that involved her family. As she said, "Chinese Americans, when you try to understand what things in you are Chinese, how do you separate what is peculiar to childhood, to poverty, insanities, one family, your mother who marked your growing with stories, from what is Chinese? What is Chinese tradition and what is in the movies?" (Kingston 1976, 215). What these readers forget is that Kingston is not Chinese, but a Chinese American who comes from a specific family background and a lifelong struggle between disparate cultural traditions. It is no surprise to the Western eye that Kingston is inevitably "Chinese"; the customs and practices vividly depicted in her book are inexorably alien. Her "Chineseness" tends to overshadow the "Americanness" that she shares with "general" Americans.

The second critique comes from the "real" Chinese such as scholars or readers from China, Hong Kong, and Taiwan, who have mastered Chinese language(s) and grown up in Chinese societies. Although some of these critics highly praise Kingston's book, a typical response has been that, being Chinese American, she has somehow "misrepresented" Chinese culture by relating only the "negative" and "shameful" aspects of an ancient, laudable civilization that has eluded the American-born, culturally disadvantaged author. They contend that Kingston has rendered descriptions of exotic foods, Chinese superstitions, values, and customs that are not really practiced by many Chinese. They quickly dismiss *The Woman Warrior* as a "poor," "inaccurate," and "degrading" depiction of high Chinese culture in an attempt to pander to mainstream American taste. In some versions of the Chinese translation of *The Woman Warrior,* a few of Kingston's myths and stories were "corrected" by the translators in order to conform to the "Chinese" way of storytelling.

These Chinese scholars further warn readers that not all Chinese women are like Kingston's mother, who displayed all the "virtueless" behaviors of Chinese women— dominant, controlling, strong, and stubborn. American readers, they argue, should realize that, though her family is from a Chinese village, the American-born writer really does not know that much about Chinese culture; that, in fact, she is not even fluent in her Cantonese dialect, let alone Mandarin, the official Chinese language. These critics question Kingston's cultural credibility, despite the obvious fact that her autobiography is not about Chinese culture, nor is it intended to reflect any experiences other than her own.

The third critique comes from other Chinese American writers. Interestingly enough, it stems primarily from Chinese American male writers such as Frank Chin, Benjamin Tang, and Paul Chan. Though they are pleased that this enchanting work has finally made its way into mainstream America, they believe that *The Woman Warrior* does not speak for other Chinese Americans' experiences. Further, these critics scrutinize Kingston's ideology as an ethnic American writer. Kingston grew up in a very peculiar family and community, they contend; many Chinese American girls growing up in this country do not think or behave like her. Despite its widely acclaimed success, they argue that *The Woman Warrior* represents a distorted view of the Chinese American experience—a "fake" Chinese American culture. They further ignore the feminist ideas, insights, and practices found throughout the book and accuse Kingston of buying into the dominant American ideology, "whitewashing" her prose to seek out white acceptance. In their minds, she does not directly challenge the issue of racism that Chinese Americans experience in this society. In other words, she is simply not radical enough.

There is some irony in these accusations, given that, as Kim (1982) pointed out, "Among some contemporary Asian American male writers . . . a strident anti-female attitude can be discerned" (197). In an interview during a visit to the University of California, Santa Barbara, Kingston countered by saying, "The content of this book is overtly feminist, although it is not the feminists' typically political rhetoric. The feminist side of this work is couched in a dramatic writing style. And the title *The Woman Warrior* was chosen to denote that throughout Chinese literature, there have always been knights and fighters who are women." The most gratifying responses to *The Woman Warrior,* she claimed, have come from Chinese American women who not only have experienced Kingston's stories in their own life, but also whose appreciation of her work is not mediated by the expectation of exoticism and foreign sensibility.

If all of us are indeed cultural interpreters, we should realize that the attempt to inscribe one's family life is no more or less than the multilayered reconstruction of what we call cultural experience. The insights into Kingston's work is derived neither from a "scientific" assessment of the veracity of Kingston's and her mother's narratives, nor by generalized comparisons of her personal life experience with that of other Chinese Americans. Rather, her revelations rely on the specificity, uniqueness, richness, ambiguity, playfulness, and sense of irony that characterize Kingston's talk-story. It is through her array of conversations, imageries, and communication practices that we learn about Kingston's bicultural experience and her ongoing struggle for a coherent cultural identity.

Despite all the controversy surrounding *The Woman Warrior,* the real issue of all these critiques is, what is this cultural construct that we call 'Chinese American?' Who defines these ethnic Americans? Who describes, articulates, and represents their experiences? In our effort to understand the wide array of such diverse experiences, whose voices are heard, and at the expense of what other voices? Even more significantly, how do we even attempt to understand a Chinese American woman's autobiography when she is constantly weaving her stories (and "lies") from a hyphenated cultural world in which she is simultaneously enmeshed and marginalized?

As for any other ethnic group, there is no single, overall Chinese American perspective from which we can decipher the myths, dreams, and fantasies in Kingston's storytelling. Nor is she attempting to present a coherent set of Chinese Ameri- can cultural narratives to the reader. Many Asian Americans' experiences can often be characterized by a kind of discontinuity and incoherence, combined with a sense of jarring reality and fragmentation, as depicted by such authors as Okada (1979), Sone (1979), Kadohata (1989), Kingston (1989), Tan (1989), Wong (1989), and Ng (1993). Mixing fictional characters with autobiographical accounts, these writers probe into immigrant family histories and the precarious nature of riding on the hyphen commonly used to describe their identity as ethnic Americans. Although the term "hyphenated identity" may seem appropriate to describe the bicultural experience that Chinese Americans grow up with, I would argue that the hyphen marginalizes these individuals in American society and would strongly advocate the de-hyphenation of Asian Americans.

Hyphenated Identity and Marginalization

. . . the paradoxical sense that ethnicity is something reinvented and reinterpreted in each generation by each individual and that it is often something quite puzzling to the individual, something over which he or she lacks control. Ethnicity is not something that is simply passed on from generation to generation, taught and learned; it is something dynamic, often unsuccessfully repressed or avoided.
—Michael M. J. Fischer

One way to conceptualize the term *identity* is not by trying merely to define who we are, but by contextualizing the term within our relationships, practices, actions, and experiences. Because our identity is inexorably bound with what we do and how we make sense of what we do, and the significance of our activities is interpretable only within the context of communication, identity can be viewed as "the actual experience of self in a particular social situation," as explained in *The Homeless Mind* (Berger, Berger, and Kellner 1973, 76). The authors described a phenomenon of the modern era: the pluralization or segmentation of lifeworlds, whereby the condition of modernity is characterized by the plurality and fragmentation of our identity. Berman (1982) made a similar point: Western cultural history virtually compels modernists to go through life experiences feeling groundless, centerless, and filled with a sense of loss.

It is certainly not unusual that our ideas and cultural endeavors do not always coexist well together; we may even face a sense of contradiction, incoherence, struggle, loss, and unbelonging in our social relationships. Surely all individuals, regardless of ethnicity, may have experienced the crossing of boundaries between lifeworlds at various stages. However, Chinese Americans' bicultural experiences are especially characterized by this pluralization of lifeworlds. It can be argued that these homeless characteristics are accentuated or exacerbated by the fact that Chinese Americans are simultaneously enmeshed between two powerful cultural traditions.

One feature of this phenomenon of pluralized lifeworlds is manifested in the commonly adopted hyphenated designation. For Asian Americans, dual cultural traditions are separated *and* connected by the hyphen that is used to describe their identity. On the one hand, the hyphen reminds them that they have a distinct ethnic heritage and are somehow different from other immigrant Americans who descended from European ancestry but are referred to simply as Americans. On the other hand, the hyphen also draws attention to the fact that they are not Asian foreigners but Americans by birthright, born and raised in this country just like other Anglo Americans.

The hyphen used to designate different Asian American groups thus functions as a paradoxical boundary continuously mediating between the two disparate cultural baggages that these individuals carry, or sometimes abandon. In a larger context, the hyphenated identity of these Americans is also mediated by the "others," the constraints in the social and historical system, the dominant American cultural institutions, and the powerful persons in their life. This multileveled and multidirectional mediation creates an important part of the context by which we can meaningfully address the issue of bicultural identity.

Feminist writer Rey Chow (1990) argued that ethnicity in America is not "voluntary" in character, and that "the consciousness of ethnicity for Asian and other nonwhite groups is inevitably a matter of history rather than of choice" (Chow 1990, 45). We also learn from Richard Rodriguez' (1982) autobiography that one's ethnicity cannot be chosen, just as Rodriguez, an American of Mexican ancestry, did not consciously choose to end his "private" childhood to enter the "public" American life. "The day I raised my hand in class and spoke loudly to an entire roomful of faces," he wrote, "my childhood started to end" (28).

The hyphen lets us assume that the two cultures on either side of the hyphen are somehow connected, that Asian Americans somehow must think and act like Asians in some ways simply because their ethnicity is visually communicated. In *The Woman Warrior*, Kingston, living in the interface between her mother's Chinese myths and her American dreams, poignantly articulated the ambiguous identity of Chinese Americans. Blessed with the warrior woman's courage, Kingston demythologized the assumed continuity between the great culture of China and the American-born Chinese. In her double voice, Kingston told us that there is no such continuity, and that "even now China wraps double binds around my feet" (Kingston 1976, 57). Therefore, she must bridge the gap between China and America. Of course, we see the irony in Kingston's denial of cultural continuity, as the whole book is devoted to the memories of her mother's talk-stories.

Kingston's writing points out that the hyphen used to describe her "apparent" cultural identity only provides some connection that is taken for granted, yet is remote and ambiguous in relation to her ethnic heritage. What she and her siblings actually experienced in their childhood was their inability to penetrate Chinese wisdom and their frustration over their Chinese relatives' unwillingness to explain Chinese folklores and customs. She wrote, "I don't see how they kept up a continuous culture for five thousand years. Maybe they didn't; maybe everyone makes it up as they go along" (Kingston 1976, 216).

One characteristic of hyphenated identity is a sense of being marginalized as one strives for a coherent life script and legitimate Chinese and American voices. In her many stories, Kingston shares such experience with us. For example, her mother often referred to her children as "You American children." She would reprimand them, "Stop being silly. You Americans don't take life seriously" (Kingston 1976, 174). Later, the mother would scold her children, "What do you know about Chinese business? Do as I say" (175). This, of course, requires that children realize they are perceived as Americans who lack knowledge of Chinese culture; but at the same time they are also expected to act like good Chinese children, obeying the parents with total deference. Indeed, this double bind is a common feature of ethnic Americans' dual cultural enmeshment, and many do not fit comfortably in either world.

Kingston complained, "They would not tell us children because we had been born among ghosts, were taught by ghosts, and were ourselves ghostlike. They called us a kind of ghost" (Kingston 1976, 213–214). Non-Chinese are referred to as ghosts in the Chinese way of thinking. Kingston wrote, "But America has been full of machines and ghosts—Taxi Ghosts, Bus Ghosts, Police Ghosts. . . . Once upon a time the world was so thick with ghosts, I could hardly breathe; I could hardly walk, limping my way around the White Ghosts and their cars" (113). To the Chinese, ghosts symbolize the alien, the strange, the incomprehensible, all with a pejorative overtone. Kingston's parents were often puzzled by their American-born and American-educated children's "foreign" behavior. The mother would complain in exasperation, "You children never tell me what you're really up to. How else am I going to find out what you're really up to?" (118). What is interesting about Kingston's case, as in other Chinese Americans' experiences, is that the "otherness" in their identity is being constructed by their family members, to whom they are ethnically related, as much as by Americans outside their families. In their own Chinese families, Kingston and her siblings were always the "other ghosts," the hopelessly ignorant and Americanized second-generation offspring. For many Chinese American children, however, ghosts are the residue of the fragmentary past, the family history, and the old tradition that seems so foreign to them, all of which must be exorcised and externalized. As Kingston wrote, "Whenever my parents said 'home,' they suspended America. They suspended enjoyment, but I did not want to go to China. In China my parents would sell my sisters and me" (116).

Being marginal also means being without a community. Just like the mythical Chinese warrior woman Fa Mu Lan, who felt that she must fight the battle away from home until her task and duty were fulfilled, Kingston found it ambivalent, difficult, and at times painful to be a Chinese American: "I've stopped checking 'bilingual' on job applications. I could not understand any of the dialects the interviewer at China Airlines tried on me, and he didn't understand me either" (Kingston 1976, 239). And "when I visit the family now, I wrap my American successes around me like a private shawl; I *am* worthy of eating the food. From afar I can believe my family loves me fundamentally. . . . I refuse to shy my way anymore through our Chinatown, which tasks me with the old sayings and the stories" (62).

Although Kingston's lack of Chineseness is ridiculed by her parents and relatives, in the larger society Chinese Ameri- cans are often portrayed as the "others" as well, the unassimilable Asians who are still sometimes told to go back to their own country after generations of settlement in America. Mainstream white America insists that Kingston writes from an exotic Eastern perspective. In response to her critics, Kingston countered in exasperation, *"The Woman Warrior* is an American book. Yet many reviewers do not see the Americanness of it, nor the fact of my own Americanness" (Kingston 1982, 58). Chinese American women indeed experience a double alienation, from the mainstream American culture because of their race, gender, and ethnic heritage, and from their own Chinese communities because of both their inevitable Americanization and the traditional Chinese marginalization of women. This double-edged social displacement can leave them homeless; Kingston found that she had to escape to survive. Even though the children told one another, "Chinese people are very weird" (Kingston 1976, 183), she still pleaded, "The swordswoman and I are not so dissimilar. May my people understand the resemblance soon so that I can return to them" (62). Where is home for individuals like Kingston? And how do they build a new route to "return" home?

Dehyphenated Double Vision

Postmodern knowledge . . . refines our sensitivity to differences and reinforces our ability to tolerate the incommensurable.

—Jean François Lyotard

Like many others, I have argued that the identity of Asian Americans is not an *either/ or* choice, but a *both/and* transformation; a new kind of integration, or sometimes a lack of integration, of two cultural lifeworlds. One reason that the use of the hyphen to designate Asian Americans has been challenged is that even the third or fourth generations of Asian Americans have a difficult time being accepted as "fullfledged" Americans in white America. Toni Morrison (1992) in *Playing in the Dark* argues that "Deep within the word 'American' is its association with race. . . . American means white, and Africanist people struggle to make the term applicable to themselves with ethnicity and hyphen after hyphen after hyphen" (47). Although Asian Americans' physical characteristics may remind others that their ancestry is indeed from a remote land, a significant part of their cultural history and knowledge is at the same time deeply rooted in American tradition. The hyphen may give the false impression that there is some middle point along the Asian American continuum that poses the ultimate triumph for these ethnic Americans—to find that golden mean which bridges the gap between Asian wisdom and American dreams, allowing any individual to be fully integrated into and accepted by both worlds.

In reality, many Asian Americans would find it indeed an American dream to conflate the hierarchical structure of the two cultural impositions. The reality is that there is a qualitative disjunction between Asian and American cultural experiences and practices. The imaginary balancing point wrongly assumes the possibility of converging the two cultural worlds into the same sphere of discourse. I have suggested that some of the intergenerational conflicts between the American-born Chinese and their immigrant parents are incommensurate, that there is no shared discourse upon which the conflicting ways of life can be adjudicated or even discussed (Chen 1992). The hyphen thus serves not only as a political boundary between Asian American and white American, but more as the illusion of an imaginary bicultural ideal than as a connective means to a perfectly blended and integrated bicultural reality.

Although I am not presuming that the simple elimination of the hyphen in describing Asian Americans would solve all the issues involved, I do believe that the hyphen

is a metaphor which highlights the boundary between minority Americans and white Americans. The hyphen often provides the locus for homelessness while marginalizing the social position of Asian Americans. To dehyphenate Asian Americans would enable us to recognize and accept their ambiguous, unequal, and often imbalanced cultural worlds, to survive the lack of continuity in their ethnic heritage with a sense of irony, and to invent new, creative ways to experience and appropriate from different cultural traditions. As Fischer (1986) pointed out, the struggle for a sense of ethnic identity is the reinvention and discovery of a vision for the future.

Kingston chose to write her autobiography as a way to sort out her childhood memories. An irony in *The Woman Warrior* is that she opens it with the chapter "No Name Woman" wherein her mother warned her to forget about a disgraceful aunt, whose name should remain unspeakable in the family history: "You must not tell anyone what I am about to tell you" (Kingston 1976, 3). Kingston, however, rebelled against her mother's wish and gave this woman's life back: "My aunt haunts me—her ghost drawn to me because now, after fifty years of neglect, I alone devote pages of paper to her. . ." (19). "They want me to participate in her punishment. And I have" (18).

The end of *The Woman Warrior* realized the making of a storytelling Chinese American daughter. Despite all the "lies" that Kingston accused her mother of telling, she let the lying go on by retelling us her mother's lies and recounting to us her own stories, which in a sense are lies themselves. "Here is a story my mother told me, not when I was young, but recently, when I told her I also talk-story. The beginning is hers, the ending, mine" (Kingston 1976, 240). The family tradition is not only "passed down" but also reinvented and made real: "Hong Kingston grows up a warrior woman and a warrior-woman storyteller herself. She is the woman warrior who continues to fight in America the fight her mothers fought in China" (Trinh 1989, 134). Kingston transformed the cultural myths and family stories through her fascinating double voice: "And I have so many words—" (Kingston 1976, 63).

Dreams, imagination, ambiguities, and visions pervade Kingston's storytelling. The entire book is full of ironies and paradoxes beyond the simple contradictions between so called Eastern and Western philosophies. What makes Kingston's feminist work so intriguing and powerful is the array of rich, specific, intimate, and personal stories that are characterized by intense conflict between the loved ones, ambivalence toward one's own family and cultural heritage, and paradoxical choices made through a double identity, which ultimately refer back to the choices that were left out. As Kingston said, "If one lives long enough with contradictions, they will form a larger vision" (Kingston 1976, 35).

Living on the fault line between cultures and trying to hold them together is like oscillating between choices in a double bind. But if indeed "modern man [*sic*] has suffered from a deepening condition of 'homelessness'" (Berger, Berger, and Kellner 1973, 82), all of us then share this sense of living on the margin at one time or another in a culture that is rapidly changing. Perhaps real people *are* hyphenated people after all.

One way to transcend the double bind that traps Chinese Americans is to build a community in which dehyphenation and double vision are the central practices. The notion of double vision for bicultural individuals points to their ability to see things from multiple perspectives, to live in these paradoxes without being entrapped by them, to appreciate the ambiguity of their bicultural world, and to create new possibilities from these paradoxes. As Kingston explained during an interview, "Even in America there's still some heritage of mythical women. Women must find a new way of being a knight in the U.S." Accompanying this double vision is what W.E.B. Dubois called "double consciousness," multiple cultural insights to construct meanings out of chaos, to deepen our awareness of the plurality of our cultural interpretations and practices. To deny this characterization of ethnic Americans is to neglect an opportunity to transcend their marginal status in this society. Perhaps the celebration of marginality is the beginning of a joint effort by all ethnic Americans to once and for all center their social marginality.

The idea of double vision takes a critical look at the cultural construction of the metaphorical hyphen. It empowers ethnic Americans to use their marginality to create a new community, a community where their double voice is articulated and heard, a community where one is steeped in several cultural traditions and discourses, and a community where multiple subjectivities are encouraged and even celebrated. One of the important messages in *The Woman Warrior* is that a marginal person derives power and vision from living with paradoxes. As Kingston put it, "I learned to make my mind large, as the universe is large, so that there is room for paradoxes" (Kingston 1976, 35).

Reconceptualizing one's hyphenated identity is the ultimate act of self-affirmation and cultural continuation. Kingston emphasized the importance of Asian Americans recognizing themselves as warriors instead of victims. Being a true warrior requires wisdom and courage. Even Kingston's act of writing *The Woman Warrior* rode on the precarious and marginalizing hyphen, risking "misinterpretation" and criticism from both sides of the hyphen, thus rendering her vulnerable in both Chinese and American communities. Nonetheless, she was determined to make public the memoirs of her girlhood among ghosts. Writing her stories thus became a powerful source of Kingston's strength as a woman warrior. In presenting her private words and feelings to the American public, Kingston also immortalized the *No Name Woman*, giving new meaning to her life. Fischer (1986) insisted that ethnic memory is and ought to be oriented toward the future, not the past. Writing *The Woman Warrior* dehyphenated Kingston and empowered her with a futuristic vision to transform the alienation and marginalization imposed by the hyphen. Kingston not only continued but even surpassed her mother's talk-story tradition; she found a home in America. As she told her mother, "We belong to the planet now, Mama. Does it make sense to you that if we're no longer attached to one piece of land, we belong to the planet? Wherever we happen to be standing, why, that spot belongs to us as much as any other spot" (Kingston 1976, 125).

Inherent in Kingston's writing is the uncertainty and ambiguity of her bicultural identity, as well as the ongoing, at times turbulent process of trying to make sense of the confusion created by the hyphen. As readers, we feel the pain in her talk-story; but we also taste her triumph. Although Kingston's creative style of writing presents a challenge for the reader to decipher multifaceted cultural imageries, she also found some stories difficult. As she wrote, "To make my waking life American-normal . . . I push the deformed into my dreams, which are in Chinese, the language of impossible stories" (Kingston 1976, 102). How do we recognize what is American-normal to Chinese American women? What are their dreams? What are Chinese dreams? How do we enter their impossible stories, written in such incommensurate language? How do they do it themselves, being enmeshed in and marginalized by two disparate narratives?

Even Kingston herself was confused: "I continue to sort out what's just my childhood, just my imagination, just my family, just the village, just movies, just living" (Kingston 1976, 239). Perhaps once this sorting begins for us as readers and students of other cultural experiences, we can redefine our questions about cultural identity, ethnicity, marginalization, and America. Without doubt, this is an ongoing effort with no guarantee of ever finding the "correct" realities, just as we never can be sure if Kingston's life stories were not mixed with "lies."

If open-ended ambiguity is an inherent feature of a woman's autobiography, perhaps it is also what empowers Kingston's double-voiced talk-story. *The Woman Warrior* symbolizes a journey of searching for self-realization and self-creation which remains still unfinished at the autobiography's close. The ultimate feminist moment in *The Woman Warrior* comes at the end, when "two powerful woman storytellers meet . . . both working at strengthening the ties among women while commemorating and transmitting the powers of our foremothers. At once a grandmother, a poetess, a storyteller, and a woman warrior"

(Trinh 1989, 135). And in Kingston's own words, "She said I would grow up a wife and a slave, but she taught me the song of the warrior woman Fa Mu Lan. I would have to grow up a warrior woman" (Kingston 1976, 24). Maxine Hong Kingston has triumphed as an enchanting storyteller, a true warrior—a Chinese American woman warrior. Her double voice has translated well.

References

Berger, P., Berger, B., and Kellner, H. (1973). *The homeless mind.* New York: Vintage.

Berman, M. (1982). *All that is solid melts into air.* New York: Simon and Schuster.

Chen, V. (1992). The construction of Chinese American women's identity. In L. F. Rakow (Ed.), *Women making meaning: New feminist directions in communication* (225–243). New York: Routledge, Chapman and Hall.

Chow, R. (1990). Politics and pedagogy of Asian literatures in American Universities. *Differences,* 2 (3), 29–51.

Fischer, M. M. J. (1986). Ethnicity and the postmodern arts of memory. In J. Clifford and G. E. Marcus (Eds.), *Writing culture: The poetics and politics of ethnicity* (194– 233). Berkeley: University of California Press.

Kadohata, C. (1989). *The floating world.* New York: Viking.

Kim, E. H. (1982). *Asian American literature.* Philadelphia: Temple University Press.

Kim, E. H. (1987, Spring). Defining Asian American realities through literature. *Cultural critique,* 6, 87–111.

Kingston, M. H. (1976). *The woman warrior: Memoirs of a girlhood among ghosts.* New York: Knopf. Reprint New York: Vintage. (All references are to the Vintage edition.)

Kingston, M. H. (1982). Cultural misreadings by American reviewers. In G. Amirthanayagam (Ed.), *Asian and Western writers in dialogue: New cultural identities* (55–65). London: Macmillan.

Kingston, M. H. (1989). *Tripmaster monkey: His fake book.* New York: Knopf.

Morrison, T. (1992). *Play in the dark: Whiteness and literary imagination.* Cambridge, MA: Harvard University Press.

Ng, F. M. (1993). *Bone.* New York: Hyperion.

Okada, J. [1957] (1979). *No-no boy.* Seattle: University of Washington Press.

Rodriguez, R. (1982). *Hunger of memory: The education of Richard Rodriguez.* New York: Bantam.

Sone, M. [1953] (1979). *Nisei daughter*. Seattle: University of Washington Press.

Tan, A. (1989). *The joy luck club*. New York: Putnam.

Trinh, T.M. (1989). *Woman, native, other*. Bloomington: Indiana University Press.

Wong, J.S. (1989). *Fifth Chinese daughter* (rev. ed.). Seattle: University of Washington Press ✦

2

Dis/orienting Identities

Asian Americans, History, and Intercultural Communication

Thomas Nakayama
Arizona State University

*If I'm not who you say I am, then you're
not who you think you are.*

—James Baldwin (1990, 5)

One morning while I was walking to the Mouton-Duvernet Métro station in Paris's 14th Arrondissement, where I was renting a room for the summer, a woman came running up to me in an obvious hurry. Out of breath, she blurted out, *"Monsieur! Pardon! Où est le métro, s'il vous plaît?"*[1] I quickly gave her directions and she ran off, disappearing around the corner.

On my way to the Latin Quarter, I thought about how odd that little interaction had been for me. Here was a woman running up to me, assuming that I spoke French. I felt dis/oriented, as if I were called into a position that I do not normally occupy. When in Europe, I have come across many people who assume that, as someone of Asian ancestry, I speak French. Living in the United States, I rarely encounter people who assume that I speak French.

I begin with this story because I think it contributes to an understanding of the way that various histories influence intercultural communication practices. France's history with Asia is different from that of other European nations and certainly from that of the United States. These varying histories position me in different ways in different cultural contexts. As an Asian American, my ties to France and French history are distant indeed; yet this past confronts me when, for example, Europeans assume I speak French. My goal in this paper is to explore the cultural and historical constructions of the "Orient" and its relationship to my communication experiences in both domestic and international contexts.

My hope is that this essay will help challenge assumptions that continue to hamper many communication interactions. If James Baldwin is correct, I want to encourage a rethinking of what "American" means as a nationality and as an identity. As Kim (1982, 22) points out: "For Asian American writers, the task is to contribute to the total image and identity of America by depicting their own experiences and by defining their own humanity as part of the composite image of the American people." My goal here is not to argue simply that Asian Americans are Americans, but to suggest *why* this definition is a problem for Asian Americans. Unlike European Americans, Asian Americans have long been considered "forever foreign."

I do not wish to confuse the already confusing difference(s) between "Asians" and "Asian Americans." Yet, I believe it is important for Asian Americans to begin seeing their identities in both domestic and international contexts. For example:

> Asian American Studies has been located within the context of American Studies and stripped of its international links. This nationalist interpretation of immigration history has also been a more comfortable discourse for second- and third- generation Americans of Asian ancestry. Tired of being thought of as foreigners, these scholars have been particularly reluctant to identify with Asian Studies and its pronouncements on the distinctiveness of Asian cultures in counterpoint to Euro-American culture. (Mazumdar 1991, 29–30)

My point is not to reinforce this binary view of "Euro-American culture" versus "Asian cultures" in which Asian Americans are invisible, marginalized, and silenced. Rather, I want to suggest that we cannot understand the experiences and histories of

Asian Americans outside of the context of *both* domestic and international contexts.

It is not enough simply to mark the difference between "Asian" and "Asian American." Asian Americans, like Asians, are diverse groups of people that can be categorized under the same discursive label. The cultural backgrounds and histories of Americans of Asian ancestry are at least as diverse as Americans of European ancestry, if not more so. It is important, therefore, to recognize the heterogeneity concealed in the construction of Asian American identity since an essentialized ethnic identity "also inadvertently supports the racist discourse that constructs Asians as a homogeneous group, that implies we are 'all alike' and conform to 'types'" (Lowe 1991, 30). The cultural and discursive construction of "Asian American," then, is certainly inadequate to describe the diversity and complexity of the differences between and among us, but it does help us understand how "Orientals" are often categorized as "Other" in U.S. culture, due to histories of discrimination.

The Specter of the 'Orient'

As *yonsei*, a fourth-generation Japanese American, I feel at home in the United States. Like many Americans of European ancestry who have not been to Europe, I have not yet visited Japan. While I would like to visit Japan, the reality of Japan is not part of my experience. Certainly, I have been influenced by Japanese culture, filtered down through the generations and experiences of my forbearers in the United States. Like many U.S. citizens whose ancestors came from overseas, my relation to the "Orient" is similar to those who trace their origins elsewhere.

There is a specter haunting the United States, the specter of the Orient. The cultural image of the Orient invades and structures much of my intercultural communication interactions. My physical features identify my Asian ancestry, and it is this identification that structures my communication interactions with others. The phenomenon of being a U.S. citizen without European ancestry is noted by Chan (1991):

The history of Asians in America can be fully understood only if we regard them as both immigrants and members of nonwhite minority groups. As immigrants, many of their struggles resemble those that European immigrants have faced, but as people of nonwhite origins bearing distinct physical differences, they have been perceived as "perpetual foreigners" who can never be completely absorbed into American society and its body politic. (187)

The question here is one of identity: Who am I perceived to be when I communicate with others? What does it mean to be a "perpetual foreigner" in one's native country? My identity is very much tied to the ways in which others speak to me and the ways in which society represents my interests. In order to begin to answer these questions, we have to understand the complexity of the cultural construction of the Orient.

It is the cultural construction of the Orient that many Asians and Asian Americans find negative. Therefore, the term *oriental* is not the preferred term; it is fraught with stigmatizing ideological meanings. The use of *oriental* to refer to people, then, should also be avoided.

Where Is the Orient?

We can sense the ideological framework that produces the cultural construction of the Orient when we juxtapose European with American visions of this imaginary place. Europeans tend to think of the Near East (Turkey) and the Middle East when they speak of the Orient. However, as Said (1978, 1) pointed out, "Americans will not feel quite the same about the Orient, which for them is much more likely to be associated very differently with the Far East (China and Japan, mainly)." The Orient is not a place with clearly defined boundaries in the way that nations or even continents are demarcated. The Orient crosses continents "from North Africa and Turkey to China and Japan"[2] (Thomas 1990, 6).

But what do Turkey and Japan share that Italy and Japan do not? How is North Africa like China, but not like France? These are more than analogy questions; they point to an odd system of categorizing, of ordering the world through a discourse in which the Orient becomes the Other, the antithesis of the West. This binary opposition between the Occident and the Orient is reflected in U.S. culture as well.

The cultural construction of the Orient is evident in the innumerable films, television and radio programs, advertisements, and cartoons that depict this "Other" place. This exotic place is occupied by odd people, as evidenced by their bizarre clothes, eyes, and the sounds emanating from "Orientals." This is not a new discovery, as "caricatures of Asians have been part of American popular culture for generations" (Kim 1981, 3).

Even when I was young, I hated seeing media and movie images of martial arts, Fu Manchu types, and other limited and distorted representations of Asians. I longed for images of Asian Americans, rather than Asians. Yet the creation of Asian American images might have upset the binary opposition between East and West. I often wonder if we still need this oppositional force in our culture, but as I watch "Japan-bashing" on television, its continuation seems assured.

How to Become Dis/oriented

Dis/orientation is a dialectical process. The first part of this process, that of Asian Americans, comprises the historical experiences of Asian Americans living in the U.S. The second part, that of non-Asian Americans, is the socially learned expectation that Asians are not American, and can never become Americans. The combination of these processes invariably constructs identity positions that rarely correspond to where we, Asian Americans, think we are; hence, we are left dis/oriented.

In order to be dis/oriented, it seems necessary that Asian Americans had to first be "oriented." The historical process by which dis/orientation happens may take several generations, but the specific time frame seems to matter little. In my family, dis/orientation began in the nineteenth century and continues today. It is part of a long struggle to distance oneself from the cultural construction of the Orient.

Obviously, there were tremendous influences that caused a split from cultures, rather than a combination thereof. My mother's family, for example, switched from being a primarily Japanese-speaking household to an English-speaking one during their internment in a U.S. concentration camp during World War II. I think they felt it was better to demonstrate their commitment to the U.S. during a time of crisis in which, based on their ancestry, their loyalty was questioned. This historical experience has been one of the most influential aspects of Japanese American identity, a shared collective memory that has bound Japanese Americans as a group and created a distinct identity. In this way, the collective memory serves an important identity function (Ng 1991). In fact, it is this historical experience that creates my need to insist that I am American, not Japanese.

For non-Asian Americans, dis/orientation is not a split from the Orient, but the disorienting inability to overcome "Orientalism." I suspect that Orientalism manifests itself in different ways in intercultural communication interactions, but it becomes problematic when distinctions between Asian and Asian Americans are not made, when English is assumed a foreign language for Asian Americans, when Asian and American are split into two unrelated terms.

Reconsidering History

"Do you speak English?" This question always dis/orients me; I am lost when asked this question. Why wouldn't I speak the language of my parents, the language of my country? The simple response "Of course I do" does not usually dis/orient the questioner's assumption that one needs European ancestors to be "American."

I once had a Vietnamese American student whose francophone parents wanted her to learn French. She steadfastly refused, saying, "French is the language of the colonizers." History has situated her relationship to French quite differently from my own. The other students in class objected, insisting that "French is a beautiful language." Once I had explained a little about the history of France in Indochina, they understood her resistance.

History is a process that has constructed where and how we enter into dialogue, conversation, and communication. It has strongly influenced what languages we speak, how we are perceived and how we perceive ourselves, and what domestic and international conflicts affect us.

On the domestic level, the histories of Asians in the United States are often difficult to find. Ignorance of these histories leads many Americans to assume that Asian Americans are recent immigrants. Although many Asian Americans trace their roots back before the tremendous wave of European immigration in the early twentieth century, our histories are hidden and silenced. We know that "the major Asian immigrant groups in the U.S. in the nineteenth century were the Chinese and Japanese, although there is evidence that Filipinos, for example, had been in Louisiana as early as the eighteenth century" (Odo 1993, 118–119). Yet, the experiences of Asian Americans in many regions of the U.S. are often overlooked, hence, "much of our [Asian American] social and cultural histories will never be recovered" (Odo 1993, 120). On the international level, the dynamic nature of international relations between Asian nations and the U.S. continues to influence the ways in which Asian Americans are seen. For example:

> Over 50 years after the bombing of Pearl Harbor, Japanese Americans are again victims of rising tensions between Japan and the United States. This should come as no surprise. The fate of Asian Americans has always been historically shaped by the prevailing state of U.S.–Asia relations. (Omi 1993, 208)

The shifting winds of international relations have driven Asian Americans in many directions in their continual struggles to find a place in the U.S. But these international relations are not limited to the U.S. and Asia; they encompass many international interactions, contemporary as well as historical, in which we find ourselves trapped.

While waiting for the RER train at the Luxembourg station in Paris, I stood on the platform near a group of European American tourists who were examining a map and discussing where to go next. One of the women looked around and complained to her friends, in English, that there were "too many foreigners in Paris." As I *am* a foreigner in France, the comment did not strike me until I realized that the tourist assumed that I did not speak English and felt that she had some claim to France that I did not, as I assume she was not complaining about herself. I have wondered from time to time about the nature of her comment. Did she expect a different Paris? Did she know about our shared history on the other side of the Atlantic? Did she know about France's history in Africa and Asia? Would such knowledge have helped her understand France in other ways?

Our many different histories have much to do with where and how we enter into communication. The complexity of these histories can seem daunting, but they are crucial to the study of intercultural communication. Perhaps it is the absence of historical understanding that is no longer tenable if we are serious about understanding intercultural communication.

Another Country?

I do not know the face of this
country.
It is inhabited by strangers
who call me obscene names.
Jap. Go home.
Where is home?
　　　　—Janice Mirikitani (1987, 7)

When I was growing up in Georgia, I began first grade at a "white school." At the time, I do not think I understood why there were two types of schools or any of the other racially segregated practices we engaged in daily. In hindsight, it seems bizarre to have lived in a black and white world when one is neither black nor white. How arbitrary these divisions are! Yet, they construct the ways in which we think about ourselves and others. Even today, when I speak to my students about history and intercultural relations, they look at me as if I am from another country.

Today, I live in central Arizona. Fifty years ago my mother also lived in Arizona, at Poston III, an internment camp. Although we might like to believe that being an American is not a matter of "a common nationality, language, race, or ancestry" (Lapham 1992, 48), the historical divisiveness of these differences and their importance in our everyday understanding of ourselves and others belies this dream.

Because of the inability of many European Americans to perceive any difference— cultural, linguistic, national, etc.— between Asians and Asian Americans, I can only be wary of recent Japan-bashing in the U.S. media. Although it has been 50 years since the U.S. concentration camps opened, it was because of similar racism that the mass incarceration of U.S. citizens was initiated. Here, then, is the irony: Asian American identities cannot be understood outside of the context of international politics and histories, and Asian American history and politics *are* a part of U.S. history and politics. Hence, my identification as an "American" seems ineffectual and, I feel, in an ongoing struggle with those who wish to identify me otherwise. These dis/orienting identities always leave me somewhere other than where I think I am. Asian Americans are trapped among larger discourses and histories, which constantly disrupt any claim to a stable identity; perhaps we are a paradigmatic example of postmodern racial identity.

I resent being considered a foreigner in the United States, asked if I speak English, or asked when I came to this country. I am angry that my family has lost what I consider to be the most important part of its cultural heritage: its language. Perhaps this is the price to be paid for living in a society that is more interested in acculturation to "the hegemonic values of white U.S. society" (Escoffier 1991, 64) than to multiculturalism. My hope is that Asian Americans will be able to inscribe their experiences and histories into other groups through "the formation of important political alliances and affiliations . . . across racial and ethnic, gender, sexuality, and class lines" (Lowe 1991, 31). In large part, this strategy would require

letting go of the dominant view of U.S. history as one of European conquest and the assumption that Americans are of European descent.

Unlike James Baldwin, Richard Wright, and many other African American expatriates, I did not find Paris as liberating as they did. They lived in a different Paris, in a different context than I did. They also came from a different United States. As much as I enjoyed Paris, it was not home.

When the Arizona desert heat becomes oppressive, I think of my mother living in a tar-paper barrack without air conditioning. I doubt that she considered Arizona "home." For me, however, I am home far from Georgia. This is my country and my home, even if I do not look "all-American."

Notes

1. "Excuse me, sir, where is the Metro station?"
2. *de l'Afrique du Nord et de la Turquie à la Chine et au Japon* (my translation).

References

Baldwin, J. (1990). Quoted in introduction: A war of images. In J. L. Dates and W. Barlow (Eds.), *Split image* (1–21). Washington, DC: Howard University Press.

Chan, S. (1991). *Asian Americans: An interpretive history.* Boston: Twayne.

Escoffier, J. (1991). The limits of multiculturalism. *Socialist Review,* 21/3–4, 61–73.

Kim, E.H. (1982). *Asian American literature.* Philadelphia: Temple University Press.

Lapham, L.H. (1992, January). Who and what is American? *Harper's Magazine,* 43–49.

Lowe, L. (1991). Heterogeneity, hybridity, multiplicity: Marking Asian American differences. *Diaspora,* 1/1, 24–44.

Mazumdar, S. (1991). Asian American studies and Asian studies: Rethinking roots. In S. Hune, H.C. Kin, S.S. Fugita, and A. Ling (Eds.), *Asian Americans: Comparative and global perspectives* (29–44). Pullman: Washington State University Press.

Mirikitani, J. (1987). Prisons of silence. In *Shedding silence* (5–9). Berkeley: Celestial Arts.

Ng, W.L. (1991). The collective memories of communities. In S. Hune, H. C. Kim, S.S. Fugita, and A. Ling (Eds.), *Asian Americans:*

Comparative and global perspectives (103–112). Pullman: Washington State University Press.

Odo, F.S. (1993). Is there a future for our past? Cultural preservation policy. In *The State of Asian Pacific America, a public policy report: Policy issues to the year 2020* (113–126). Los Angeles: Leadership Education for Asian Pacifics and UCLA Asian American Studies Center.

Omi, M. (1993). Out of the melting pot and into the fire: Race relations policy. In *The state of Asian Pacific America, a public policy report: Policy issues to the year 2020* (199–214). L:os Angeles: Leadership Education for Asian Pacifics and UCLA Asian American Studies Center.

Said, E.W. (1978). *Orientalism.* New York: Random House.

Takaki, R. (1989). *Strangers from a different shore: A history of Asian Americans.* New York: Penguin.

Thomas, Y. (1990). Présentation. Special issue: La Tentation de l'Orient. [Introduction. The Temptation of the Orient]. *Études françaises,* 26/1, 6–8. ✦

3

How I Came to Know 'In Self Realization There Is Truth'

Sidney A. Ribeau
Bowling Green State University

A recent reading of *Multi-Cultural Literacy: Opening the American Mind* (1988) prompted this paper. In this anthology, the editors present a number of essays which challenge readers to analyze critically their world through the writing of women and men who see a diverse America. Education, history, and culture are discussed from a critical perspective which includes groups traditionally considered "outsiders." The authors provide cultural critiques in a manner designed to expand our understanding of America, and thus strengthen the fabric of our culture. bell hooks (1990) has referred to this approach as education for a critical consciousness. Through speaking and writing, she suggests, academics can make critical interventions which lead to altered perceptions of social reality. "A Journey Into Speech" by Michelle Cliff, a selection from this collection, is particularly useful in understanding the difficulty of overcoming personal alienation and establishing an empowered ethnic identity.

Issues discussed in *Multi-Cultural Literacy* seem especially important for those interested in the study of culture and communication. In this chapter, I use these issues to establish the context for a discussion of my personal search for an African American academic identity to guide my career. Michelle Cliff insightfully describes her struggle to find her literary voice after years ". . . of assimilation, indoctrination, passing into the anglo-centricism of British West Indian culture. . . ." She describes the British domination of Jamaican culture as leading to the internationalization of white supremacy which marginalized her culture and traditions. Works written in the "King's English" were literature, while indigenous stories written in patois were not. This led to a gradual alienation from her ethnic identity which culminated in the completion of her education at the Warburg Institute.

> My dissertation was produced at the Warburg Institute, University of London, and was responsible for giving me an intellectual belief in myself that I had not had before, while at the same time distancing me from who I am, almost rendering me speechless about who I am. At least I believed in the young woman who wrote the dissertation—still I wondered who she was and where she had come from. (57)

The inception of an academic career further immersed Cliff in the culture of dominant society. Her academic success depended on her ability to create knowledge in a form and for an audience rooted in cultural hegemony. Academically trained and intellectually prepared, she found herself personally isolated and marginalized. Psychological introspection and participation in the feminist movement enabled her to "approach herself as subject," and begin to reveal who she was in her work. As subject, she was required to rediscover her ethnocultural past.

> To write [she says] as a complete Caribbean woman, or man for that matter, demands of us retracing the African part of ourselves, reclaiming as our own, and as our subject, a history sunk under the sea, or scattered as potash in the cane fields, or gone to bush, or trapped in a class system notable for its rigidity and absolute dependence on color stratification. On a past bleached from our minds. (59)

The transformation from a muted, detached, alienated outsider to a centered, connected, articulate actor is not unique to

Cliff. In *Breaking Ice*, Terry McMillan (1990) describes a similar realization:

> I couldn't believe the rush I felt over and over once I discovered Countee Cullen, Langston Hughes, Ann Petry, Zora Neale Hurston, Ralph Ellison, Jean Toomer, Richard Wright, and rediscovered and read James Baldwin, to name just a few. . . . My world opened up accumulated and gained a totally new insight about, and perception of our lives as "black" people, as if I had been an outsider and was finally let in. (xvi)

While reading about the experiences of Cliff and McMillan, I was drawn to memories of my graduate school years. Communication theory, interpersonal communication, research methodology, the list continued, but none of the courses listed considered the African American experience, nor the experience of Latinos, Asians, or Native Americans. There was, in our requirements, no intercultural communication course or mention of the ethnic experience. The "Message from the Grass Roots," a speech by Malcolm X, was brought up in one class, but other than that, rhetoric, communication theory, and all other areas of the discipline were decidedly Eurocentric. During this period, I maintained intellectual balance by taking courses in African American literature and anthropology. Like Terry McMillan, literature enabled me to experience the aesthetic life of the African American while groping for a connection between my experience and the discipline which seemed to ignore it. Was there an African American rhetorical tradition? Did interpersonal communication theory consider the unique cultural history of African Americans here and in Africa? Was there form and content which distinguished African American communication from that of the dominant group? These questions and other similar ones were felt but not stated as I struggled with Greek rhetorical tradition and social scientific theory which seemed to render me invisible. I should add that my graduate program was an excellent one. The faculty was nationally recognized; the research facilities exceptional. It was not the quality of the program that was restricting;

it was the limitations placed on curricula by a Eurocentric paradigm that dominated graduate work in my disciplinary area—and in most others. I was briefly connected to another dimension of communication study by Arthur L. Smith (1969, 1972, aka M.K. Asante). His *Rhetoric of Black Revolution and Language, Communication and Rhetoric in Black America* ignited in me a desire to expand my understanding of the communication processes to include a voice, albeit muted, which recognized my presence.

Graduate school reflections were quickly replaced by the demands of my first full-time university teaching position. I felt prepared to teach courses in interpersonal and group communication, my areas of concentration, and was beginning to develop an interest in intercultural communication. My colleagues were supportive, and academic life was fine. However, as time passed I was compelled, for personal and professional reasons, to prepare a paper for submission to a scholarly journal. This decision vividly reminded me of the absence in the literature of non-mainstream voices.

African American rhetoric had surfaced momentarily, but faded with the dissipation of the Black protest movement. Papers on the subject were not being published. Intercultural communication was considered an interesting instructional area because of its focus on improving race relations (Rich 1974), but was not represented in the scholarly journals. Surely, I thought, ethnicity and culture were variables that significantly influenced communication; my time would come. When it didn't, I forged ahead with a colleague, who shared similar interests, and conducted an empirical study on what we called "domestic ethnic cultural groups." It was submitted to a regional speech communication journal and rejected by the reviewers because African Americans did not constitute a unique culture. They were merely a "subcultural" group. My colleague and I wrote a rebuttal, citing the works of W.E.B. DuBois (1903), Melville Herskovits (1941), and Geneva Smitherman (1977), which clearly traced the evolution of African American culture from the shores of West Africa to America. The editor was not persuaded by our evidence, and the paper was not published. My anger slowly cooled and assumed the form of quiet resignation. The ethnic culture which was not included in my formal education, but gave form and definition to my life, was casually dismissed. As in graduate school, again I did not exist.

Eventually the paper was resubmitted and accepted for publication in an international journal outside of my discipline. I recount these events to make a point: the academic experience can empower or silence. It empowers through the inclusion of content that speaks to the breadth of the human experience; it silences through the exclusion of those outside the mainstream. In America we readily identify these groups. The examples discussed above consider the process by which academics of African descent come to a sense of ethnic identity which focuses their intellectual interests and creates a cultural foundation for their work. Academic training alone, in programs dominated by a Eurocentric paradigm, do not equip one to conduct research, write, or teach about issues that grow from cultural experiences. A recent issue of *Liberal Education* (June 1991) considers the limitations of traditional educational approaches that lack diversity and argues for a more pluralistic approach.

> Most commonly . . . applicant institutions report a pervasive parochialism among their students: they lack either knowledge of or interest in both the complexity of their own society and the variety of cultures, claims, and world views mingling across the boundaries of nations and societies. (4)

Parochialism is not only a characteristic of the students, but also it grows from school curricula that ignores the experiences of outsider groups. These omissions separate the academic world from the realities students encounter in daily life and see on television or film. Many students live in a world very different from the one studied in school. Because of this, it is easy for them to become academically isolated and psychologically removed from the intellectual stimulation that schools should provide. This situation is intensified for many ethnic stu-

dents whose language, family structure, and traditions move them further from the mainstream culture. Years of such educational experiences can extinguish natural intellectual curiosity, or significantly dampen it. The results, all too often, are invisibility or silence.

This does not have to be. Along with Cliff, McMillan, and others, I discovered an intellectual space through an awareness of my African American ethnic identity. Ethnic identity is the ethnic culture with which one identifies. It includes traditions, "peoplehood," heritage, orientation to the past, religion, languages, ancestry, values, economics, aesthetics, and social organization. The term currently used by academics to explain the intellectual framework for African American identity is *Afrocentricity*. The intellectual threads of this idea date back to the early work of W.E.B. DuBois (1903) and Carter G. Woodson (1933), but the most articulate of its current advocates is Molefi K. Asante (1987). Five central measures undergird the approach:

1. People of African descent share a common experience, struggle, and origin.

2. Present in African culture is a non-material element of resistance to the assault upon traditional values caused by the intrusion of European legal procedures, medicines, political processes, and religions into African culture.

3. African culture takes the view that an Afrocentric modernization process would be based upon three traditional values: harmony with nature, humaneness, and rhythm.

4. Afrocentricity involves the development of a theory of an African way of knowing and interpreting the world.

5. Some form of communalism or socialism is an important component of the way wealth is produced, owned, and distributed. (Covin 1990, 126)

Although these measures are both descriptive and prescriptive, they gain their greatest potency from the ability to connect the African diaspora to its early cultural roots. Connection to a nation, philosophy, languages, and cultural values enables the Afrocentric scholar to replace noticeable curricular omissions with substantive information leading to a sense of self-awareness. This in turn redefines the role of the outsider and can help remove the mantle of invisibility.

Afrocentricity is mentioned here to illustrate a mechanism through which a people alienated by educational institutions and social practice can discover a sense of ethnic identity which leads to renewed positive self-awareness. It suggests how an outsider group can confront the paradoxes of a racially stratified America. This approach, however, is also of value for other marginalized ethnic academics, especially communication scholars. In addition to being a powerful liberating force, Afrocentricity frames significant questions regarding communication and social interaction. Asante suggests that it involves

> the systematic exploration of relationships, social codes, cultural and commercial customs, oral traditions and proverbs, and the interpretation of communicative behavior as expressed in discourse, spoken or written, and techniques found in jazz studies and urban street vernacular. (16)

This focus is replete with research opportunities for the scholar interested in African American communication. It grounds the field in expressive forms and rituals central to African American culture. From it, one can begin to formulate a perspective on African American communication which begins with the fundamental cultural experiences of the people. Oral traditions, for example, are key elements in understanding African American communication and cultural continuities which connect Africa to the African American experience. Smitherman (1977) explains this important point:

> Naturally, Black Americans, having to contend with slavery and Euro-American ways, have not been able to practice or manifest the traditional African world view in its totality. But, as we shall see in closely examining the many facets of the oral tradition, the residue of the African world view persists, and serves to unify

such seemingly disparate groups as preachers and poets, bluesmen and Gospelettes, testifiers and toast-tellers, reverends and revolutionaries. (76)

Here we see a meshing of world views which gives rise to a number of African American expressive forms. The Afrocentric perspective, through its foundational assumptions, guides the researcher to fundamental questions regarding African American communication.

Thus far my discussion has focused on the African American experience, for through it I have established an academic ethnic identity. I am convinced that this identity has enabled me to focus professional interests in a manner consistent with the way in which mainstream scholars research and write about the reality that defines their worlds. For them, years of education identify, explain, and validate their intellectual interests because the curriculum mirrors them. The controversy surrounding multicultural education hinges on a belief that liberal education should be inclusive rather than exclusive, thus capturing the varied intellectual wealth of our nation. To accomplish this objective, ethnic scholars must be empowered to interpret the world through the eyes of those who have been forgotten. We all have much to learn, for example, from the lives of American Indian women. Paula Gunn Allen (1986) comments on the importance of the female in Indian culture:

> There are many female gods recognized and honored by the tribes and Nations. Femaleness was highly valued, both respected and feared, and all social institutions reflected this attitude. Even modern sayings, such as the Cheyenne statement that a people is not conquered until the hearts of the women are on the ground, express the Indian's understanding that without the power of women the people will not live, but with it they will endure and prosper. (16)

This information can help both feminist scholars and social historians extend the debate regarding the role of patriarchy in the development of American culture. Also, this information might ignite a spark of ethnic awareness for an American Indian woman psychologically buried in Eurocentric culture and searching for a sense of self. In both instances, new information enlightens and empowers.

Certain factors of racism and discrimination are shared by people of color in America, whatever their cultural group. These factors significantly contribute to outsider status and lend themselves to similar remedies. African Americans, Native Americans, and Latinos have all been subjected to *de facto* and *de jure* segregation. History documents the evolution of these events (Zinn 1980), while sociology describes the vestiges of this legacy found in ghettos, barrios, reservations, and other communities of the marginalized. In these areas, ethnic marginalization is usually accompanied by its economic counterpart, poverty. The combination is often a death sentence to the dreams of the young (Kozal 1991). With limited educational opportunities, the clouds of alienation begin to settle. Those who escape this trap must still grapple with curricula that ignore them and a society largely indifferent to the plight of their people. But they are the ones who might defy the odds and make it into the academy. If they are fortunate, an opportunity for a university degree affords a range of new possibilities. But there is a price. Achievement in the academy requires a kind of acculturation that can challenge the foundation of one's cultural life. Mainstream values designed to prepare one for success in a capitalist society are usually not derived from traditional ethnic cultures. All too often the price for academic success is the loss of self, described earlier by Michelle Cliff. Fortunately, there are ways to obtain educational goals and maintain a healthy ethnic identity. This process, however, begins with an education based on the premise of inclusion. Those in the communication discipline must take a new leadership role in this process.

The study of human communication assumes as its domain the formulation, transmission, and interpretation of messages. It is bound by a cultural context which frames interactional patterns. The history of the discipline is grounded in classical rhetoric and British public address, which places it well within the Eurocentric paradigm. As mentioned previously, this paradigm does not speak to the diversity that constitutes our nation. Implicit in our field is the assumption that most communication is a social act that emerges from a context. It is a short distance from these assumptions to a culturally sensitive communication perspective. What are the outlines of the requirements of such an approach?

Communication research must utilize a perspective on ethnic communication based on the cultural experiences of the group being studied. Just as an Afrocentric approach attempts to ground African American communication research in established cultural traditions of African Americans, research pertaining to other ethnic groups should begin with the cultural experiences of the people rather than theories developed on data from mainstream groups. The current methodological sophistication of our discipline makes this quite possible.

New initiatives must be taken to encourage ethnic students to pursue graduate work. The study of a culture differs from the experience of it. Insights gained from "living a culture" are assets in the study of cultural life. Ethnic students trained in communication theory and research methods can combine these with insider insights to explain the complexity of inter- and intracultural communication.

In the instructional area, intercultural communication must focus on the problematic aspects of intercultural encounters. Many of the problems in contemporary society are the result of cultural misunderstanding. We read of them in newspapers, see them on television, and experience them in our lives. For the most part, unfortunately, they do not find their way into the classroom to be analyzed. We must use our theory and skills to develop intercultural improvement strategies. We must connect the academy with the larger society.

The communication discipline has much to offer a truly liberal education. I have briefly discussed what I consider to be some possibilities. More importantly, I have attempted here to describe a space characterized by W.E.B. DuBois as "behind the veil." As I emerge from it, a new academic environment seems possible. One which is inclusive, empowering, and sensitive to the challenges which face our contemporary world.

I would be remiss, in closing, not to mention how the emergence of my ethnic identity has directly influenced the direction of my career. The implied impact is probably apparent to the careful reader, yet there are more pronounced manifestations. I mentioned earlier that I could not have written this essay prior to my search for a personal ethnic identity to ground both teaching and research interests. Unknown to me was a world of ideas, constructs, and feelings which would eventually direct my professional life. A result of this self-realization process was the acceptance of the chair position in the Pan African Studies Department at my university, a decision which forced me to confront alternative ways of experiencing and interpreting the communication discipline and long-range professional objectives. I interacted regularly with social scientists, literary scholars, and film critics who connected teaching, learning, and scholarship to ethnic issues and community service. In addition, my emerging personal and professional ethnic identity led to a redirection of career plans. It became apparent through discussions with a number of colleagues that the educational experience that had fostered my sense of personal alienation was not an isolated case. If this was to change, I reasoned, university policy must change. Thus, I embarked on an administrative track which has led me to serve as chair, dean, and now academic vice president. In my current position, it is possible to mobilize institutional resources to confront race, class, and gender bias while promoting an environment of inclusion which values the unique attributes of each individual.

Organizational change is a process that takes place over an extended period of time. Success in this area must begin, however, with personal self-realization. The intellectual journey described in this paper has brought me to a place where the personal and professional are fused in ways that affect my work, who I am, and what I might become.

References

Allen, P.G. (1988). Who is your mother? Red roots of white feminism. *Multi-cultural literacy: Opening the American mind.* Saint Paul, MN: Graywolf Press.

Asante, M.K. (1987). *The Afrocentric idea.* Philadelphia: Temple University Press.

Cliff, M. (1988). A journey into speech. *Multi-cultural literacy: Opening the American mind.* Saint Paul, MN: Graywolf Press (originally published, 1985).

DuBois, W.E.B. (1903). *The souls of black folk.* Greenwich, CT: Fawcett.

Herskovits, M. (1941). *The myth of the Negro past.* Boston: Beacon.

hooks, b. (1990). *Yearning: Race, gender, and cultural politics.* Boston: South End.

Kozal, J. (1991). *Savage inequalities.* New York: Crown.

McMillan, T. (1990). Introduction. *Breaking ice: An anthology of contemporary African-American fiction.* New York: Penguin.

Rich, A.L. (1974). *Interracial Communication.* New York: Harper and Row.

Schneider, C. (1991). Engaging cultural legacies. *Liberal Education*, 77(3), 4.

Simonson, R. and S. Walker (1988). *Multi-cultural literacy: Opening the American mind.* Saint Paul, MN: Graywolf Press.

Smith, A.L., aka M.K. Asante (1969). *Rhetoric of black revolution.* Boston: Allyn and Bacon.

Smith, A.L., aka M.K. Asante (1972). *Language, communication, and rhetoric in black America.* New York: Harper and Row.

Smitherman, G. (1977). *Talkin and testifyin: The language of black America.* Boston: Houghton Mifflin.

Woodson, C.B. (1933). *The mis-education of the American Negro.* Washington, DC: Associated Publishers.

Zinn, H. (1980). *Peoples' history of the United States.* New York: Harper and Row. ✦

4

Names, Narratives, and the Evolution of Ethnic Identity

Dolores V. Tanno
University of Nevada, Las Vegas

When being an "American" does not yield empowerment and acceptance, marginalized groups look for labels around which to proclaim identity and rally for political and communal purposes. The emergent theory of ethnic identity proposed by sociologist Felix Padilla in *Latino Ethnic Consciousness* (1985) suggests that ethnic identity is adaptive and evolving. It adjusts to the institutional and structural forces of the dominant culture. In the process, ethnic identity evolves in several ways. There is ethnic identity based on symbolic themes such as a common language, rituals, or shared world views. There is ethnic identification as historical consciousness, a sequence of events and struggles over time that reflects continuity from past to future. There is also ethnic identity as social consciousness, a seeking after communal or group acceptance. Finally, there is ethnic identity as strategy, a way of gaining political voice. Padilla's focus is on the evolution of communal ethnic identity, but individuals also go through a similar process in understanding and coming to terms with their ethnic identity.

The individual process may be understood by examining the different terms or names persons use to identify themselves over the course of their lives. Each "name"[1] is a rhetorical device insofar as it communicates a particular story. Walter Fisher's (1987) narrative paradigm suggests that every person has life experiences that become his/her own "story." According to Fisher, these experiences are biographical, cultural, historical, and moral, and they define the efforts of reasoning and valuing beings to conduct their lives in some semblance of order. Padilla's definition of ethnic identity and Fisher's focus on the narratives of our lives come together to help us understand the rhetorical impact of names placed on individuals and groups by themselves and by others. These names are "not merely a dilemma of self-identity, but of self-in-group-identity" (Rendon 1971, 324). In this essay, I will trace the unfolding of my own ethnic identity from Spanish to Mexican American, to Latina, and to Chicana by briefly examining the story behind each name. I will also address the value of, indeed the necessity for, multiple names.

Unfolding Ethnic Identity

Over the course of my life one question has been consistently asked of me: *What are you?* I used to reply that I was American, but it quickly became clear this was unacceptable because what came next was, "No, really, what are you?" In my more perverse moments I responded, "I am human." I stopped when I realized people's feelings were hurt. Ironic? Yes, but the motive behind the question often justified hurt feelings. I became aware of this only after asking a question of my own: "Why do you ask?"

The answers sometimes astounded me and almost always saddened me. I was astonished by outright hostility based on the assumption that I am where I am today because of "an easy affirmative-action ride." My sadness resulted from a growing knowledge of the desperate need of students who timidly ask, "What are you?" in the hopes of finding a role model. The combined result of my responses to "What are you?" and others' responses to "Why do you ask?" has been an enlightenment. Confronting the motives of people has forced me to examine who I am. In the process I have had to critically examine my own choices, in different times and contexts, of the names by which I am "placed" in society. The names are "Spanish," "Mexican American," "Latina," and "Chicana."

'I Am Spanish'

Behind this label is the story of my childhood in northern New Mexico where I was born and raised. New Mexico was the first permanent Spanish settlement in the Southwest, and New Mexicans have characterized themselves as Spanish for centuries. My parents, grandparents, and great-grandparents considered themselves Spanish; wrongly or rightly, they attributed their customs, habits, and language to their Spanish heritage, and I followed suit. In Fisher's terms, this was the biographical aspect of my life story. From Padilla's perspective, this would be considered ethnic identity based on symbolic themes such as rituals and practices. The rituals and practices included covering paths with flower petals for religious processions, speaking Spanish with some regional peculiarities, and listening to the religious ballads of the Penitentes. We never talked about whether we were *really* Spanish. Only in later years did I hear the argument that the intermarriage of Spaniards with Indians invalidated the use of the name "Spanish." Its continued use, according to Mario Garcia (1989, 281), communicates the idea that "racially and culturally they [New Mexicans] had to do more with Spain than with Mexico;" therefore, to be Spanish is to consider oneself "racially pure" or an "anglicized Mexican American." Garcia's argument may or may not be valid, but, in my young mind, the story of being Spanish did not include concepts of racial purity or assimilation; what it did do was allow me to begin my life with a clearly defined identity and a place in the world. For me, the story of being Spanish incorporates into its plot the innocence of youth, before the reality of discrimination became an inherent part of the knowledge of who I am.

'I Am Mexican American'

When I left New Mexico, my sense of belonging did not follow me across the state border. When I responded to the question "What are you?" by saying, "I am Spanish,"

people corrected me: "You mean Mexican, don't you?" My initial reaction was anger; how could they know better than I who I was? But soon my reaction was one of puzzlement, and I wondered just why there was such insistence that I be Mexican. Reading and studying led me to understand that the difference between Spanish and Mexican American could be found in the legacy of colonization. Mirandé and Enriquez (1979) make a distinction between the "internal" colonization of the Southwest and the "classic" colonization of Mexico. A central consequence of internal colonization is that "natives are deposed from power and native institutions are completely destroyed" (9). There is no formal or legal existence; it is as if the natives are re-invented in the conqueror's image. Therefore, behind the name "Spanish" is the story of internal colonization that does not allow for prior existence.

On the other hand, classic colonization "allows for more continuity between the pre- and post-conquest societies" because "native institutions are modified but retained," allowing formal and legal existence of the natives (9). Thus, behind the name "Mexican American" is the story of classic colonization that allows for prior existence and that also communicates duality. The name itself signifies duality; we are, as Richard A. Garcia (1983) argues, "Mexican in culture and social activity, American in philosophy and politics (88)." As native-born Americans, we also have a dual historical consciousness—the history of America and the history before America—that we must weave into the narrative of our lives to create a collective "biography." We have dual visions: the achievement of the American Dream and the preservation of cultural identity. To be Mexican American means "'navigating' precariously between both worlds, inhabiting both in good faith, and finally . . . forging a span between . . . original Mexican and . . . acquired American enculturations" (Saldívar 1990, 168).

'I Am Latina'

If the story behind the name Mexican American is grounded in duality, the story behind the name "Latina" is grounded in cultural connectedness. The Spaniards proclaimed vast territories of North and South America as their own. They intermarried in all the regions in which they settled. These marriages yielded offspring who named themselves variously as Cubans, Puerto Ricans, Colombians, Mexicans, and so forth, but they connect culturally with one another when they name each other Latinas.

Renato Rosaldo (1989) argues that culture encompasses "the informal practices of everyday life (26)." One of the most fundamental practices that unites those belonging to the Latino culture is religion, probably because Catholicism was another Spanish legacy. The Virgin Mary is appealed to in the course of daily living; the title by which she is known changes, but her importance is never questioned. For example, she is *La Virgen de Guadalupe* in Mexico, *Nuestra Señora de la Caredad del Cobre* in Cuba, *La Virgen de la Macarena* in Colombia, and *La Conquistadora* in New Mexico. She symbolizes the deep spirituality that is a definitive characteristic of the Latino culture. To use the name *Latina* is to communicate acceptance and belonging in a broad cultural community. This is ethnic identity as a type of consciousness that addresses the cultural aspect of Fisher's conception of the life story.

'I Am Chicana'

This name suggests a smaller community, a special kind of Mexican American awareness that does not invoke others (Cubans, Puerto Ricans, etc.). In *Chicano Manifesto*, Armando Rendon (1971, 320) argues that "to be Chicano[a] means that a person has looked deeper into his [her] being." To appropriate the name for oneself signifies the most intense ethnic identity, because, as Arnulfo Trejo (1979, xvii) suggests, "Chicano/a" is "the only term that was especially selected by us, for us." Padilla would define this ethnic identity as a strategy, and he would be right; the name was the primary political as well as rhetorical strategy of the Chicano movement of the 1960s. Mirandé and Enriquez (1979, 12) argue that a dominant characteristic of the name "Chicana" is that it admits a "sense of marginality." There is a political tone and character to "Chicana"

that signifies a story of self-determination and empowerment. As such, the name denotes a kind of political becoming. At the same time, however, the name communicates the idea of being American, not in a "melting pot" sense that presupposes assimilation, but rather in a pluralistic sense that acknowledges the inalienable right of existence for different peoples (Trejo 1979).

The Worth of Multiple Names

What, then, am I? The truth is that I am all of these. Each name reveals a different facet of identity that allows symbolic, historical, cultural, and political connectedness. These names are no different than other multiple labels we take on. For example, to be mother, wife, sister, and daughter is to admit to the complexity of being female. Each name implies a narrative of experiences gained in responding to circumstance, time, and place and motivated by a need to belong. As such they possess great rhetorical force. So it is with the names Spanish, Mexican American, Latina, and Chicana. They reveal facets of complex cultural beings. In my case, I resort to being Spanish and all it implies whenever I return to my birthplace, in much the same way that we often resort to being children again in the presence of our parents. But I am also Mexican American when I balance the two important cultures that define me; Latina, when I wish to emphasize cultural and historical connectedness with others; and Chicana, whenever opportunities arise to promote political empowerment and assert cultural pride.

It is sometimes difficult for people to understand the "both/and" mentality that results from this simultaneity of existence. In *To Split a Human*, Carmen Tafolla (1985) traces the theme of duality that gave rise to the both/and mentality. Beginning with pre-Columbian civilizations, the mythic polarities of life/death, half male/half female, and the Mother/Father god represented dual natures. In contemporary times, this duality manifests itself rhetorically as "otherness," which Alberto González (1990, 276) defines as "expressions of the [Mexican American] cultural identity. . . that includes simultaneous themes of separation and desire for inclusion." While some may lament this duality, Tafolla finds joy in it. Chicana women expressed to Tafolla their feelings about living in the midst of two cultures: "What is most exciting. . . is the constant thought in my mind that I am actually two;" "Being bilingual and bicultural has sensitized me. . . I can then live intensely and not merely exist;" "There are several words that we can use to describe a feeling, thing, etc. that cannot be translated into English . . . and some that cannot be translated into Spanish. We have both" (93–94).

We are indeed enriched by belonging to two cultures. We are made richer still by having at our disposal several names by which to identify ourselves. Singly, the names Spanish, Mexican American, Latina, and Chicana communicate part of a life story. Together they weave a rhetorically powerful narrative of ethnic identity that combines biographical, historical, cultural, and political experiences.

Note

1. *Name* is the term I use to describe the confluence of historical, cultural, biographical, political, and symbolic themes that express membership in a particular group.

References

Fisher, W.R. (1987). *Human communication as narration: Toward a philosophy of reason, value, and action.* Columbia: University of South Carolina Press.

Garcia, M.T. (1989). *Mexican Americans: Leadership, ideology, and identity, 1930–1960.* New Haven, CT: Yale University Press.

Garcia, R. (1983). The Mexican American mind: A product of the 1930s. In *History, culture, and society: Chicano studies in the 1980s* (67–93). Ypsilanti, MI: Bilingual Press.

González, A. (1990). Mexican "otherness" in the rhetoric of Mexican Americans. *Southern Communication Journal, 6,* 276–291.

Mirandé, A. and Enriquez, E. (1979). *La Chicana: The Mexican American woman.* Chicago, IL: University of Chicago Press.

Padilla, F. (1985). *Latino ethnic consciousness.* Notre Dame, IN: University of Notre Dame.

Rendon, A.B. (1971). *Chicano manifesto.* New York: Collier.

Rosaldo, R. (1989). *Culture and truth.* Boston: Beacon Press.

Saldívar, R. (1990). *Chicano narrative: The dialectics of difference.* Madison: University of Wisconsin Press.

Tafolla, C. (1985). *To split a human: Mitos, machos y la mujer chicana.* San Antonio, TX: Mexican American Cultural Center.

Trejo, A. (Ed.). (1979). A word from the editor. In *The Chicanos: As we see ourselves* (xv–xviii). Tucson: University of Arizona Press. ✦

Part II

Negotiating Sexuality and Gender

5

Jewish and/or Woman

Identity and Communicative Style

Sheryl Perlmutter Bowen
Villanova University

More than ten years ago, my graduate school mentor revealed to me that only when I stopped complaining would she begin to worry about me. Over time, she had come to expect my continual complaints of work load, crises that got in the way of completing tasks, gripes about my family, and other such minutiae of life. She had learned that, as long as I "bitched," I was really doing fine. That meant that, despite all my verbiage, I was still functioning normally.

Recently, in separate incidents, two young men in leadership positions in a student organization that I advise asked me why I was "mocking them." I thought I was just having good-natured conversation with them, harmlessly teasing, trying to create identification with them. I might ask how the weekend went or perhaps retort, "Oh, you just like to have a good time." On another day I might ask how their classes were going and respond in a way that wouldn't paint me as "the professor," saying something such as, "You can't take this academic stuff too seriously." When one of these young men brought this so-called mocking to my attention, I attributed it to not knowing him very well and assumed that perhaps he was more sensitive than I had imagined. When the second man made the same comment, I recalled the earlier episode and became pensive. I tried to identify what they had found so troublesome.

Most of us do not spend considerable amounts of time ruminating about our own styles of communication. Usually it is only when our communication becomes problematic, when we fail to achieve a communicative goal or are called out for something we said or how we said it, that we really begin to notice how we communicate with others. This self-awareness is quite different from the relative ease with which we can characterize someone else's interactive style.

I have begun to understand that the complaining aspect of my interaction with my mentor (and countless others since) is in part a result of my cultural identity. I will often list the impediments to the work I *should* be getting done. My frequent teasing of students is also a part of my cultural identity, as I try to connect with students on a personal level without prying into their lives. Symbolic interactionist theorists tell us what most of us already know: all of us play a variety of roles in our daily lives and often alter our communicative styles based on the roles we perceive for ourselves. What has not been well discussed, however, is how variations in that communicative style can be highly influenced by one's cultural or ethnic heritage. Often the influences are not conscious, and surely they are also affected by individual differences among people.

In this essay, I will explore two conditions that may account for the complaining and teasing aspects of my communicative style. Specifically, they are being Jewish and being female in late twentieth-century America. Each of these aspects of my identity has shaped my being, my goals and aspirations, my lifestyle choices, interpretations of my experiences, and my communication with others.

The problematic episodes related above have come to symbolize for me the tension that exists between certain aspects of identity. What I hope to show in the pages that follow is that being Jewish accounts for some aspects of style and being a woman accounts for others. Now, there are surely other influences on my communication, such as my education and socioeconomic background, but cultural influences are dominant in the complaining and teasing episodes mentioned above. Consistent with the style of this book, I will not bother to detail the scholarly literature on these topics, but rather analyze the two episodes in light of my understanding of my own cultural experiences. Perhaps readers can use this essay to learn a bit about how it feels to be Jewish and female, or to reflect on the ways in which their own cultural identities may influence aspects of their communication with others.

Jewish Identity

I am, besides being Jewish and female, a non-traditional Jew and a feminist. I was raised in a traditional Jewish home, heavily influenced by two aunts who are Orthodox Jews. I went to religious school at least once a week from age 6 to 15, and spent one year in a Jewish parochial school where the day was divided between secular and religious studies. I learned to read Hebrew with fluency and to understand a portion of what I read. The Jewish calendar was very important in marking the passage of time in my home. As my immediate family was affected by the death of a parent, remarriage to a non-religious Jew, and a move to the suburbs, my experiences in Jewish institutions were with conservative and Reform synagogues. By the time I was in high school, my Jewish identity was primarily expressed through my active involvement with a statewide Reform youth organization. Here I celebrated Jewish rituals and culture with other adolescents in a social setting. I even flirted with the idea of becoming a rabbi.

Although I have a fairly traditional Jewish background and upbringing, as an adult I choose to affiliate with a "spiritual activist synagogue" which places emphasis on joining Jewish life and Jewish renewal with modern secular work. This synagogue is part of the Reconstructionist movement, the fourth branch of Judaism. Reconstructionism is heavily influenced by the thinking of Mordecai Kaplan and retains elements of traditional Jewish ritual and observance with understandings relevant for living in the modern multi-cultural world. I have found the Reconstructionist movement to be highly compatible with my understanding

about life from my academic training, and I am able to connect my secular and religious life.

Culturally, I am a Jew. This means that I am influenced by the historical experiences of Jews in this country, in my family's Eastern European origins and, indeed, in today's Middle East. I am a product of the ways that I have received Jewish training, participated in Jewish ritual, and interacted with others, Jews and non-Jews.

I have felt a closeness to the feminist ideals espoused in academic and activist presses. I am not content to perpetuate traditional sex roles, as I am not content to perpetuate traditional Jewish roles. My personal choices have involved discovering methods to reconstruct and reaffirm aspects of both female culture and Jewish culture in ways that disturb the male-female inequities that have characterized our society. My group affiliations and political perspectives force me to continually question and evaluate situations in which I find myself.

In addition to taking a Jewish perspective, I must also consider the fact that my experiences are influenced by my gender. As many Jewish women have been describing over the last 15 years or so, being a Jewish woman is different from being a Jewish man in this country. Differing access to religious and cultural experiences has meant that Jewish women and men traditionally have lived in different worlds. To provide an oversimplified sketch, men were responsible for public prayers, traditionally said three times per day, and for working outside of the home; while women were responsible for the domestic aspects of family life, including raising the children and keeping the household according to Jewish law to preserve traditions (for example, following *kashrut*, the Jewish dietary laws). Aside from the particulars that differentiate Jewish life, the traditional sex roles parallel those dominant in the larger culture.

Consistent with feminist moves in a variety of other areas, Jewish feminists have recently begun to appropriate some of the symbols and rituals that previously were open only to men. For example, in traditional Orthodox Jewish circles, only men were able to be counted in the prayer group, or *minyan* (which must consist of at least ten men to allow saying all of the prescribed prayers in a given service). Orthodox women in many cities across the country are gathering to pray among themselves, and some have protested their invisibility in a male prayer service, because in Orthodox synagogues, women and men sit in separate areas divided by a screen or curtain. Some groups of women have reclaimed *Rosh Hodesh*, the celebration at the new moon each month, as a women's holiday. Women's groups have developed rituals of their own to commemorate and celebrate their experiences as Jews and as women (e.g., celebrating life cycle events). Women are ordained as rabbis in most of the major Jewish dominations and can fully lead and participate in religious services and conduct rituals that were previously performed only by men. In short, over the years, many changes have been made.

Vivian Gornick (1989) has written about being "twice an outsider," expressing many of the dilemmas faced by women who struggle for cultural identity within the patriarchal confines of Judaism. Gornick notes that in American culture, being Jewish and female involves two stigmas, although ostracism for being Jewish is less prevalent than in previous decades. Put-downs for being a woman, however, have not yet been rejected in many circles. Letty Cottin Pogrebin (1991) details many of the feelings I myself have had as I confront being female and Jewish in American society. She particularly attacks the Women's Movement for its anti-Semitic undertones. In my view, these phenomena surely have an impact on individuals' behaviors.

In the communication discipline, we learn that one's communicative style is shaped and influenced by the historical and cultural events surrounding one's life, and my case shows no exception. Further, my speech may be characterized by at least some of the elements of what Deborah Tannen early on described as New York Jewish conversational style (Tannen 1981; curiously, by 1984, she refers to this simply as New York style). Although I am not from New York, I am from a mid-Atlantic state and share recent Eastern European Jewish immigrant history as a member of my family's second generation of Americans.

Tannen (1981; 1984) describes this conversational style as "high-involvement," which comprises a number of elements that seem to be consistent with the two "problematic" examples described in this essay. My own speech, for that matter, is often marked by a preference for personal topics, abrupt topic shifts, storytelling (in which the preferred point is the teller's emotional experience), a fast rate of speech, avoidance of inter-turn pauses, quick turn-taking, expressive phonology, pitch and amplitude shifts, marked voice quality, and strategic within-turn pauses (Tannen 1981, 137). Given these characteristics, my complaining and teasing should both be seen as normal interaction strategies. Because the others in this episode did not share the same style, my conversational style became an issue. Such ill-perceived attempts to communicate might be best understood as simply strategies using humor to "keep the conversation going."

Jewish Humor

The examination of humor as one aspect of communicative style offers a perspective for understanding some of the influences on Jewish women's style. Humor provides an avenue of communication, for it includes not only jokes and stories but witticisms and sometimes sarcastic statements that punctuate everyday interaction. Humor is also somewhat ambiguous, in that one can intend to be funny and not succeed, or that something one says can be taken as humor when it was not intended as such. As feminist and Jewish styles of humor interact in today's changing world, there are often few markers that indicate "this is humor" in routine interaction.

For many years, people have tried to isolate what constituted Jewish humor and determine why it was characteristically different from other types of humor. One explanation derives from the historical experiences of Jews. Novak and Waldoks (1981) describe some of the mis- conceptions about Jewish humor. They contextualize Jewish humor in the nineteenth- and twentieth-century Jewish experience with such momentous influences as pogroms, anti-Semitism, the Holocaust, immigration, and assimilation. Nineteenth-century Jewish humor arose partially out of persecution, poverty, and uprootedness. On the other hand,

> For every joke about anti-Semitism, poverty, or dislocation, there are several others dealing with less melancholy topics: the intricacies of the Jewish mind, its scholars, students, and schlemiels; the eternal comedy of food, health, and manners; the world of businessmen, rabbis, and schnorrers (beggars); the concerns of matchmaking, marriage, and family. (Novak and Waldoks, xiv)

Although the humor carries into the twentieth century, these authors see anxiety and skepticism as twin currents underlying much of Jewish humor of that century. As Jews increasingly moved into the American experience of the twentieth century, jokes about anti-Semitism became less central and were replaced by jokes about assimilation, name changing, conversion, and fund raising. Many of these jokes arose as a way to cope with surrounding hostility and rapid changes to ways of living which had been transplanted from Europe. Novak and Waldoks, in their attempt to summarize Jewish humor, have come up with five descriptors: (1) it is usually substantive, and the topics often illustrate a fascination with mind and logic; (2) as social or religious commentary, it can be sarcastic, complaining, resigned, or descriptive; (3) it is anti-authoritarian; (4) it has a critical and often political edge; and (5) it mocks everyone, including God, while simultaneously affirming religious traditions (xx–xxi).

As I read through the jokes and stories included in Novak and Waldok's anthology, I felt a deep connection and familiarity with much of the contents. The witticisms sounded like comments I might interject into some of my own interactions. It is no accident in my mind that the sarcastic, mocking, and complaining notions included in the characteristics of Jewish humor fit the pattern of how others view my own interactions. Could I be witnessing my own Jewish roots playing themselves out in this way? I believe so.

A complaining style, despite continued productivity (as in the case with my graduate school mentor), could function in several ways. It might diffuse the tension felt between doing work and not wanting to brag about it. In the Jewish context, I was taught as a child not to be too boastful, not to call too much attention to myself, especially as a female. The complaints could also be a way of drawing attention, commiseration, or support. A stereotypical "Oy vey," a Yiddish response cry (Tannen, 1981) uttered with a sigh, would be an appropriate response from another Jew.

Complaining, therefore, would not necessarily seem to be depressing to the listener nor even a sign of depression in the speaker. Rather, it could function in a social context to maintain the connection between speaker and listener. In other circumstances, complaints from one could generate complaints from another in a "Can you top this?" fashion. But in the setting described between student and mentor, this seems unlikely. The mentor in my case accepted the complaints of the student without interjecting her own complaints. Perhaps because she did not share the same cultural identity with the student, she did not enter into the language game of comparing complaints but rather simply accepted the complaints as clues to what was happening in the student's life.

Feminist Humor

What of the episode of the two male students? Is there a way to account for it within the Jewish context? It does not seem so, unless one compares the in-group/out-group phenomena of Jew and non-Jew to women and men. Jewish humor traditionally has not included many celebratory notions of women. Gornick's connection between being an outsider because of Jewish identity and being female may invoke similar in-group/out-group aspects of humor. The demarcation of the in- and out-groups is one of the types of humor found by Cindy White (1988).

In an essay about feminist humor, White lists characteristics of the humor that in some ways parallel Novak and Waldok's characterization of Jewish humor. She notes that feminist humor "exposes sources of imbalance and attempts to eradicate them" (78). It comes out of a desire for equity, an attempt to bond people together, and a need to obliterate the myths and stereotypes that have plagued women since time immemorial. White collected instances of feminist humor from feminist comics and feminist social actors in their everyday interaction. These humorous incidents often poke fun at mainstream expectations, just as they take jabs at feminist expectations. The uncertainties reflected in the changing notions of women's roles and behaviors are mirrored in this type of humor. At the same time, feminist humor is used to connect people, to point up shared experiences, and to affirm the positive strengths of women. At times, the humor can also be anti-male.

From a feminist perspective, an interpretation of my teasing behavior with the two male students suggests several things. I may have been attempting to close the gap between us. I am older, female, and perceived as an authority figure in my role as advisor. They are younger, male, and subordinate in the hierarchy of the university. In my desire to close the distance between us—because feminists often see equality as a prerequisite for satisfactory interaction or negotiation—my teasing may have functioned to show them that I could "play" with them, indeed that we could have playful interactions. Our relationship did not have to fall into the usual superior-subordinate norm. On the other hand, simply because they were men and assumed greater knowledge of everyday operations within their student organization, my attempt at nonthreatening communication could have served as a safe feminist ploy to equalize roles of women and men, despite the other differences between us. Had these two leaders been women, I doubt that I would have used the same teasing behaviors with them. More likely, I would have used a strategy that would have appealed to our common

womanhood, perhaps juxtaposed against the predominantly male membership of the organization. When I recall my feelings and level of awareness in these interactions, I was more conscious of being a woman than of being Jewish, even though the young male students were not Jewish.

Conclusion

The somber side to analyzing each of these episodes resides in the potential for conflict as the styles of being Jewish and being female collide, especially in interactions with Jewish men or with women who are very male-centered. Pogrebin (1991) recalls her 1982 article in which she labelled one problem faced by Jewish women as "invisibility, insult and internalized oppression." She was speaking particularly of the problems of Jewish women within the broader women's movement, but the same descriptors could be used for other situations. Jewish women are often rendered invisible because of either their Jewishness or their femaleness. The analysis offered for each of my two experiences perpetuates the invisibility of one or another dimension of my being. Jewish women are often seen by outsiders as loud, pushy, or motivated by material wealth in stereotypically negative ways. Because of a number of factors, Jewish women often face personal feelings of self-hatred and denial, thus internalizing the oppression that has been waged from outside.

In attempting to overcome the negative forces that can lower Jewish women's self-esteem and contributions to society, I would argue that micro-level communication should be examined for the strategies in which Jewish women can continuously face their challenges. As most Jewish women today interact with others who are not Jewish, as well as with men, flexibility in communicative strategies seems to be warranted. Humor provides one arena of options for overcoming obstacles to satisfactory interaction.

References

Gornick, V. (1989). Twice an outsider: On being Jewish and a woman. *Tikkun*, 4 (2), 29–31, 123–125.

Novak, W. and Waldoks, M. (Eds.). (1981). *The big book of Jewish humor.* New York: Harper Collins.

Pogrebin, L.C. (1991). *Deborah, Golda and me: Being female and Jewish in America.* New York: Crown.

Tannen, D. (1981). New York Jewish conversational style. *International Journal of the Sociology of Language*, 30, 133–149.

Tannen, D. (1984). *Conversational style: Analyzing talk among friends.* Norwood, NJ: Ablex.

White, C. (1988). Liberating laughter: An inquiry into the nature, content, and functions of feminist humor. In B. Bates and A. Taylor (Eds.), *Women communicating: Stud*ies of women's Talk (75–90). Norwood, NJ: Ablex. ✦

6

Remembering Selena

Alberto González
Bowling Green State University

Jennifer L. Willis-Rivera
Southern Illinois University

Prelude/Postlude

It *was March 2, 1991, at the San Antonio, Texas, Convention Center Arena. On this evening, several nominees and winners from the previous night's 11th Annual Tejano Music Award ceremony are performing to raise a scholarship fund. Mazz does a set, then Shelly Lares, and Adalberto; there is an act for every generation. The music is great, but so far, we have been hesitant to go for the stage; after all, we are Mexican Americans from Ohio, our Midwestern accents alienate us from many tejanos from the valley.*

One performer, however, gets us off of our table and out to the stage. One performer brings us all together—Selena Quintanilla. As she performs her set, she gives little waves to people close to the stage. She seems to delight in her newly choreographed motions; her voice seems to rejoice in her newly learned Spanish. Soon men and women take turns climbing the steps to the stage. They cross to Selena to give her a brief hug. Some give her a polite kiss on the cheek. Several fans respectfully pose so that their companions can snap a picture. (Invariably, a camera's flash fails, and Selena invites another attempt.) During the instrumental portions of the songs, Selena engages in small talk with those who come up to the microphone. Through all of this, Selena is laughing and smiling. She makes the interactions part of the music rather than a distraction from it.

This is the earliest memory of Selena because it provides a first picture of the living artist-in-performance. It is also the most recent memory because it is a lasting commentary on whatever we hear about her. It is the best memory.

Borderlands in Society

Like so many images in our lives— speeding tracer bullets in the Gulf War or ill-fitting gloves at the O.J. Simpson trial—the first images of a tragedy appeared on television. On March 31, 1995, a distraught Yolanda Saldávar sat in her parked car outside a Corpus Christi Days Inn. A Texas SWAT team surrounded Saldávar as she spoke by cellular telephone to police negotiators and members of her family. She was taken into custody and booked for the murder of Selena Quintanilla Perez. That same evening CNN and other news programs, in particular the Spanish-language TV network *Univision*, broadcasted a vast array of tributes to Selena.

Ironically, Selena achieved far greater fame in death than in life during her career as a singer, recording artist, and products spokesperson. In the months that followed, she would become a constant fixture in the popular media. In the spring of 1995, *People* magazine published a commemorative issue on Selena's life and music. In October of that year, *Newsweek's* lifestyle section featured "Mexamerica: Selena Country" (Adler and Padgett 1995).

It's an easy drive from San Antonio to Corpus Christi. It was rainy in San Antonio, but when we got close to Corpus the sun came out. We got off the freeway at Navigation Boulevard and stopped at a nearby Denny's to eat. We really didn't think much about where we were until we discovered that around the corner was a Days Inn.

In *Borderlands: The New Mestiza* (1987), Chicana poet and essayist Gloria Anzaldúa describes the U.S.-Mexico border experience and the consciousness born of living between two cultures. A *mestiza* with a mix of Spanish and Native American blood, Anzaldúa has learned to juggle cultures, operating "in a pluralistic mode—nothing is thrust out, the good the bad and the ugly, nothing rejected, nothing abandoned" (79). Selena offers a case study of the pluralistic mode which Anzaldúa attributes to the contemporary Chicana.

This essay will explore how the events after Selena's death, the mourning, the remembrances, and our own journey to the place where Selena lived and died have revealed the extent of her border sensibility. By comparing the treatment of Selena by the mainstream Anglo media with the ways in which *mestizos* experience her music, we argue that cultural borders are symbolically recognized and negotiated.

Borderlands in Selena

More than an international marker, the current U.S.-Mexican border is a site of struggle against poverty, environmental neglect, and political exploitation as well as for justice, self-worth, and social respect. People living along the border have had to find ways to accommodate multiple (and often conflicting) histories, cultural identities, and social practices. To the extent that Anglo and Mexican values and references intermingle, the border is a region of mediation and innovation. Mediation occurs when the preferences of two or more cultures are reconciled; innovation results when the preferences of those cultures are transcended.

In addition to the legal border, a symbolic space exists where diverse meanings come together through imposition, by invitation, or by accident. Border people often question those meanings and remold them into new interpretations that fit into their border world.

Tejano music is an example of a border innovation. The sounds of the *ranchera* are a rich mixture of cultural influences: Spanish (guitar and violins), Mexican (trumpet and emotional vocal delivery), country and western, and pop. In a review of Linda Ronstadt's *Mas Canciones* and Anna Gabriel's *Mi Mexico*, Daisann McLane (1992) writes, "A theatre of human emotion, written in vernacular poetry of pain, pride and sexual braggadocio, *ranchera* is dramatic, at times hyperbolic, never merely pretty" (79). By contrast, *cumbia* is a dance with simple and repetitive

lyrics that function to reinforce the rapid rhythm of the instrumentation. Musically the *cumbia* often displays the German/ Czech influence from East Texas with its accordion and polka-like rhythm.

The musical tradition that Selena inherited is a border creation that reveals a particular historical moment. Her sound can be understood as a symbolic integrating of Aztec empires, Spanish/Arabic conquest, Mexican devotion, and Anglo colonization. Through integration and transcendence, tejano music avoids capitulation to any one influence. The *grito*,[1] a cry given out during many tejano songs, is as much an expression of defiance as one of solidarity with the singer's pain.

We found Bloomington Street and turned right, moving slowly westward. Soon we came to a washeteria on whose wall was painted Selena's logo and the words, "Always in Our Hearts. A Neighborhood Tribute to Our Fallen Star." Further down the street tied to a chain link fence was a homemade sign we recognized from several news reports and magazines. It read, "Heaven Needed Another Angel. We'll Miss You!!!" The sign displayed concert photos of Selena. After months of exposure to both the coastal rains and the Texas sun, the sign was faded.

Linguistic Borders

José E. Limon in his ethnography of south Texas *bailes* notes the symbolic borderland that tejano youths occupy: "While their hold on and sense of anything that could be called *Mexican* is tenuous and flat, they do not conversely think of themselves as *Americans* in any ideological sense. . ." (1994, 112). This is not necessarily problematic, however. The *mestizo* identity possesses an ever available opportunity for improvisation and creation. Like many young *mestizos* in the United States, Selena had only recently begun to think explicitly of her Mexican heritage (Patoski 1996, 89) and was in the process of reinventing herself.

Such a border identity is full of unexpected linguistic creation, nowhere more apparent than in the pronunciation of Selena's name. Three pronunciations circulated in the discourse surrounding her death: Se-*len*-a, Se-*leen*-a, and Se-*lain*-a. The first pronunciation (Se-*len*-a) is correct Spanish, the one heard in northern Mexico and on *Univision*. But Selena was considered tejana rather than Mexican, giving this particular sound change a unique status. Anglo newscasters (especially in the North) usually used the third pronunciation (Se-*lain*-a), thus revealing their unfamiliarity with tejano music.

In the aftermath of Selena's death, new aspects of the borderland developed, especially for those outside South Texas and the tejano culture. Prior to her death, few outside the Mexican American community had ever heard of Selena. Even when she won a Grammy, she was not any major topic of media discussion. Today, however, she has captured a new audience as a result of the sensationalism of her demise.

Upon Selena's passing, the Anglo media was confronted with an image for which they had neither background nor history. She was consequently typecast in the role of a "Mexican Madonna," so labeled because of her sparkling bustiers and flashy costumes. Using this misguided comparison with Madonna, those Americans unfamiliar with Selena accepted an easily accessible though inaccurate reference by the news media. A *Rolling Stone* review of *Dreaming of You*, her final album (and first one in English), noted that Selena "loved dressing skimpily onstage so you could see her navel and cleavage" (Eddy 1995). Although this description of Selena may have been visually accurate, it varied drastically from the descriptions of her by those who had celebrated her in life. No one who knew tejano music ever referred to Selena as the Mexican Madonna. She was always *la Reina de la Música Tejana. Mi reina* ("my queen") is a common term of affection used for a girlfriend, a female child, or one's mother. The expanse of this expression from the casual to the intimate to the professional is typical of *mestizo* wordplay. By contrast, "Mexican Madonna" is severely limiting.

By portraying Selena as such, the media also assigned to her many of the derogatory images reserved for Madonna: promiscuous, opportunistic, and disrespectful. This depiction conflicted directly with the values ascribed to Selena by those in her own culture. Another review of *Dreaming of You* offered a different perspective: "Selena stays true to her roots yet brings both worlds together. . . " (Flores 1995). She was celebrated by those who shared her cultural self-view as the girl next door or the girl from the barrio.

When we finally reached her street, we were surprised by the fact that the houses were very modest. This was no Brentwood. The majority were one story ranch style houses, most in need of painting or slight repair. Nothing very big. When we reached the end of the street, we found the Quintanilla houses. It was obvious that these houses were a bit out of place in the neighborhood. They were newer and larger than any of the other houses, though they weren't mansions by any stretch of the imagination.

Because of her death, Selena broadened the spaces for negotiation along the symbolic border. Those who knew her or came from her tejana roots created a new discursive space to celebrate her people, her values, her culture, and Selena herself as she was in life. This allowed for the definition and examination of the border sensibility that she represented.

Enacting Borders

The diverse interpretations of cultural understanding have also united through the enactment of mourning and celebrating for Selena. Invisible communities suddenly shed their cloaks of obscurity as they gathered to write, parade, grieve, sing, and perform her memory throughout the country. In front of her house, at her grave, at her boutique, and in their own homes, people erected *descansos* ("resting places") dedicated to Selena. These symbolic creations, often referred to as "shrines" in the Anglo media, have allowed tejanos to express their grief and joy.

Selena's memory was celebrated not only in her hometown but all across the United States. The procession at the funeral viewing in the Bayfront Convention Center numbered more than 60,000 people (Patoski 1996). Selena's final album sold 175,000 copies in one day (Leland 1995, 80). Her music was played as a tribute on numerous radio stations in the Southwest and elsewhere, yet another factor that brought the cultural borders between Anglo and *mestizo* closer together.

The gravestone itself was a black marble face with the word "Selena" carved in white. On top of the gravestone sat two angels, blowing kisses. One of the angels had a red plastic crucifix wrapped around its neck. The other angel held a white carnation. A very young mesquite tree was planted behind Selena's grave. On every surface of this tree, on every branch, were carved and written messages to Selena. Here was a living testament to Selena. It was on this living part of her memorial where the grief of her fans poured out.

Re-forming Borders

Mediation of the borderlands did not end in the weeks after Selena's death. Americans have been newly introduced to various interpretations of tejano culture and tejano music. The negotiation continued as Selena's song *I Could Fall in Love* (Selena 1995) hit the top 20 on *Billboard's* pop charts. Those who had never heard a song in Spanish were introduced to her Spanish whispers intertwined with English verses. Tejano music was suddenly transformed in the eyes of the dominant culture from background music in Mexican restaurants into a person, a place, and an event.

The voice of a culture once formed in isolation has now spoken to a national audience. In his study of tejano music and culture, Peña (1985) notes that "tejanos remained culturally isolated from the rest of American society, as a result of ethnic prejudice and segregation. Under such circumstances the retention of Mexican culture was inevitably encouraged" (136). Peña argues that much of this retention was accomplished through the use of music. He also emphasizes the pedagogical aspects of music-centered events in the tejano community in that "the musical events were a special sort of rhetorical play form... that both defined symbolically what a tejano was and prescribed how he or she should behave culturally" (135).

In one way, Selena has been promoted as a pedagogical ideal for many tejanas. Her message lives on for many young people, in their memories and in their dreams. For

example, one young fan writes, "Selena has effected [*sic*] my life because she is a role model for me and all Mexicanas. . . . "[2] Another tells of a dream in which Selena came to her and told her to do well in school. "It was so real to me. She told me, 'Don't let anybody stop you.' I took her advice and my school grades have gotten a lot better" (Blosser 1995, 24). Because of her position as a cultural idol, Selena's message has become even stronger, reaching the larger audiences who were once inaccessible.

Moreover, through her music *mestizos* have been able to share their culture with the entire nation, allowing for a (re)formation of symbolic borders and the (re)introduction of mainstream American culture to many aspects of tejano culture. Gloria Anzaldúa (1987) celebrates the (re)making of cultural spaces: "What I want is an accounting of all three cultures—white, Mexican, Indian. I want the freedom to carve and chisel my own face.... And if going home is denied me then I will have to stand and claim my space, making a new culture—*una cultura mestiza*" (22). Through Selena, that possibility has awakened, creating a new space on this symbolic border.

Conclusion

She blazed and shimmered in the spotlight, but it was the fact that Selena was happily, proudly *del pueblo*—"of the people"— that forged a powerful, personal bond between her and her audience. (*People Weekly Tribute* 1995)

We found Selena's boutique situated in a row of houses that had been turned into little shops. Her boutique was modest and small with a neon sign on the wall that read "Selena Etc." The walls inside were covered with pictures of Selena, gold records, newspaper and magazine stories, and Coke advertisements featuring Selena. A magazine article hung on one wall: "Haven't heard of Selena? If not, you will."

Tenemos un recuerdo. . . . Siempre nos hace tan feliz. . . .

Notes

1. Typically, the tejano songs during which *gritos* are expressed are love songs or songs of pain, such as those of lost love.
2. This quote was taken from a "memory book" passed around during a Mexican-American dance. The book was later sent to the Quintanilla family.

References

Adler, J. and Padgett, T. (1995, October 23). Mexamerica: Selena country. *Newsweek*, 76.

Anzaldúa, G. (1987). *Borderlands/la frontera: The new Mestiza*. San Francisco: Spinsters/Aunt Lute.

Blosser, J. (1995, August 24). Selena reaches out from the grave. *National Enquirer*, 24.

Eddy, C. (1995, September 7). Reviews. *Rolling Stone*, 72–73.

Flores, R. (1995, October). Music. *Hispanic*, 82.

Leland, J. (1995, October 23). Born on the border. *Newsweek*, 80.

Limon, J.E. (1994). *Dancing with the devil: Society and cultural poetics in Mexican-American South Texas*. Madison: University of Wisconsin Press.

McLane, D. (1992, February 6). Recordings. *Rolling Stone*, 77–79.

Patoski, J.N. (1996). *Selena: A biography*. Boston: Little, Brown.

Peña, M.H. (1985). *The Texas-Mexican Conjunto: History of a working-class music*. Austin: University of Texas Press.

People Weekly Tribute. (1995, Spring). Remembering Selena. 7.

Selena. (1995). *Dreaming of you*. EMI Records. ✦

7

When Miss America Was Always White

Navita Cummings James
University of South Florida

I am a child of the American baby boom. I am a person of color, and I am a woman. All of these factors have influenced the creation of the person I am today, just as the time and place of each of our births, our genders, races, and ethnicities influence the people we are today. On some level, we all know that the configurations of these factors is intertwined with the unique life stories we each have to tell. But some stories are not as well known as others. For example, the lived experiences of everyday Black[1] women are not reflected very well in the academic knowledge base. Any student of the Black female experience in the United States, who is interested in how this female and racial identity has emerged, would be better served by studying the music written and performed by Black women, their novels, short stories, essays, and poems, or their oral and written life histories—rather than relying on traditional social scientific research.

In this essay, I will use my own life history and personal narrative to illustrate how family stories about race that I heard as a child influenced the development of my racial identity. These family stories were a powerful counterforce to the negative images of Blacks in the dominant culture, and they helped me to grow up believing that I could be a doctor, a lawyer, or whatever I wanted to be, assuming that I had the talent and that I worked hard. Nevertheless, I also knew a "colored girl" in the 1950s, no matter how smart, talented, or attractive she was, could never grow up to be President of the United States or Miss America.

Two related conceptual frameworks for studying the human experience inform my analysis of racial identity. The first framework assumes that individuals take an active role in constructing themselves within particular cultural contexts. The second framework assumes that one's personal story is a powerful way to gain insight into the way people construct their lives and social worlds. Each of these approaches is briefly addressed here.

The first framework undergirds much contemporary thinking on human behavior and is sometimes labeled social constructivism. It is based on the works of Berger and Luckman (1967), who argued that reality, culture, and personal identity are socially constructed by humans. The construction of personal identity, they suggest, is a dialectic between the self and the culture in which it evolves. Individual personal identities or selves evolve differently in given cultures, in part because those cultures provide different scripts and experiences for different people. What script one receives is based on socially significant constructs in the culture. For example, in the United States, gender, race, age, and class are socially significant. In other cultures, other social constructs might be important. Because cultures change over time, the scripts and resulting meanings of gender, race, class, and age in a given culture may also change. So the meanings of gender, race, and class are not only culturally but historically bound. Another way to phrase this is that being a "colored" middle-class girl in the 1950s was not the same as being an "African American" middle-class girl in the 1990s.

The second framework of this essay addresses the role of narrative or personal story in social inquiry. The personal story is an important research strategy that gives us new insights into how people construct their lives. Anthropologist Mary Catherine Bateson in *Composing a Life* (1990) studied the personal stories of five extraordinary women. She revealed how women of significant achievement constructed their lives in a society that did not provide role models for female success outside the family.

Stories are memorable in ways that statistical studies are not. As they are recalled and given meaning, stories are not "right" or "wrong." Facts can be challenged, but a person's story *just is*. Also, as individuals and their life experiences are products of particular sociocultural milieus, no one story is so unique or idiosyncratic that it cannot provide us insight into the overall human experience. One of the most powerful ways to gain an understanding of "the other" (e.g., a person from a culture other than one's own) is to hear or read the story of "the other" *in his or her own words*.

Family Stories

The telling of family stories not only informs children about their past, but also passes on family values and helps prepare them to live in the world beyond the family. I was born in 1952 in Columbus, Ohio. One of the duties of my parents in the 1950s and 1960s was to help prepare my sister and me for a world that would attempt to put limitations on what we could achieve because of our race. Our family always refuted the dominant culture's message of what it meant to be "colored" or "Negro." Race was a frequent topic of discussion in our family, especially among the adults.

The most vivid race-related stories of my youth were about the treachery and violence of White men, how Whites could get away with any crime committed against Black people. These stories led me to believe that Black life was not highly valued by White people and that, in the eyes of White society, Black women had no virtue worth respecting or protecting.

The single most upsetting story I can recall, related to me by an aunt, happened to a young Black girl in Georgia in the 1920s. Two young school girls were walking down a road and met a drunken White man carrying a gun. He pulled one of the girls aside, put the gun in her mouth, and began to play a form of Russian roulette. One of the chambers was loaded, and he blew the back of the girl's head off. I expected my aunt to say that the man was punished and sent to jail. But *nothing* happened to him. Instead, White people felt pity for the man because he was drunk and had to witness his own folly, rather than for the murdered child and her family. I remember my horror that such a man could get away with killing a little Black girl *like me*.

The story taught me that White men were violent and not to be trusted. Other stories I heard about lynchings only served to reconfirm this for me. I was horrified when I learned about the practice of castrating Black men during lynchings and placing their genitals in their mouths or in jars to be displayed in community stores as trophies or warnings.

The other family stories I vividly recall were about the Cummings family from my father's side and the Pearson family from my mother's.

The Cummings Family

According to my father, my great-grandfather "Gramps" was a slave in his youth and always carried the scars of the beatings he received as a child. One of the stories I recall was about Gramps' mother. She was the child of a slave woman and a White Virginia plantation owner. Apparently she resembled her father so much that the owner's wife became upset and had the child sold off. Because of her father's betrayal, the child hated Whites so intensely that she married the darkest man she could find.

There were several interesting stories about Gramps himself. At the age of 16 he was freed from slavery. As an adult he became a landowner in Laurens County, Georgia. He learned to read and passed his love of reading on to his children and grandchildren. He gave his daughters an education so they would not have to work in "Miss Anne's"[2] kitchen, and he gave his sons land. Gramps was one of the first people in his county to own a car. As the story goes, the Whites did not like the idea of a Black man owning a car when the vast majority of Whites could not afford them. So Gramps had to carry a shotgun with him to protect himself from jealous Whites.

The stories about Gramps and his family reinforced what I had been told about the evil of White men. I was shocked that a father would sell his own flesh and blood. As I grew up, I came to believe that being White was nothing to be proud of and that the light skin color of some Blacks (including myself) was a badge of shame. It seemed to me that Whites would resort to any means—even murder—to keep Blacks beneath them.

I later learned other families in the Black community educated their women so that daughters would not have to work in the homes of Whites. This strategy helps to explain, in part, why Black women often had more education than Black men and why this difference did not create tension in the Black community.

My father's stories about his own life also influenced me. Among the most vivid were those of his experiences during World War II. My father was a Tuskeegee Airman. He was very proud to have been part of a U.S. Army experiment to test whether Black men were intelligent enough to fly airplanes. The Tuskeegee Airmen units that ultimately served in Europe and North Africa had one of the most distinguished records of the war. After the war, however, Black pilots were not hired by the airlines unless, perhaps, they were interested in being janitors.

Some of the most painful memories of my childhood revolve around my father's business. Since he couldn't get a job as a civilian pilot, he fell back on skills he learned as a boy in Georgia—masonry and carpentry—and started his own contracting business. But racial discrimination followed him here as well. My father often complained that when Whites contracted with him, they would pay him less than what they paid the White contractors for the same work. Even after he finished the work, some would not pay him for weeks or months. However, I began to notice that not all Whites were alike. Jews seemed to be different. They would pay for quality regardless of whether a Black or White man did the work. At least they were more likely to hire and less likely to delay payment.

Perhaps the most important lesson I learned from my father's stories, that would later be reflected in my own life and the lives of my children, was the idea that many Whites fail to see the talents and accomplishments of Black people—even when the evidence is right before their eyes.

The Pearson Family

The stories about Whites from my mother's family were less violent and shocking. Nat Pearson, my grandfather, was also a landowner. He lived in Wheeler County, Georgia. According to my mother, Whites respected "Mr. Nat" and his children. He was a hard-working and fair man. His wife was also respected in the community. She took food to the sick and the poor, Black or White, in addition to taking care of her nine children.

The Pearson family emphasized the importance of getting a college education. My mother and her eight siblings all attended college and earned degrees. (In my generation it was just expected that all 26 of us would earn at least *one* college degree.) In my mother's generation, the older children helped the younger ones through college by providing financial support. The family stuck together, helping one another. That was very important.

My mother emphasized different things than my father did when she talked about race. For example, she stressed how my grandmother helped poor Whites. My mother did not believe in any way that Blacks were inferior to Whites. She was very proud of her family, and there was no false humility here. However, as the mother of daughters, she did give us one race-related warning: "There is only one thing a White man wants from a Black woman." She warned that Black women should be wary of White men, because, in the event of rape, the White man would probably go unpunished. We should never think of marrying a White man, because, according to her, a Black woman's virtue meant nothing to Whites.

My Pearson cousins were another source of information about race. While I was going to racially integrated schools in the North, most of them attended segregated schools in the South. I was amazed that they had all Black teachers, just as they were amazed that mine were all White.

My cousins and their friends loved to tease and tell jokes. They sometimes used profanity just out of hearing distance of the adults. During one of our visits to Georgia, I learned an interpretation of the origin of the word *motherfucker*. They said it was used by the African slaves in the Old South to describe White men who raped their African slave mothers.

Beliefs and Stereotypes of My Youth

From these significant stories of my youth emerged a set of beliefs and stereotypes which provided a backdrop for my own lived experience. These beliefs and stereotypes about Blacks and Whites can be summarized as follows:

Black People

- Black people are "just as good" as White people—and in some ways (e.g., morally) better.
- Black people are just as smart and capable as White people, if not more so.
- Black people should always be prepared to fight for fair treatment from Whites.
- Black people have to be twice as good as Whites to be considered half as good.

White People

- White people are often violent and treacherous.
- White people probably have some kind of inferiority complex which drives them to continually "put down" Blacks and anyone else who is not White.
- White men often rape Black women. If they say they love a Black women, they are doing so to gain sexual favors. A White man would never marry a Black woman.
- Most White people do not want to see Blacks rewarded for their abilities and accomplishments.
- Most Whites, especially Northerners, cannot be trusted. They can hardly ever be a real friend to a Black person.
- White men are usually arrogant. White women are usually lazy.

- There are some good White people, but they are the exceptions.

These childhood beliefs and stereotypes, however, did *not* become an intellectual prison of my self-identity or beliefs about Whites. Below, I address how these beliefs and stereotypes blended with my own experiences. From this dialectical interaction, my racial identity emerged.

The Dialectic of Family Stories, Culture, and Identity

Earlier, I suggested that the construction of personal identity is a dialectic between self and culture. In some circumstances, families may reinforce the messages of the dominant culture, but as we have seen in my case, my family's messages ran counter to it. The social-cultural milieu of the integrated North in the 1950s was rife with overt and covert messages about Blacks. Whites often pretended that there was no prejudice in the North. Yet the dominant culture portrayed Black people as stupid, lazy, dirty, dishonest, ugly—and invisible. We were unwelcome in many public places, even if it was legal for us to be there. If my self-image had relied solely on the messages of the dominant culture, I might have grown up with low self-esteem and seen no value in being Black.

Instead, my family's stories gave me pride in my people and in myself. They encouraged me to reject the dominant culture's scripts and embrace those from my family and the Black community that said I was a person of value and worth. The stories became a sort of metaphorical shield that protected me from the larger, hostile culture. In high school, I learned that there were many times I did not need the shield, e.g., with some of my White schoolmates. But I also learned that, because racism is a constant feature of our culture, I would be a fool to ever throw that shield away.

Moreover, I had to revise my stereotyped ideas about Whites and Blacks—hence about myself. For example, I learned that race was not a good predictor of violence— gender was; and that race was not a good predictor of intelligence—income and opportunities were. I further came to believe that all people, regardless of color, deserve to be treated with dignity and respect. We are all equal in God's eyes and in principle in American cultural mythology. Finally, I learned that prejudice existed on both sides of the color line, but sometimes for different reasons.

Through this dialectical process, my beliefs and stereotypes changed and evolved. I made definitive choices about how I would relate to others. Unlike some Blacks who preferred to socialize only with Blacks, I chose to have friends of diverse backgrounds, including Whites.

I am now the mother of two girls. What is the role of family stories related to race in *my* family? I have already had to reassure my 4-year-old that "brown" people are good and beautiful. I have stressed the importance of reading and education in our family—values which span generations. And I have passed along my parents' stories, along with my own experiences. For example, I have told my 12-year-old how, as children, my sister and I used to run excitedly into the living room whenever there was someone Black on TV. In the 1950s, it was a rare occurrence to see someone Black on TV. And I told her how beauty pageants such as the Miss America Pageant celebrated only European standards of beauty, so Miss America was always White.

In the course of my daughters' childhoods, Black women have finally been crowned Miss America. But when I was a child, I secretly yearned for a Black Miss America. To me that would have been a sign that our culture was learning to value Black women—that we could be viewed as beautiful, smart, and virtuous.

As I grew up, I fantasized about what my life might have been like were race not such a socially significant construct in the United States: after World War II my father would have been hired as a commercial airline pilot

and our family would have flown the world for free. I would have been able to afford the Ivy League school I could not attend for lack of funds. I would have studied in Paris, become an anthropologist/pilot, and gone to Africa. . . .

As for Miss America? I would have been too busy traveling to have cared about her.

Notes

1. The use of the upper case "B" in the word "Black," when Black refers to African Americans, is a convention dating back to the 1960s and is still currently utilized by some writers. In the late 1960s and early 1970s, the common usage of the word "Negro" changed to "black." However, because black referred to a people and not just a color, some writers thought the upper case "B" in Black seemed more appropriate and dignifying. (Some of these writers also adopted the equivalent use of the upper case "W" when referring to Whites.) Also, since terms used to describe other ethnic and racial groups utilized upper case first letters, for the major descriptor for Black to appear with a lower case "b" seemed an unfortunate, yet grammatically correct, way to reinforce the stereotypical view of Blacks as less important. Black writers using this convention recognized the subtle power of language and that rules of language and grammar are arbitrary and evolve over time. These writers chose to take an active role in promoting what they viewed as a useful change.

2. "Miss Anne" is an unflattering term referring to White women.

References

Bateson, M.C. (1990). *Composing a life.* New York: Plume.

Berger, P.L. and Luckman, C. (1967). *The social construction of reality.* Garden City, NY: Anchor.

Leeds-Hurwitz, W. (1992). Forum introduction: Social approaches to interpersonal communication. *Communication Theory, 2,* 131–139. ✦

8

Illusive Reflections

African American Women on Primetime Television

Bishetta D. Merritt
Howard University

Images of African American women in popular culture have run the gamut from the oversized, sexless mammy and yellow gal of nineteenth-century race literature to the boisterous comediennes and witty lawyers of contemporary situation comedies. Television, one of the most ubiquitous forms of popular culture, exposes its audiences to a refined, updated version of these images and has become for many Americans, particularly white Americans, their only window on the African American world. Through this window, television viewers have been exposed to characterizations of African American women that seldom reflect their myriad numbers or diverse roles in society. This essay will review the imagery of African American women on television and suggest a fairer, more multidimensional portrayal of this ethnic group.

The history or development of the black image on network television reflects a picture of stereotypes, tokenism, paternalism, and neglect. Early television offered the promise of developing as a color-blind medium. Yet as network schedules were created, this promise became an unfulfilled dream for African Americans, particularly African American women (MacDonald 1992). Images crystallized in film and radio became the order of the day on the small screen, unless one viewed the *Ed Sullivan Show* on which blacks appeared as performers or were recognized as members of the

audience. (We phoned excitedly to tell our neighbors to watch a particular show whenever an African American personality was scheduled to appear. Frequent visitors to the Sullivan program included Sarah Vaughn, Hazel Scott, and Pearl Bailey.) As D. W. Griffith's epic silent film, *Birth of a Nation*, crystallized the image of African American women on the large screen, *Amos 'n Andy* performed the identical role for blacks on television. Black images in *Birth of a Nation* ranged from the devoted slave to the vamp. African American women were either cast as mammies or mulattos. Portrayed as sexless, aggressive females devoted to their owners or employers, or as wild, untamed "party girls" whose lives generally ended tragically, African American women retained remnants of these early characterizations well into the 1980s (e.g., Nell Carter in *Gimme a Break* and Sondra in *227*). Louise Beavers, a mammy in such films as *Imitation of Life* (1934) and *The Last Gangster* (1937), moved to television and starred in the 1950s comedy *Beulah*. The hardy, pervasive, and long-lasting mammy image of film became the central image of African American woman on television after the airing of *Amos 'n Andy*. To her other characteristics were added the role of "nag" and "shrew" through the portrayals of Ernestine Wade as Sapphire and Amanda Randolph as Mama. The name Sapphire became synonymous with an African American woman who raised her voice beyond a certain accepted level and who spoke harshly to African American men. She was an extension of the mammy character created in film, only more vocal and assertive. These roles made a significant contribution to establishing the image of African American women in the consciousness of the television audience. In addition, women were featured as secretaries or romantic interests for Andy. The latter characters were seldom discussed or remembered by the viewers of the program.

As a child, I enjoyed the show. It was not until I gained some maturity and a more critical view of the world, television, and the power of images that I realized how pervasive and detrimental these portrayals were to African Americans and black women in particular. The contribution of this program to the molding of perceptions about African American women on television and, by extension, in society is significant and irreversible.

As the civil rights movement flourished in the 1960s, one of the most significant characters to develop was Julia, played by Diahann Carroll. Completely different from Sapphire in temperament and physical appearance, Julia represented an educated African American woman with a successful career, raising her son in a wholesome environment. On another level, however, the image was shallow and one-dimensional, merely a reflection of what most whites thought of middle-class black women. Although set in the late 1960s, Julia and her son Cory never discussed racism, the civil rights movement, what it meant to be black and male in the United States, or African American culture and history. Like the sexless mammies characterized in films, Julia's life was devoid of romance. She was husbandless because of the Vietnam war and manless because the writers on the show decided that her only contact with black men would be fleeting romances.

Julia seemed very far removed from the married, middle-class Southern women I knew, who all seemed constantly surrounded by family and friends. Yet these women were proud of her and pleased with the relationship she shared with her son. I, on the other hand, the young, so-called revolutionary woman, viewed her as an unrealistic fantasy. She didn't have an Afro hair style, wear dashikis, or discuss Malcolm, Rap, or Stokley with her son. It seemed that every African American, save Julia, was touched in some way by the exciting and turbulent period when sit-ins, marches, and rallies were everyday occurrences. Moreover, I could never understand her closeness to the white woman who lived in the apartment upstairs or to other people at her job. I also could not understand her lack of family and lack of black female friends. Julia was for my generation what we called an "Oreo"—a person who is black on the outside and white on the inside.

During a lecture I attended at Fisk University, Nikki Giovanni spoke on the authenticity of Julia. She indicated that Julia was a beginning, and the portrayal of black women would hopefully expand and develop positively from this initial image. She encouraged us to use Julia as a stepping-stone, and, as media consumers, to demand better and less stereotypical images of African American women. But our voices were never heard, and any attempts at airing relevant television images of black women disappeared as the 1970s approached and public interest shifted to the Vietnam war. African American women in this decade were reminiscent of minstrel show caricatures. Situation comedies began to flourish and the Norman Lear comedies, among others, featured women in starring or co-starring roles. From *That's My Mama* to *The Jeffersons*, black women were portrayed as over sized females with boisterous voices and numerous problems.

However, Isabel Sanford's Louise Jefferson (*The Jeffersons*) and Esther Rolle's Florida Evans (*Good Times*) did make a significant contribution to the image of African American women on primetime television during the 1970s. Through these series, the television audience was exposed to women who were no longer isolated from their families and communities like Julia, but who were people with nuclear families and female friends. Media critic William Henry (1983), in his analysis of *The Jeffersons*, described Louise as the long-suffering wife of George Jefferson, the owner of a chain of dry cleaning businesses. Louise may have appeared submissive, but in reality she outmaneuvered and outfoxed George in most episodes. Assisted in her housework by the live-in maid, Florence (Marla Gibbs), Louise smoothed over the faux pas George committed in his quest to climb the social ladder and make more money (Henry 1983). Through this activity, the wit and intelligence of her character was revealed.

Louise worked constantly to maintain a pleasant relationship with George's mother in addition to serving as a bridge between George and their son Lionel. Louise volunteered at a community center and adjusted to her newly acquired middle-class status with little difficulty. She became very close to her neighbor Helen Willis, the female half of an interracial marriage. The bond between the two women deepened once their children, Lionel and Jenny, married. Louise and Helen worked at the community center and enjoyed shopping excursions. Helen's appearance on the program was a positive experience for me. She was statuesque, assertive, and articulate. I ignored her marriage partner and her status as a housewife because her physical appearance broke the mold of most black women on television. She shed the mammy stereotype and presented another dimension, however shallow, of the African American female.

Florence, Louise's maid, completes the circle of women on *The Jeffersons*. Her relationship with Louise was positive and supportive, yet the distance between employer and employee was maintained. Florence was not treated like and did not act like a typical maid—another milestone.

Florida Evans, mother and housewife, depicted a black woman diametrically opposed to Louise Jefferson. Her home was a tenement in Chicago and her husband, though industrious, was seldom employed. Florida controlled and attempted to overcome her environment through a positive attitude. She lived for her three children and husband, pushing them to excel. Promoting strong family values, Florida and James worked as a team in their household and attempted to make the best of their meager circumstances.

Florida and her neighbor/confidante, Winona, were similar to Louise and Helen, save for their class differences. Winona portrayed the stereotypical single African American female. However, her friendship with Florida proved genuine and a positive element in the series.

Louise and Florida portrayed earth mothers and, because of their physical appearance, reflected mammy characters from 1950s television. Neither character behaved like Sapphire, yet their size and "presence" in their families made them appear stronger and more secure than their husbands. Though Helen, Florence, and Winona played traditional roles, they offered a glimpse of black women released from the physical restrictions usually reserved for African American women in the media. In addition, the friendships created by these women kept them from being isolated, one-dimensional characters as Julia had been in the 1960s. Progress, though linear, could be detected in the development of the image of the African American woman.

Primetime dramas aired during this decade provided meaningful portrayals of African American women with the introduction of made-for-television specials like *The Autobiography of Miss Jane Pittman*, *A Woman Called Moses*, and *Roots*. These dramas offered a break from the situation comedies that dominated the 1970s; yet, the main themes of these specials and the driving force of the characters focused on suffering, struggle, and the will to survive—not the will to change the system *and* survive.

African American women on primetime television in the 1980s were defined by the home and family, even though they were often cast as professional women such as school teachers (Gladys Knight of *Charlie and Company*), attorneys (Phylicia Rashad of *The Cosby Show*), or university students and administrators (Cree Summer and Jasmine Guy of *A Different World*). A study by Stroman, Merritt, and Matabane (1990) indicates that portrayals of African American women have changed in their socioeconomic milieu and physical appearance since the Kerner Report (1968), but remain controlled by the dominant myths regarding female social roles.

The Nell Carter character in *Gimme a Break* paralleled the maids' roles black women have played for generations. Carter, aware of the image she depicted, parodied Butterfly McQueen's role in *Gone with the Wind* in one episode and defended her mammy-like behavior in another. Ever the dominating mammy, Nell neglected her own personal development and career possibilities while she physically abused the white youngsters under her supervision. Nell promised the children's dead mother she would raise them as her own and, when their aunt threatened to take the children, she fell to her knees crying and beseeched the judge to let her keep "her" children. For an African

American woman to perform this obsequious act on network television in the 1980s was astounding (Dates 1993).

Nell's friend Addie (played by Telma Hopkins) encouraged her to break from this family and develop her own musical talents. Nell rejected this advice and often physically abused Addie. Their friendship lacked the warmth associated with Louise and Helen or Florida and Winona. The program, its main characters, and the friendship between Nell and Addie represented a step back for African American women on television. Watching it was worse than viewing old movies starring Louise Beavers and Hattie McDaniel. Nell's character embarrassed me as an African American woman and represented every stereotype my friends and I had worked to dispel through our research and daily behavior. We all celebrated the cancellation of *Gimme a Break*.

In the late 1980s, the Marla Gibbs character in *227*, Phylicia Rashad of *The Cosby Show*, and Anne Marie Johnson of *In the Heat of the Night* made contributions to the images of African American women in a more positive manner. Mary, the Gibbs character, though cast as a housewife, portrayed a vital, strong black woman with a reliable husband and lively teenage daughter. *227* added another dimension to the black female image: a female friendship circle.

There were three other woman living in the apartment building where Mary resided: Sondra, Rose, and Pearl. They offered the audience a picture of four different types of African American women in one series. Sondra, the vamp, represented the single black woman who used her physical appearance to attract men with financial stability. Initially, Rose portrayed a widowed mother. After the first season, however, her daughter was dropped from the series and it was eventually revealed that she owned the apartment building where they all lived. She remarried before the program ended. Pearl, the grandmother of a young teen male, was cast as an older African American woman rarely depicted in primetime television except for Mother Jefferson on the *Jeffersons* and the grandmother on *Family Matters*. Pearl, true to her name, frequently shared "pearls of wisdom"

with the younger women. Mary, as described above, was the housewife, mother, and chief "cheerleader" for her husband Lester, a construction company supervisor. She portrayed a middle-class, intelligent woman whose skills at organization were utilized in her home and community. Various episodes focused on serious concerns that the women addressed within the context of their mutual friendships.

Clair Huxtable, mother, wife, and attorney, also depicted a type rarely seen on primetime television: the multidimensional, upper-middle-class, African American professional woman with a professional husband, children, and a career. Clair not only had daughters but female friends, a mother, and a mother-in-law who visited her New York brownstone. This generational bond was a first for a black family on television. In contrast to *227* where the generational links were represented through friendship, the Cosby women were family. From little Winnie to grandma Cosby, the women shared family remedies, memories, and keepsakes. In one episode Clair and her friends gathered to plan a tribute for one of their college instructors. Through their discussions, the influence this woman had on their development as African American women was explored, as well as the growth and development of their friendships during the years since their graduation from Hillman.

Trashed by the critics as unrealistic, *The Cosby Show* and its characters were never accepted as rooted in the black experience, but rather as Bill Cosby's idea of black family life—*Leave It To Beaver* in blackface. African Americans considered this evaluation further proof of the lack of knowledge whites have of the black community. There was a failure to understand the diversity of our community and to continuously group us at one end of the socioeconomic scale. African American women, however, viewed the diverse storylines on the Cosby series as an opportunity to see themselves, frailties and all, through the multidimensional Cosby characters. Women like Clair, her children, her mother, her mother-in-law, and her friends permeated African American households and workplaces in every major city in this country.

One of the few African American women in the early 1990s to have had a continuous role in a primetime drama was Anne Marie Johnson who portrayed Althea, the wife of Virgil Tibbs, on *In the Heat of the Night*. A teacher by profession, Althea became the mother of twins. Regarded by her husband and the chief of police as a very intelligent and intuitive woman, Althea's opinions and counsel were highly valued. Althea, however, suffered from the isolation Julia experienced, for she had few close female friends. In the 1991–92 season, Althea and the city council member portrayed by Denise Nicholas began to bond and share a friendship. Althea represented the only black female cast in a continuous dramatic role since the women of "Palmerstown, U.S.A." in 1981.

During the Fall season of 1993, S. Epatha Merkerson began her portrayal of an African American police officer on the long-running drama series *Law and Order*. As Lieutenant Van Buren she supervised other New York homicide detectives. In a rare episode Van Buren, accosted by three African American teens, shot one of them in self-defense while her own sons watched from the family van. The character's judgment was challenged when she stood trial for the shooting. Viewers were given new insight into Van Buren's multidimensional character and background, her career difficulties, her communication with her children, and her relationship with her colleagues. However, the episode never revealed what impact the exposure of intraracial violence had on her young sons. Reminiscent of Julia, the Van Buren character struggled on without a support system of either family or friends. Again the African American female was depicted without parents, extended family, or husband.

During the Spring season of 1995, one bright spot appeared with the premiere of *Under One Roof*, a series starring James Earl Jones as a widowed police officer sharing half of a Seattle duplex with an adult daughter and a teenage foster son. His older son, a Marine Corps retiree, lived upstairs with a wife and two children. The female characters from the two families represented three generations of African American women who were striving for their individuality and

a place in a world where values changed and shifted like the tides on Puget Sound. This drama had it all—complex, realistic stories that reflected a slice of African American life with characters of depth and quality. Its extended black family exemplified real life in the 1990s, dealing with such issues as children living with parents for financial reasons, the challenges of peer pressure versus values learned at home, racism, intergenerational conflicts, male-female relationships, and urban crime.

Finally, there was a television drama that explored a functional black family without all the maladies that usually plagued primetime-television households. Unfortunately the series lasted only six weeks before it was canceled. African American audiences were stunned. Many asked why and wrote the network, pleading for the series' return. Donna Britt, a newspaper columnist for *The Washington Post*, devoted an entire column to lamenting the show's abrupt cancellation. The network's answer was simply low ratings.

If the program's ratings in the African American community had been taken into account, a different picture might have emerged. For example, a survey conducted by BJK & E Media Group concluded that in the fourth quarter of 1994 *Living Single, Martin*, and *New York Undercover* comprised the three top-rated primetime shows among African Americans. White audiences ranked the programs 95th, 96th, and 98th, respectively (Britt 1995). This disparity emphasized how different audiences reacted to the same programs and how networks made decisions regarding series that starred African Americans. The network view seemed to be that dramas depicting realistic images of African American family life had no place on primetime television.

The Fall season of 1994 marked the arrival of *Touched by an Angel*, a fantasy series that co-starred Della Reese as Tess, a heavenly supervisor. This role further broadened the image of African American women on primetime television but did not compare to the weekly insights of *Under One Roof* on the influence of black women in family life and their diverse roles in society.

More recently, *ER* and *New York Undercover* have depicted African American women in recurring, supporting, and guest roles. Two black women were cast as nurses on *ER* and appeared weekly as competent assistants to the doctors in the emergency room of a Chicago hospital. Any information regarding their personalities, however, was disclosed through their limited but assertive interactions with others. Gloria Reuben portrayed the recurring role of a physician's assistant whose part was upgraded to regular cast member in the 1995–96 season, the only African American character to actually star on *ER*. Other than the guest-starring role of a highly competent visiting surgeon played by C.C.H. Pounder, these women served mostly as auxiliaries to the male characters. The audience was always left to wonder who these women really were and what life was like for them outside the hospital.

African American women appearing on *New York Undercover* were cast as the black male lead Williams' girlfriend and his son's mother. Both gave multidimensionality and depth to the Williams role but served merely as props to highlight his character. They also represented a throwback to the black female stereotypes portrayed in films during the 1920s.

Situation comedy continued to prevail as the genre of choice for African American female stars, co-stars, and members of ensemble casts on primetime television. From Phylicia Rashad on *Cosby* to Sheryl Lee Ralph on *Moesha* and JoMarie Payton-Noble on *Family Matters,* black women continued to provide comic relief for American television audience.

One of the most popular comedy series with black audiences was *Living Single*. This series centered on the friendships shared between black female characters, principally magazine owner Khadijah James portrayed by Queen Latifah, and depicted them as upwardly mobile black women in situations that attracted a diverse African American audience. *Living Single* was not only the top-rated primetime program with black viewers but also the number-one show with Hispanic audiences (Collier 1996). The program also stood out as one of the few ever produced and written by African Americans.

Exposed to the ups and downs of being twentysomething, black, single, and living in New York, audiences enjoyed the diverse female voices of this series' stars. Honest and bright, these characters argued, cried, laughed, supported, and criticized one another. They all represented a type of African American female portrayed on television in the past; yet their multidimensionality saved them from becoming stereotypes. Viewers related to these women as *whole* people rather than as cardboard replicas of Julia or Sapphire.

Living Single, initially canceled for the Fall 1997 season, was reinstated by FOX after an outpouring of audience support spearheaded by Travis Smiley, host of *BET Talk*. The series, canceled for a second time in December 1997, did not return to the network for the Spring 1998 season. Though popular with its audience for four and one-half seasons, this support could not save the series. Fox made plans to change the network and refocus its programming from urban to more mainstream. The void created by the cancellation of this series in the image of African American women on primetime television was not filled with the new programs scheduled for the 1998–99 season.

In addition to the roles of African American women discussed above, portrayals that receive little or no attention today are the background characters that merely appear as *scenery* on television programs. These characters include the homeless person on the street, the hotel lobby prostitute, or the drug user making a buy from her dealer. They may not be named in the credits or have recurring roles, but their mere appearance can have an impact on the consciousness of the viewer and, as a result, an impact on the imagery of the African American woman. These nameless women have not been accorded the respect, competence, and friendships of Clair, Mary, or Khadijah, yet their presence cannot be ignored.

Of course, African American women are much more than the characters portrayed on primetime television indicate. They are multidimensional people who make daily contributions to the success and failure of their homes, places of employment, extended families, and recreational sites. They are resourceful, intelligent, sensitive people who show human frailties. They are large, fat, short, tall, slender, petite, brown, tan, black, cream, and caramel. They are presidents of universities, tellers at banks, and talk-show hosts. They also teach school, dig ditches, own businesses, perform heart surgery, plan civil rights demonstrations, fight wars, paint houses and portraits, serve as judges and mayors, preach the gospel, are elected to the House of Representatives, make movies, and write and produce television programs. Yet, when one watches primetime television, these images are illusive.

In order to provide a more multi-dimensional portrayal of African American women, the television industry must recognize the diversity of these women and create programs and series like *Under One Roof* that reflect their variety and resourcefulness. Accomplishing this objective is far from impossible as evidenced in the myriad roles depicted by white women in programs as diverse as *Chicago Hope, ER, NYPD Blue, Mad About You, Home Improvement, Veronica's Closet, The X-Files, Melrose Place, The Profiler, Caroline in the City, Friends,* or *Promised Land.*

The impact of the image of African American women on audiences' perceptions should not be dismissed by the television industry. The constant reinforcement of a particular image has an effect on how a person or idea is perceived. If the majority of black women the television audience is exposed to are homeless, drug-addicted, or maids, and if viewers have no contact with African American women other than through television, what choice do they have but to believe that all women of this ethnic background reflect this television image? Furthermore, what image is transmitted to African American children regarding black women, their worth, and their contributions to this society? It is, therefore, important, as

the twenty-first century approaches and the population of this country includes more and more people of color, that the television industry broaden the images of African American women to include their nuances and diversity.

I would argue that even though the commercial television industry's primary interest is ratings supremacy and profits, the medium should serve as an accurate window on the world by creating programs that go beyond old stereotypes and develop fleshed-out characters for African American women to portray. Universal situations and themes must be explored and examined in dealing with black culture and the black female experience. An increase in the number of roles for African American women on television would also broaden the types of images represented. Most importantly, African American women producers, directors, writers, and technicians with a special sensitivity to the diversity of the African American female population should also be hired and given the responsibility to ensure that these characters do not rely on archaic television stereotypes.

References

Britt, D. (1995, May 5). A TV show worth raising the roof over. *Washington Post,* 1–2.

Collier, A.D. (1996, February). Behind the scenes of *Living Single. Ebony,* 27–34.

Dates, J.L. and Barlow, W. (Eds.) (1993). *Split-image: African Americans in the mass media.* Washington, DC: Howard University Press.

Henry, W. (1993, March) *The Jeffersons*: Black like nobody. *Channels,* 62–63.

Kerner Commission (1968). *Report on the national advisory commission on civil disorders.* New York: Bantam.

McDonald, J.F. (1992). *Blacks and white TV: Afro-Americans on television since 1948.* New York: Bantam.

Stroman, C., Merritt, B., and Matabane, P. (1989–90). Twenty years after Kerner: The portrayal of African Americans on primetime television. *Howard Journal of Communications,* 1, 44–56. ✦

9

Black Queer Identity, Imaginative Rationality, and the Language of Home

Charles I. Nero
Bates College

Home and the human relationships within it are recurring referents in the artistic, critical, and theoretical discourse of late twentieth-century black queers in the United States. Home performs a dual task. On the one hand, it grounds our identities within African American culture. This grounding is necessary, as Ron Simmons (1991) asserts, in order to further "the development of a progressive view of homosexuality in the African American community" (211). Too often African Americans view homosexuality as alien to our communities or as a pathological response to white racism (Nero 1991).

Afrocentric and black feminist scholars have emphasized the importance of perspective in theoretical discussions of meaning and epistemology. In *The Afrocentric Idea*, Molefi Kete Asante (1987) asserts that the "critic's chief problem is finding a place to stand. . . in relation to Western standards, imposed as interpretive measures on other cultures" (11). Patricia Hill Collins (1990) in *Black Feminist Thought* contends that "experience as a criterion of meaning with practi-

cal images as its symbolic vehicles is a fundamental epistemological tenet in African-American thought systems" (209). Collins (1990) emphasizes the importance of the experiential in the production of meaning and knowledge in order to challenge the dominance in the social sciences of positivist approaches which "aim to create scientific descriptions of reality by producing objective generalizations" by removing "all human characteristics except rationality" from the research process (205). For Collins (1990), an experiential approach leads to understanding a black woman's standpoint, a stance that functions "to create a new angle of vision on the process of suppression" (11–12).

In this essay, home provides a perspective from which to theorize about black queer identity. The first part of this essay is a brief overview of some of the meanings and uses of home in black queer discourse. The second part is an auto-biographical exploration of home as a site of contradiction and contention in the formation of my own identity.

Home in Black Queer Discourse

In the preface to the path-breaking *Homegirls: A Black Feminist Anthology*, Barbara Smith (1983) declared, "There is nothing more important to me than home" (xix). Smith, a black lesbian feminist, chose the radical maneuver of identifying home as the origin of her intellectual and political consciousness. Her maneuver was radical in the sense that it located her queerness within a black communal setting. Kitchen Table: Women of Color Press, the publishing company that Smith founded, also alludes to home imagery. Writer and critic Jewelle Gomez confirms the importance of home in black lesbian fiction. Gomez (1983) has identified a longing for home as "the driving force behind most strong writing by black Lesbians" (120).

Home is also a metaphor for black community. Audre Lorde (1984) referred to familial relations and her status within the home in the title of her collection of essays and speeches *Sister Outsider*. Poet Donald Woods (1986) in *Sister Lesbos* used the home imagery of the family in referring to the possibility of any connection between male and female black queers:

What we've shared

is the strength

to be apart

what we seek

is the strength

to be together.

Liberation to love ourselves

fiercely, in the family way.

—(105)

In *Brother to Brother: Words From the Heart*, the late essayist and anthologizer Joseph Beam (1986) defined home as "not only the familial constellation from which I grew, but the entire black community: the black press, the black church, black academicians, the black literati, and the black left" (231). Beam's "brotherhood is community" metaphor has influenced the work of Essex Hemphill (1991) in the acclaimed *Brother to Brother: New Writings by Black Gay Men* and of Marlon Riggs (1989) in the controversial and award-winning film *Tongues Untied*. Actors chanted and recited portions of Beam's *Brother to Brother* essay in Riggs' film. Hemphill (1991) extended Beam's concept of home to invoke a powerful call to black gay men:

Our mothers and fathers are waiting for us. Our sisters and brothers are waiting. Our communities are waiting for us to come home. They need our love, our talents and skills, and we need theirs. They may not understand everything about us, but they will remain ignorant, misinformed, and lonely for us, and we for them, for as long as we stay away hiding in communities that have never really welcomed us or the gifts we bring. (xx)

Home thus suggests a perspective from which black queers can articulate their reality and negotiate meaning.

'When I Think of Home. . . '

For me, home is a site both of contradiction and contention. As a site of contradic-

tion, home is experienced as a mediated event. As a site of contention within the home, my childhood was a mixed environment of liberation and domination.

Home as a Mediated Event

Home has been mediated by imagery from popular culture. The title of this section, "When I Think of Home," is from the black gay anthology *Brother to Brother*, which is a song from the Broadway musical and subsequent film *The Wiz*. As I write this section of the essay, I imagine Rodgers and Hammerstein's *My Favorite Things*. Although I am familiar with versions of the song by Mary Martin in the Broadway cast recording of *The Sound of Music* and the straight-no-chaser jazz version by Betty Carter, it is the cloying Julie Andrews version that I am humming now. Andrews sang *My Favorite Things* in the movie version of *The Sound of Music*. Although I did not see that movie until I was in graduate school, *My Favorite Things* mediates my understanding of home. Often imagining my home to be like the one in *The Sound of Music*, with a fun-loving ex-nun for a governess and mother figure. All day and night I could have sung "Raindrops on roses and whiskers on kittens/Bright copper kettles and warm woolen mittens/Brown paper packages tied up with strings/These are a few of my favorite things" (Rodgers and Hammerstein II 1960, 29). My home, however, was never like this.

Nevertheless, I reject the scenario popularized by many intellectuals that a powerful media creates unrealistic images that necessarily lead to personal frustration. Such a notion would rob me of my own power. I was not a passive victim consuming media images. Let me use two examples to illustrate my point.

It was through television that I first imagined the possibility of being gay and living as a member of the African American post-civil rights professional middle class—the group I was being educated to enter. I vividly remember watching Hal Holbrook, Hope Lange, and Scott Jacobi in the 1973 television movie *That Certain Summer*, in which a white man divorced his wife for a male lover. I was a junior in high school and I remember being emotionally moved by poignant scenes such as the one in which Lange, the wife, tells Holbrook, her husband, that she doesn't know how to compete with a man and the anger of young Scott Jacobi, the sensitive son with whom I identified, when he discovered that his father was gay.

Did this film create unrealistic expectations for me? Did they lead to personal frustration because I could not attain the image of home as presented in the media? No, because I also remember several disquieting moments in the movie. Holbrook and his lover, played by Martin Sheen, never displayed affection toward each other. (I had recently viewed Marlowe's *Edward II* on PBS, and it seemed to me that for the entire program the King and Gaveston did nothing but kiss.) It also occurred to me that Holbrook and Sheen, for all intents and purposes, were not the least bit effeminate like me. Yet, *That Certain Summer* allowed me to imagine the possibility of being in love with another man. It also reinforced the idea that personal happiness was a worthy goal, and, on later reflection, that one's quest for personal happiness might be a cause for the unhappiness of others. In other words, I realized that announcing I was gay would require me to weigh my happiness against that of my parents. For me that became an intellectual task beyond homophobia—a critique of heterosexuality itself. This critique was aided by the music of Stephen Sondheim. In Sondheim's music, heterosexuality and marriage were often sources of profound unhappiness. For example, in his 1970 musical *Company*, one character who has been married "three or four times" sings, "The concerts you enjoy together/Neighbors you annoy together/Children you destroy together/ That keep marriage intact" (Sondheim 529). At the end of *Company*, Robert, the bachelor protagonist, appears to have accepted the idea of marriage as desirable. His final song, however, is not about marriage, but about love within a relationship. Moreover, the gender of the lovers in Robert's final song is never specified. Instead, the love interest in Robert's final song, "Being Alive," is signified by the genderless pronouns "someone" and "some-

body." These genderless pronouns recur over twenty times in the song. "Being Alive" contained phrases such as "But alone is alone, not alive" and "Somebody need me too much/Somebody know me too well/Somebody pull me up short/And put me through hell and give me support/For being alive" (Sondheim 570). The deliberate absence of gendered third person pronouns affirmed the possibility of love and commitment outside marriage and heterosexuality. Sondheim's music enhanced my defenses against the forces of compulsory heterosexuality. Marriage would not guarantee me happiness. Rather, it might be more desirable to resist compulsory heterosexuality and to imagine, as it seems Sondheim's Bobby did, the possibility of that "someone" being a man.

Home as Lived Event

My behavior was a site of contention in my home. I was an effeminate boy, a so-called sissy. My parents did not want me to be effeminate. Frequently, I was chastised, told that I held cups too much like a girl, that I should try to act tougher, play football and basketball, talk in a deeper voice. I acquiesced to some of these demands. I actually practiced how to hold a cup in a more masculine manner and how to shake hands with a firm grip. But my parent's verbal and physical abuse drained my confidence. Although I know that they loved me, I began to realize that their efforts threatened the loss of my own sense of self. At a very early age, I learned not to trust my parents. Even to this day, I rarely tell them about the ordinary, everyday events in my life. This lack of trust hurts me; yet, I believe that it is necessary for my survival. Domination hurts, even when it is done to protect.

What my parents feared, of course, was that I might be gay. Social scientists, however, have shown that male childhood effeminacy is an inaccurate predictor of homosexual tendencies (Bell, Weinberg, and Hammersmith 1981). My parents number among the millions of people and institutions who do not see the existence of gay people, as Eve Sedgwick (1991) has stated, "as a precious desideratum, a needed condition of life" (23). In other words, the battle waged over my effeminate traits reflected a larger wish endemic in our culture: "the wish that gay people *not exist*" (Sedgwick, 23). I would like to show how this wish manifested itself in my relationship to sports and my decision to become a scholar.

At my request, my parents bought me a basketball, and I learned how to play the game. But when the ball was stolen, I lost interest and stopped playing. I really did not have an aversion to athletics; I was just not overly enthusiastic about football, baseball, basketball, or track and field. But as a teenager, I discovered sports that I liked. I learned how to play tennis which eventually led to volleyball, the sport that I most enjoy and continue to play. However, neither tennis nor volleyball is a masculine sport in African American communities, so there were few occasions to engage in these sports within my neighborhood. Moreover, even at white high schools, there was little enthusiasm from either parents or physical education instructors for boys to play volleyball.

The idea that some sports are more masculine than others harmed me, as I am certain it has harmed many other boys. I missed the opportunity of experiencing the benefits of physical activity, such as hand-eye coordination and cardiovascular maintenance, that accrue from early participation in sports.

I also experienced a great deal of resistance to my interest in a career in scholarship. The African American feminist bell hooks (1991) has written movingly about the resistance she experienced:

Many black females, myself included, described childhood experiences where the longing to read, contemplate, and talk about a broad range of ideas was discouraged, seen as frivolous activity, or as activity that indulged in too intensely would lead us to be selfish, cold, cut off from feelings and estranged from community. In childhood, if I did not place household chores above the pleasures of reading and thinking, grown-ups threatened to punish me by burning my books, by forbidding me to read. Although this never happened, it impressed on my consciousness the sense that it was somehow not only "wrong" to prefer being alone reading, thinking, writing, but was some-

how dangerous to my well-being and a gesture insensitive to the welfare of others. (155)

Unlike hooks, who grew up poor, my parents were school teachers with graduate degrees. Yet they opposed my desire to become an intellectual. They gave me the best education they could afford with the hope that I would become a professional, preferably a medical doctor. They were delighted by my childhood announcement that I wanted to become a pediatrician. When I later decided instead to apply for teaching and research assistantships to attend graduate school, however, their disappointment was palpable. My mother lamented, "I'm not giving you any money; who is going to pay you to go to school?" My father was more resigned. When I got my first tenure track job in academia, he said, "Well, I guess you are just going to be a teacher." Two or three years ago, he criticized my desire to write and do research by informing me that Alex Haley's *Roots* was the last book by a black person that he had seen on the shelves at his neighborhood drugstore.

hooks (1991) suggests that being an intellectual in African American communities "meant that one risked being seen as weird, strange, and possibly even mad" (149). Moreover, hooks (1991) ponders the fate of "gifted black children raised in homes where their brilliance of mind was not valued but made them 'freaks' who were persecuted and punished" (149). Certainly, as a young, effeminate black male, I risked falling into the category of freak, a term often used in my community to describe gay men and lesbians. My desire for isolation in order to read and indulge in contemplation, as well as my absence from organized sports, raised the level of my parents' anxiety about me.

The desire for isolation, I have recently discovered, is historically connected in science and popular lore with pathology and criminology. The 1949 *Encyclopedia of Criminology* includes activities that require isolation in its description of the narcissistic homosexual. The people in this category included "eccentrics of all kinds, misers, collectors, *book-worms* [emphasis added], also exaggerating lovers and protectors of animals who prefer pets to men, because animals are no danger to them" (Wittels, 193). In the insightful ethnography *Ways With Words*, Shirley Brice Heath (1983) gives the following account of a small town black community in North Carolina and its reaction to a young man who enjoyed reading in isolation:

> Aunt Berta had a son who as a child used to slip away from the cotton field and read under a tree. He is now a grown man with children, and he has obtained a college degree, but the community still tells tales about his peculiar boyhood habits of wanting to go off and read alone. In general, reading alone, unless one is very old and religious, marks an individual as someone who cannot make it socially. (191)

It should also be remembered that the hermit who lives in isolation is a popular stereotype for men who deviate from heterosexual intercourse. In her brilliant debut novel *The Bluest Eye* (1974), Toni Morrison chillingly manipulated this stereotype of the hermit as a homosexual and child molester to create the character Soaphead Church.

'Alone Is Alone, Not Alive'

My description of home seems reminiscent of Esther Phillip's recording of Gil Scott Heron's "Home Is Where the Hatred Is." It certainly has not been my intention to say that home was an absolutely terrible place. It wasn't. Yet home was a place I associate with domination and resistance. My parents did not want me to be gay, and they tried to force me to alter such behaviors that they attributed to gayness. Because of their social class standing and their desire to educate me, they supported my attendance of the opera, ballet, and theatre. I could purchase books and music and, as long as I didn't remain cloistered in my room for unreasonable periods of time, I could consume them with abandon. My parents did not, however, realize that the activities and events they sanctioned and associated with class mobility also enabled me to oppose their wishes for my future.

The home I have created today does not resemble the one in which I was raised. For the past nine years, I have shared a home with a man whom I love deeply. The desire to be free from domination by loved ones is a constant issue in our home, and we have struggled with the issue of monogamy when our careers have forced us to live apart. Neither of us believes that we have the right to police each other's body. Belief and praxis, however, are not the same. So we struggle to avoid domination. We just want to be happy.

My parents and I have cordial relations. I speak with my mother on a weekly basis, but sometimes weeks pass before I speak to my father. Seldom do we speak of my relationship with my partner.

References

Asante, M. K. (1987). *The Afrocentric idea*. Philadelphia: Temple University Press.

Beam, J. (1986). *Brother to brother: Words from the heart*. In J. Beam (230–242).

Beam, J. (1986). *In the life: A black gay anthology*. Boston: Alyson.

Bell, A. P., Weinberg, W. S., and Hammersmith, S. K. (1981). *Sexual preference: Its development in men and women*. Bloomington: Indiana University Press.

Collins, P. H. (1990). *Black feminist thought: Knowledge, consciousness, and the politics of empowerment*. Boston: Unwin Hyman.

Gomez, J. L. (1983). *A cultural legacy denied and discovered: Black lesbians in fiction by women*. In B. Smith (110–123).

Heath, S. B. (1983). *Ways with words: Language, life, and work in communities and classrooms*. New York: Cambridge University Press.

Hemphill, E. (Ed.). (1991). *Brother to brother: New writings by black gay men*. Boston: Alyson.

hooks, b. (1991). Black women intellectuals. In b. hooks and C. West, (Eds.), *Breaking bread: Insurgent black intellectual life*. Boston: South End.

Johnson, L. (Director). (1973). *That Certain Summer* [Television Film].

Lakoff, G. and Johnson, M. (1980). *Metaphors we live by*. Chicago: The University of Chicago Press.

Lorde, A. (1984). *Sister outsider*. Freedom, CA: Crossing Press.

Nero, C. I. (1991). *Towards a black gay aesthetic: Signifying in contemporary black gay literature*. In E. Hemphill (229–252).

Rich, A. (1980). Compulsory heterosexuality and lesbian existence. *Signs,* 5, 631–60.

Riggs, M. T. (Producer and Director). (1989). *Tongues untied* [Film]. San Francisco: Frameline.

Rodgers, R. and Hammerstein, O. (1960). *The Sound of Music.* New York: Williamson.

Sedgwick, E. K. (1991). How to bring your kids up gay. *Social Text,* 29, 18–27.

Simmons, R. (1991). Some thoughts on the challenges facing black gay intellectuals. In E. Hemphill (211–228).

Smith, B. (Ed.). (1983). *Home girls: A black feminist anthology.* New York: Kitchen Table, Women of Color Press.

Sondheim, S. (Music and Lyrics), and Furth, G. (Book). (1973). *Company.* In S. Richards (Ed.), *Ten great musicals of the American theater.* Radnor, PA: Chilton.

Wittels, F. (1949). Homosexuality. In V. C. Branham and S. B. Kutash (Eds.), *Encyclopedia of criminality* (189–194). New York: Philosophical Library.

Woods, D. W. (1986). Sister lesbos. In J. Beam (104–105). ✦

Part III

Representing Cultural Knowledge in Interpersonal and Mass Media Contexts

10

Negotiating Cyberspace/ Negotiating RL[1]

Radhika Gajjala
Bowling Green State University

Radhika Gajjala
Bowling Green State University

What does "personal is political" mean within the context of this list? A highly oppressive mechanism where-by little brown women are given a "voice" as long as we say certain things (not necessarily on this list though). Or within the context of commodification of the personal voice on the internet? It is institutionized and commodified not only on the internet but also in academia and the art world.

—a post on sa-cyborgs
(October, 1998).[2]

"Ignorance" and "knowledge" are constructed relative to specific socio-cultural contexts, within various powerfields. The continental philosopher Michel Foucault (1977) points out that we (subjects) are discursively produced as "docile bodies" through the workings of power. As docile bodies, we are constructed as ignorant in relation to the authorities who control the flow and production of knowledge as well as the legitimization and mystification of certain kinds of knowledge as more worthy than others.

Most non-Western regions are in the state they are because, historically, their cultural identities, belief systems, as well as social and economic structures were eroded and stripped away by certain authorities. For example, during the British rule, traditional modes of local production in India were forcefully replaced by industrial mass pro-duction, which was more beneficial to the British economy than to the people on the Indian sub-continent. In the new industrial mass production era, the traditional products lost markets and the traditional producers, their confidence. The resulting outmoding of traditional forms of community and production, under the ideological cover of Western progress, led to a loss of self among local producers. People with expert knowledge of local modes of production were declared "ignorant." In the presence of Enlightenment from the West, several non-Western modes of thought and life were implicitly and explicitly constructed as "backward," "traditional," and "ignorant." The peoples of these regions were thus dis-empowered.

Verhelst suggests that the nature of under-development in this context is a stripping away of identity, which leaves people without the capability of self-determination (Verhelst 1990). Within this context, how can the Internet and other digital technologies be used to self-empower people in "Third-World" dis-empowered contexts, whether located geographically in the West or the East? Even as the Internet and digital world construct many as "ignorant" yet again, can we possibly use these tools for self-empowerment? In the words of one of the members of the E-mail discussion list called sa-cyborgs:

> what is it that will give me "iden-tity". . . alot of it is how I am perceived by someone else. Today I seem to have given away this power to people who have a vested interest in seeing me as one thing or the other . . .I am constantly in the position of negotiating for more space . . .do I get more people to negoti-ate on my side do I decide that I and only I will decide my identity and in an rl world where my identity is already threat-ened by my own ignorance . . .will not the net just be one more place where I am "ignorant" . . . .[3]

The present chapter discusses my negoti-ation of cyberspace as a woman of color and a Third-World woman of cultural and mate-rial privilege in relation to the very real structures of power that extend from "RL" (real life) into "VL" (virtual life) and repro-duce the same old hierarchies even online. I use the term *negotiation* to refer to our everyday transactions of meaning-making from within hierarchies and power structures. Negotiation thus refers to the tactics that we adopt in the process of interpersonally and socially co-constructing meaning in our everyday lives. I will discuss information communication technologies (ICTs) in the context of the vision of a global village, in relation to the current (im)possibilities of empowerment and cross-cultural dialogue. My theoretical approach is an interweaving of postcolonial, feminist, and critical-cultural theories. I will first narrate my introduction to cyberspace and my negotiation of cyberspace as both an academic and a creative writer, then I will discuss ICTs within the context of the rhetoric of global village. I will end the chapter with an sa-cyborgs lis(t-s)tory and briefly describe the founding of an E-mail list.

Cyberspace, the Academy, and Me

Whenever I need to use personal anecdotes and my experiences as a Third-World woman or woman of color or both in writing from within academic spaces, I struggle. Although I have often interspersed the personal within fictional and mythological narrations, as a poet and a writer of fiction, I am wary of explicitly writing about my experiences. Yet I have made myself vulnerable in many ways, in both academic and creative writing, by working in ways that required bringing in the personal because the topics I work on are in a sense very personal. I have written about myself in various ways even in my dissertation and on many online spaces (Gajjala 1998a; Gajjala 1998b; Gajjala 1999). However, I am never comfortable doing so. I am always aware that what I write will be read within frameworks that might peg me as a "victim" of typical Third-World cultures or as a "victor" who supposedly transcended the life of a Third-World woman. I can never write about myself in public spaces without agonizing over the fact that I may yet again be invoked and commodified within both academic and non-academic spaces as a model informant from the Third World. This awareness arises from the fact that much of what I have done and continue to do in my research, creative work, and online is directly and indirectly related to the issue of "personal is political" in relation to the commodification of personal voice of colored women within Western powerfields of knowledge.

Over the years, as an Indian writer who is able to write and read no other language but that of her colonizers, I have learned to disguise my various "ignorances." I have multiple voices in which I write, and these voices have transmuted over the years and within various lived contexts. Negotiating language, negotiating social spaces from in-between spaces, is what I have always done and continue to do. My multiple voices speak from multiple traveling locations. Traveling has been my life and translating myself has been my mode of negotiation, whether in Nigeria as an Indian child, in India as an African-at-heart child, in "International" schools as a nonwhite child marked by cultural practices that were different, as in Catholic schools as a Hindu child. In India I was not colored; in Nigeria I was not colored. In both these places, I was culturally and materially more privileged than many others. Even as a female child and later a' woman, I had access to cultural and material capital that many who live even in the First-World nations do not. In the United States, I am marked as an "ethnic" woman of color. In the United States, I identify with "women of color." As is the case with any prismatic narrative of self-identity, the way I am telling the story here is true, but it is one of many ways to tell it. Within the narration of such partial stories, I will discuss my experience of cyberculture.

In cyberspace, I translate in various ways as cyberdiva, cyborgwati, and Radhika Gajjala. I am cyberdiva most often within the anglicized spaces online—both on E-mail discussion lists and on MOOs.[4] I use cyborgwati within certain contexts when emphasizing my difference for rhetorical and performative effect. Because my usernames "cyberdiva" and "cyborgwati" tend to confuse some people and create the impression that I am "weird," I use "Radhika Gajjala" when I feel that the person on the other end might not have enough experience of cyberculture to understand the playful, ironic trend to use psuedonyms online.

But what do terms like *intercultural* and *woman of color* mean in the context of cyberspace/cyberculture? If, as the famous *New Yorker* cartoon says, "On the Internet no one knows you're a dog," why bother with theories of culture and difference when discussing computer-mediated communication? One of my cotravelers in cyberspace has the following signature file attached to his E-mail messages:

> *New Yorker* cartoon (Internet Savvy Dog): "On the Internet, no one knows that you're a dog."
> Art McGee (Internet-Ignorant Dog added to cartoon): "What's wrong with being a dog?"[5]

This signature file questions the need to disguise who we are. Indeed, why should it be assumed that it is wonderful for "dogs"— women and colored people—to be able to hide who they are and to be able to disguise their gender, race, and culture in favor of passing as Caucasian? Why must we be ashamed of being women or colored or both? What's wrong with being colored, whats wrong with being a woman?

Cyberspace today looks white. We are wired and connected within a Westernized, Anglicized and white cyberspace. As Kali Tal[6] writes,

> In cyberspace, it is finally possible to completely and utterly disappear people of color. I have long suspected that the much vaunted "freedom" to shed the "limiting" markers of race and gender on the Internet is illusory, and that in fact it masks a more disturbing phenomenon— the whitinizing of cyberspace. The invisibility of people of color on the Net has allowed white-controlled and white-read publications like *WIRED* to simply elide questions of race. (Tal 1996)

Having said that, and also having claimed that I am a woman of a fair amount of cultural and material privilege who chooses to identify as a woman of color in the United States, what have I done about this situation? Is it up to me as an individual to "do something" about such a white cyberspace?

Does anything I have done so far qualify as a "doing"? These are questions I cannot directly answer, but they most definitely are tackled in electronic environments. Examples are what we do on the sa-cyborgs and Third-World-women E-mail lists. Interactively, the members have been trying to maintain an online presence that counters and resists mainstream assumptions and appropriations of Third-World women's stories and opinions. At the beginning and end of this chapter, I have included excerpts from posts by members of sa-cyborgs in relation to the commodification of the personal voice of Third-World women in various spaces. It is interactions such as these that continue to feed my interest in sensitive political topics and electronic environments.

Although I first gained access to E-mail in 1992, as a graduate student at Duquesne University, I began "traveling" cyberspace in 1994, a semester after I joined the doctoral program at the University of Pittsburgh. My traveling started with a quest for communication with women from the South Asian community. In the isolation of my graduate student-cum-mother life, I sought out "community" through the windows offered by my most salient work-tool, the computer. Because I needed to negotiate my complex life as graduate student, mother of a 9-year-old, and wife of a graduate student, my husband and I had invested in a computer. Having a computer with modem at home meant that one of us could be at home when the child came home from school, see that the child was fed and did his homework, while still squeezing in time to work on papers and dissertations. We took turns doing "being at home."

With the sound of cartoons and a child talking in the background about his imaginary airplanes and Lego™ creations, I launched off into a textual world of Usenet bulletin boards and E-mail discussion lists. I volunteered to be part of the moderator's pool for the South Asian Women's Network.[7] In 1995, I volunteered to co-moderate the postcolonial list and joined the Spoon Collective. A few months later, I started my own list via the Spoon Collective called the Third-World-women list. Subsequently, I started the sa-cyborgs list and the women-writing-culture list.[8] At about the same time, I attended a two-hour workshop and learned the basics of HTML, which led me into the webbed world. Personally, I was fascinated by the potential for connecting.

Connectivity meant possible dialogue. Intercultural dialogue with anyone in the world was potentially made available as I sat in my roach-infested graduate student apartment in Pittsburgh, Pennsylvania, typing messages to e-friends I had never met face-to-face. In addition, being a creative writer since I was a teenager, the ability to virtually "publish" my writing to an audience was a very tempting prospect.

Of course, being a graduate student of media studies, a way to feed my growing "addiction" with cyberspace emerged by doing research about cyberculture.[9] My dissertation dealt with issues of identity in relation to South Asian women in diaspora and the formation of postcolonial virtual communities.[10] Issues were raised in relation to diasporic South Asian women's use of ICTs within the rhetoric of the global village.

ICTs and the Global Village

If communication is power, how can we ensure that people all over the world are able to use the powerful information and communication technologies (ICT) tools for their material, social, and cultural empowerment? Within our present-day context, an important question that needs to be considered asks what kind of communication might be possible across the "vast experiential gulfs" that divide different regions of the world "especially when it is mediated by inequalities in power and resources" (Eade 1998, 5). How do we ensure that, in the use of these technologies, we hold each other accountable for the silence of the less privileged peoples of the world, while acting responsibly towards each other? How do we ensure that this silence is not filled up with voices that remain unaccountable to the rest of the world as it basks in its haven of choices? The complexities of these questions have only begun to be addressed.

Information communication technologies (ICTs) are increasingly being touted as the magical tools for establishing a new, democratic Utopia—the Global Village. The global village is seen as a space where all men, women, and children will enjoy the benefits of a modemized, networked liberal humanist society with its implicit underpinning of U.S. views on the nature of democracy. The virtual global village in cyberspace, it is presumed, will be a postmodern day Atlantis where all men and women can indulge in the individualist "choices" offered by the free market economy and the consumer culture. Coca Cola™ or Pepsi,™ AOL or Prodigy, MSN's Internet Explorer or Netscape Navigator, IBM or Mac, Anarchy or Neo-Nazism. We are offered flashing webbed choices between different brand-names and different ideologies all under the umbrella of an already existing power structure. These choices will liberate people from the world of everyday misery, we are told. We are supposedly creating, and interactively composing, a Utopia in which we will be able to turn off the world at our convenience when it rudely intrudes upon the privacy of our individualistic dreams of power and money. Thus, every member of the global village will achieve the "American Dream" through virtual reality and live forever in digital harmony.

In addition, popular narratives about the Internet do not make obvious the connection between what has come to be termed as RL (real life) and VL (virtual life). Issues of virtual accountability to RL ways of being are not addressed. Within our current information age, information distribution, knowledge production, and communication are equivalent to power. Scholars like Foucault (1988) have discussed the relationship between knowledge production and power. What we write, communicate, and do in social spaces enabled by ICTs feeds into the construction of everyday social realities. Our active engagement within social spaces (whether face-to-face, in print, or online) has the potential to effect and transform the way people interact and construct communal realities. The social climate of such a space is determined by the people who have the power to voice their opinions within any context. For example, in my examination of postcolonial communities online, I found that cultural and material access to these virtual communities is fairly class-specific (Gajjala 1998a). In general, the celebratory attitude to digital existence gives the impression that "the social and political turbulence of our time—ethnic conflict, resurgent nationalism, urban fragmentation—ha[ve] nothing at all to do with virtual space" (Robbins 1995, 137), when in fact they do. Researchers (Rai 1995; Gajjala 1998a) have found that, in fact, interaction online tends to replay many of the social tensions and problems that arise in RL existence. The net has become yet another place where people from non-Western contexts are positioned as informants, representative of their "native" cultures and societies. As Everard points out, "the Internet is far from global but it serves to appropriate the idea of the global for western consumption" (Everard 1998, 1).

Social spaces created online are discursive spaces. Books, magazines, and newspapers can also be regarded as discursive spaces. However, online the discursive spaces are uniquely interactive and typically somewhat like live (textual) broadcasts. Discursive spaces affect RL all over the world. As David Holmes points out, "we may never have watched television or 'surfed' the net, but in information societies these forms nevertheless frame our lives" (Holmes 1997, 30). Through no fault of theirs, most people all over the world have no cultural or material access to this cyberspatial discursive realm. They have no choices, not even the illusion.

The Internet Superhighway Utopian scenarios are immersed in what Kevin Robbins (1995) terms the "Technological Imaginary." Robbins is referring to an intoxication with the notion that technology will deliver us from the imperfections of our present world. Within this technological imaginary, ICTs will deliver us from our everyday oppressions. As Cees Hamelink points out:

> This line of thought emphasizes historical discontinuity as a major consequence of technological develop- ments. New social values will evolve, new social relations will develop, and the 'zero sum society' comes to a definite end, once ICTs have realized worldwide access to information for all. (Hamelink 1998, 68)

Such narratives that automatically equate Western technologies with the transformation and emancipation of society in various ways, avoid issues related to the forced disappearance of some older, more environmentally, communally, culturally friendly technologies (Pacey 1992; Shiva 1995). They ignore the fact that, if the adoption of technology changes social/ cultural/economic structures, the change is not always liberatory.

Social/cultural/economic structures sometimes change in undesirable ways when technology is adopted inappropriatly within the lived contexts of a community.[11] Most often, the simple carrying over of Western technological practices into non-Western contexts merely provides "technological and managerial fixes, rather than addressing or solving basic . . .problems" and creates new problems by "destabilizing livelihoods in the Third-World" (Shiva 1994, 1). As a member of sa-cyborgs (who is also a member of Third-World women) pointed out from her Third-World geographical RL location, "entire concepts of time, space, or economics which are developed in one circumstance fail in another because of a lack of an adequate internalization process."[12] This lack of internalization is labeled as "ignorance" and the people who have not adequately internalized are told they have not learned to "change" with the times, and are therefore inferior. "Old" modes of production are arbitrarily replaced by the "new" not necessarily improved modes of production, and community structures that enabled excellence within previous modes of production are unable to perform well with the new modes, because the new modes have not been adopted in culturally and socially sensitive ways. As Sharona Ben-Tov cautions, we must be wary of imposing First-World technology myths and strategies "on people who might have oppositional strategies of their own, drawn from their own cultural resources" (Ben-Tov 1995, 145).

In addition to the above problems, Dale Spender suggests that simply "giving computers to the poor" is not a solution to the inequalities of wealth between various regions of the world. Contrary to popular belief, technology cannot be the "great equalizer." She argues that,

> the more advanced technology is in the first world, the more difficult it will be to live, work, and communicate in the Third World, which has no such resources. And the further the Third World will be removed from the centers of wealth and influence. . . in life-threatening circumstances, to convince the poor of the desirability or necessity of [the Internet as] a technological solution. . . could be taken as yet another version of Marie Antoinette's derisory contribution: "Let them eat cake!" (Spender 1995, 250)

Having said that, I do not want to debunk the possible use of Internet technologies for empowerment of men and women all over the world. Some of the discussions and conflicts on the Third-World women list and the sa-cyborgs list reflect the tensions and dilemmas that I have discussed above in relation to ICTs and the global village. In the next section of this chapter, I will narrate an sa-cyborgs lis(t-s)tory as an example of an attempt to create a space online for perspectives and voices that are not necessarily possible in a majority of other online spaces.

An Sa-cyborgs Lis(t-s)tory

Several members of the E-mail list sa-cyborgs are deeply invested in the above issues. This is apparent from many of the exchanges we have had in the various manifestations of the list since I started it[13] in March 1996.[14] The list was conceived out of concerns in relation to South Asian women's identity with South Asian diasporic communities. In my efforts to study South Asian women and national identity on the E-mail list SAWNET (South Asian Women's Network), I encountered issues that led me to begin a discussion on a Spoon Collective seminar list (seminar-13). Several women and men interested in issues of identity and South Asian women joined the list and we started a discussion to explore our locations in relation to each other and in relation to the kind of

research we were doing. So, in March 1996, sa-cyborgs began out as a continuation of something we had started on seminar-13. The focus of the list was to be,

> "South Asian" (a label which no doubt needs to be problematized) women's identity—especially in relation to nationalism(s) and sexual politics. . . a place where both academic and non-academic discussions (theory, personal accounts, fiction, poetry. . . and more) will intersect.

The critical focus of list interactions was made apparent right from the start, even though many of the exchanges were in the form of poetry. The list description was changed subsequently, to encourage an exchange of creative writing in relation to the above stated focus. For a while I had a co-moderator helping me run the list. After several re-focusings of the description of the list, the current description reads thus:

> Sa-Cyborgs Is a List Brought to You by the Spoon Collective

What are the boundaries between "RL" (real life) and "VL" (virtual life) if any— what are the boundaries between "global" and "local"—where are we going with writing (wrything) online, where writing is existence and not-writing disappears voices. . . . What are the possibilities and (im)possibilities of our transborgized selves merging textually into each other's context—the implications of which are not yet fully (may never be fully) understood. . . .

What can we produce in these dangerous encounters of the "self" and "other" and "other" as "self"— the blurring, the surfing, the wrything. . . .Cyberculture and identity. Wrything the cyborgian body. Cyberchronicles, "rl" chronicles, sci-fi articulations, doing the cyborgian dance on a cyber-kailasham—the fears, the uncertainties, the excitement, the cynicism, the transborgification. . . this is the list. Some purposes of this list are to:

1. Share creative works and to discuss ongoing creative works by members.

2. Discuss issues concerning writing/producing and/or publishing, problems of

audiences, reception and critiques of our works. . . .

3. Provide support, encouragement, and constructive criticism to writers.

4. Discuss issues that come up in different people's work—especially issues pertaining to gender, race, cyberculture and identity.

5. Engage in collective exercises to unblock writer's block or just for fun such as collective poems, stories, or other forms of experimental writing while avoiding hierarchy, sexism, racism, classism, heterosexism, ethnocentrism, and any other oppressive, repulsive views.

Other long-term (and ambitious) goals may include the following:

1. Set up an archive of creative works.

2. From this archive, perhaps set up an editorial collective to put together an anthology which we can try to have published.

3. Network and outreach.

4. Provide a resource on how to go about publishing.

An information sheet ("info sheet") draws a broad outline of the possible topics to be discussed on the list. It also contains any other community rules determined either by the list founder or by the majority vote of the participants. Therefore, the info sheet for sa-cyborgs attracts members interested in the focus of the E-mail list. Occasionally, people who don't "belong" drift in and out of the list, but longtime subscribers are the ones who maintain an ongoing interest in what is happening. Most Spoon Collective moderators neither actively monitor posts to the lists or approve or censor posts actively. I see my role as a moderator/administrator to be one of subtle control and diplomacy, in addition to being purely technical. The purely technical back-stage work for running a list via the Spoon majordomo involves sharing Spoon Collective administrative/ technical work with other members of the collective as well as keeping a watch over my

lists in order to fix any spams, etcetera. Most Spoon lists are at least partially "self-regulated" in terms of content, in that the list members interactively control and allow content. I am (like any other list-member) able to exercise subtle and not-so-subtle modes of interpersonal and textual modes of control in relation to the tone, topics, and form of interaction on lists that I moderate and co-moderate. The nature of list interaction is such that a moderator can never have total control of list interaction unless he or she chooses to perform tasks that a journal editor usually does.

To edit list interactions in this manner, at the very source, however, would be to restrict the interesting aspects and potential of online interaction by merely replicating processes involved in the production of print documents. Print publications—like books and magazines that carry their own ideological labels and sanctions in the form of book and magazine covers, publishers' names, comments from reviewers, and even explanatory prefaces and acknowledgments, and so on— are packaged within definite ideological frameworks. We cannot actually witness the process of change in the ideological positioning of any author published in print, because the very publication in print by a certain publisher, under a certain category, fixes the author's ideological position for the readers.

In the case of E-mail lists, this function is usually performed by the ideological positioning of the E-mail list on which someone might post his or her work. When someone posts a piece that is unacceptable to the ideological framework of the list, the process of censuring occurs after the work has already been posted to the list. The writer is "flamed" or unsubscribed, depending on how democratic the moderators of the list pretend to be.

Email lists are not "free" spaces where individuals have the freedom to post anything they want. The censorship and the ideological "fixing" of the content of E-mail lists are different from the censorship and labeling that are done in the print world. The censorship that happens on E-mail lists, for example, relies to a large extent on interpersonal verbal cues and power dynamics (Gajjala 1998a).

Some Last Words

In spite of work being done by several critical scholars, cyberfeminists, and real world activists, the dominant rhetoric concerning cyberculture and community online continues to be uncritically celebratory (see Rheingold 1993 for a sample of uncritical celebration). In addition, much of the rhetoric surrounding cyberspace and cyberculture views the Internet as a virtual world where men pick up "chics." The Internet, according to this rhetoric, is where teenage boys look for pornography, children have their innocence snatched from them the minute they go online, while adult men and women promiscuously engage in safe "net-sex" (a form of virtual masturbation) away from RL consequences like AIDS and VD.

If ICTs are seen as a source of power for women and men, whether in the more affluent regions of the world (North) or the underprivileged regions of the world (South), they are viewed as such mainly because ICTs enable "other" men and women to stay connected to the center of (economic) power located in the North. The power that ICTs and such technologies grant to men and women in developing countries is currently minimal compared to the power that was taken away by colonial and neo-colonial political, economic, and cultural structures set in place several decades ago. Men and women in developing countries and in less privileged race and class locations, even in rich Western nations like the United States, use ICTs within this framework of already existing (unaccountable) hierarchies.

There are no exhaustive and direct answers to the questions posed at the beginning of this chapter. But we must ask such questions—over and over and over again. At least those of us with access to both the South and the North must continue to ask them and make people aware of the silences. It is our responsibility to turn these silences into *audible silences*. The discomfort that arises from having to encounter such audible silences may one day enable us to find

solutions. Within this context, and in order to once again express my own discomfort as possibly being read as an informant from the "Third-World," I end this chapter with a relevant quote from a message sent to me by a member of sa-cyborgs:

> *Taking personal grievances to the public domain and calling it feminism. . . it's a lack of objectivity that we have to be careful to avoid because we then take away the legitimacy of people less privileged than we are. . . I don't like an articulation where we come across as victims or victors. . . .*

—off-list comment from
a member of sa-cyborgs[16]

Notes

1. I wish to acknowledge M. Annapurna's role in helping me construct some of the arguments in this paper. My dialogues with her or various E-mail discussion lists (Third-World woman, sa-cyborgs, and millenium-borgs) as well as our exchange of E-mails and telephone conversations during the process of putting together this chapter have influenced some of what I have written here. I also wish to thank Paige Edley, Al González, and Melissa Spirek for patiently helping with revising and structuring this chapter. Finally, I wish to thank the members of sa-cyborgs for participating on and being members of the list.

2. I thank Shashwati Talukdar for giving me permission to use her post to sa-cyborgs. See (http://lists.village.virginia.edu/~spoons) for public archives. This exchange can be found in the sa-cyborgs archives for November 98 (sa-cyborgs.9810) under the thread heading "a few quotes—stray thoughts—in relation to this list."

3. From an off-list message sent to me by M. Annapurna.

4. Multi-User Domains Object-Oriented—these are (text-based) synchronous online interaction/communication spaces.

5. Art McGee first made this statement on the "Computers, Freedom, and Privacy" conference in 1995. Also see Art's page of links at (http://www.igc.org//amcgee/e-race. html).

6. See (http://www.kalital.com/text/writing/whiteness.html).

7. See website . . .I am currently one of several volunteer moderators.

8. I recently "shut down" the women-writing-culture list—an e-lis(t-st)ory that I will save for another time.

9. Just for the record, I don't think I am "addicted" to the Internet.

10. See (http://ernie.bgsu.edu/~radhik/sanov. html).

11. In this context, see some of the exchanges in the discussion archives of the Gender Perspectives section of the *Virtual Conference: The Right to Communicate and the Communication of Rights* at (http://commposite.uqam. ca/videaz/wg3/).

12. From an E-mail exchange with M. Annapurna off-list.

13. The archives and history of this list can be accessed via the Spoon Collective website— (http://lists.village.virginia.edu/~spoons).

14. Malgosia Arkansas of the Spoon Collective was kind enough to help with the technicalities and programming needs for setting up the list, as she has done with my other lists.

15. Lakshmi Gopinath Nair was a co-moderator of sa-cyborgs until I lost cyberspatial contact with her sometime in 1998.

16. Reproduced with permission of the author. Sa-cyborgs is an E-mail discussion list that I run via the Spoon Collective (see http:// lists.village.virginia.edu/~spoons).

References

Ben-Tov, S. (1995). *The artificial paradise: Science fiction and American reality*. Ann Arbor: University of Michigan Press.

Eade, D. (1998, February). Editorial. *Development in practice*, 8.1 (Feb. 1998): 5–7.

Everard, J. (1998). *Virtual states: Internet, globalization, and inequality*. New York: Routledge

Foucault, M. (1977). *Discipline and punish: The birth of the prison*. New York: Vintage.

Foucault, M. (1980). *History of sexuality*, vol. 1. (Translated by Hurley, R.). New York: Vintage.

Gajjala, R. (1998a). The sawnet refusal: An interrupted cyberethnography (Doctoral dissertation, University of Pittsburgh), Dissertation Abstracts International, 99–00131.

Gajjala, R. (1998b, December). There are no last words online. *Cybersociology: Magazine for social-scientific researchers of cyberspace*, issue 4.

Gajjala, R. (1999, Winter). Cyberdiva. *New observations*. Issue on cultures of cyberspace.

Hamelink, C. (1998, February). The people's communication charter. *Development in practice*, 8

Holmes, D. (1997). *Virtual politics: Identity and community in cyberspace*. Gold Coast Campus: Griffith University.

Pacey, A. (1992). *The culture of technology*. Cambridge: MIT

Rai, A.S. (1995). On-line: Electronic bulletin boards and the construction of a diasporic Hindu identity. *Diaspora*, 4, 1.

Rheingold, H. (1993). *The virtual community: homesteading on the electronic frontier*. New York: HarperPerennial.

Robbins, K. (1995). Cyberspace and the world we live in. In *Cyberspace, cyberbodies, cyberpunk: Cultures of technological embodiment*, Featherstone and Burrows. London: Sage.

Shiva, V. (1994). *Close to home: Women reconnect ecology, health, and development*. India: Kali for Women.

Spender, D. (1995). *Nattering on the net: Women, power, and cyberspace*. Australia: Spinifex.

Tal, K. (1996, October). The unbearable whiteness of being: African American critical theory and cyberculture *WIRED*. (http:// www.kalital.com/Text/Writing/Whiteness.html).

Verhelst, T. (1990). *No life without roots*, London: Zed Books. ✦

11

The Rhetoric of *La Familia* Among Mexican Americans

Margarita Gangotena
Blinn College

"You are going out so soon? At what time will you be back, *hijo?*" the mother asks as she approaches her son and fixes the collar of his shirt. She touches his cheek with the palm of her hand while looking at him with love and pride. Manuel, a six-foot-tall, 25-year-old man, checks the rest of his attire then embraces his mother and kisses her farewell on the cheek.

"I will be back soon, no later than eleven," he replies. "Jenny and I are going to the movies. And, yes, *Mami, I left the money for the rent on your night table, where Cristina left the money for the food.*"

As he departs, his sister Cristina enters the apartment. "Have fun, Manuel," she says and turns around to kiss her mother on the cheek. "Hola, Mami. What are we having for supper? Is Dad still at work? Where is Uncle Beto? Is Grandma asleep?" She sits on a couch.

"Cristina," the mother says without answering any of her questions, "when are you going to get married to Joe? He is four years older than you; you are 22, and you will be graduating from college this year. We will help you get started and help you along. Joe is a good, hard-working young man."

"I don't know, sounds all right, but. . . " Cristina sighs. "We have only known each other for a couple of months, and, you know how it is, he wants to have everything clear and organized before we even talk about marriage. He will have to move out of his parents' house, and there are still younger kids in the family, they need support. . . ."

If this same episode had transpired in an Anglo family, the dialogue would most likely have been different.

"See you, Mom," Tom says as he opens the door to leave. Noticing that his sister Cary has arrived, he adds, "I better leave, she's back!" Cary glares at him as he goes by. As she walks in, she says, "I have a lot of work to do, Mom." She marches off to her bedroom and closes the door. Throughout this exchange, the mother does not take her eyes off what she is doing, nor does she respond to her children's statements.

Two typical households, one Mexican American and the other Euro-American, reflect two very different underlying values and assumptions of what a family is and what it provides for its members. The communication of the Mexican American family in the above episode points to the continued interdependence of its members across generations. It also makes explicit that sharing time in conversation is a valued form of family interaction. Touch, affection, and greeting rituals are means of affirmation. In contrast, the communication in the Anglo family points to some basic assumptions about the value of individualism and the need to maintain it through more restricted communication and contact. In the Mexican American family, the formality given to greeting rituals is intended to keep both familiarity and distance. In the Euro-American family, cultural valuations seem to limit interdependence and affiliation to the family, so as to make the children leave the "nest" and form other independent, nuclear families. In my opinion, the Euro-American family rarely uses touch in its casual interactions and even less so with grown children. The cultural perception of touch for Euro-Americans seems to work as (1) a means of control and preventing any tendency toward individualism and (2) a communicative device reserved mainly for sexual encounters. The need for independence and individualism apparently fosters an emotional distance between the generations that severely impairs significant bonding among family members.

72

The Mexican American family is the source of many of the cultural values, attitudes, and assumptions that Mexican Americans carry with them into their interactions with mainstream society. This composite of cultural elements that influences the Mexican American character is what Mexican Americans call *la familia* (the family). Consequently, the analysis of the rhetoric that frames Mexican American family values and activities will facilitate Euro-Americans' understanding of Mexican Americans. Moreover, awareness of the Mexican American valuation of the family provides a model for society of such productive attributes as community, solidarity, respect, and discipline.[1]

The purpose of this essay is to describe the rhetorical devices that comprise and sustain la familia (the Mexican American family) in the United States. The essay begins with a critique of traditional social science research that has advanced a negative image of *la familia*. Then it discusses the contributions rhetorical analysis can offer toward clarifying the Mexican American valuation of the family. Finally, it introduces a new theoretical approach not yet present in the literature on Mexican Americans, nor in the Euro-American interpretation of Mexican American culture. Theoretically, this essay is significant, because it provides (1) a process for analyzing Mexican American culture and (2) a more accurate interpretation than would be the case from a Euro-American perspective.

This essay describes five rhetorical devices that emerge in family discourse among Mexican Americans: harmony/silence; rationality/emotionalism; the concept of personhood; respect for hierarchy, age, and gender; and solidarity and a sense of community. One qualification must preface this analysis: the devices described herein occur in various ways among Mexican Americans. The rhetorical vision of *la familia* is often manifested in the discourse and behavior of most of its adherents. However, one's perception of this rhetorical vision may differ if one is neither of Mexican American background nor is an actual participant of *la familia*. Nevertheless, the vision of *la familia* holds a strong allegiance among most Mexican Americans. Any participant of *la familia*, upon hearing this discourse, should immediately feel a sense of familiarity and comfort, become emotionally moved, and consciously recognize the layers of meaning embedded herein.

La Familia and Traditional Social Science Research

Traditional social science research has studied the Mexican American family for several decades. Although it has brought *la familia* to the focus of scholarly work, it has not always been able to understand it clearly. Because of this, social science studies tends to blame *la familia* for most of the problems of Mexican American acculturation.[2] Hence, *la familia* has become a scapegoat for the lack of both understanding and intercultural sensitivity.

Social science discourse on *la familia* has been biased by Euro-American conceptions of the family. Some of the elements that characterize the Euro-American vision of the family include nuclear structure; non-generational, indivdualistic, non-extended, detached, permissive child-rearing practices; and flexible gender roles, all of which tend to grant respect on the basis of individualism.

Another factor may be involved in the social sciences' assessment of *la familia*: conclusions are often based on assumptions derived from incomplete information on the psycho-social background of Mexican Americans. It has been postulated that the changes *la familia* undergoes are due to Mexican Americans moving from rural to urban life. Mexican Americans have high mobility within the United States. Needless to say, as they relocate, they have to undergo some changes. However, these changes are not pronounced, because their movement is from one urban center to another. We know this is the case because a large proportion of Mexican Americans have lived mainly in urban centers. A large percentage of those who migrate to this country are already city dwellers—many of them skilled and semiskilled industrial laborers (Schick and Schick 1991). The unfounded conclusions by U.S. social scientists that the Mexican American family is neither "developed," "Western," nor like middle-class America and, therefore, of a lesser, peasant-like quality, derive from generalizations based on studies of the rural enclaves of Mexican Americans. Because of such conclusions, the Mexican American population at large has been stereotyped. For example, stereotypes portray the Mexican American husband as a dictator in the family and the wife as weak and spineless. When these stereotypes are not corroborated by the urban data, researchers attribute the differences to the influence of urbanization and modernization on a peasant population. I would argue that previous studies of the characteristics of the Mexican American family may have reflected the reality of the locale or the people researched, but they were not really representative of Mexican American people as a whole.

Social scientists have relegated the slow progress of Mexican Americans toward assimilation on their strong attachment to *la familia*—or "familialism"—not to mention their dependence on the extended families. But they do not take into account that the reaction of Euro-Americans to Mexican Americans contributes to segregating the latter from social interactions, job opportunities, and overall advancement. I personally experienced this Euro-American perception when I was traveling by bus to a high-level seminar at the University of Portland. During most of the trip, I talked with a senior citizen, while across the aisle sat a friendly couple. The husband would occasionally eavesdrop on our conversation. Later, he queried about my destination. When I told him I was going to the University of Portland, he asked with apparent sincerity, "Are you going there to learn to serve tables better?" He had automatically pegholed me into a specific socioeconomic structure.

Researchers on the Mexican American family have not brought to bear certain historic facts about *la familia*. Influenced by the slow but persistent erosion of the importance of the Euro-American family, their data has distorted the relevance of *la familia* for Mexican Americans and for the nation.

Both the Meso-American and the Spanish ancestors of the contemporary Mexican American were highly urbanized, and the religious beliefs of both cultural groups valued the basic family structure. The Meso-American ancestry is obvious in Mexican American food, Mexican American discourse, and much of its folklore. The Spanish imprint on Mexican Americans today is manifested, for example, in their preference for language usage, music, family structure, and religion. Undoubtedly, one of the symbols that has strengthened the Mexican American valuation of the family is the Christian image of the Holy Family (Joseph, Mary, and Baby Jesus). This rhetorical type is continuously reinforced through the discourse of the Catholic Church. It also coincides with basic rhetorical themes commonly valued by Western culture, i.e., love, a need to belong, mature interpersonal relations, and deliverance from guilt. Thus, the force of the vision of *la familia* has its source in discourse that supports (1) life, (2) self-identity based on family belonging, and (3) human communication. The dialogue at the beginning of this essay illustrates some of the elements that sustain the rhetoric of *la familia* for Mexican Americans. For example, through Manuel, Cristina, and Mami, we see the importance of touch, caring, and nurturing in *la familia*. Some of social science's misunderstanding of Mexican American culture can be overcome by a proper analysis of rhetorical visions through symbolic convergence theory. Applying this theory, commonly known as fantasy theme analysis, is not only innovative but practical, because the methodology allows the culture to speak for itself without the influence of the system of analysis or the researcher's bias.

Contribution of Communication to Understanding La Familia

La familia is a concept embedded with meanings developed by Mexican Americans through five centuries. As we gain an understanding of these meanings, we will be better able to view *la familia* from the perspective of its participants. Thus, we can develop a deeper appreciation of the inner richness of *la familia.*

To help us comprehend the meanings associated with *la familia,* communication theory and methodology allow us to focus on the discourse of Mexican Americans. As dialogues, narratives, and symbolic references to la familia are analyzed, the rhetorical critic will be able to understand the development of meaning as a manifestation of the deeper layers of values and value attributions. The dialogues and narrative data found among Mexican Americans are quite rich.[3] Because of the culture's valuation of narratives as a means to transfer tradition and to interact, one of the best methods to understand *la familia* is through symbolic convergence theory.

Ernest Bormann developed symbolic convergence theory at the University of Minnesota, where he analyzed data on leaderless groups. He found that these groups seemed to create narratives on themes outside of the topic of discussion which involved their members emotionally (Bormann 1972). When the discourse of a group's narratives was analyzed, it was found to contain such dramatic elements as heroes, heroines, and villains, and performed "action sequences somewhere other than in the 'here and now'" (Smith 1988, 271). Furthermore, the drama, plot, characters, and discourse of the group were found to be symbolic of what was happening in the dynamics of the group's interaction. For example, when a group studied the benefits of the social security system, one of its members offered only minimal participation. Digressing from the topic at hand, the others told jokes and stories about the importance of working together and making contributions, which revealed the group's disapproval of the more reticent member's lack of involvement.

Bormann and his associates researched message stories in interpersonal, small groups and organizational settings, both in writing and over the electronic media. They found dramatizations of fictitious and nonfictitious events with a specific message, which Bormann labeled as "fantasy themes" (Bormann 1972). The recurrence of these fantasy themes, or "stock scenarios repeated in various forms within a body of discourse," were deemed fantasy types. Bormann defined rhetorical views as "the more global symbolic realities consisting of fantasy themes and fantasy types, often including metaphors and analogies" (Gangotena 1980, 24). Groups of people sharing in the same rhetorical vision comprised what was called a rhetorical community. In using the term *fantasy,* Bormann did not mean that the narratives were negative or reflected negatively on the people researched, nor did he interpret them as imaginary or unreal. Rather, the term *fantasy* was used to indicate that the themes and types made reference to events not in the "here and now" of a group's task.

> When a communicator dramatizes some event, the listeners may share the drama in an appropriate way or they may ignore it, ridicule it, or reject it in some other way. Only the communication associated with the sharing of fantasy serves to build a common social reality for the participants. When people constituting a community have shared a large number of similar fantasy themes, they may allude to the basic scenarios in general terms in the form of a fantasy type. (Gangotena 1980, 24)

Thus, if several Mexican Americans dramatize incidents in which a person has not displayed behaviors that in Mexican American culture demonstrate respect, and/or they praise those who have displayed those behaviors, we can safely assume that a fantasy type of respect has been introduced into the group's discourse. Once the fantasy type is present, the entire meaning for a class of fantasy types can be brought about through such expressions as *malcriado* or *sin crianza* (both terms meaning "poorly trained at home by the parents").

By utilizing this kind of rhetorical criticism, the researcher needs to look at the dramatic elements of the discourse (the plot, heroes, heroines, villains, and scenarios) to uncover the basic themes, types, and rhetorical visions involved. Subsequently, the critic focuses on the artistic manifestation and value of the discourse, the consequences of that discourse for the rhetorical community, and the consequences of that vision for the enhancement of humanity. "Did the rhetorical vision emancipate and enrich human experience, did it enslave and degrade the people affected by it?" (Smith 1988, 273).

When using symbolic convergence theory, the objective is to unravel the themes, i.e., the fantasy themes, that predominate in a group or in a cultural community. These themes, each time they are repeated, create fantasy types that are shared by groups of people. The rhetorical community which shares in these themes creates a unique rhetorical vision, or paradigm, of the world. The convergence of these themes captures the imagination and emotion of people by way of a shared symbolic reality. (For further discussion on this topic, see Bormann 1972.)

Fantasy theme analysis of discourse is one way of describing the cultural meanings expressed by members of a rhetorical community. As we uncover the basic framework of discourse through symbolic convergence, we are able to see a culture from its own perspective rather than from that of the "biased outsider." Bormann has used fantasy theme analysis to interpret the elements of Euro-American rhetoric that have helped shape this nation in his book, The Force of Fantasy: The Making of the American Dream (1985).

Reports of Mexican American discourse on *la familia*, gathered by the author from participant observation, point to the existence of various fantasy types that support the rhetoric of *la familia* among Mexican Americans. It is through these themes that the Mexican American community comes to share in a common symbolic reality. The fantasy types that emerge regarding *la familia* are: harmony and silence; rationality and emotionalism; the concept of personhood; respect for hierarchy, age, and gender; solidarity and the sense of community.

Harmony and Silence

One of the main fantasy types that supports the rhetoric of *la familia* among Mexican Americans is that of maintaining harmonious relationships. The basic fantasy type is that of a person who values relationships, gets along well with others, fulfills all family obligations, does not place others in compromising situations, and does not bring shame to the family. In this fantasy type, Mexican Americans resist creating external conflicts such as those that would draw them out of their shell, have them lose face, or cause insecurity. Not only are relationships valued, but, when faced with choices that go against harmony, their preference would be to avoid conflict through compromise. Mexican Americans generally dislike conflict, considering it to be of no social value in maintaining relationships. Only when discourse has failed to prevent conflict will they choose antagonistic exchanges. For example, if faced with a situation where the choice is between assertiveness and harmony, Mexican Americans will compromise. This is not to say, however, that they will not fight abuse and oppression from external sources. They will come out against injustice once other channels have failed. The fantasy type that will justify assertiveness and aggressiveness is the fantasy theme of "the intrinsic honor of the person" and "the honor of the family."

Much like in other Latin cultures, Mexican Americans have a cultural need to protect themselves from external influences, thus maintaining some control over their own lives and circumstances. They usually accomplish this with silence and compromise. To attain harmony, silence is often necessary. Mexican Americans may choose to grow silent and introverted rather than become a source of disharmonious relationships. This fantasy type of harmony/silence is supported by what González (1990, 281) has called "defense against intrusion."

The importance Mexican Americans give to maintaining relationships offsets a natural human inclination toward selfishness and the Mexican American tendency to self-absorption described by González (1992). It also tempers the cultural trait of undeterred individualism passed on by the Spanish. The characteristics that conform to the Spanish individualistic fantasy type of the sixteenth and seventeenth centuries are a preference for private property, the freedom to be one's own agent, the freedom to speak one's own mind, the freedom to have a divergent point of view from another, self-trust, mistrust of others until proven reliable, freedom of mobility and decision making, and freedom of enterprise. In the rhetorical vision of la familia, these characteristics are incorporated as qualities of the Mexican American family. Thus, trust is placed on *la familia* and not on the self alone. This familia is one that includes relatives on both the mother's and father's sides, both generationally (e.g., great-grandparents, grandparents, children, and grandchildren) and laterally (e.g., uncles by blood and marriage, first, second, and third cousins, brothers- and sisters-in-law, sons- and daughters-in-law, nephews and nieces by brothers, sisters, and first and second cousins).

This fantasy type of harmony and silence never includes the trust of strangers, only the trust of family members. When Mexican Americans want to trust a friend or a business partner, the fantasy type allows for two types of fictive kinship: (1) the granting of a family title (and the respect that goes with it) to the family and/or person with whom a closer association is desired; and (2) the integration of an individual into the *compadrazgo* system, which refers to "coparents." The *compadrazgo* system is established between the parents and the baptismal godfather and godmother of a child. Originally established by the Catholic Church to oversee the Christian upbringing of the child, the relationship carries with it obligations of education and upbringing of the godchild, especially in the event of the parents' death. Among Mexican Americans, the bond between the adult members of this fictive system replaces the possible lack of blood relationship and is cultivated by both parents and godparents. A couple with three children could have six coparents. For the sake of the child, the relationship is made "like family" and the godparents are included in *la familia's* networking structure.

The titles that express this fantasy theme of family-like closeness are *hermano, hermana,* (brother, sister), *tio, tia* (uncle, aunt), and *compadre*. Other expressions that will indicate this fictive kinship are *como hermana, como hermano* (as a sister, as a brother). With the family role title, each new member receives the treatment of that role

within the family and with the trust of that family's members.

Another theme in the fantasy type is the care for others, for *la familia*, and for relationships. In this scenario, care should not be sacrificed for the sake of self, because one's sense of self comes through caring and being cared for in the context of relationships.

One of the advantages of this discourse on care is that it provides Mexican Americans with a system for avoiding conflicts that can destroy relationships. The second advantage is that the circle of people Mexican Americans trust and depend on for support is larger than what an individual would usually have in the mainstream culture. The existence of a support system serves two basic purposes. First, it is relational. Mexican Americans need not be alone in the fight against the "rat race"; they have a greater choice of support networks on which to depend. Thus, when needed, the rebuilding of self-esteem after interacting with the outside world can be done within the "safe" *familia* network. Within *la familia*, many not only rest their minds by speaking Spanish but are also cared for through the sharing of familiar stories and through expressions of love and understanding. Expressions such as *"Mijita/mijito, mi amor, cómo le fue?"* (My child, my love, how did it go?) are used to establish a scenario of care and nurturing for both children and adults. Second, this support is not only psychological but also pragmatic. *La familia* provides help with food, clothing, child care, contacts for jobs, referral to community and government services, education, citizenship instructions, and legal procedures.

Because the structure of services in this country is organized and oriented within an individualistic frame of mind, community and government institutions and services not only do not know about *la familia*, they do not have the flexibility to attend to it. In most hospitals, for example, beds are not provided for family members to stay with an adult family member who is ill. When Mexican Americans are interviewed by government agencies in most states, their request that a family member be present is often met with disapproval. The same is true when Mexican Americans visit a physician: the examination room is often blocked, and only the patient is allowed inside. The difficulties Mexican Americans encounter are often misconstrued by agencies as the problems of individuals without support systems. In leaving out the family and its influence, a great measure of support is discounted. The use of public services, therefore, may prove ineffective. If Euro-American institutions and services would pay more attention to the particular discourse of *la familia*, the social and economic advancement of Mexican Americans would be greatly enhanced.

Rationality and Emotionalism

Mexican Americans are brought up in *la familia* with a fantasy type that encourages the expression of emotion and rationality. This contrasts with the Euro-American background that usually emphasizes, in my opinion, the use of reason over emotion—á la Sherlock Holmes. One popular Euro-American vision subscribes to a scenario in which the hero displays aggressiveness, sexuality, and forcefulness with cool reasoning—á la Rambo.

For males, the themes that tend to prevail in the Mexican American fantasy type of rationality/emotionalism are those of courage, self-defense, honor, the defense of *la familia*, and the defense of women's honor. Other themes include the control of certain expressions of emotions (e.g., crying and fear) when these expressions may be seen as weakness by an opponent or interactant; and their display, for example, when celebrating with friends of the family. The social display of emotions such as romantic love, caring, and enthusiasm, however, is more encouraged in the fantasy type of rationalism and emotionalism. Hence, Mexican American men may have no problem in defending their honor physically, yet see no contradiction in reciting poetry, giving serenades to their fiancées, writing ballads or short stories, raising their voice with emotion in social circumstances, and crying when among the family or among friends. In this scenario, a typical villain is unemotional, detached, calculating, manipulating, two-faced, and a bit

of a coward. In contrast, the hero is *"todo un hombre"* (a total man, i.e., expressive, intelligent, caring, tender, physically and psychologically strong, masculine, emotive, assertive, understanding, honest, forward, chivalrous, romantic, pragmatic, respectful, and caring toward women and children).

The Mexican American rhetorical vision excludes any conflict between the simultaneous expression of emotion and the use of reason and logic. This apparent contradiction is resolved in a scenario of caring within which the heroes and heroines of *la familia* develop actions and discourse. (In fact, one way to distinguish a villain in Mexican American discourse is by his or her coolheaded, dispassionate yet sensual attitude, and by lack of love, caring, relating, or self-sacrificing behavior. When a person in this vision stops caring, reason and logic predominate; therefore, all sense of relationship ends. In this fantasy type, interactions acquire meaning through nonverbal expressions of emotion, e.g., gestures, maintaining an appropriate space in interactions, taking the time to relate, and para-language. Caring is one of those meanings expressed nonverbally. Consequently, when the nonverbal communication of this fantasy type is not allowed expression, emotion is subdued and turns to introversion. Under this circumstance, the only option left for the participant is to play the role of the villain. Logic without caring means severing relationships, negating people's inner worth and thus fostering individualism and human expediency.

Some of the puzzling behavior of Mexican American gangs could be better understood if these concepts were brought to bear on the analysis of their behavior. Particular attention should be given to the gangs' strong need for affiliation to a *la familia*-like network, as well as to the alienation they feel toward society, because Euro-American society does not understand that their idiosyncrasies stem from cultural differences.

The consciously enacted script that encourages the use of nonverbal communication enables Mexican Americans to be more perceptive, receptive, and understanding of the discourse of other rhetorical visions. But in turn, this same asset can leave them frustrated, disappointed, and mistrustful when their depth of insight is not appreciated or reciprocated by those visions.

The fantasy type of rationality/emotionalism can be better understood through an explanation of the facial gestures that a Mexican American is likely to use when talking and listening. At times the Euro-American culture emphasizes the use of permanent facial expressions for some discursive situations. Usually the upper lip is fixed, while the lower lip moves to produce sound, while the eyes remain detached. In the case of the Mexican American, especially for a close descendant of a first-generation immigrant, emotion can also be conveyed through the smile and through the eyes. The seriousness of a topic is usually expressed verbally, although relationship is often expressed through the seriousness of the face ("I do not care for you") or through a smile while talking ("you are okay"), or through the expression in the eyes. If the receiver of the communication is not conversant with the cultural discourse, he or she may choose not to pay attention, as the smile for some Euro-American groups is likely to mean that he or she is not serious and does not really mean what is being said. When the topic is serious and the nonverbal expression of a Mexican American is excited and friendly (e.g., a smiling mouth and/or eyes, a rapid rate of speech, a higher pitch of the voice, and a louder volume), the listener will react attentively. They will be neither bothered, bored, nor otherwise react adversely to the message and the speaker, if they are knowledgeable about the social discourse. The reverse will be true if the listener is not familiar with Mexican American rhetoric.

The Concept of Personhood

The fantasy type of personhood is summarized by the words *la persona* (the person). Understanding the meanings and elements that conform this structure allows us to gain deeper insights into the rhetoric of *la familia* for Mexican Americans. The themes that predominate in this fantasy type are

that *la persona* has a soul, or spirit, and is superior to lower animals and endowed with qualities an animal cannot possess. In addition, a person has life, dignity, and a heart which is considered sacred. Therefore, no one has a right to use other persons, play with them, or mistreat them. A person has the right to keep his or her thoughts private, to be one's own self; in the face of conflict, he or she has the right to neither show emotions nor expose the inner self in public— though amongst the family it would be acceptable to do so. In this fantasy type, "People's definitions of persons. . . did not. . . depend on being a biologically defined human being or on other physical characteristics, but on some other way of being in the image of God, such as having an inner nature of a certain kind" (Sewell 1989, 91). Hence, people, or *personas*, must be treated with dignity, courtesy, and deference.

The importance given to the person does not mean that the holders of this vision are naive and easily deceived. Mexican Americans are very aware of the evil nature in human beings: people are "difficult to understand, egoistic, tricky, often covertly hostile, prone to offensive gossip, and competitive . . . " (Sewell 1989, 92). Yet, because humans are persons, they deserve respect and humane treatment.

One of the themes that holds this fantasy type together is that of good upbringing or *educación*. In turn, this theme manifests itself through two other fantasy themes: courtesy and good manners. Examples of courtesy would be greeting people cordially or offering a chair to a guest. Good manners are expressed when conversation is deferred to those who are older, or when one takes time to talk with people. If people are to be treated with respect, rules on behavior are necessary. Hence, good manners or the rules of *educación* are in order. If *personas* have undesirable qualities, rules have to be developed to test these people and to keep them at arm's length until proven reliable. These approved behaviors minimize the opportunities for people to feel offended and disregarded. Once the person proves to be reliable, basic, culturally approved rules for good manners are maintained. But many of the restrictions on psychological closeness can be relaxed. An example would be the writing of thank you cards. Mexican American culture usually does not see the necessity for thank you cards among *la familia* or with friends (except where this custom has been adopted from Euro-American culture), but it deems them necessary with formal acquaintances.

Needless to say, this fantasy type clashes with contrasting types when Mexican Americans come in contact with cultures that do not share fantasy themes that support the discourse of personhood. For example, Mexican Americans may feel deeply offended by someone raising their voice to them in public or not greeting them. Many individuals of a Euro-American background do not have this rhetorical element in their discourse and hence are not always sensitive to what the Mexican American experiences. Clashes of rhetorical visions like the one just described only serve to increase the suspicions that Mexican Americans have toward Euro-Americans, because the Euro-Americans' behaviors closely resemble those of a villain. In this rhetorical vision, the villain is one who has no regard for the personhood fantasy type.

One of the main reasons why Mexican Americans may never fully integrate with Euro-American culture is because they do not see in the latter the elements of personhood. Above all, they do not find in the Euro-American rhetorical vision the more evolved valuation of human dignity inherent in the term *persona*. Hence, they prefer to remain apart because they do not believe that Euro-American culture has these superior values to offer them.

Respect for Hierarchy, Age, and Gender

Besides the need by people to be respected because they are *personas*, a fantasy type in the rhetoric of *la familia* dictates that they should be treated with deference because they have status in the family due to their age and their gender. Of these three themes, age is the most significant characteristic that supports the theme of status in the rhetoric of *la familia*. Hence, the grandparents and great- grandparents are given more defer-ence because of their age and birth order. In the same way, parents throughout their lives should be respected and treated with special care by sons and daughters. Uncles and aunts are given respect according to their birth order, the oldest having the most authority and deference. For example, younger individuals never look directly into the eyes of those of higher status, particularly parents and grandparents, when being addressed, nor when they are being disciplined verbally. To do so would be challenging authority.

Contrary to the usual stereotype of Mexican American women, in the rhetorical vision of *la familia*, women are never considered weak, passive, or of lesser stature than any other family member. Although age is a more important criterion for respect than gender, women are important *because they are women*. They hold the family together by transmitting the values, assumptions, and beliefs of *la familia*, which enables it to remain a viable institution. Furthermore, women are vital to the sustenance of relationships and social networks, particularly when they have to establish one-parent households. This is not the case with the men. Once a Mexican American male marries, it is the new wife who takes charge of recreating the vision of la familia. One popular proverb verifies this essential truth: *la mujer es el centro del hogar* (a woman is the center player in the home).

To understand the Mexican American rhetorical vision of women, consider the following response of one such male when asked his view on women: "From the time we were kids, we were taught to respect girls and women, not to hit them, but to protect them from harm. We were taught to take care of them." Then he added that taking care of women did not mean that they were inferior, but that they were special "and had to be respected and especially cared for." Although Euro-American women may perceive this attitude as patronizing and chauvinistic, Mexican American women are better aware of two basic facets of their culture: (1) the rhetoric of Mexican American culture does not hold that women are inferior, and (2) the attitude of Mexican American men lies within the context of the fantasy type of respect and honor toward women.

The importance of women does not exclude the importance of men. In this rhetorical vision, *la familia* contains two sources of power, but only one leader—the father. In his absence, the head of household is the mother with the support of the male family members. The oldest son, especially if he is already in late adolescence or early adulthood, is delegated more responsibility. Every male role in this rhetorical vision must represent and act as a spokesperson for *la familia* in the society at large. Hence, any humiliation or disregard of the Mexican American male by Euro-Americans can be detrimental to the culture's participation in the mainstream. Both males and females would rather communicate with those who would encourage and understand them and their vision of *la familia*.

The Mexican American male has yet another role in *la familia*: preserving order and discipline, and giving direction to the family. Studies show that both Mexican American men and women share in the disciplining of the children. The men consult with the family regarding decisions and encourage their wives to do the same. The responsibility of the decision, however, is carried by the male.

In a rhetorical vision where the conception of personhood is vital to relationships, women cannot exist as non-persons. It follows, then, that daughters are highly regarded. The Mexican American vision equalizes the sexes, because it does not deny the nature and contribution that these two important *personas*, man and woman, provide to *la familia*.

Solidarity and the Sense of Community

Although *la familia* is an almost self-sufficient unit in regard to relationships, it still has to interact with other institutions and groups of familias. Their rhetorical vision of *la familia* also carries over into the barrio, which includes the group of households around the home. The limits of the barrio may be decided by the individual in relation to one's home, or by the community. In the Hispanic tradition, barrios were usually lim-

ited to the Catholic parishes. This limitation no longer applies to the Mexican American experience in this country. Each barrio is a communal unit composed of groups of familias, which allows each persona in this vision to overcome their "resistance to intrusion" in order to fulfill social and practical goals. They can engage in discourse with those outside the barrio because (1) relationships are important and (2) knowing their neighbors enables them to keep some control over strangers' intrusions. The *barrio* is also a place where one can live by *la familia's* principle of solidarity, thus making urban survival that much easier. In contrast, mobility only tends to fragment the network of the barrio, as every new neighbor may not share the same rhetorical vision or may even reject it.

In the rhetorical vision of *la familia*, solidarity is one fantasy type that contributes greatly to family unity. A basic theme in this context is that of sacrifice. Although love and caring are part and parcel of relationships, a member of *la familia* must also give up rights, interests, and desires for the family's welfare. If child members of *la familia* have been orphaned or their mothers can no longer support them, for example, relatives of *la familia* will take the children in and raise them in spite of the sacrifice involved. This kind of sacrifice means staying together through thick and thin and giving loyal support to the family member undergoing difficulties. This would explain the lower rate of divorce and family breakdown among Mexican American families (Schick 1991, 38). The social sciences, influenced by the rhetorical vision of "the deficiency theory of minorities," does not consider the influence of solidarity and sense of community when examining the stability of the Mexican American family.

Conclusion

This essay has covered some salient points of the Mexican American rhetoric of *la familia* in order to better understand the discourse associated with the rhetorical visions of Mexican Americans. It has provided a theoretical framework by which to analyze Mexican American culture in a new light and offer an alternative to the typical misrepresentation made by Euro-American studies of Mexican American culture. The communication methodology of symbolic convergence was used to identify five main fantasy types: harmony/silence; rationality/emotionalism; the concept of personhood; respect for hierarchy, age, and gender differences; and solidarity and the sense of community. Some basic fantasy themes under each of the above categories were described to better explain the rhetorical vision.

When two rhetorical visions come into contact, the two visions either blend together or not. Corroboration is the term used in symbolic convergence theory to refer to the ability of one rhetorical vision to incorporate another (Gangotena 1988). Visions that are empirical in nature tend to be sensitive to corroboration; that is, if a vision embraces "facts" or "observations" as the ultimate basis for argument or proof, it will tend to be more flexible and more easily altered by other themes and visions. Those visions which are insensitive to corroboration tend to be more rigid and more idealistic (Gangotena 1980, 217–218). We could expect the Euro-American vision to be more sensitive to corroboration, as it is more pragmatic and logical in nature, and the Mexican American vision to be less sensitive because of its more idealistic view, but in practice this is not the case. Euro-American culture is less sensitive to corroboration when influenced by the Mexican American rhetoric of *la familia*.

In the search for themes in the Euro-American rhetoric that render it less flexible, we find one possible fantasy type with two supporting themes. This fantasy type is based on the principle of homogeneity by which Euro-Americans will accept those who are "like them" and will disregard those who are Spanish and Catholic. This harks back to the so-called "Black Legend," when the leaders of Great Britain in the 1600s and 1700s (and the United States in the 1800s) found it convenient to spread legends about the evil nature of the Spanish and their descendants, and of the Catholic Church and its supporters, in their attempt to prevent

Spain and other European powers from controlling the Americas. Although the rhetorical vision of *la familia* is alive and well in America, Euro-Americans do not identify it as a valuable source of support for Mexican Americans. The rhetorical vision of Euro-American society is not flexible enough to include either contrasting rhetorical visions or alternate themes and fantasy types. In contrast, Mexican Americans can incorporate elements of the Euro-American vision into their own rhetoric, because their rhetorical vision is more flexible and lends itself to corroboration.

The Mexican American rhetorical vision of *la familia* has long been under siege by Euro-American culture. When the vision of *la familia* comes in contact with Euro-American culture, it loses adherents from its own ranks. This disenfranchisement is caused by a clash of visions in which the adherents to the Mexican American rhetorical vision encounter others who have succumbed to the Euro-American script of a hero and his uncaring conception of relationships. Every time one of the fantasy types and themes of the rhetorical vision of *la familia* is lost, Mexican Americans are left without the integral system of discourse that helps them survive in an alien culture. Hence, they are easy prey to the most negative elements of the Euro-American vision. Gangs, violence, child abuse, substance abuse, and crime, as portrayed through the communication channels of the Euro-American vision (i.e., public schools, radio, television, and cinema), supplant the more beneficial fantasy types and themes of *la familia*.

As the Euro-American community becomes more aware of the rhetorical vision of *la familia* and comes to respect it, Mexican Americans will be granted a more distinguished place in American life. Regardless, the vision of *la familia* continues to be a form of discourse that provides Mexican Americans with identity, support, and comfort in an often hostile environment.

Notes

1. This "call for the family" was verified by *U.S. News and World Report* of December 9, 1991. The report indicates that 93 percent of Americans interviewed by the Gallup Poll say that

the family is very important. This contrasts with an 82 percent in 1981. The increase in 1991 was stronger among the 18–29 age group. The report also indicates that two-thirds of voters believe the family to be the basic core unit of the society.

2. An extensive discussion on this topic is provided in the following books: Buriel, R. (1984). "Integration with traditional Mexican American culture and socio-cultural adjustment." In J.L. Martinéz and R.H. Mendoza (Eds.), *Chicano Psychology*. Orlando: Academic Press, 95–129. Mirandé, A. (1982). "The Chicano family: A reanalysis of conflicting views." In Duran, L.I. and Bernard, H.R. (Eds.). *Introduction to chicano studies*. New York: Macmillan, 430–444; Mirandé, A. (1985). *The Chicano experience: An alternative perspective*. Notre Dame, IN: University of Notre Dame Press.

3. I found the Mexican American narratives to be longer, more detailed, and more vivid than those of Euro-Americans. The discourse of Mexican Americans has more interplay of characters, plot, script, and drama.

References

Bormann, E.G. (1972). Fantasy and rhetorical vision: The criticism of social reality. *Quarterly Journal of Speech, 58*(4), 396–407.

Bormann, E.G. (1985). *The force of fantasy: Restoring the American dream*. Carbondale: Southern Illinois University Press.

Gangotena, M. (1989). Curanderas and physicians: Contrasting rhetorics of healing. Intercultural Communication Association Mid-Year Health Communication Conference. Monterey, CA.

Gangotena, M. and González, A. (1980). Rhetorical visions of medicine compared and contrasted: Curanderismo and allopathic family practice as held by Mexican American and Anglo patients and practitioners. (Doctoral dissertation, University of Minnesota, 1980). *Dissertation Abstracts International, 41,* 5A.

González, A. (1989, Fall). "Participation at WMEX-FM: Interventional rhetoric of Ohio Mexican Americans." *Western Journal of Speech Communications, 53,* 398–410.

González, A. (1990). Mexican "otherness" in the rhetoric of Mexican Americans. *The Southern Communication Journal, 55,* 276–291.

Schick, F.L. and Schick, R. (1991). *Statistical handbook on U.S. Hispanics*. Phoenix, AZ: The Oryx.

Sewell, D. (1989). *Knowing people: A Mexican-American community's concept of a person*. New York: AMS.

Smith, M.J. (1988). *Contemporary communication research methods*. Belmont, CA: Wadsworth.

Walsh, K. (1991, December 9). The retro campaign. *U.S. news and world report, 111,*(24), 32–34. ✦

12

When Mississippi Chinese Talk

Gwendolyn Gong
The Chinese University of Hong Kong

As an undergraduate at the University of Mississippi during the early 1970s, I can recall thinking about how I spoke and how I sounded to others. I remember boasting proudly to a classmate of mine from Illinois that a native Mississippian with a true Southern drawl could enter an elevator on the ground floor, push five, say "Delta, Delta, Delta," and—lickety split—the doors would open on the fifth floor, long before even the second "D-el-l-ta" had been uttered.

While this anecdote makes an amusing conversation piece, it is not really true that most Mississippians with Southern accents speak slowly. In fact, when I consider my own siblings, all native Mississippians with genuine Southern twangs, I know that, if anything, Southern talk can be lightning fast and full of the colorful expressions and melodic rhythms of dialogue from a Faulkner novel. Given that my siblings—in truth, my entire immediate family—serve as classic, prolific producers of Southern speech, I found it peculiar that, when I went to graduate school in Indiana, my Hoosier peers and professors saw me as some sort of enigma—an oddity. They would joke, "The picture's fine but adjust the sound." This same type of remark followed me to Texas, where indeed another version of English is spoken. "Adjust the sound." What did that mean? Hadn't these folks ever encountered a Mississippian before? The truth was that they had. But I was different. I was a Chinese Mississippian.

Though my family heritage traces back to an ancestral village in Canton, China, I am a Chinese American, born and reared in the Mississippi Delta:

> In the northwest corner of the state of Mississippi lies a vast alluvial plain, formed from the rich black flood deposits of the Mississippi and Yazoo Rivers. Almost perfectly flat, rimmed by low bluffs to the east and south, the basin is called the Yazoo-Mississippi Delta. The Delta stretches over nearly the entire 185-mile distance from Memphis to Vicksburg, though it includes neither of those cities, and at its widest point it extends sixty miles east of the Mississippi River. (Loewen 1988, 1)

Since the late 1800s, this lush farming area has served as a homeland for approximately 1200 Cantonese Chinese from Southern China who have gradually assimilated into being Southerners of another ilk: Mississippi Chinese (MC). As a consequence, the MC represent a melding of primarily Confucian and Southern Genteel cultures, distinct yet powerfully complementary in terms of thought and action. For example, despite the apparent geographic and physical European-versus- Asian or Western-versus-Eastern contrasts, both cultures valorize the past, family, elders, traditions, secular rituals, land, business, hospitality, and propriety. And it is this mutuality of values, along with an unyielding emphasis on education, that has allowed the MC to adapt successfully in the Mississippi Delta, not only surviving but flourishing in a place lost in time, a place time has lost.

My family operated a general store in Boyle, a small, dusty town located on Main Street. This location—like most everything in the Delta—represented for us a strange and wonderful cross-cultural intersection. Our store sat in close proximity to the Post Office, City Hall, and the defunct Fire Station and Depot—landmarks that suggested the Caucasian milieu of the plantation South. Our business was also tightly sandwiched between two dirt and gravel alleys where most of the African Americans in town lived. Thus, my family and I were situated in the middle of a populace whose convictions, behaviors, and social and linguistic conventions epitomized Southern Genteelism. It is from this perspective that I now write about the communicative interactions of the MC with others and among themselves.

In my experience, one of the most interesting ways by which I have observed how Southern Genteelism and Confucianism reveal themselves is in the talk of the MC. A major rhetorical feature that typifies MC speech is deference, the courteous yielding to others, which may manifest itself in two forms: accommodation (i.e., making the non-MC speaker feel comfortable and welcome) and topic shifting (i.e., changing the subject of the conversation). Ironically, accommodation that may provide comfort for the non-MC listener may, on occasion, result in discomfort for the MC speaker; conversely, topic shifting oftentimes provides relief and control for the MC speaker but frustration for the non-MC listener. As an MC, I know that the discomfort and frustration which non-MC listeners may experience is very recognizable by MC listeners. As an in-group participant in this communicative act, I find myself keenly aware of the MC speaker's conversational shifts, which are designed to manage the conversation and my level of involvement in it, no matter how deftly and graciously these rhetorical strategies are executed. My recognition of the linguistic turns enables me to interact felicitously and reciprocate with my own conversational deference: accommodation. For non-MC speakers and listeners, understanding how deference operates among the MC helps to provide a more effective, informed exchange between these two groups.

Deference and Accommodation

Deference refers to the submission or acquiescence to the opinion, wishes, or judgment of another speaker. The courteous yielding of the floor results in an MC accommodating the topic designated by a speaker, whether or not it may be interesting, logical, tasteful, or pertinent. Part of the motivation of this act may be to seek approval, to demonstrate respect, to allow others to perceive that they are respected or even "superior" to the speaker, or simply to cooperate and not "make waves."

Most of the time, accommodating others' topics in conversations can be quite easy, mutually satisfying, and pleasant. I recall customers like Mr. Schaefer (the town sheriff, who insisted we call him "Uncle Charlie") and Preacher (an African American Southern Baptist lay minister), who would stop in the store at supper time to pick up groceries and chat with my father about the weather and fishing.

> "K.W., how hot was it today, anyhow?" Uncle Charlie would ask Daddy, chomping on his King Edward cigar. "Summers are gittin' hotter every year, don't ya think?"
>
> Daddy would reply, "It was a scorcher, all right. But I didn't see no monkeys dancin'. Now that's when I know it's really hot."
>
> "Monkeys dancin'. Yep, that'd be mighty hot, hell yeah," the sheriff would agree.
>
> Then Preacher would break in, "Good thing we wasn't on the lake in this heat, though, Mr. K.W. The water's probably so hot the fish ain't bitin'—they just put out a sign sayin' 'Out to lunch' or some such."
>
> They would all laugh and lean on the counter top, while my mother or I totaled their bill, took their money, and sacked their groceries. The chit-chat would end at this point, everyone feeling as if an enjoyable conversation had taken place and that something significant had been said.

As I reconsider this snippet of talk, I realize now it was more than mindless chatter and mere politeness. These three men, all of different races, professions, ages, and socioeconomic backgrounds, were interacting socially and linguistically. The Caucasian sheriff initiated the talk and the subject, and my MC father accommodated him, as did the African American minister. This exchange illustrates deference and accommodation in its purest form as both a Confucian and Southern Genteel phenomenon. The MC speaker, as well as the Southern non-MC preacher, courteously participated and played the linguistic game, partly out of respect for the sheriff, partly out of a code of social etiquette—convention or propriety—and partly out of their own genuine interest in the topic and their ability to communicate as equals in this informal rhetorical situation.

This example of deference is one in which all participants—MC and non-MC alike—accommodated one another and felt "at home" with the conversation, but this is not always the case. For MC, certain topics or types of discussion are simply inappropriate, in both an MC to MC as well as non-MC to MC context. Topics such as death (especially a violent one), terminal illness, and sex are seen as particularly personal and private. MC subscribe to the notion that living things, good fortune, and happiness should never be intermixed with the dead, bad luck, or inauspiciousness in either their conversations or their activities. Consequently, in my parents' home, my mother would never place a photograph of my deceased older brother, Dwight Arnold, among other family pictures of the living. In fact, until I was 6 years old, I never knew I even had another brother, for Arnold was never talked about.

My first memory of Arnold was when I noticed his name on a headstone at the cemetery one day when our family went to "bow three times in silence" to pay honor and respect to our ancestors. Though his bronzed baby shoes and faded snapshots were treated with reverence, I later learned, these reminders of him were segregated from all other items that families typically display—reunion and wedding pictures, annual school photos, trophies, awards, baby books, and so on. Even in my siblings' and my own home, no picture of Arnold is displayed. I keep my photographs of him in a filing cabinet drawer, along with the portraits of my father's deceased parents. Moreover, I have never queried my parents about the brother I never knew. To accommodate myself about this topic would have caused them great pain and discomfort. Even writing about this now is troubling for me and would be unsettling for my family, were they to read these words. As this clearly illustrates, the MC valorize the family, the past, and secular rituals in very specific, often non-verbal ways.

That example shows how I, an MC speaker, could have engendered discomfort for other MC listeners, such as my parents, in order to satisfy my own need to know. Instead, I understood the delicate nature of death and the need to respect my elders, as well as family, ritual, and MC's tendency to accommodate others; thus, I refused to invoke the tragic subject of Arnold. There are other people and events I long to know more about: my father's involvement in World War II and the Korean War; the KKK's burning of our original family store in Merigold, Mississippi; and Principal Akins, who had a fist fight with a prominent school board member in his attempts to ensure Chinese Americans would be allowed to attend the Boyle public school. Out of my sense of deference and accommodation, however, I have never asked my parents to explain these parts of our family past that surely must have shaped our lives over the years. For propriety's sake, I have refrained from mentioning anything from the past, especially if it was traumatic. Most MC hold that the "unlucky" past lies behind us, yet the past also represents auspicious events and times such as weddings, births, and family traditions. Consequently, most MC can learn from the auspicious past how to proceed with the present and the future.

Unfortunately, however, this sensitivity in regard to accommodating others may not always be contemplated or realized in conversations between MC and non-MC speakers. A number of years ago at the institution where I was teaching, I developed a friendship with a colleague. This woman was a master teacher who spoke with authority and often openly revealed to me her earnest but prejudicial concerns about me as a person. Occasionally, we would see each other in passing and chat:

"Hi, Gong. I went to a Thai restaurant on Sunday. I asked for some soy sauce, and the waiter looked at me like I was crazy. What was wrong with askin' for some soy sauce? The food was so bad—like bad Chinese food—that I covered everything with it. Why was the guy so mad at me?"

"Asking for soy sauce isn't a crime. I don't know why your waiter was upset," I replied sheepishly. I was not certain why she was broaching me on the topic of

Thai food; I'm no expert on it, though I do enjoy that particular cuisine.

"We ought to have lunch. What's your schedule?" my colleague inquired.

"I've already eaten. Plus, I've got so much work to finish in my office today. Sorry that I can't join you while you eat." I was uncomfortable, yet truthful.

"What'd ya eat? Betcha had egg rolls, eh? Gong, you're always eatin' egg rolls—at least you used to. Remember when you first came here years ago? I couldn't believe it—a Chinese, teaching English—with a Southern accent, too. I used to share an office with a fellow named Joe, who'd eat tacos and avocados all the time, and then I'd see you across the hall, eatin' egg rolls. Right, Gong? Don't ya remember?"

"Well, no, I really don't remember, but I suppose it's true," I replied, trying to go along with my colleague. "I do recall Joe and I ate take-out food sometimes. It was a quick way to have lunch," I added, my voice trailing off, diminishing with every syllable.

I wished I was anywhere else but here, "talking" with this person. It was embarrassing enough that she made these kinds of remarks to me at all, much less within earshot of other faculty and students. Where could I hide? I thought to myself: "Hang in there; it'll be over soon."

This is only one conversation among many that this professor and I have shared. Out of my deep belief that she did care about me and out of my respect for her professional accomplishments, I always accommodated this individual's topic selection and conversational moves. I self-consciously defended her, rationalizing that she was just "tone-deaf" and didn't understand her audience very well. She admitted that she never knew an American-born Asian like me before. As a result, I reasoned to myself that I should give her a break, help her avoid "losing face," and prevent her from feeling awkward. Despite my desperate efforts to excuse her inappropriate comments, I always experienced regret that I voluntarily subjected myself to being bullied, demeaned, and belittled by someone espousing true friendship. Yet I can still hear her explanation regarding her response to me as a colleague: "I've never known a 'foreigner' who wasn't a foreigner,

like you are." She proudly offered this remark with great gusto.

In these types of conversations, the non-MC speaker initiates talk and the MC allows it to continue. In other words, I reluctantly contributed to the communication pattern created in this relationship. Why? Were my attempts to ignore this colleague's insensitivity somehow linked to gender? I don't think so. Was it linked to age? After all, this woman was older than myself. Again, I don't think so. Instead, so that the non-MC speaker didn't lose face, I deliberately chose to let her go on at my own expense—despite the extreme distress and humiliation she was causing me. I wondered to myself: "If I were an African American, would she announce that surely I must eat fried chicken and watermelon in the office?" In this way at least, she would be treating all the people in our office "equitably." This passive strategy in speech is mirrored in most MC behaviors, giving rise to perpetuating the stereotype of Asian submissiveness.

This kind of tolerance can be likened to a Southern Genteel social convention, wherein Southern speakers will casually invite folks to "stop by and visit us whenever you're in the neighborhood; we've got lots of room." True Southerners realize that, while the warm intent of such a speech act is very genuine, it is rarely meant literally. As a result, when those folks—virtual strangers—do appear on the speaker's doorstep, no one is more surprised than their host. All make the best of the situation: The host extended the invitation and must now honor it. It would be impolite to do otherwise; these guests have no idea that they have just missed the implicature (the underlying meaning in, or "real" function of, the literal utterance). Here, accommodating actions reinforce verbal accommodation. MC act too, but they often do so through inaction. For example, I now carefully avoid this colleague, aware that, if I don't cross paths with her, then I won't have to endure her abusive talking—thus, action through inaction. In this non-confrontational and Confucian way, I can prevent this non-MC speaker any opportunity to control our conversations and my role in them, while still "accommodating" her if I have to.

I do not always tolerate her racist talk with passive and indirect accommodation. Sometimes I pursue her subject, refuting her views with vociferous debate. When this occurs, it usually pertains to subjects beyond "self"; that is, when her attacks are personal, I try to ignore or avoid interacting with her. But when they are directed toward others or issues, I am compelled to respond. This is certainly true when she once asserted, for example, that there is no difference between the KKK and the NAACP. If we in society can see the NAACP as respectable, she adamantly asserted, then we should do likewise for the KKK. After all, "they're both merely special interest groups." I wondered, how can she broach such matters with me? Should I be honored that she looks at me, hears my Southern drawl, and then "accepts" me as just a salt-of-the-earth country woman? Or should I be absolutely offended that she fails to realize that I am a person of color whose family has experienced firsthand the ways that groups like the KKK mete out their own particular brand of "special interest?" At times like this, I cannot be silent and passive. Deference and accommodation serve no purpose in these instances. As I illustrated earlier, I believe that I can hear this person's verbal jabs directed at me, and I can weather and survive them by staying above the fray. But I have to defend other people, values, causes, ideas, and ideals.

This is an opportune time to present another conversational strategy that enables MC speakers to participate conversationally with greater ease and comfort: deference and topic shifting.

Deference and Topic Shifting

Ironically, accommodations that may at times provide a sense of deferential comfort for the non-MC speaker may instead result in estrangement and embarrassment for the MC speaker. Accordingly, MC often use a second strategy: topic shifting. This is a linguistic strategy which turns the tables, oftentimes providing relief and empowerment for the MC speaker and confusion and frustration for the non-MC listener. To understand this type of conversational move requires that we explore when and why topic shifting may occur, as well as consider which topics MC speakers may commonly switch to.

Topic shifting happens most frequently when an MC speaker is the subject of discussion, whether being complimented or spoken of in any positive way, but does not want to respond to the issue. For example, consider this scenario:

"Good morning, Annie," says Mrs. Alexander warmly, wearing a floral-patterned knit dress.

"Hello," replies my mother, Annie Gong, busy hauling two massive platters of food into Fellowship Hall. Annie and Mrs. Alexander are both in their early 60s, attending a Sunday potluck lunch at the Boyle Baptist Church.

"I made deviled eggs, my specialty. They go like hot cakes ever' time I make 'em. You make sure you sample one." Scooting over a crystal bowl containing a mustard potato salad, Mrs. Alexander positions her egg plate smack dab in the center of the long table dedicated to salads. "Whatcha got there? I surely do hope it's Chinese food. You make the best Chinese food, Annie."

"I love deviled eggs," my mother says to shift the topic, as she concentrates on removing tin foil from her cashew chicken and sweet and sour pork. She continues to talk, never looking up. "How do you make your filling so tasty?" Garnishing her dish, she persists in her egg-talk: "Some folks just put Miracle Whip or mayonnaise in their filling; some like Underwood deviled ham mixed in with their mashed yolks. What do you think, Mrs. Alexander? I trust what you do."

Mrs. Alexander, however, prefers to talk about Annie's food. "How do you do it? How did you learn to cook like this, Annie? Now, that's sweet and sour, isn't it? And what's that other dish with the nuts? Can it be chicken almond ding? No, well. Last year, you brought fried rice, too. There wasn't a grain left inside of 10 minutes when the line started moving. Wish you'd give lessons on Chinese cookin'. Everybody at the church would be your student in nothin' flat. Mark my words."

But Annie just coyly smiles and begins her egg talk once more. "Your eggs, do you boil them all at once? Put sweet or dill pickles or relish in them? And what about white or black pepper, because that's something I've never understood about makin' that." Annie stuffs her tin foil back into her bag and looks Mrs. Alexander in the eye. "I'm fixin' to go back to the car to get the chow mein. Before I do, though, you tell me about your recipe, okay?"

At this juncture, Mrs. Alexander commences telling Annie her deviled egg recipe. "Well, you know, I always go out and buy the freshest dozen of eggs I can find. I put all my eggs in one pot at room temperature. Never try to boil an egg straight out of the ice box."

Relieved by this egg talk, Annie listens intently, nodding her head as each ingredient and instruction is described. "I never had anybody teach me about cookin' in the formal way," she then says. "I just learn from good cooks like yourself and by doin'—makin' mistakes."

With that, the small MC woman saunters out of Fellowship Hall to fetch her noodles, breathing a sigh of relief that she avoided having to talk about herself or her cooking without being perceived as rude by not accommodating Mrs. Alexander.

As is evident, Annie diverts attention and conversation away from "self," a subject that she is uncomfortable with, despite the fact that Mrs. Alexander's topic selection would allow this MC speaker a chance to showcase her personal accomplishments as a cook. Annie can't take a compliment, a common phenomenon among most MC. Rather than demonstrate her deference to Mrs. Alexander by accommodating her topic selection, Annie is deferential—polite and respectful—through her topic shifting to high- light the culinary skill of the other speaker. To cap it off, she is even a bit self-effacing at the end of the exchange, thus countering the compliment. This topic shifting, consequently, is a move to accomplish modesty. That is, by persistently re-introducing her egg talk, she eventually leads Mrs. Alexander to talk about *herself* and *her* dish, two topics in which any Southern Genteel woman excels. Hardly any other region of the U.S.

compares to authentic Southern cooking and the talk that goes with it.

While Annie didn't choose to talk about the entrees that she prepared, she does engage in talking about food. This is a topic to which most MC shift routinely, especially with in-group speakers or non-MC they regard as close friends. To share food talk with an MC is, by and large, a sign of trust and acceptance. In my own MC family, food talk epitomizes being Chinese. Be it good or bad fortune, the event can be ritualized with sumptuous, bountiful amounts of food. The more impressive or auspicious the occasion, the longer the menu. Rituals require ceremony, and ceremony always entails food. For example, weddings call for nine-course dinners; births—"red egg and ginger" banquets and a vat of *gai djil gahng,* a chicken-whiskey soup often referred to as "mother's brew"; birthdays—chicken, noodles, and a cake with some shade of Chinese red in or on it. (Chocolate cakes and frostings are perceived by many superstitious MC as inappropriate for happy celebrations.) Red is a good-luck color and a standard for every celebration; in fact, brides often don bright red, silk *cheung sahms* (a type of Chinese dress) at their wedding receptions and banquets.

Although food talk is not the focus of this essay, it is such an unquestionably important subject to all Chinese that it deserves further mention here. After all, one conventional way to greet someone in Chinese is "Nay heck fan?" (Have you eaten your rice?) The MC maintain this traditional valorization of food and the Confucian notion of dining rather than eating. As I was once admonished by my sister, "When planning any MC event, always remember that, if everything else is a disaster but there are lots of good, exotic dishes, then you're okay. Everyone will leave bragging about what a great time they had because all they'll remember and tell others about is the food."

Here is another example of topic shifting. Every week I phone my parents in Mississippi. Inevitably, I always spend the majority of the call reviewing the MC current affairs with my mom. She and I cover the general topics—health, work, and family—rather swiftly. Then, without any linguistic cue at all, Mama commences with the food talk:

"Grilled chicken, that's what we ordered. Daddy and I went to our exercise class at the Mall this morning and ate at the Food Court. I like that. It was grilled, yes, not pan-fried with no liquid smoke," Mama speculates. She carried on this dramatic monologue of sorts: "Daddy didn't like it 'cause of the mayonnaise; he likes his sandwiches dry." Reminded of my sister-in-law's poultry, Mama then reminisces: "On Monday, Josie barbecued chicken. It was real good—she left the skin on."

I hear my daddy's voice in the background. "The girls didn't have tennis or basketball—they're all playing sports now, you know—so we all went over there and watched football," he says, alluding to my brother Stephen's big-screen TV and the Monday night NFL game.

Without skipping a beat, my mother returns to revealing the supper guests and their contributions to the buffet. "And Annette made homemade rolls and a broccoli-rice casserole—too rich, but Daddy likes it. Ginger and Eddie ate there, too; think Ginger had a tin of brownies, still warm from the oven. And that Lynette. She made a batch of cookies, and I sampled one—everybody fussed at me, said 'Mama, better watch your diabetes.' Juanita just phoned and told Josie she and her family had already eaten, but she'd come on over later, if she had time. She had laundry and house cleaning to do. Just like a family reunion."

Throughout this part of the phone call, I never get a word in edgewise—nothing but an intermittent "a-huh," barely audible amidst Mama's recollection of the communal meal (i.e., an important interpersonal function that unites everyone, strengthens family ties, and provides a sense of "village" life from Canton) at sister-in-law Josie's. From her food talk, I intuit that everyone there is fine. My siblings and their spouses are well; the grandchildren are doing well in school; Daddy's blood pressure and cholesterol are reasonably low, but Mama's sugar is high. Among MC speakers who know each other well, food talk can be as natural, effortless, and meaningful for MC speakers as alternating between English and Cantonese in a single conversation. One MC's divulgence of the context, people, and events, along with a cataloguing of the edibles, can provide informa-

tion for another MC—data that could only be otherwise fathomed by folks who were present at the family gathering. This food talk demonstrates our common bond as individuals in family and culture; it serves as a vehicle to express our love and respect for one another as members of a single, cohesive community whose "separateness" is merely geographic. A seasoned food talker myself, I usually sense there is more to the story than the abbreviated menu suggests. I ruminate on my suspicion, wondering what Mama *isn't* telling me in what she *is* saying.

There is a pregnant pause on the other end of the line, and I chime in, "What was the reason y'all decided to eat at Stephen and Josie's, Mama? Didn't y'all do turkey and dressing for Stephen's birthday the day before? Goodness, what'd y'all do with all the leftovers, anyway?"

"Oh, C.W. had a stroke, and Audrey drove him to town to see a specialist." C.W. is Mama's nephew, Audrey his wife. "They were supposed to stop by Stephen's to see all of us and have a bite before the drive back, but all they did was call. They have a daughter in town here now, see." There's another lull in the conversation. "We warmed 'em up. Flavor's the best the next day when the turkey and dressin' have set awhile," Mama then says. "We don't waste leftovers here."

I understand now, having discovered the missing link: Mama had arranged the family's Monday night communal potluck at my brother's house because relatives were in town; they had expected C.W. and Audrey to drop by and visit. But the couple never showed up. Never mind that their expectations were never fulfilled. They still enjoyed their own informal reunion, an interpretation that my mother construed. And even more important was this ultimate reality: They had lots of delectable home cooking. Given a satisfying meal, a body can strive to overlook the out-of-town guests who never came to dinner—and C.W. was, after all, sick. The graciousness with which Mama handles this situation is both very Confucian and Southern. But one should never be deceived by the surface politeness: C.W. and Audrey's minor transgression will not be soon forgotten. And you can bet your last shiny penny that I'll hear about this matter next week, when Mama shifts into food talk. Her message will be loud and clear.

Food talk is but one topic that MC speakers are predisposed to shift toward. It is a rather clever, witty, and powerful topic, though, for it enables speakers to shift to or intermingle with additional topics. These topics tend to be in narrative form, stories of self-disclosure about the MC's family, historical past, or cultural traditions. Some of the narratives are "stock" or "ritualized" tales, repeated in public again and again; others are akin to "sacred texts," seldom uttered under any circumstances. The more "ritualized" the narrative, the less trustworthy or familiar the MC speaker may feel toward the other speech participants. Conversely, the more "sacred" the text, the more the MC speaker may identify with and have regard for the other speakers in the communicative act. To break out of the safe, ritualized narratives in topic shifting means risking greater self-disclosure and thus greater vulnerability.

Perhaps my best example of the trust and deference involved in topic shifting is apparent when examining the narratives that I have chosen for use in this essay. I really don't know you, my readers. Yet, I am convinced that you will be as interested in MC talk as I am, as I have topic shifted to some very "sacred" subjects: my family, its cultural and historical past, and its rituals. The conversations reconstructed here are the embodiment of one of the most precious revelations of all: the way we MC talk to ourselves and to others.

Lotuses in the Land of the Magnolias

When I was in high school, I remember Mama, brother Stephen, and myself driving an old aunt from Canton to visit my cousins in Duncan, a neighboring town some 35 miles north of Boyle. It was fall, the weather was cold and wet, and the expanse of rice and cotton fields was flooded, reflecting an eerie mirror image of the full moon on the black water. The ribbon of road we drove along was surrounded on either side by encroaching rainwater. We were all concentrating on the road, silent; my brother drove fast, nonetheless. Then the silence was broken by our elder's deep voice, difficult to decipher because she really spoke no English. She muttered softly. Mama translated: "This looks like Canton." The old aunt scanned the landscape, waving her hand toward the window as if to bless the land itself. We heard her utter more sounds. "No wonder you live here; it's just like home," relayed Mama, fixing her own eyes on the blackness. My mother broke the silence once more: "Home." With this, she peered out her fogged window and reached over to grasp the old woman's hand. Three generations of our family drove the narrow Delta road that night—Chinese with cultural and linguistic roots in two Southern regions: Canton and the Mississippi Delta.

* * *

To explain and exemplify deference as it manifests itself in accommodation and topic shifting during MC talk, I have offered here a very small sample of the linguistic interaction of Chinese Americans from the Mississippi Delta as I know it; the milieu that I depict is from my own perspective, as seen through my own eyes. Furthermore, the conversational strategies that I have selected represent linguistic phenomena drawn from my own experiences as an MC speaker.

As mentioned in the introduction, I have always been sensitive to voices—mine and others'. I have always been conscious of how I and other MC were distinct yet complementary in the way we sounded and expressed ideas. My hope is that understanding deference and the ways by which it can be expressed through specific rhetorical strategies will provide keys to greater appreciation for the culturally distinct communicative acts of the Mississippi Chinese-lotuses living in the land of the magnolias.

Reference

Loewen, J.W. (1988). *The Mississippi Chinese: Between black and white* (2nd ed.). Prospect Heights, IL: Waveland. ✦

13

The Reason Why We Sing

Understanding Traditional African American Worship

Janice D. Hamlet
Shippensburg University

Someone ask the question,
Why do we sing?
When we lift our hands to Jesus,
What do we really mean?

—Kirk Franklin (1993)

Growing up in the South, I fondly remember Sunday morning worship services at my predominately African American church. Regardless of what kind of week the worshipers had experienced, they entered the church immaculately dressed, heads held high, all in search of spiritual renewal and the comfort of each other's company. The service would begin when the pastor stood and read the scripture, "This is the day which the Lord hath made. We will rejoice and be glad in it" (Psalms 118: 24). Then he would say, "Let us stand to receive the choir." And the choir would come down the aisle, swaying from side to side, in step with the music from the organ. Sometimes there would be drums and tambourines. The voices were melodious and filled with excitement and praise. Some members of the congregation would clap their hands in time with the music while others would wave their hands over their heads. Once the choir reached the choir stand, the singing would drop to a whisper while the pastor prayed. Afterward, the choir and congregation would sing the morning hymn. Sunday morning worship was now in progress.

When finally the last song had been sung, testimonies given, announcements read, tithes and offerings taken up, the pastor would approach the pulpit where his great Bible awaited him and a spirit-filled aura was about him as if there was no doubt in his mind that God had placed him there. A hush would fall over the congregation as the preacher "took his text." What followed was a strong sermon, which was never less than an hour, punctuated by a great deal of animation and "talk-back" from worshipers.

Even as I began to visit other African American churches, I came to accept without question that what I was experiencing was religious culture, a universal phenomenon shared by all cultural groups. It was an experience that I took for granted. It was not until I became an adult and began to visit churches outside of my culture that I began to realize that there is something distinct about African American worship. The purpose of this essay is to explain this distinction.

African American Worship

At the onset, it is important to note that it is often difficult for a visitor outside of the culture to understand what is going on in a traditional African American worship service. However, one cannot approach this experience as an outsider intending to simply observe and take notes on how "black folks" behave in church. Visitors should also not come expecting to see stereotypical notions of the African American church played out based on mediated comedic portrayals. One must come as a participant, willing to be transformed by the presence of the "spirit." African American congregations have literally claimed God's promise whereby, "Where two or three are gathered together in my name, there I am in the midst of them" (Matthew 18:20). It is this belief that creates the distinctive style of the traditional African American worship service.

In her work on black language, Geneva Smitherman (1986) notes that to speak of the traditional black church is to speak of the holy-rolling, bench-walking, spirit-getting, tongue-speaking, vision-receiving, intuition-directing, Amen-saying, sing-song preaching, holy-dancing, and God-sending church. This church may be defined as one in which the cognitive content has been borrowed from Western Judeo-Christian tradition, but the communication of that content has remained essentially African, deriving from the traditional African worldview. This worldview assumes a fundamental unity between spiritual and material aspects of existence. Though both are necessary, the spiritual domain assumes priority.

The heart of traditional African religions is the emotional experience of being filled with the power of the spiritual. Its legacy thrives in traditional African American church and culture. African American worshipers believe that soul, feeling, emotions, and spirit serve as guidelines to understanding life and others. All people are moved by spirit forces, and there is no attempt to deny or intellectualize this fact (Smitherman, 92). This convergence of Judeo-Christian content and African delivery is found in Protestant denominations, particularly Baptist, Methodist, and Holiness, where the worship patterns are characterized by a spontaneous preacher-congregation relationship, intense emotional singing, spirit possession, and extemporaneous testimonials to the power of the Holy Spirit (Smitherman, 90).

A major aspect of African American Christian belief is found in the symbolic importance given to the word "freedom." Throughout African American history the term freedom has had significance although its meaning has changed depending on the time period. For example, during slavery, freedom meant release from bondage. After slavery, it meant the right to opportunities, and to move about as respectable human beings.

Freedom also manifests itself in the structure of worship services. African American worship is a collective experience wherein the worshipers experience the truth about their lives as a people in the struggle for freedom and held together by "God's spirit." It is this presence of the spirit that accounts for the intensity in which African Americans engage in worship. Spirit is essential and phenomenal in the worship service. There is no understanding of African American worship apart from the presence of the spirit who descends upon worshipers.

One way in which freedom manifests itself is in the unpredictable, oftentimes uncontrollable length of worship services. One Sunday the service may end at 12:30 p.m. (but don't count on it); on another Sunday, the service may last as long as 1:30 p.m., 2:00 p.m., 3:00 p.m. This unpredictability may be irritating to an outsider, but African American worshipers believe "you can't hurry God," so it is an acceptable characteristic of the traditional African American worship service.

In the act of worship itself, the experience of freedom becomes a component of the community's being. Worshipers come prepared to be uplifted and to become a part of a sacred community. They also come prepared to be healed from the pains caused by racism, sexism, and other evils that exist in their lives. This healing may come from the sermon, the songs, from the choir, someone's testimony, or the power of the spirit alone. And like their oppressed ancestors, who created "hush harbors" where they could, out of the sight of their oppressors, enjoy the warmth of their commonness and give vent to their emotions, by speaking, singing, crying, or shouting, African American worshipers experience a catharsis through the freedom in which they are allowed to express themselves in church. The "hush harbors" of the enslaved Africans were the forerunners of the African American church service. Because African Americans know that they are more than what has been defined for them by the dominant culture, they struggle to achieve in society the freedom they experience in their worship service. And, they celebrate life and give praise to the creator for making it through another week. This is why it is often hard to sit still in an African American worship service. African American worship demands involvement. For the people claim that "if you don't put anything into the service you won't get anything out of it."

Role Behaviors

Both past and present, the African American church provides a structured religious and social life in which African American worshipers can give expression to their deepest feelings and at the same time achieve status and find a meaningful existence. In addition to serving as a buffer and source of release against oppression, what is also significant is the way African Americans are treated in their churches. A school janitor in the dominant culture could be a deacon in the African American religious culture. A domestic worker in the dominant culture could be the assistant pastor in the African American religious culture. In other words, the "invisible people" who are at the bottom of the socio-economical ladder and often rejected by the larger culture, receive status, recognition and appreciation in the African American religious culture. Equally significant, worshipers are shown respect. They are known as "brother" and "sister" or "Mr. and Mrs." Even children are given responsibilities and respect as members of the church. And one can see the worshiper's pride in their new identities exemplified by the way they walk and talk and dress and their whole demeanor.

This transformation is found not only in the titles members have and the roles they perform but also in the culture of the worship service.

Some critics have argued that this practice has kept African Americans down as an inferior race. But others (Hamilton 1972) have pointed out that African American churches have been the only places where they could see the potential of what they could become.

The African American Preaching Style

Finally, because African American worshipers believe that no worship service can exist without the presence of "the spirit," a high premium is placed on the role of the pastor, most importantly his (or her) preaching ability. Throughout the history of the African American church, the sermon has served a wide variety of functions and purposes. Its primary purpose had been to "win souls" for God. But it has also served as theo-

logical education, cultural education, ritual drama, and therapy—all rolled up onto one.

To be considered a good preacher in the African American religious culture, does not necessarily mean that the preacher is grounded in critical reasoning or systematic theology, but that he or she has the ability to communicate within the cultural milieu of the people. Through the use of dramatic storytelling, identification of heroes, both biblical and from within the culture, use of repetition, poetic diction and rhythm, the organizational culture of the African American church develops into a symbolic world where identification with the scripture as well as cultural history is enhanced and celebrated and creates a way for people to make sense out of what is going on around them and within their lives. Each one of these components will be briefly discussed.

Dramatic Storytelling

Although African Americans believe that academic degrees in theology, philosophy, and so forth are commendable credentials for their preachers, the dominant criterion in accepting a pastor has been "Can he or she preach?" This simply means "Can he or she tell the story?" Hermeneutics is an essential tool for telling the story. As it relates to religion, hermeneutics may be defined as the process through which the Bible is read, examined, interpreted, understood, translated, and proclaimed (Stewart 1984, 30).

In the following excerpt from the sermon "Recipe for Racial Greatness," African American preacher Dr. Manuel Scott paraphrases the story told in Joshua 17:14–15. Through application of the hermeneutics process, the story of the children of Israel is told. The preacher argues that African Americans should use the Israelites' lifestyle as a role model.

> They would not permit four hundred years of bondage, biological distinctiveness, material meagerness, educational retardation, and exaggerations by their enemies to strip them of a sense of worth and dignity. Without apology or ambiguity, they affirmed to Joshua: "We are great people." This was another way of saying that they liked themselves without being ashamed. They were not inclined to

mimic, mindlessly, other people. They had a sense of being somebody. They comprehended in themselves usefulness and a capacity to meet meaningful needs. They included in their self-image the idea of equality with the rest of mankind. They were not cringing and crawling and bowing and blushing before anyone. (Scott, 93)

The preacher took the bare facts of God's story and wove them into the structure of the audience's own lives.

Identification of Heroes

Illustrations from within the culture and the Bible are effective because they are down to earth and deal with the issues of African American existence. This is illustrated in the following excerpt from a sermon entitled, "When You Have Had Enough."

Joe Louis, Dr. Martin Luther King, Jr., Elijah, and even Jesus Christ—all faced discouragement, but each felt his work was so important that he refused to be defeated. With the faith and knowledge that God the Father would see them through, they accomplished what they had to do. With this same faith, we can do it too. (Gillespie 1977)

Through repetition, the preacher ensures that the gist of what he or she is saying is not lost in the emotionalism of the audience. An example of repetition can be noted in the following excerpt from the Rev. Jesse Jackson's celebrated "I Am Somebody" message:

I am somebody.

I may be poor.

But I am somebody.

Respect me.

Protect me.

Never neglect me.

I am somebody.

—Jackson (1987, 205)

Poetic Diction and Rhythm

African American preachers have always understood that poetry is the language of emotion and imagination, and their sermons have appealed to both of these as well as to reason. Poetic diction uses symbolic and presentative words and sets up a musical structure of alliterative expression. In utilizing poetic diction, sentences are short, crisp, and clear. Verbs are filled with energy. Sentences build to climax.

An equally significant feature of this preaching style is rhythm. The voice is considered the preachers trumpet for proclaiming the gospel. It can challenge, convince, comfort, and charm. An example of the use of poetic diction and rhythm is illustrated in the following sermon excerpt.

It's not the color of your skin, brother. It's what you have in your heart and in your mind that makes you a man or a woman. Remember that. And if you will stand together, there's nobody in this world that can stop a united mass of people moving as one. . . .

Standing together

Working together

Picketing together

Loving together

Worshipping together

You'll win together

Walk together children, don't you get weary. There's great camp meeting in the Promised Land.

—Powell (1990)

Call and Response

The African American preacher is also a performer of sorts. The preacher's job is to transform the congregation into an actively participating group. As described by Dona Richards (1985) there is no passive audience. Calling the spirits correctly implies total involvement. For the ritual to be successful, the preacher must move the congregation to the point that they come outside of their ordinary selves.

He speaks, but it is not so much the meaning of the words which is important, it is their sounds which make the magic. He punctuates them, putting them together in musical phrases which have tonal variation. The phrases rise and fall. He pauses, he hesitates, he whispers, he moans and grunts. He repeats and he listens for our responses. We have begun to participate, because his words have touched something in us and so we say "Amen". . . and then we say it again. (220)

This passage vividly captures the interactive experience between the preacher and congregation which gives worshipers the opportunity to release pent-up frustrations and achieve a catharsis, an escape from the harshness of their daily realities.

This interactive experience commonly referred to as call-response is an African derived process between speaker and listener. It is not uncommon for African American preachers to receive responses from their congregations during their sermons. Some preachers may call out for a specific response, such as "Can I get a witness?" or "Somebody ought to say Amen," thereby soliciting responses. The responses may also come voluntarily from members of the congregation as an affirmation of the presence of "the spirit" and/or encouragement to the preacher. Such responses as "Amen," "Preach!" "Tell it" or "Go on pastor," are compliance and essential in traditional African American worship. Whether solicited or unsolicited, this participatory technique makes the listeners believe that they are experiencing God's presence in their midst.

If the people do not say "Amen" or some other passionate response (and they don't always respond), it could mean that the spirit has chosen not to speak through the preacher at that time. The absence of the spirit could also mean that the preacher was too dependent on his own word instead of the spiritual word, or that the congregation was too involved in its own personal quarrels to receive the word. Whatever the case, the absence of feedback is typically uncharacteristic of traditional African American worship for African American worshipers believe that if you don't put anything into the service, you won't get anything out of it.

African American preaching is not simply a religious presentation. It is the careful orchestration of the Biblical scriptures interpreted in the context of a people's culture and experiences. It is presented with logic blended with creative modes of expression, and tonal and physical behaviors from a tradition that emphasizes emotionalism, interaction, spirituality, and the power of the spoken word.

Summary

The African American church has been and will continue to be a very dominant institution in America. That which began as a weapon to combat human degradation has become a successful means of sustaining a people.

Sunday after Sunday, African American preachers have breathed new life into a downtrodden people. They have interpreted the Bible in view of their historical, cultural and daily experiences. Their tones are powerful, their gestures natural, and their words keep audiences spellbound.

Every culture attempts to create a universe of discourse for its members, a way in which people can interpret their experiences and convey it to one another. We tend to take this interplay between communication and culture for granted without exploring its effect within the culture and on other cultures. Although this essay has focused on the former, hopefully it has enlightened those of other cultures as to the reason "why we sing."

And when the song is over

We've all said Amen.

In your heart just keep on singing

And the song will never end.

And if Somebody asks you,

Was it just a show?

Lift your hands and be a witness

And tell the whole world NO!

—Kirk Franklin (1993).

References

Franklin, K. (1993). Why we sing, in *Kirk and the family*, (cassette), Inglewood, CA: Gospocentric.

Gillespie, W.G. (1977). When you think you have had enough. In *Black preaching in the Presbyterian tradition*. Philadelphia, PA: Fortress.

Hamilton, C.V. (1972). *The black preacher in America*. New York: Morrow.

Jackson, J.L. (1987). It's up to you. In Hatch, R.D. and Watkins, F.E. (Eds.), *Jesse Jackson: Straight from the heart*. Philadelphia, PA: Fortress.

Powell, Jr., A.C. (1990). *Adam Clayton Powell*. Washington, DC: Public Broadcasting System.

Richards, D. (1985). The implications of African American spirituality. In Asante, M.K. and Asante, K.W. (Eds.), *African culture: The rhythms of unity*. Trenton, NJ: Africa World.

Scott, M. (1973). Recipe for racial greatness. In *The gospel for the ghetto*. Nashville, TN: Broadman.

Smitherman, G. (1986). *Talkin' and testifyin.'* Detroit, MI: Wayne State University Press.

Stewart, Sr., W.H. (1984). *Interpreting God's word in black preaching*. Valley Forge, PA: Judson. ✦

14

When Black Women Talk With White Women

Why the Dialogues Are Difficult

Marsha Houston

University of Alabama, Tuscaloosa

> *My conversations with white women of equal social status involve much competition, aggression, and mutual lack of trust, intimacy, and equality. However, there are exceptions.*
>
> —A black woman
> graduate student

Gender and communication researchers have demonstrated that women's conversations with each other are different from their conversations with men. For example, they are more egalitarian and mutually supportive. Certainly, many conversations between African Americans[1] and white women are of this sort. Yet I and nearly every other African American woman I know can recall many conversations with white women that were neither egalitarian nor supportive, conversations that we would describe as stressful, insensitive, and in some cases even racist. Like the graduate student quoted above, many African American women are likely to consider such "difficult dialogues"[2] with white peers to be the rule and open, satisfying conversations the exception.

The difficulties in black and white women's interracial conversations are the focus of this essay. I do not intend to give a definitive or an exhaustive analysis of women's interracial talk, but to explore two reasons why black women so often find conversations with white women unsatisfying and to suggest three statements to avoid in interracial conversation. I write from an African American woman's perspective, from within my ethnic cultural group, but I hope this essay will spark dialogue about both the differences and commonalities between black and white women speakers.

A History of Suspicion and Distrust

Wed., Sept. 12,1855. . . . I have met [white] girls in the schoolroom—they have been thoroughly kind and cordial to me—perhaps the next day met them on the street—they feared to recognize me; these I can but regard now with scorn and contempt. . . . . Others give the most distant recognition possible—I, of course, acknowledge no such recognition, and they soon cease entirely. These are but trifles, certainly, to the great public wrongs which we [black people]. . . are obliged to endure. But to those who experience them, these apparent trifles are most wearing and discouraging; even to a child's mind they reveal volumes of deceit and heartlessness, and early teach a lesson of suspicion and distrust.[3]

This quotation is taken from the girlhood diary of Charlotte Forten, who was born into an affluent, free, black Philadelphia family in 1838. Like many modern communication scholars, Forten saw her everyday conversations as microcosms of the larger social and political relationships of her time. To her, the "trifles" which defined her relationship to her white schoolmates were a reflection of the "great public wrongs" of slavery that defined the relationship of African Americans to U.S. society during her youth. Her words remind us that even a life of social and economic privilege does not protect African Americans from racist encounters.

Charlotte Forten's words are also a reminder of the long history of "wearing and discouraging" conversations between black and white women. Her experience with her white classmates is an example of what Philomena Essed has termed "everyday racism," that is, racism that is expressed by a range of acts that may appear to be "trivial" or "normal" to whites, but are a constant source of stress for African Americans.[4] Essed points out that everyday racism results in a communication climate in which blacks can never take for granted that whites will respect them, treat them with courtesy, judge them fairly, or take them seriously. In her study of African American professional women of the 1920s and 1930s, Gwendolyn Etter-Lewis reports an act of everyday racism that was told to her by a successful composer and music teacher:

> I can think of things that happened to me in high school, for example a young white girl, whom I thought of as being my friend and she considered me a friend. But I remember how I felt one day when going up the broad steps of City High School. There were only ten black people at City High at that time. She spoke to me and smiled as she was passing me . . . as she always did. And her friend must have said something to her about speaking to me, like why did you speak to that black person. And I heard my friend say, "Well, she can't help it because she's black." And that jarred me. . . . [5]

This woman was so taken aback when her high school friend spoke about her color as if it were an affliction, that she never forgot the encounter and recounted it for Etter-Lewis at the age of 75.

Although not every contemporary conversation between black and white women is stressful, uncomfortable, or unpleasant, much talk between black and white women takes place against a backdrop of long-standing suspicion and distrust. This often unspoken distrust is illustrated by the contrasting attitudes of black women interviewed by Essed in the Netherlands and the United States. Most of her interviewees in the Netherlands were recent immigrants from Suriname who were surprised when Dutch whites treated them with duplicity or hostility; but *every one* of her African American interviewees mentioned that as a girl she was "ingrained" with the expectation of encountering insensitive or racist communication from whites and with defenses against it.[6] African American women's defenses against everyday racist talk may not consist of verbal retorts but rather an attitude of imperviousness to racial insensitivity, that is, cognitive skill in dismissing insensitive discourse, perhaps by thinking, "That's just the way *they* (whites) are." Some interracial conversations between women may appear untroubled because black women have learned to mask or ignore their dissatisfaction and distrust, rather than because white women have learned to be more sensitive than they were in Charlotte Forten's day.

In one research project I attempted to probe beneath black women's defenses, to lift their mask a bit by asking comparable groups of black and white women to describe their own communication style and that of the opposite group. Their most frequent descriptions are summarized below. They suggest that one reason women's interracial dialogues are difficult is that black and white women pay attention to different features of talk.

Mutual Negative Stereotypes

A basic concept of contemporary communication theory is that a speaker does not merely respond to the manifest content of a message, but to his or her interpretation of the speaker's intention or meaning. In other words, I respond to what I *think* you *meant* by what you said. Such factors as the setting and occasion, the language variety or dialect, and the interpersonal relationship between speaker and listener influence message interpretation and response.

In addition, some understandings of talk are influenced by a speaker's gender or ethnicity. For example, researchers have found that when the same message is delivered in much the same manner by a woman or by a man, listeners interpret it quite differently, in part because they expect women and men to use different styles of talk and to have knowledge of different subjects.[7] Thomas Kochman has pointed out how the different non-verbal vocal cues that working-class African Americans and middle-class whites use to express the same emotion (e.g., sincerity or anger) can create diametrically opposed attributions regarding a speaker's intentions.[8] Each ethnic cultural group has come to expect the expression of various emotions or attitudes to sound a certain way. Thus, sincerity, when uttered in a high-keyed, dynamic, working-class black style, may sound like anger to middle-class whites. And when uttered in a low-keyed, non-dynamic, middle-class white style, it may sound like disinterest or deceit to working-class blacks. Because expectations for talk are culturally learned and seldom violated by speakers *within* a cultural group, they appear to be natural or normal to the members of that group. Misunderstanding and conflict can result when cultural expectations for how to express specific attitudes and emotions are violated.

By asking African American women to describe their communication style ("black women's talk" or "talking like a black woman") as well as that of white women ("white women's talk" or "talking like a white woman"), I endeavored to discover some of their expectations for talk.[9] Below are examples of these African American women's most frequent responses:

Black women's talk is:

- standing behind what you say, not being afraid to speak your mind
- speaking with a strong sense of self-esteem
- speaking out; talking about what's on your mind
- getting down to the heart of the matter
- speaking with authority, intelligence, and common sense
- being very sure of oneself; being very distinguished and educated
- reflecting black experience as seen by a black woman in a white patriarchal society

White women's talk is:

- friendly (with an air of phoniness)
- arrogant
- know-it-all

- talking as if they think they're better than the average person
- mainly dealing with trivia
- talking proper about nothing
- weak, "air-headish"
- silly but educated
- illustrating fragility; seemingly dependent and helpless
- passive, submissive, delicate

I asked a comparable group of white women to describe their talk and that of black women. Here are their most frequent responses:

Black women's talk is:

- using black dialect
- saying things like "young 'uns," "yous," "wif," and "wich you"
- using jive terms

White women's talk is:

- all kinds of speech patterns
- distinct pronunciation
- using the appropriate words for the appropriate situations
- talking in a typical British-American language with no necessary accent and limited to "acceptable" middle-class women's topics

The above suggests that African American and white women hear very different things. Not only does each list contain positive descriptions of the group's own talk and negative descriptions of the other group's talk, but each focuses on different features. African American women concentrate on both their own and white women's interpersonal skills, strategies, and attributes. They see themselves as open, forthright, intelligent speakers and white women as duplicitous, arrogant, and frivolous. White women, on the other hand, concentrate their descriptions on language style—vocabulary, grammar, pronunciation—describing themselves as standard or correct and African American women and non-standard, incorrect, or deviant.

Because they concentrated on language style, white women described only those African American women who use African-based black English as "talking like a black woman." Their descriptions suggest that black women who use General American Speech, the prestige variety of language in the U.S.[10], are "talking white" (or talking "normally"). In contrast, African American women described themselves as speaking in "black women's talk" whenever they used particular interpersonal strategies (e.g., "standing behind what you say"; "getting down to the heart of the matter"), communication that is independent of language variety.

One reason why African American women perceived "black women's talk" as independent of language variety may be that many of us are bistylistic (able to speak two language varieties) while most white women are relatively mono-stylistic. College-educated, middle-class women who grew up and learned to speak in predominantly African American communities usually have a command of both black English and General American Speech. Those of us who are bistylistic speakers switch language varieties to some extent[11] according to situations and conversational partners, but we do not feel that we shed our ethnic cultural identity when we use General American Speech. Barbara Smith describes black women's perspective on their two speaking styles in this way:

> Now, I don't think this is about acting white in a white context. It's about one, a lack of inspiration. Because the way you act with black people is because they inspire the behavior. And I *do* mean inspire. . . . [W]hen you are in a white context, you think, "Well, why bother? Why waste your time?" if what you're trying to do is get things across and communicate and what-have-you, *you talk in your second language.*[12]

In describing their style, African American women were able to look beneath the surface features of language choice and concentrate on underlying interpersonal skills and strategies. White women, unfamiliar with how language and interpersonal interaction work in black communities, defined only that black women's talk most different

from their own in vocabulary, pronunciation, and grammar as "black."

Perhaps African American women's greater awareness of differences in language and style accounts for the final difference in the lists above. White women tended to describe their own talk as normal or universal ("all kinds of speech patterns") and African American women's talk as deviant or limited. But African American women described both their own and white women's talk as particular speaking styles.

The attention to different aspects of talk may be one reason why mutually satisfying dialogue between the two groups is often difficult. For example, researchers have noted the high value African American women place on talk that is forthright, sincere, and authentic, as did the women who responded to my questionnaire (e.g., "not being afraid to speak your mind").[13] This may sometimes conflict with the high value white women have been taught to place on politeness and propriety in speech, as several white respondents to the questionnaire indicated (e.g., "using appropriate words for the . . . situation").[14] Thus, white women may sound "phony" to black women because they have learned to be more concerned about being proper and polite than "getting down to the heart of the matter."

However, There Are Exceptions

The picture of black and white women's conversations painted here may seem particularly gloomy. The unequal power relationships that generally define the places of blacks and whites in the U.S. social order continue to intrude on our everyday interpersonal encounters, much as they did in Charlotte Forten's time. Our perceptions of one another as communicators are often riddled with stereotypes and misattributions. And yet open, satisfying conversations between African American and white women do occur; many black and white women are amicable colleagues and close friends.[15] As an African American woman who has been a student or professor at predominantly white universities for almost 30 years, I have many white women colleagues whose conversation I enjoy and a few friends whom I can count on for good talk. Even the graduate student whose stinging criticism of conversations with white women peers is quoted at the beginning of this essay admitted that "there are exceptions."

What is the nature of those exceptions? What communicative acts enable African American women to perceive white women's talk as authentic rather than "phony"? This is a complex question for which there may be as many answers as there are black women speakers (or as there are black and white women conversational partners). I would like to briefly suggest a response gleaned from my own interracial relationships and those of the members of my large network of African American women friends, relatives, students, and acquaintances.[16] I have chosen to phrase my response by offering three statements that a white woman who wants to treat black women with respect and friendship should never utter: (1) "I never even notice that you're black"; (2) "You're different from most black people"; (3) "I understand what you're going through as a black woman, because. . . . "

(1) 'I Never Even Notice. . . . '

The first statement sometimes comes as "We're all the same, really—just people." It expresses what I have come to call "the myth of generically packaged people." It is based on the incorrect assumption that cultural, sexual, or generational differences do not result in different social experiences and different interpretations of shared experiences.

Although intended to be non-racist, statement 1 actually denies the uniqueness of black women's history and contemporary experiences. It suggests that the speaker regards blackness as something negative, a problem that one "can't help" and, therefore, as something that one's white friends should overlook. It denies the possibility that blackness could be something to be valued, even celebrated. Yet many black women view our blackness as a source of pride, not only because of the many accomplished African American women and men who have overcome racism to make significant contributions, but also because of our knowledge of

how our personal histories have been influenced by our blackness. In addition, as one white woman scholar has noted, when a white woman says, "We're all alike. . . . " she usually means, "I can see how *you* (a black woman) are like *me* (a white woman)"; she does not mean, "*I* can see how I am like *you*."[17] In other words, "Just people" means "Just *white* people"—that is, people who are culturally and behaviorally similar to me, just people who share my values and beliefs, just people who do not make me aware that they are culturally or historically different and who do not insist that I honor and respect their way of being human. It is an ethnocentric statement.

Despite the non-racist intentions of the white women whom I have heard utter "I never even notice. . . . " I interpret it as blatantly racist. It erases my ethnic cultural experience (a part of who I am), redefines it in white women's terms.

(2) 'You're Different. . . . '

This statement is closely related to the first; I see it as an effort to subtract the blackness from the woman. Sometimes the statement precedes other negative or stereotypical statements about black people ("The black girls I went to high school with in South Georgia. . . . " "Those black women on welfare. . . . ") It indicates that the speaker perceives there to be "acceptable" and "unacceptable" black women or some groups of black women whom it is okay to hate.

Although I am eager for white women to see that there is diversity among African American women, and although some African American women desire to separate themselves from elements of our community that they (and whites) perceive as undesirable, I believe that few of us fail to see the racism lurking behind this "divide and conquer" statement. I am different from the poor black woman on welfare; I have a different personal history, more education, the ability to provide a better lifestyle and better life-chances for my son. But I am also the same as her; we share an ethnic cultural history (in Africa and the U.S.), and we share a life-long struggle with both racism and sexism. When I hear "You're different. . . ." I always wonder, "If I can respect and accept white women's differences from me, why can't they respect and accept my differences from them?"

(3) 'I Understand Your Experience as a Black Woman Because. . . .'

I have heard this sentence completed in numerous, sometimes bizarre, ways, from "because sexism is just as bad as racism" to "because I watch *The Cosby Show*," to "because I'm also a member of a minority group. I'm Jewish. . . Italian. . . overweight. . . ."

The speaker here may intend to indicate her effort to gain knowledge of my cultural group or to share her own experiences with prejudice. I would never want to thwart her efforts or to trivialize such experiences. Yet I hear in such statements examples of the arrogance perceived by the black women who described "white women's talk" in the lists above. Similar experiences should not be confused with the same experience; my experience of prejudice is erased when you identify it as "the same" as yours. In addition, there are no shortcuts to interracial relationships, no vicarious ways to learn how to relate to the people of another culture (e.g., through reading or watching television). Only actual contact with individuals over an extended period of time begins to build interracial understanding.

I believe that "I understand your experience as a black woman because. . . " represents white women's attempt to express solidarity with African American women, perhaps motivated by the assumption that, before we can begin a friendship, we expect them to understand our life experiences in the way they understand their own. I make no such assumption about my white women friends, and I think they make no comparable assumption about me. There is much about white women's life experiences and perspectives that I may know about, but will never fully understand. Whether my friend is black or white, I do not presume to understand all, just to respect all.

The above three statements are words I have never heard from white women whom I

count among my friends. Rather than treating our ethnic cultural differences as barriers to be feared or erased before true friendship can emerge, they embrace them as features that enrich and enliven our relationships.

Notes

1. In this chapter *black* and *African American* will be used synonymously.

2. The phrase "difficult dialogues" was first used to describe talk between different social groups in J. Butlers "Difficult Dialogues," *Women's Review of Books* (February 1989).

3. R.A. Billington. (Ed.) (1953) , *The Journal of Charlotte L. Forten: A Young Black Woman's Reactions to the White World of the Civil War Era* (74). New York: Norton. Charlotte Forten married the Reverend Francis J. Grimke in 1878; she was a prominent equal rights activist until her death in 1914.

4. P. Essed. (1991). *Understanding Everyday Racism: An Interdisciplinary Theory*. Newbury Park, CA: Sage.

5. G. Etter-Lewis. (1991). Standing up and speaking out: African American women's narrative legacy, *Discourse and Society*, II, 426–27.

6. Essed, 144.

7. B. Thome, C. Kramerae, and N. Henley (1983). Language gender, and society: Opening a second decade of research, in their *Language, Gender, and Society*, (7–24). Rowley, MA.

8. T. Kochman. (1981). *Classroom Modalities in Black and White: Styles in Conflict*. Urbana: University of Illinois Press.

9. 135 African American women (professionals, undergraduate, and graduate students) responded in writing to an open-ended questionnaire in which they freely described the talk of several social groups, including their own. A comparable group of 100 white women also responded to the questionnaire. Initial findings were reported in M. Houston (Stanback) and C. Roach, "Sisters Under the Skin: Southern Black and White Women's Communication," and M. Houston, "Listening to Ourselves: African-American Women's Perspectives on Their Communication Style," both papers presented to the Southern States Communication Association, 1987 and 1992 respectively.

10. The speaking style I refer to as *General American Speech* others sometimes call *Standard English*. I prefer the former term because it

connotes the way of speaking (rather than writing) English that is accorded preference and prestige in the United States; thus, *General American Speech* is both a more communicatively and culturally accurate term than *Standard English*.

11. Some black women change only their intonation patterns, and not their grammar or vocabulary, when they "switch" to a more black style. See discussions of the "levels" of Black English speech in M.R. Hoover. (1978). "Community attitudes toward black English." *Language in Society*, 7, 65–87.

12. B. Smith and B. Smith. (1983). Across the kitchen table: A sister to sister conversation. In *This Bridge Called My Back: Writings by Radical Women of Color*, (119). (Eds.), C. Moraga and G. Anzaldúa. New York: Kitchen Table, Women of Color Press

13. A.K. Foeman and G. Pressley. (1989). Ethnic culture and corporate culture: Using black styles in organizations, *Communication Quarterly*, 33, 293–307; and M. Hecht, S. Ribeau, and J.K. Alberts. (1989). An Afro-American perspective on interethnic communication, *Communication Monographs*, 56, 385–410.

14. R. Lakoff. (1975). Why women are ladies, in *Language and Woman Place*. New York: Harper and Row.

15. M. McCullough, Women's Friendships Across Cultures: An Ethnographic Study (Unpublished Manuscript, Temple University, 1989).

16. I admit that I chose these three state-ments in an "unscientific" manner, on the basis of their high experiential validity, rather than through any statistical sample. They are the statements that the women in my large network of black women friends, relatives, students, and acquaintances most often discuss as problematic in their conversations with white women; whenever I have shared my analysis of the statements with a group of black women whom I do not know (e.g., during a public speech for professional women or guest lecture at another university) they also have indicated that they hear them often and consider them insensitive.

17. E. Spelman. (1988). *Inessential Woman: Problems of exclusion in Feminist Thought*. Boston: Beacon. ✦

15

Latina/o Experiences With Mediated Communication

Diana I. Ríos
University of Rhode Island

The mass audience was once mythologized by marketers as homogenous in terms of race, ethnicity, cultural background and socio-economic class. This conception provided ease of mind for media commercialists who, especially since the introduction of television in the 1950s, when companies kept focus on European American middle class ideal to whom to pitch consumer products. This way of thinking about the mass audience began deteriorating in the 1960s era of national unrest when Civil Rights and counter culture movements challenged constructions of the dominant order. A coloring effect took place, where the mass audience was slowly reconceived as heterogeneous. The mass audience was indeed more than just white; it was black, brown and more! This coloring and other reconfigurations of the mass audience with regard to gender, class and sexual orientation continues today, as media marketers and researches continuously update their perceptions of the audience mosaic. This reworking is necessary in order to be in touch with the development of U.S. audience co-cultures.

In the years 2000–2010, non-white co-cultures are projected to represent about one-third of the United States. Latinos will become the nation's largest ethnic group, reaching 14 percent of the U.S. population by 2010 (U.S. Bureau of the Census 1996). Over the years, I have seen Latinos draw the lion's share of attention as a prominent ethnic and language group. Many segments of average folks, politicians, media professionals and others who consider themselves part of the mainstream of society have been perplexed about the ethnic group persistence of Latinos. While European immigrants tended to follow suit. Latinos are proud to participate in and contribute to U.S. society but choose to do so on their own terms—without disappearing into a melting pot.

As a Chicana[1] user of mass media, my ethnic identity, my cultural-based values and attitudes, and my social experiences with ethnic, class, and sex discrimination all come into play when I engage with mediated communication. My cultural and social characteristics and interests are not just self-consciously utilized; they are an ever present part of who I am. Thus my expectations, cultural needs, and desires comprise my point of view when I am watching movies such as an *Alien* sequel, a television program such as *Star Trek: Voyager,* Spanish-language international news on *Telemundo,* or the Spanish-language soap opera *La Duena* on *Univision,* or when I am looking for familiar names in the Latino newspapers across the country. With mainstream media, I have always kept a vigilant eye for people who looked like me and for issues that pertained to the Latino heritage of people like myself. Growing up in a professional, lower-middle income family in grape-picking Fresno, California, in the early 1960s, I became dissatisfied with pink dolls with blue eyes and yellow hair who did not look like they could sing "Bendito Sea Díos" at a Mexican mass. So I learned to view the visual and print media from a discreet distance until I found someone or something with which to identify, picking and choosing with very discriminate brown eyes.

This essay is intended to explore the significance of ethnicity and culture in relationship to Latinos' dual use of mass-mediated forms of communication. I will focus on bilateral functions in terms of how the media serve Latinos: (l) their acculturation to mainstream values and norms, and (2) the preservation and fortification of their ethnicity and culture. Mass-media research on Latinos, as well as personal insights, are presented in regard to audience functions, dual functions of the media, media use for acculturation, and media use for ethnic and cultural self-preservation.

Audience Functions

Communication functions have been studied within the mass communication field for a number of years (Hsia 1988). More recently, researchers have moved away from the consideration of what media does *to* individuals and have focused more intensively on what audiences do *with* media. Researchers now address more the mitigating impact of audience-member needs and goals in the selection of each medium and in its usage. When engaging with the media, audience members are viewed as "free agents" who are not constrained or so easily influenced by media messages (Lindlof and Meyer 1987, 3). Researchers who support this view do not treat audiences as "lumps of passive clay ready to be molded by what they view, read, and hear" (Severin and Tankard 1992, 269), but as people taking active roles in the way they select media and in the manner by which they decide which form of mass media is most useful for them. This "audience function" approach is especially empowering to Chicanos, because they are a powerful minority group.

An audience function focuses not on what a media form does *to* a person, but rather on what a person does *with* a media form. Consider, for example, how I viewed the sequel *Aliens* at a northern California theater and what I drew selectively from this film. A female Hispanic was introduced in the movie who was not stereotyped either as a virgin, whore, maid, or mother-saint. Pleasantly surprised to see such a strong supporting character, I was excited that this courageous and beautiful woman actually had olive skin and dark hair like myself. As her image appeared on the screen, my brother who accompanied me exclaimed, loud enough for other Chicano audience members to hear, "Hey, they put a Chicana in there!" Most of the Anglos in the audience did not seem to share our enthusiasm. The film character's lightly accented intonations reminded me of the working-class Latinas whom I had known in the San Francisco Bay area. This image of a Latina leader was what I had long been missing in popular media. She projected a positive image which I could relate to as a Latina. But then, amidst the action sequences, she was suddenly killed off. I had to settle with rooting for Sigourney Weaver's Anglo heroine—a brave woman but no Latina, and definitely not a Mexican American. Once the Latina character was gone, the film ceased to serve any affirming Chicana cultural function for me.

A film that better serves an affirming cultural function for me might be a film about a persistent, independent, likable Mexican American woman played by Salma Hayek in *Fools Rush In*. In this film, the lead female character successfully maintains cultural and ethnic identity while in a love relationship with a European American man from the U.S. East Coast. Issues of personal cultural identity struggle during long-term interactions with the dominant European American co-culture strike a chord for Latina audiences. They may live in communities where European Americans are the majority co-culture or interact closely with European Americans as friends, lovers, co-workers, supervisors or teachers. Among these casual, romantic or formal relationships Latinas still wish to keep cultural and ethnic integrity. The process of keeping, maintaining, nurturing and sharing Latina and Latino culture is one that the character and real life Latinas find challenging.

Dual Functions

Two media-centered functions merit attention because they underscore the special relationship Latinos have with mass communication when the functions are thought of as audience centered. These are the functions of acculturation (or the more encompassing terms *socialization* or *assimilation*) and ethnic and cultural self-preservation. Though there is a dearth of scholarly studies that addresses these functions for ethnics, especially Latinos, selected works which have dealt with these kinds of relationships include Park (1922); Warshauer (1966); McCardell (1976); Gutiérrez and Schement (1979); Burgoon, Burgoon, Greenberg and Korzenny (1986); and Subervi-Vélez (1984; 1986). McCardell, Gutiérrez, and Schement, Burgoon et al., and Subervi-Vélez have focused on Chicano and Latino media functions, while Park and Warshauer have touched on Spanish-language communities.

The media function that has attracted attention from the government, because of institutionalized efforts toward societal homogenization, has been the socialization power of media. For example, Park (1922) examined the role of the press for United States, European, and some "Spanish" communities early in this century. Park's study on the press was part of a collection of materials sponsored by the "Division of the Immigrant Press of Studies of Methods of Americanization" (Park 1922, vi). Ethnic presses are described as serving as tools of adjustment and as expressing a group's values, heritage, and changing sense of identity (Miller 1987, xvi). What I perceive as a cultural fear still exhibited by xenophobic individuals, who push such initiatives as "English Only," is what Park describes as the self-preservation role of ethnic print media for ethnic communities. During Park's time, there was a concern that ethnic-oriented newspapers could act as bridges to ethnic homelands and offer access to foreign political ideologies through the dissemination of information from outside the United States. This xenophobic concern will most likely intensify as ethnic minorities such as Latinos gain longer histories within the U.S. and use presses for self-preservation more efficiently than ever before. Latino presses, such as those found in several major cities, are supportive of a bicultural American ethnic community which does not want to be considered as either culturally foreign or linguistically alien.

Latino-targeted media such as community presses provide a certain content of which audiences can take advantage. However, there is always the concern that the positive role of Latino media may be diminished by the promotion of consumerism, through advertising to the economically disenfranchised. Warshauer (1966) and Gutiérrez and Schement (1979) contend that the dual functions of broadcast media such as Spanish-language radio may provide linguistic support; however, this is incidental when the mother tongue is used on behalf of a commercialistic form of Americanization. While listening to commercial Spanish-language radio in Austin, I have found that "Tex-Mex" and Latino Caribbean music are available to me but hardly as a Chicano community service, given the deluge of car and furniture advertisements, pitched by native Spanish speakers, which I am forced to endure. In Hartford, Connecticut, I can hardly wait for one radio station's key sponsor, McDonald's™, to finish its long appeals or for another to stop reminding me about the best *sofrito*, a Puerto Rican condiment, in the world. I consider myself a selective listener, and yet I and others who listen to Spanish-language radio must be bombarded constantly by appeals to buy the American dream—or buy some product that will change our lives. Chicano and Latino radio music and news are culturally affirming; but, as Gutiérrez and Schement (1979) have warned, other parts of the broadcast package essentially perpetuate "the unequal and internally colonial relationships between Anglos and Latinos in the United States" (102). We, as Chicano listeners, should be especially aware of the culturally affirming limitations that exist in the offerings of our own media.

Arguably, this observation can be generalized as applicable to other ethnic broadcast media, since co-culture-oriented media is not typically designed for the sake of social service interests, but rather that of capital gain. One exception is public broadcast stations, which have historically preserved non-commercial ideologies. Not all public broadcast stations completely fulfill the goal of public service. I have listened to some Texas stations that seem to want to maintain a culturally high-brow Anglo image for potential foundation funds rather than cater adequately to Mexican and African American listeners with limited resources in their service area. Public radio stations in the New England region fare no better. However, public radio stations offer far more opportunities and responsibility for uplifting, non-mainstream co-cultures (q.v. the case study by González 1989).

Media-centered research with Latinos and media in various U.S. cities support the idea that dual media functions, and the potential for purposive audience utilization, are simply not isolated phenomenon. Subervi-Vélez' (1984) work, based on Cubans, Mexican Americans, and Puerto Ricans in the Midwest, found that mass media exposure reflected dual functions for mainstream social integration, as well as for sustained ethnic differentiation. In McCardell's investigation of socialization factors in the Spanish-language newspaper *El Diario-La Prensa,* the author finds that the content serves to socialize the New York Latino audience to American mainstream society as well as support ethnic and cultural self-preservation by promoting socialization within "Spanish-speaking society."

Part of a study conducted by Burgoon et al. (1986) in the Southwest describes the importance of a number of general media functions to Mexican Americans. These include: information about local events; local vigilance and publicity; relaxation, escapism, and pleasure; cultural information, cultural pride, and identity; language acquisition (Spanish or English); and conversation topics (113–115). Such findings indicate that Chicanos use media for the purposes of self-preservation and acculturation, along with general uses.

Two main functions have been presented as having a special significance for Chicanos. In previous research on media and ethnics, there has been a tendency to focus on relationships that are media-centered rather than audience-centered. A media-centered approach provides only limited insight into audiences, because media users are perceived as subordinate to potential media effects. From a new view, audiences are less likely to be perceived as undiscerning dupes than as empowered, selective individuals.

Media Use for Acculturation

The aspect of media use for the goal of acculturation has been explored in a large body of work on ethnics and mass media. It has been argued that this research is rooted in the belief that media can be used as an agent to stamp out ethnic and cultural diversity in a society that prizes Euro-American culture over others. Acculturation, which involves changes in ethnic values, customs, and cultural elements toward a dominant norm, has been a highly promoted process in the U.S. Often researchers view Latinos as caught in an uneasy bind between the cultural processes of self-preservation within their own community and outside acculturation. However, Latinos have access to both ethnic-oriented and general market (English-language) media, having acquired the tastes and needs for both.

The use of media for acculturation is not inherently bad. Many ethnics use media to assist then in adapting to new environments. One problem, however, is that some Latinos accept the nativist philosophies of Anglo-Saxon cultural superiority and, as a result, use mass media to exhibit an acceptance of these beliefs in ways that I consider to be self-defeating. For example, some individuals use mainstream media as part of a program of Americanization for themselves and children. I have observed Latino children watch large amounts of mainstream serials and "kiddie" television, then heard justifications from immigrant Latino parents that this is good for their children because it helps them to master English. Although mass media may indeed help co-cultural members improve their knowledge of English, as well as U.S. society, some Latino parents harbor the false perception that acculturation will offer such members automatic access to the economic social structure.

One of the myths of the American melting pot suggests that losing one's mother tongue "makes more room" for English. Another myth offers the illusion that learning how to be "American" by Euro-American standards is the golden key to opportunity in this country. I have often looked with ethnic pride upon children with hereditary tan complexions and jet black hair, who could communicate competently in Spanish and English by necessity, and who favored their mothers' tamales or pasteles. And yet I found it such a shame that their own parents believed so adamantly that watching TV would help these children become white and successful like Batman, Perry Mason, or the oil barons J.R. and Bobby Ewing from *Dallas*. They did not even stop to consider the discreet social barriers that people of color face because they do not *look* right or know the right kind of people on the Anglo side of town. The sad truth remains that, though numerous ethnics in the U.S. have acculturated, the "Anglo-Saxon center" has largely refused entrance to non-white minorities (Novak 1972; Glazer and Moynihan 1963, 20).

It is important for Latinos to realize that, because of their unique biculturalism, they have access to media outlets in addition to those of the mainstream population. For example, Latinos who are Spanish-language dominant use mainstream media as a tool to help improve their English, while still retaining their cultural identity through ethnic-oriented media and interpersonal communication. The mass media, though distorted, does offer a window of sorts to the values, attitudes, and norms of American society.

Media Use for Self-Preservation

In my view, the function of media, for purposes of ethnic and cultural self-preservation, needs to be emphasized more positively in audience studies (Ríos 1995; Ríos and Gaines 1997). The number of media outlets for Latino audiences has not been in fair proportion to the number of Latinos in this country. Nevertheless, this does not preclude Latinos from utilizing local media to strengthen their cultural foundation.

In the capital cities of Austin, Texas, and Hartford, Connecticut, for example, Latinos have access to several community newspapers that feature artistic, cultural, political and business news relevant to them. The news coverage varies from local city stories to regional, national and international events. In Central Texas, Chicanos have access to *Arriba*,[4] a free periodical which is delivered to small grocery stores, restaurants, and other public locations. Mexican Americans also read *La Prensa*,[5] a paper with a much wider circulation that caters to Mexican Americans residing in Austin and San Antonio. Ethnic group pride and solidarity are reinforced as social activists, artists, and school-age children read stories about themselves and announcements about Chicano events. Though Chicanos do not often find themselves reflected in the mainstream media limelight, the Chicano- oriented print and broadcast media cover such events as Chicana and Chicano politicians running for local offices, community "Cinco de Mayo" and "Diez y Seis de Septiembre" celebrations, accomplishments by Chicano students, and works by local Chicano artists.

In greater Hartford, Latinos read *El Extra News*, *La Voz Hispana*, *El Reportero* and *El Vocero de Puerto Rico*. These can be picked up during your trip to buy *gandules*, or beans, on special at your corner Latino grocery store. The first three newspapers have a mission to report on positive events involving Latinos in Connecticut and neighboring states. Reading issues during 1997 and 1998, one can see that these papers made special effort to cover U.S. language policy, elections, and the Puerto Rican island status issue. These stories had direct relevance to Latino socio-cultural, educational and economic development.

The media offerings for Latinos in Austin and Hartford are not as grand as in such cities with higher Hispanic population densities as Los Angeles, California, or New York, New York. However, Austin's Chicanos do have access to a myriad of Latino-oriented television and radio stations, newspapers, magazines, music recordings, and videos in Spanish, English or both—originating in the U.S. as well as in Mexico and other parts of Latin America. In the Hartford area Latinos listen to WRYM(AM), WLAT(AM) and WPRX (AM). These three radio stations play "merengue" and other popular Latin American-Caribbean dance music.

The newspaper *Arriba* tends to print in English; *La Prensa* is bilingual. Chicanos with continued ties to Mexico seek out both local or international news stories from either small newspapers or the Spanish-language television network Univisión, as well as access to mainstream broadcast and print media such as the *Austin American-Statesman*. Latino popular culture, such as found in music and film, often deal with contemporary issues and shared feelings among Chicanos and other Latinos (Padilla 1989). To this end, for example, the large video rental store "Acapulco" in the Chicano section of Austin specializes in offering Spanish-language film videos. One can walk in, indulge in an iced fruit *agua fresca,* and select movies from Mexico's golden age of cinema or American-made films dubbed in Spanish. There are two main Spanish-language radio stations at the time of this writing. KELG (AM)[6] offers "Tropical" Latino music as well as news broadcasts in Spanish. KTXZ (AM)[7] is a bilingual "Tejano" station. Both these stations are popular among immigrants and the U.S. born, though community people have often complained that they need more Spanish language stations from which to choose (Ríos 1993).

During my field work among Mexican Americans in Austin, I encountered two women who were particularly conscious of and labored hard to strengthen their biculturalism. One was "Lupita," an immigrant who described to me how she cut out English-language stories from the newspaper to figure out unfamiliar American words, trying to utilize both English and Spanish print media. She also carefully monitored her children's cable television viewing of shows in English and Spanish. In her cultural values and attitudes, Lupita was unequivocally "Mexicana" and strived to retain this even in her efforts to function well in her new society. Dedicated to promoting *la comunidad* (the community), she became one of a group of neighborhood organizers who networked with other Latinos to address burning demands with the city of Austin. The other woman was "Lorena," a long-time Texan Mexican who took advantage of mainstream media, particularly professional trade media, in order to keep up in her area of expertise. She competed well in the Anglo world, yet always maintained her cultural ties through Mexican American newspapers, her family, and other Chicanos she had grown up with in the neighborhood.

Concluding Remarks

Latinos must rely on communication among themselves in order to fulfill the need for self-validation. As this essay has illustrated, mass-mediated communication can be attained by Latinos so that they can exercise cultural maintenance, strengthen ethnic identity, and gain the sociocultural tools necessary to function within the dominant coculture. Even when Latinos live in areas of high ethnic concentration, they must interact with a mainstream society that has limited tolerance for linguistic and cultural diversity. Cultural dualism has long been a process by which I and others of Mexican heritage, and other U.S. Latinos, have balanced the conforming agents of mainstream socialization, such as private and public educational institutions and government bodies. Ethnic-oriented media, selected mainstream media, Chicano-Latino churches, professional and social groups all help to advance our co-culture in America.

Notes

1. *Latino* is a preferred term of reference over the imposed *Hispanic* term (see Hayes-Bautista and Chapa 1987, for discussion).

2. The term *Chicano*, most popular during the civil rights era, connotes a political and ethnic consciousness. (For a historical account, see Acuña 1988.) *Chicano* will be used here interchangeably with *Mexican American* to avoid repetition, as well as draw attention to this group's continued struggle for social equality.

3. Mechanca's (1989) case studies describe how nativistic philosophies are enforced within Chicano communities.

4. *Arriba* was established in 1980 as a response to poor Chicano cultural events coverage by Austin's main city paper, the *Austin American-Statesman*. Interview with *Arriba* publisher and editor Romeo Rodriguez, February 21, 1992.

5. *La Prensa,* founded in 1986, is a free weekly paper distributed to Chicano parts of the city and elsewhere. The publisher and editor is

Catherine Vasquez-Revilla. The co-publisher is State Senator Gonzalo Barrientos.

6. Founded by Jose Jaime Garcia, Sr., in 1985, KELG is a family-owned and operated business that plays many types of Latino music. It is currently managed by Jose Jaime Garcia, Jr. Interview with Jose Jaime Garcia, Jr., February 24, 1992.

7. This has been a bilingual "Tejano" music station since 1986, geared to Texan Mexicans who were born and raised in Texas as well as others of Mexican origin. It is owned by SCAN Communications. Interview with Douglas Raab, general manager, February 24, 1992.

References

Acuña, R. (1988). *Occupied America: A history of Chicanos,* (3rd ed.). New York: Harper and Row.

Burgoon, J.K., Burgoon, M., Greenberg, B.S. and Korzenny, F. (1986). Mass media use, preferences, and attitudes among adults. In Greenberg, B.S., Burgoon, J.K., Burgoon, M. and Korzenny, F. (Eds.), *Mexican Americans and the mass media* 79–146 Norwood, NJ: Ablex.

Glazer, N. and Moynihan, D.P. (1963). *Beyond the melting pot: The Negroes, Puerto Ricans, Jews, Italians, and Irish of New York City.* Cambridge, MA: The MIT Press and Harvard University Press.

González, A. (1989). "Participation" at WMEX-FM: Interventional rhetoric of Ohio Mexican Americans. *Western Journal of Speech Communication, 53,* 398–410.

Gutiérrez, F.F. and Schement, J.R. (1979). *Spanish-language radio in the Southwestern United States.* Austin: The University of Texas at Austin, Center for Mexican American Studies.

Hayes-Bautista, D.E. and Chapa, J. (1987). Latino terminology: Conceptual bases for standardized terminology. *American Journal of Public Health, 77,* 61–68.

Hayes-Bautista, D.E., Schink, W.O. and Chapa, J. (1988). *The burden of support.* Stanford, CA: Stanford University Press.

Hsia, H.J. (1988). *Mass communications research methods: A step-by-step approach.* Hillsdale, NJ: Erlbaum.

Lindlof, T.R. and Meyer, T.P. (1987). Mediated communication as ways of seeing, acting, and constructing culture: The tools and foundations of qualitative research. In Lindlof, T.R. (Ed.), *Natural Audiences* 1–30, Norwood, NJ: Ablex.

Menchaca, M. (1989). Chicano-Mexican cultural assimilation and Anglo-Saxon cultural dominance. *Hispanic Journal of Behavioral Sciences, 11,* 203–231.

McCardell, W.S. (1976). Socialization factors in *El Diario-La Prensa,* the Spanish-language newspaper with the largest daily circulation in the United States. Unpublished doctoral dissertation. University of Iowa.

Miller, S.M., (Ed.). (1987). The ethnic press in the United States: A historical analysis and handbook. New York: Greenwood.

Novak, M. (1972). *The rise of the unmeltable ethnics: Politics and culture in the seventies.* New York: Macmillan.

Padilla, F.M. (1989). Salsa music as a cultural expression of Latino consciousness and unity. *Hispanic Journal of Behavioral Sciences, 11,* 28–45.

Park, R.E. (1922). *The immigrant press and its control.* New York: Harper and Brothers.

Ramos, H.A. and Morales, M.M. (1985). U.S. immigration and the Hispanic community: An historical overview and sociological perspective. *Journal of Hispanic Politics, 1,* 1–17.

Ríos, D.I. (1995). Chicano cultural resistance with mass media. In De Anda, R.M., (Ed.), *Chicanas and Chicanos in contemporary society,* Needham Heights, MA: Allyn and Bacon.

Ríos, D.I. (1993). Mexican American audiences: A qualitative and quantitative study of ethnic subgroup uses for mass media. Unpublished doctoral dissertation. University of Texas at Austin.

Ríos, D.I. and Gaines, S.O. (1997). Impact of gender and ethnic subgroup membership on Mexican American use of mass media for cultural maintenance. *Howard Journal of Communication, 8,*(2), 197–16.

Severin, W. and Tankard, J., Jr. (1992). *Communication theories: Origins, methods and uses in the mass media,* (3rd ed.). New York: Longman.

Subervi-Vélez, F.A. (1984). Hispanics, the mass media, and politics: Assimilation versus pluralism. Unpublished doctoral dissertation. University of Wisconsin-Madison.

Subervi-Vélez, F.A. (1986). The mass media and ethnic assimilation and pluralism: A review and research proposal with a special focus on Hispanics. *Communication Research, 13,* 71–96.

Traudt, P.J. (1986). Ethnic diversity and mass mediated experience. In Thomas, S. and Evans, W.A., (Eds.), *Communication and culture: Language, performance, technology, and media.* Norwood, NJ: Ablex.

U.S. Bureau of the Census (1991). *Census and You*. Resident population of the United States: Middle series projections. Washington, DC: Government Printing Office.

U.S. Bureau of the Census (1996, March) Resident population of the United States: Middle series projections. Washington, DC: Government Printing Office.

Warshauer, M.E. (1966). Foreign language broadcasting. In Fishman, J., *Language loyalty in the United States*. London: Mouton. ✦

16

Native American Culture and Communication Through Humor

Charmaine Shutiva
Isleta Elementary School

> *One of the best ways to understand a people is to know what makes them laugh.*
>
> —Vine Deloria, Jr.
> *Custer Died for*
> *Your Sins* (1969, 146)

Contrary to popular belief, Native Americans are not a stoic, quiet people (Deloria 1969; Giago 1990; Hill 1943; Opler 1938). They are generally a joyful people (Deloria 1969; Hill 1943; Miller 1967; Obamsawin 1983) who appreciate and dote upon humor. Although the role and function of humor have been components of the religious, social, and political lives of Native Americans, it has rarely been acknowledged (Deloria 1969; Ortiz 1984) or examined as an element of communication in social and interpersonal settings (Deloria 1969; Ortiz 1984).

This essay will explore Native American humor, its form and function, and its usefulness in interpersonal communication in various Native American secular and sacred social settings.

Native American Humor and Group Cohesiveness

In the lively world of the Native American, many religious, cultural, and social events are breeding grounds for humor. Humor permeates even the most serious tribal council meetings. Parliamentary procedures are repeated, but in the "Ini'n way"—which invariably involves much humor (Miller 1967). The pace of meetings is often slow, with wandering topics, drawn-out discussions, and inevitable exchanges of humorous stories and asides.

Although each tribe is different and has traditions and ceremonies that are tribally specific, researchers (Eyster 1980; Faas 1982; Hanson and Esienbise 1983; Miller and Garcia 1974; Sanders 1987; Supaka 1972) have developed lists of values and beliefs that can be considered cross-tribal. The use of humor among Native Americans has aided in helping to maintain many of these values and, conversely, these values and beliefs have aided in helping to establish humor as an intrinsic component of Native American communication. Two of the cultural values that strongly influence this humor are perception of time and group orientation.

Native American Perception of Time

The Native American perception of time is different from the dominant Euro-American perception of time (Attneave 1982; Faas 1982; Hanson and Eisenbise 1983; Sanders 1987), which is linear and segmented. For the latter, punctual activities are the norm. In contrast, among the various tribal societies, the perception of time is circular and flexible. The predominant attitude is that the activities will commence "whenever people are ready; when everyone arrives" (Pepper 1976). According to Garrison (1989), "[Native American] people see no need to control time or to let it control them . . . .The goal is not to limit the time, but to experience and enjoy time as it passes" (122). This consideration of time symbolically reinforces the Native American religious belief of achievement and maintenance of harmony with nature because "nature is allowed to take its own course."

This somewhat "laid back" attitude about time has been jokingly referred to as "Indian

113

time" (Anderson, Burd, Dodd, and Kelker 1980; Lockart 1978; Marashio 1982) and has contributed to the development and maintenance of humor in the Native American world. "Indian time" has provided Native Americans unstressed, unpressured time to teach younger generations the "proper way" to greet friends and relatives and to exchange stories and anecdotes. While patiently waiting for cultural festivities to begin, the individual is provided the opportunity to entertain the "audience with his/her talent and flair for the spoken word." For example, according to Steve "Raising" Kane, a Northern Pauite comic orator, a Native American operating on Indian time is an individual who is either early or not so early, but never late (Giago 1990).

Native American Group Orientation

A second traditional Native American value that has had an impact on the use of humor is an emphasis on group and community rather than on individualism (Eyster 1980; Faas 1982; Garrison 1989; Hanson and Eisenbise 1983; Light and Martin 1986; Miller, Garcia 1974; Supaka 1972). A harmonious balance with self, others, and nature is emphasized; cooperation with others is stressed. Competition is regarded with disdain by traditional Native Americans. Individual achievements are viewed as contributions to the group, not to personal glory (Pepper 1967).

Attneave (1982) noted that when the needs or goals of a group conflict with individual decisions and preferences, the group will exert stronger influence, whether the group is understood as the tribe, a band of the tribe, the family, or any other coherent cluster of people. In Native American culture, to excel for personal fame is frowned upon because it sets one above and apart from the others. This disturbs the group's cohesiveness and the balance that tribal members endeavor to maintain. The solidarity of tribes and the group cohesiveness that Native Americans value have been supported and reinforced by the use of humor. It has been a significant and instrumental fac-

tor that has helped maintain unity and traditional cultural values.

Studies on humor conducted by McGhee (1970) have shown that humor can serve to facilitate social acceptance by producing an "in-group." The shared knowledge of in-groups is especially important in the Native American world, where humor functions to guide social situations when various tribal communities interact (Deloria 1969; Giago 1990). Deloria (1969) has noted that "rather than embarrass members of the tribe publicly, people used to tease individuals they considered out of step with consensus of tribal opinion." (147). "If someone is out of line, that person [is kidded to convey] that he's doing wrong, and that realization gives value to teasing. The one doing the teasing is not trying to be better than the person being teased but is trying to make a point" (Giago 1990, 52). For example, the young Native American girl is teased about dragging her swal on the ground."Are you trying to catch your supper?" she is asked (i.e., to collect bugs). The teenage boy is kidded about falling asleep while prayers are being recited in the kiva. "Your mouth was open so big we could have put a whole fried bread in it."

Deloria (1969) also noted that, when various tribal people get together for social and cultural functions (such as a pow-wow), "everything is up for grabs" (163). Sioux tease Chippewas; Chippewas tease Pueblos; Pueblos tease Sioux, etc. Their ability to laugh, to take a tease, and to share jokes creates a bond and a "solid feeling of unity and purpose to the tribe" (Deloria 1969, 147). For example, Pueblos tease Sioux that their hamburgers bark when they bite into them. (Sioux traditionally ate dogs.) Chippewas tease Pueblos that their outdoor ovens would make good bomb shelters.

Giago (1990) observed that the development of cross-tribal teasing may have gained increased popularity when Native Americans were sent away to attend Bureau of Indian Affairs boarding schools. The humor helped "to lighten the lonely feeling and harsh conditions at the schools" (Giago 1990, 52). According to Giago (1990), the adaptability and tenacity of Native Americans, combined with their spiritual beliefs (of a harmonious balance with life and nature), have enabled them to survive centuries of orchestrated hardships and devastation. Humor, Giago notes, was vital because it created a link that connected Native American people.

Native American Humor

In addition to the rampant teasing, many other forms of humor are also prevalent: puns (Navajo, Arapaho, $50-a-night-ho), practical jokes (gluing high heels to the bottom of a pair of moccasins for an "evening look"), ribbing and sexual innuendo ("He just likes long-haired Native American girls so he can get all wrapped up in them." "Custer wore Arrow shirts." "It is a good thing Columbus was not looking for the country of Turkey or else we would be called Turkeys instead of Indians"). Many Native Americans are excellent mimics and mimes, with a superb sense of timing and climax (Giago 1989; Hill 1943).

The Sacred Clown

No better example of this humor is the role of the sacred clown in the various tribes' religious ceremonies (Giago 1989). This religious yet entertaining figure facilitates group unification through humor that brings together all who are within sight and hearing. Heib (1984) stated that "the ritual clown is the embodiment and articulation of humor from a structural perspective. . . . If it is to be fully understood [it] requires an understanding of a great complexity of structural relationships extending beyond the ritual process itself to the larger context of how [Native Americans] live" (190).

During the religious ceremony, no one is exempt from the exaggerated, often embarrassing, acts and mimickings of the tenacious clowns. Governors and other tribal officials often become the target of each clown's jest and fun. The clown's obvious disregard for authority helps to unify the group.

Koestler (1964) refers to this social phenomenon as a participatory or self-transcending tendency in that "the self is experienced as being part of the larger whole" (54). The sacred clown tests individuals' ability to

take a joke and laugh at themselves and others. For example, the sacred clown will walk behind an elderly woman and mimic her slow, deliberate steps. This teaches the audience not only a great appreciation for humor and group solidarity, but the sacredness of humor (Beck and Walters 1977). Although the majority of the sacred clown's actions are comical, there are lessons that the clown teaches about how Native Americans treat each other. For example, if two boys are caught fighting by the sacred clown, he and his fellow clown friends may mimic the boys' fighting and make the boys kiss each other to make up. By embarrassing the boys, he not only teaches them that it is wrong to fight, he teaches others observing the action that this type of conduct is inappropriate. Often, after people have observed this type of interaction, the adults will use this opportunity to admonish their children. "See what the clown did? You better behave yourself." Thus, the sacred clown functions not only to teach the lesson of not being too serious, but to protect and teach traditional values and beliefs that reinforce the tribal cohesiveness that is critical for tribal survival.

Pow-wows

Another avenue for the expression of humor in the Native American world occurs at social gatherings called "pow-wows" and "49ers." Young and old participate and share in the pageantry, laughter, and merriment. Speakers noted for their colorful personalities and ability to captivate audiences are often asked to be the emcees at pow-wows (Giago 1989). Their knowledge of ceremonialism and ritual is shared with the audience, along with their jokes, wisecracks, and puns. Humorous stories such as predicaments resulting from the Native Americans' unfamiliarity with some customs, mannerisms, and language patterns of the dominant Euro-American society are often the favorite topics of the pow-wow announcer. For example, one pow-wow announcer spoke about his recent experience on a plane. When he saw the flight attendant demonstrate the use of an oxygen mask, he thought it was a breath-analyzer and put his wine back in his boot.

49ers

After the conclusion of the pow-wow ceremony, a "49er" is often held. There is no simple way to describe what a 49er is, nor is there one accurate or authentic way to relate it to history. There are as many images associated with the 49er as there are stories told about how "49ing" first originated. It is a kind of "night capper" after a fine evening of pow-wow dancing and singing; an R-rated campfire sing-along that allows rookies, as well as master singers and drummers, a chance to learn old songs and make up new ones using English and various tribal languages. Bystanders are free to enjoy the relaxed atmosphere and impromptu performances. The atmosphere is full of gaiety and laughter as Native Americans stand around the fire "milking" their jokes. Making up lyrics to each beat of the drum, the comedian receives continual reinforcement from cohorts. A special favorite at 49ers is a song entitled "One-eyed Ford." This is a song about a man taking home his "snag" after the 49er has ended. There are various versions of "One-eyed Ford." One rendition is as follows:

When the dance is over, sweetheart

I will take you home

in my one-eyed Ford, one-eyed Ford.

Whay yah hi, whay yah hi, whay yah hi yooooo.

When I'm dry and sober, sweetheart

I will take you home

in my one-eyed Ford, one-eyed Ford.

Whay yah hi, whay yah hi, whay yah hi yooooo.

Storytelling

Another important element in the Native American world is its oral tradition and history. Among Native American circles, there has always been an orator or storyteller (Sando 1976; Tafoya 1982). Like the sacred clown of Native American religious ceremonies, storytellers have delighted young and old with their oratorical talents, using tales and myths, humorous in context and content, that are told and retold (Deloria 1969). Their use of humor serves to captivate the audience, as well as to forcefully make points of social and cultural importance. For example, stories about Custer, Columbus, and the Pilgrims are given a different flair and unusual twist.

Conclusion

Humor plays an important role in helping to maintain and reinforce traditional Native American beliefs. Two cultural values, group cohesiveness orientation and circular time perception, are especially emphasized and have a great impact on the Native American's use of humor. To effectively communicate with Native Americans, an awareness of these two cultural values, plus an awareness of the Native American's spiritual belief of harmony with nature, must be acknowledged.

However, just because a Native American's choice of solving a problem may be humorous, this does not necessarily mean that he or she is not taking the task seriously. A supportive, non-judgmental, and accepting attitude is important in understanding how humor has served as a survival mechanism to help Native Americans deal with the complexity involved in living in two different worlds.

References

Anderson, B., Burd, L., Dodd, J. and Kelker, K. (1980). A comparative study in estimating time. *Journal of American Indian Education*, 19,(3), 1–4.

Attneave, C. (1982). American Indians and Alaska native families: Emigrants in their own homeland. In McGodrick, M., Pearce, J.K. and Giordano, J., (Eds.), *Ethnicity and Family Therapy* (55–83). New York: Guildford.

Beck, P.G. and Walters, A.L. (1977). *The sacred: Ways of knowledge, sources of life.* Tsaile, AZ: Navajo Community College Press.

Deloria, V., Jr. (1969). *Custer died for your sins.* New York: Macmillan.

Exum, H.A. and Colangelo, N. (1981). Culturally diverse gifted: The need for ethnic identity development. *Roeper Review*, 15–17.

Eyster, I. (1980). *Culture through concepts: A teachers' guide.* Norman, OK: Southwest Center for Human Relations Studies. (ERIC Document Reproduction Services No., ED 176 928).

Faas, L. (1982). *Cultural and educational variables involved in identifying and educating gifted and talented American Indian children.* (ERIC Document Reproduction Service No. ED 255 010).

Garrison, L. (1989). Programming for the gifted American Indian student. In Maker, C.J. and Schiever, S., (Eds.), *Critical issues in gifted education: Defensible programs for cultural and ethnic minorities* (116–127). Austin, TX: Pro-Ed.

Giago, T., Jr. (1990). My laughter. *Native peoples: The arts and lifeways,* 3(3), 52–56.

Hanson, W.D. and Eisenbise, M.D. (1983). *Human behavior and American Indians.* Rockville, MD: National Institute of Mental Health. (ERIC Document Reproduction Service No. ED 231 589).

Heib, L.A. (1984). Meaning and mismeaning: Toward an understanding of the ritual clown. In Ortiz, A., (Ed.), *New perspectives of the Pueblos* (163–195). Albuquerque: University of New Mexico Press.

Hill, W.W. (1943). Navajo humor: Methods for identifying the gifted and talented American Indian student. *Journal for the Education of the Gifted,* 11(3), 53–63.

LeBrasseur, M.M. and Freark, E.S. (1982). Touch a child—they are my people: Ways to teach American Indian children. *Journal of American Indian Education,* 21(3), 6–13.

Light, H.K. and Martin, R.E. (1986). American Indian families. *Journal of American Indian Education,* 26(1), 1–5.

Little Soldier, L. (1985). To soar with the eagles: Enculturation and acculturation of Indian children. *Childhood Education,* 61, 185–191.

Lockart, B.L. (1978). *Cultural conflict: The Indian child in the non-Indian classroom.* (ERIC Document Reproduction Service No. ED 195 397).

Marashio, P. (1982). "Enlighten my mind:" Examining the learning process through native American ways. *Journal of American Indian Education,* 21(2), 2–10.

McGhee, P.E. (1979). *Humor: Its origin and development.* San Francisco: W.H. Freeman.

Miller, D.L. and Garcia, A. (1974, May). Mental issues among urban Indians: The myth of the savage-child. Paper presented at the Annual Meeting of the American Psychological Association. (ERIC Document Reproduction Service No. 129 485 0).

Miller, F.C. (1967). Humor in a Chippewa tribal council. *Ethnology,* 6(3), 263–271.

Opler, M.E. (1938). Humor and wisdom of some American Indian tribes. *New Mexico Anthropologists,* 3, 3–10.

Ortiz, A. (Ed.) (1984). *New perspective on the Pueblos.* Albuquerque: University of New Mexico Press.

Pepper, F.C. (1976). Teaching the American Indian child in mainstream settings. In Jones, R.L., (Ed.), *Mainstreaming and the minority child* (133–158). Minneapolis, MN: Council for Exceptional Children.

Sanders, D. (1987). Cultural conflicts: An important factor in the academic failures of American Indian students. *Journal of Multicultural Counseling and Development,* 15(2), 81–90.

Sando, J.S. (1976). *The Pueblo Indians.* San Francisco, CA: The Indian Historian.

Tafoya, T. (1982). Coyote's eyes: Native cognition styles. *Journal of American Indian Education,* 21(2), 21–33. ✦

Part IV

Celebrating Cultures

17

Capturing the Spirit of *Kwanzaa*

Detine L. Bowers
Harmony Blessings, Inc.

Three hundred people stood together in an old Milwaukee library, now the home of the Wisconsin Black Historical Society and Museum. We followed the call of the evening's libation leader for the first night of *Kwanzaa* 1995. "Habari Gani," he intoned.

The celebrants responded with "Umoja," the principle we observe on the first night of *Kwanzaa*.

"Habari Gani," he repeated, waiting for a more passionate response.

A loud, highly charged "Umoja!" reverberated in the room. The echoes of pounding drums fed and nourished our spirits as the libation leader, an elder from Ghana, West Africa, pronounced the magical words that inspired everyone to join in the experience of this healing ceremony: "Let us call forth the ancestors from the East, from the West, from the North, and from the South." He poured water on the ground from a *kibombe cha umoja* (a unity cup).

As the leader directed us to turn south, I gazed at the walls of this historic building, remembering the power of libation when Maya Angelou was guest speaker at a 1993 lecture at the W.E.B. DuBois Center in Accra, Ghana. Then I recalled the time I spent at the Slave Castles in Elmina, Ghana, during the 1993 National Council for Black Studies Conference. In my mind's eye, I could still see the sacred ceremony at the site of a holding station for captured Africans destined to board slave ships that would separate husbands from wives, parents from children, siblings from siblings, and families from families.

At Elmina we had hummed the African National Congress anthem, poured libation with blessed water from the Nile, and experienced the presence of our loved ones from whom we were parted by space, time, and water—but not by spirit. In that moment of stillness, we all felt a sense of magic as we stood in a close-knit circle and looked upon the heavens, feeling the earth shift beneath our feet as the pilgrimage spoke of the pain of separation and the bliss of reunion. We were filled with the harmony of the past folding into the present as the wind passed through our feet and filled our hearts with renewed energy. That same energy now returned to me at this Milwaukee *Kwanzaa* gathering more than two years later.

As we all turned south in the old library to remember our ancestors, I could hardly believe my eyes when I noticed a young couple who had also been on the Ghana tour with me. It was a moment of blissful reconnection.

Together we celebrated the *Nguzo Saba*, the seven principles embodying the value system of *Kwanzaa*.

This moment was a powerful one in my understanding and appreciation of *Kwanzaa*, the African American cultural holiday that Maulana Karenga established in 1966 in response to the Watts riots in Los Angeles. I had been to a few other *Kwanzaa* celebrations but had not experienced such a powerful spiritual awareness. Other celebrations had seemed ritualistic, empty, and without real meaning for me. What made this experience different, in part, was my own act of calling forth my grandparents, William and Naomi Thomas, in whose name I was in the process of creating the William A. Thomas Harmony Center, a spiritual-psychological center project in Brunswick County, Virginia.

The principles and the order of Kwanzaa ceremonies are aligned with harvest festivals in traditional West African cultures. The opening of the ceremony invites the audience to call forth ancestors after the libation leader's presentation, during which many in the audience call forth the names of deceased loved ones whom they fondly remember. I felt spiritually invigorated as I stood and requested the presence of those who had proceeded me both in building a community and in helping those seeking guidance in life. The spirit of harmony filled the room where large gatherings turned out each of the four nights of the museum's *Kwanzaa* celebration. Each night, the seven principles that embody the *Nguzo Saba* value system were proclaimed and honored as many youths led the candlelit part of the ceremony, explaining the history and meaning of *Kwanzaa*.

Kwanzaa, a Swahili term for the first fruits of harvest, represents a time (December 26 to January 1) to encourage healing through the common bonds that nurture community. Children and youths, as symbolized by the *muhindi* (or corn) are the center of these celebrations, because they represent hope for the future. Local youths led the first night's celebration of *Umoja* with enthusiasm, vigor, and the spirit of love as they sang, recited poetry, and spoke with wisdom and confidence. Though many consider *Kwanzaa* to be a religious holiday, it is not affiliated with a particular religious group or sect; it is intended to promulgate principles and values to enhance an individual's spiritual life.

Each night the museum's table was colorfully decorated with a candleholder that held seven candles (*mishumma*) to symbolize ancestors—one black, three red, and three green, each representing a principle of *Kwanzaa*. *Mazao*, fruits and vegetables symbolizing the harvest along with *muhindi* were carefully placed upon the *mkeka*, a unity mat symbolizing a firm foundation. The *kibombe cha umoja*, the unity cup used earlier during the libation, was used by the younger members of the gathering. It symbolized the value of unity within families and communities. The youth leading this part of the ceremony cheerfully proclaimed the seven principles, the *Nguzo Saba*, and the meaning of this value system to the community:

1. *Umoja* (unity): to strive to help family, community, nation, and race.

2. *Kujichagulia* (self-determination): to define, name, and create for ourselves.

3. *Ujima* (collective work and responsibility): to build and maintain our community.

4. *Ujamma* (cooperative economics): to build and maintain community businesses.

5. *Nia* (purpose): to build toward restoring the traditional greatness of a people.

6. *Kummba* (creativity): to foster and build upon the gift of beauty in the community.

7. *Imani* (faith): to believe in ourselves, our ancestors, and the righteousness of the struggle.

A wave of cultural pride filled the room and echoed from the smallest child to the oldest adult. Two youths sang *His Eye Is on the Sparrow*, a song that symbolized our past, our present, and the recommitment to our future as a community.

On the second day of *Kwanzaa*, which emphasizes the principle of self-determination (*Kujichagulia*), I was filled with the spirit of determination to exercise committed action within the community of humanity. In the hours before our evening *Kwanzaa* ceremony, remembrances of my travels on the pre-Civil War-era underground railroad through New York, Massachusetts, and Rhode Island came to my mind and heart. At that time I had also visited nearly 20 towns and cities where African Americans had followed the North Star to celebrate universal freedom during the First of August celebrations in commemoration of abolition in the British West Indies on August 1, 1833. I recalled my visit to Harriet Tubman's home in Auburn, New York, and how impressed I was by the power of a woman who had devoted her life to freedom, sacrificing comfort and safety for a higher mission. I also recalled the warmth I had felt at Frederick Douglass' gravesite in Rochester, New York, and I envisioned his powerful presence at Washington Square on the First of August as people gathered to hear his words prophesying universal freedom and justice for all.

It was a sacred time of commemoration and dedication to ancestors and philanthropists across the ages who believed in humanity and divine equality. These First of August celebrations focused on the philanthropic deeds of British activists, freedom fighters around the world, and the sons and daughters of Africa. One hundred years later, Karenga called for a new order of business, through a celebration that would seek out specific African-inspired values to praise generations of people whose work has gone unsung in many European societies.

Today these ceremonies have special value for reuniting people of African descent with their ancestors, reconciling individuals and families in their efforts to overcome the painful memories of years of forced separation across continents. The ceremonies are blessings that honor the brave spirits of the past and the rich healing power of nature found in colors and harvest crops. The ceremonial praises involved promulgate healing across the ages. One can sense the power of the ancestors as the drums echo, bringing the core of our humanity into sync with the rhythms of the universe. People dance and move with the spirit of all times as they transport the spirits of their special loved ones into present space and time. Participation in the ceremonial experience is euphoric, much like the traditional West African harvest ceremonies that praise long-lost loved ones and the universe for the gifts of nature and the harvest, thus symbolizing the beginning of human settlement on earth. For instance, the Yam Festival of the Aburi of Akuapem, in the eastern region of Ghana, praises the spirits of the ancestors in prayer. Opoku (1970) quotes one such prayer:

When I call one of you

I have called all.

Ye departed spirits of the seven

Akan clans,

Receive drink.

Today is your lustral day.

I have brought you a sheep, drink and new yam.

Receive these and visit us

This new year with a good harvest,

Wealth and prosperity, fertility and long life,

Peace and fame and rain and sunshine

At their appropriate times.

If ever we are called upon

To share three things with any other nation,

Let us have two.

Let the evil one that plans evil for us

Receive evil in return.—(30–31)

Even the ancient Greeks and Romans experienced the euphoria of harvest festivals and ceremonies, of ancestral worship and praises of nature embodied in the Eleusian Mysteries. There is little record of these secret rituals. What survives today are a few reports as recorded in the writings of Cicero:

> Nothing is higher than these mysteries. They have sweetened our characters and softened our customs: they have made us pass from the condition of savages to true humanity. They have not only shown us the way to live joyfully, but they have taught us how to die with a better hope. (Hamilton 1969, 48)

The joy Cicero spoke of could be felt in the beat of drums that engaged the crowd in powerful moments of call and response during the second night of *Kwanzaa* in Milwaukee. Children led with sounds of joy, their hands steady on their instruments and their expressions full of intensity and a touch of the spirit. They incited the same feelings in the crowds of people who were determined on that same night of *Kujichagulia* to increase African American voting in the city and confront local issues affecting the poor and oppressed.

The guest speaker that night, Molefi Kete Asante, spoke of a history of struggle and emphasized the contributions of Harriet Tubman, the Moses of her people. Asante voiced his high esteem for her vision and sacrifice that led people to a new consciousness when she helped make the underground railroad an alternative to slavery. Her persuasion aroused the courage of the uncommitted and fearful to take action.

The remaining nights of the *Kwanzaa* celebration echoed the spirit of the previous nights. The sounds of gospel, the words of poets coupled with African drumbeats, and the voices of educators charting issues, challenges, and pledges of unity helped us reunite with wise spirits across the ages.

When the doors of the Wisconsin Black Historical Society and Museum closed on the final night, a security guard escorted me to my car amidst the snow and ice. He expressed surprise that I had left every previous night for my car without the protection of an escort. Strangely, it had never occurred to me that I had been in any danger. Here I was, an unescorted woman in the heart of Milwaukee, but I never felt alone. The power of the spirit of love and spiritual connection had surrounded me after every *Kwanzaa* ceremony, and I never felt unprotected.

References

Bowers, D.L. (1995). A place to stand: African-Americans and the first of August platform. *Southern Journal of Communication, 60,* 348–361.

Copage, E.V. (1991). *Kwanzaa: A celebration of culture and cooking.* New York: Morrow.

Hamilton, E. (1969). *Mythology: Timeless tales of Gods and heroes.* New York: Mentor.

Karenga, M. (1989). *The African American holiday of Kwanzaa: A celebration of family, community and culture.* Los Angeles, CA: University of Sankore Press.

Opoku, A.A. (1970). *Festivals of Ghana.* Accra, Ghana: Ghana Publishing.

Wiggins, W.H., Jr. (1987). *O Freedom!: Afro-American emancipation celebrations.* Knoxville: University of Tennessee Press. ✦

18

A House as Symbol, a House as Family

Mamaw and Her Oklahoma Cherokee Family

Lynda Dee Dixon
Bowling Green State University

> *It is the grandmother who often is the storyteller, the preserver of the past, and the strength of the future.*
>
> —Bataille and Sand (1984, 134)

The role of family in American society is diverse and culture-bound. This essay describes an Oklahoma Cherokee family's efforts to remain an extended family despite the pressures of mainstream Euro-American society.

Families in various cultures react to internal and societal changes with varying degrees of intensity. Sociocultural changes, the aging of the children of matriarchs and patriarchs, the birth of children and grandchildren, and the transient work and living patterns of family members contribute to the evolution of family life. Cultural differences are part of the multiculturality of the United States, but their maintenance in addition to individuals' and families' adaptability to Euro-American culture creates conflict. The dominant culture encourages the splintering of families into sub-units as children marry and have children. They become the family center while grandparents, great-grandparents, aunts, uncles, and cousins become less and less involved. This concept of non-extended family subsets is con-trary to the ideals of many cultures in this country, including that of the Cherokee.

The members of one Cherokee family—my family—managed to maintain an extended family. According to Bataille and Sand (1984), Indian women have kept up the old ways and passed them on in "measures they deemed appropriate in a changing society" (130). My Oklahoma Cherokee family has remained intact and experienced its own resurgence largely through the efforts of our oldest matriarch—"Mamaw." Mamaw was the Cherokee mother, grandmother, great-grand- mother, aunt, and great-aunt who, through her decisions regarding the family home, encouraged her family to remain together.

In an attempt to understand the efforts of my family, I have used the principles of a research methodology that my research partner and I have applied to intercultural ethnographic studies. This methodology examines the perspectives of people to identify major "sites of conflict" that create contention in organizational contexts such as media, commercial corporations, healthcare systems, government agencies, correctional institutions, cultural groups, and educational organizations (Shaver, in press; Shaver 1995). I sought answers to why this particular Cherokee family struggled to retain its extended family structure and how Mamaw succeeded where many contemporary Cherokee women had failed.

A House as Symbol, a House as Home

Before moving to Arkansas in the early 1800s, various branches of Mamaw's Cherokee family were ejected from the South before the enforced death march (the "Trail of Tears") that took the lives of more than 4,000 men, women, and children (Mankiller and Wallis 1993; Wright 1992). Later, as southern Cherokees were forced into what is now Oklahoma, many Arkansas Cherokees followed, as did our family. Ours was typical of many Cherokee families: its members married early, often in intermarriages with the Scots, Irish, and English; were poor with only basic educations in seasonal rural schools; were both traditional believers and Christian fundamental Protestants; had large families with extended relatives living together; were farmers who depended on family rather than outsiders; feared Euro-American authority and government; and were isolationists. The clan membership of Cherokees derives through the matrilineal line. Before the 1800s most children were raised by the mother and her brothers. Even today Cherokee mothers are honored and influential in family decisions and structure.

Mamaw was wooed by and married a young man of Scot-Irish descent. According to her, one of his most appealing qualities was that he was the first man she had ever known who did not carry a gun. Together they, along with Mamaw's mother and their nine children, made a move from the tents and sod houses of the rural area to a small town in a Cherokee-Creek county. They lived in several rented houses while Mamaw's husband—"Papaw"—sought employment as an auto mechanic. Because of Papaw's career in the new automobile industry, Mamaw's family was the first of her clan to leave the land and pursue nonagricultural lives.

Mamaw's life in a small Oklahoma town in the early twentieth century was very similar to the lives of her clan who lived in the country. She and her mother cooked and cleaned, used the traditional healing methods passed from mother to daughter for centuries, sewed the family's clothing, planted trees and a garden, and preserved and canned garden goods for the winter.

In 1935 Mamaw's dream was fulfilled when the family moved into a house of their own. When the Great Depression and the drought in the West and Midwest hit Oklahoma, Mamaw's extended family traveled to southern California to work in the orchards to cover their mortgage. After two years they returned home to rejoin the rest of their Oklahoma family. The mortgage was paid and they bought the blacksmith shop next to her husband's garage. Having survived the Depression, the family finally had a house and a home.

The house was small, a mere 1,000 square feet in size. Originally there were four rooms, without running water or an indoor bathroom. It had electricity, but heat was provided by a potbelly, coal-burning stove. Over time, indoor bath facilities and more rooms were added. Today the house is shaded from the severe Oklahoma summers by surviving elm trees, and flowers and bushes still bloom from Mamaw's many years of tending. The grape vines that she planted at age 90 have matured and the last tree that she planted in 1988 is now taller than the house.

Mamaw died four months before her 97th birthday. She had begun talking about her wishes for the house 10 years before her death. The following describes her decisions and the ensuing family responses.

The Family

When Papaw died in 1947 Mamaw remained the center of the family. Many families seem to reach a disengagement crisis when a parent dies, but Mamaw's family continued without major upset because of the sheer strength of Mamaw's actions. Her decisions resulted in a reunited and recognizable family unit that still exists today. As a middle-aged widow, Mamaw refused to consider remarriage, as her role as head of the family would have been altered by becoming the wife of an outsider. She continued persistently in the Cherokee role of clan mother, the sustainer of life through food and care giving, and the permanent keeper of the family history and its stories.

Mamaw appeared matronly, with her dark-colored clothes, bun-rolled hair, and lack of make-up—the stereotype of a doddering old woman. But this was hardly the case. Overcoming her fear of traveling, she flew by plane or rode by cross-country bus on a regular basis to visit her children in Virginia, Missouri, Arkansas, Arizona, Alaska, Wyoming, Texas, Oregon, and California. Though she preferred to live quietly in her own home, she became a traveling nanny, babysitter, nurse, and comforter to her children and grandchildren until her 93rd year. To remain the clan mother this stalwart Cherokee woman brought herself to her family when they were too far away to come to her.

Just as land is culturally vital to Native Americans (Mankiller and Wallis, 1993; Wright, 1992), so is home vital to the Cherokee woman. In her youth, Mamaw's first home was Indian allotment land that was stolen by a local physician when her mother was very ill. Mamaw long mourned the loss of what should have been her children's land. She and our family sometimes drove by the rural acreage where Mamaw described the tent they had lived in and shared with us her childhood memories.

Mamaw's hands-off style of hospitality always encouraged family members to gather at her house for succor, holidays, reunions, and peace. She never fussed over people, and the expectation was clear that either she would serve or you could serve yourself, because this was your home. The house became a refuge, a sanctuary, a time-out zone for any family member.

In Mamaw's later years, her family began comparing notes. Ironically each child, grandchild, and great-grandchild who had thought themselves to be Mamaw's best loved child soon discovered that every one of their cousins also felt they were her favorite. Some found to their surprise that they weren't the only 1960s cross-country refugees who got food, gas money, and a bath at Mamaw's. One traveling son-in-law always stayed with her even though his parents and many siblings lived in the same community. He sometimes had difficulty explaining to his own mother why he preferred to stay with Mamaw, a mother-in-law.

Formal family reunions continued after Papaw's death in 1947, though after 1964 various events seemed to prevent further group gatherings. In 1979 the oldest grandchild asked Mamaw if she would mind her organizing a family reunion. Typically, Mamaw replied that she wouldn't mind if the children would enjoy it. The result on July 4, 1981, was the first triennial all-family reunion. To this day more than 100 of Mamaw's Cherokee children and relatives still return from around the country to those special 4th of July reunions.

One of the results of these gatherings was that the generations of Mamaw's family who had given up their Cherokee identity became reacquainted with their nation, their clan, and their traditions. Mamaw, who had let family demands separate her from tribal matters since her youth, was taken by her youngest son in 1985 to the installation of Wilma Mankiller, the Principal Chief of the Cherokees. At the ceremony Mamaw was honored as the oldest living Dawes enrollee.[1] It was her homecoming to her Cherokee Nation.

After her death in 1990 some believed that the family would disintegrate. Because Mamaw was gone they feared that the reunions would end and that this would sever the Cherokee family connections. The remaining seven of Mamaw's nine children, however, knew differently. During her last 10 years of life Mamaw had talked to each of them about her plan for the house, the family, and the reunions.

With the approval of her children and their spouses, Mamaw made the decision to will the house and land to them. A provision of the will was that the home be left as it was: furnished, operational, and structurally maintained so that "if anyone needs it, it would be there as it always had been." The home would be the center of reunion for the family. The will also gave her children the option not to do so if they were not in total agreement. At any time the majority could vote to sell the house and all the children would share the revenue.

As word of this passed through the different generations of family members, the fears of family disintegration soon ended. And the reunions have continued. The 1995 reunion after Mamaw's death was as big an event as the 1992 gathering; another is planned for 1997. At various times of the summer family members still return "home" to Mamaw's house.

Today's House, Today's Family

Nothing remains the same. Mamaw's family is certainly different today than when she was alive; so are the reunions and so is the house. Yet the family is still Cherokee, the reunions continue, and the house is still home. It is the symbol of the family but not necessarily a shrine that must be kept inviolate. Inevitable changes have occurred without conflict.

One child who lived there for several months changed the wallpaper in Mamaw's bedroom. Another spent part of a summer there and painted the woodwork a different color. Rearrangement of the furniture seems to happen whenever anyone is in the house for more than a day. When someone stays at the house, various repairs are done. When specific repairs cost more than the small trust fund can cover, family members share the expense. However, no one has ever replaced the 1960s princess telephone that was a Christmas gift to Mamaw. Some things are sacred.

All the members of this Cherokee clan are family—because of Mamaw and this house. In 1996 one of Mamaw's great-grandsons, a 23-year-old university senior, wrote the following about his feelings toward Mamaw's house and provided some insight into the perspective of the youngest generation:

> Her [Mamaw's] house had always been the center of activity. . . . This in turn became the focal point in my mind of the . . . family. Being able to sit in the house where so many memories were established was a special feeling. I saw the chair where Mamaw . . . would sit and talk to us. I saw the items on the table beside the chair, which she used with her broken [arthritic and misshapen] beautiful hands. I walked through her bedroom and remembered her sleeping curled up on the bed. The kitchen was the same as always from the butterfly magnets on the fridge to the small table on the other side. The only difference was the cast present. Now instead of our immediate family there were many others who shared the love given and received from the home made by Mamaw. . . . When I mention home I do not refer to the wood and nails but rather to the concept of family which roots itself in such structures. Today, I do not pass through town without driving by the old little house, the center of my family.

The family continues to change through death and birth. One more of Mamaw's children has died since 1990, many great- and great-great-children have been born, two of her children have moved back to retire in their hometown, grandchildren are buying land close to the original Indian allotment, and the reunions continue. The house is changing architecturally. The need for a family symbol is still present, but the mutability of that symbol is evident. What will be interesting for me as a researcher and family member is to observe the transitions. Will there be a time when the house changes to such a degree that it is no longer the family symbol? As family members move back to retire, will another family member's home become the symbol? Will the family change so much that it is no longer recognizable as Mamaw's family? Or will the house continue as long as Mamaw's stories are told?

Family is defined by culture. Mamaw's Cherokee family needed to remain so even without Mamaw.

Note

1. The Dawes Commission was a federal plan for an Indian census that began in the late 1800s. Today the first Dawes Roll is still a part of the federal government's involvement in the labeling of who is a legal Cherokee. This involuntary enrollment of Cherokees and other nations remains a point of contention between the federal government and Native Americans.

References

Bataille, G. and Sand, K. (1984). *American Indian women: Telling their lives.* Lincoln: University of Nebraska Press.

Mankiller, W. and Wallis, M. (1993). *Mankiller: A Chief and her people.* New York: St. Martin's.

Shaver, L.D. (1995, August). The dilemma of human rights and commerce: Cultural conflict between U.S. and other transnational organizations. A paper presented at the Fifth International Conference for the Cross-Cultural Institute for Research, Harbin, China.

Shaver, L.D. (in press). The dilemma of Oklahoma Native American women elders: Traditional roles and sociocultural roles. In H. Noor Al-deen (Ed.), *Cross-cultural aging.* Hillsdale, NJ: Erlbaum.

Wright, R. (1992). *Stolen continents: The Americas through Indian eyes since 1492.* Boston: Houghton Mifflin. ✦

19

Communicating Good Luck During the Chinese New Year

Mary Fong
California State University, San Bernardino

In the city of Long Beach, California, in the early 1970s we were the only Chinese family in a predominantly Euro-American community. At the age of 10 I experienced reverse cultural shock when my family moved to Chinatown in Los Angeles. I had never before socialized with other Chinese girls and boys, and although I was a Chinese American I felt different from them. I did not know what being Chinese really was. On the other hand, I always knew I was Chinese and different in some respects from my classmates when I lived in Euro-American-dominated Long Beach.

Before long I developed friendships with my Chinese peers who welcomed me into their group. One 10-year-old girl among them advised me on do's and dont's during their celebration of the Chinese New Year. "Don't wash your hair on New Year's Day," she told me.

"Why?" I asked.

"It makes you look like a white lady, a white ghost. It's bad luck. Also, we don't clean our house, throw out trash, or sweep the floor on Chinese New Year's Day. It's bad luck. It's like throwing or sweeping your money away."

As a little girl, this brief conversation struck me as odd and intriguing. Reflecting today, however, I'm fascinated at how culturally rich this interaction was. This essay offers an insider's view of how the Chinese New Year holiday [which is considered the most significant holiday of the year] is celebrated and how "appropriate" and "inappropriate" communications during the Chinese New Year are linked to the Chinese concept of good and bad luck.

In the fifth grade at Castelar Elementary School in Chinatown, I drew and painted Chinese birds and dragons in celebration of the New Year. As a class we made a six-foot-long papier-maché dragon piñata, decorating it with fluffy orange and red tissue paper. Among my vivid memories of this holiday were the popular dragon and lion dances. Firecrackers were set off in the front of homes and businesses, a ritual performed to scare away evil spirits so that good luck would abound.

On New Year's day, I always looked forward to wearing brand new clothes to symbolize a new and fresh beginning. During the New Year celebration and on special happy occasions, it would be common to wear the color red to mean happiness and good luck. And I will never forget my parents and relatives' generous gifts of Chinese red envelopes with money enclosed, called *Lei sei*. I had heard that red *Lei sei* were given especially to children so that they would be protected from mythical dragons.

The dragon, along with 11 other animal signs of the Chinese horoscope are significantly linked to defining each new year. The Chinese horoscope and the new year holiday are based on the lunar calendar year rather than on the western solar calendar year; it can begin as early as January 21st or as late as February 19th. With each lunar year, according to legend, Buddha summoned all the animals to come to him before he departed from earth.

Each animal reigns throughout its respective year, and each year is influenced by the animal's unique characteristics. For example, February 16, 1999, to February 4, 2000, marks the ruling period of the rabbit. The rabbit corresponds to the Western astrological sign of Pisces, which rules from February 20th to March 20th. The year of the Rabbit is said to bring good luck through peace or at least a respite from conflict or war. Likewise, a person born in the year of the Rabbit will do everything within one's power to restore harmony or to retreat from a tension-filled scene. Simply put, the Rabbit leaps over the obstacles in one's path and recovers from calamities with striking resilience (Lau 1995).

Moreover, many people who follow the forecast of their Chinese animal signs will find a venue to seek information and advice regarding their luck and fortune for the coming new year, if it may be through a fortune teller or a horoscope book, similar to the western astrologists. The horoscope followers would be particularly interested in knowing if their animal sign this coming year will bring good luck in terms of getting married, having a child, starting a business, and other inquiries related to their circumstances. The animals ruling the year and the hour the person is born are believed to have a profound influence on one's personality and inquire about how well they will fare in a particular year that is ruled by an animal (Lau 1995). For instance, a fortune teller will perhaps begin a reading session describing general qualities about the inquirer's animal sign of the tiger, and then proceed to the hour one is born as a horse, and to other finer details of interest during the year of the rabbit. For instance, I was born in the year of the Dog and believe that I reflect the qualities of this animal.

Only 12 animals came to wish him farewell. As a reward, Buddha named a year after each animal in the order of its arrival. First came the Rat, then the Ox, the Tiger, Rabbit, Dragon, Snake, Horse, Sheep, Monkey, Rooster, Dog, and Boar.

Moreover, the animal ruling the year in which a person is born is believed to have a profound influence on one's personality and life (Lau 1979). For instance, I was born in the year of the Dog and firmly believe that I reflect the qualities of this animal. Generally, people born in the year of the Dog are honest, intelligent, and straightforward. They also have a deep sense of loyalty and a passion for justice, objectivity, and fairness. A Dog person is an open-eyed, open-minded observer interested in preserving social goals and guarding the interests of the public at large.

The Dog is neither materialistic nor ceremonious; he or she prefers plain talk and usually sees through people's motives (Lau 1995).

In terms of the hour I was born, I also have the qualities of the snake. The snake person is considered the deepest thinker and the enigma of all the Chinese horoscope animals (Lau 1995).

In every Chinese community around the world, the ruling animal of that year will be commercially marketed. In a variety of shops, consumers will see an assortment of pictures, sculptures, lanterns, kites, key chains, and so forth—all for the celebrators to create an ambiance of the reigning animal and the good luck that it brings.

The words *good luck* and *bad luck* have many meanings to the Chinese people. *Good luck* refers to good hope, health, or wealth, getting good news, and so forth. *Bad luck* means misfortune, loss of money, frustrations in business, evil people, poverty, premature death, sickness, discord, and so on. During the Chinese New Year holiday, my parents and relatives would repeatedly use the Cantonese words /hou^2 tsoi^2/, /hou^2 men^6/, or /hou^2 wen^6/, synonyms meaning *good luck.*[1] *Bad luck* is represented in Cantonese words pronounced as /ng^4 hou^2 tsoi^2/, /ng^4 hou^2 wen^6/, and /han^4 soey^1 wen^6/. The beliefs in good and bad luck underlie the use of this language, illustrated by five types of speaking rituals: Greetings and Wishes, Breaking an Object, Speaking Positively, Chinese New Year Foods, and Prosperity Food Rhymes (Fong 1992). Cantonese-speaking Chinese engage in these activities especially during the first three days to bring good luck and avoid bad luck throughout the coming year.

One popular greeting is *Gung Hay Fat Choy* ("May you have a happy and prosperous New Year"). This expression is said to bring good luck to both the giver and receiver. Other wishes usually refer to good health, wealth and fortune, abundance, and improvement. Expressions of good wishes are often written on red and gold paper called *fai chun* and attached to walls and doors, offering good fortune, wealth, health, and so forth. Also, the five blessings—old age, wealth, health, love of virtue, and a natural death—are written on fai chuns. These blessings are typically written in a poetic style, believed to possess the power to ward off evil influences (Williams 1976).

The Chinese avoid shattering any objects during the first three days of the New Year because this is believed to be a sign of bad luck. However, if an object is shattered by chance, the Chinese use two strategies to counteract the unfortunate incident. One way is to play with words and their meanings by the use of implied statements representing a positive idea. For instance, the unfortunate incident of breaking an object is transformed into a fortunate one when a person uses a positive verbal expression believed to counteract the negative occurrence so that a balance is reestablished. The Chinese expression /lok^9 dei^6 hoi^1 fa^1/ means "falling down to the ground, may the flowers blossom." The expression /fu^3 gwei^3 win^4 wa^4/ implies becoming prosperous and wealthy. Thus, when an individual drops some- thing and it shatters on the floor, it blossoms up at which point the person will acquire wealth.

The use of homonyms is another method for converting mishaps into positive events. Broken pieces are translated as /soey^3 dzo.^{2}// Soey^3/ sounds the same as another Chinese character, /soey^3/, meaning year. The expression /soey^3 soey^3 ping^4 on^1/ means peace in every year, *ping* referring to peace. Hence, broken pieces become peace in every year, and a negative act turns into positive good wishes by using homonyms.

Another luck ritual observed by the Chinese during this holiday is the avoidance of saying anything negative. Everyone is conscious of speaking positively, carefully avoiding any mention of such unlucky topics as death, sickness, or misfortune. It is believed that any negative utterances will bring bad luck in the coming year.

In her observations of a Cantonese-speaking family living in Mississippi, Gong (1994) reports that Chinese are highly accommodating during interactions, always courteously yielding on topics whether or not other speakers' comments may be interesting, logical, tasteful, or pertinent. The motive for this accommodating behavior is either to seek approval, demonstrate respect, allow others to perceive that they are respected or even superior to the speaker, or simply not to "make waves." In my own experience with Cantonese-speaking Chinese, however, we are far from accommodating on topics that are negative during the New Year celebration. Strategic options are quickly used if a speaker does say something negative. This listener may reply, /tou^3 heu^2 soey^2 dzoi^3 geng^2 gwa^3/, meaning "spit out your saliva and speak once more." Other expressions used for this situation include /tsoi^1/ or /tsoi^1 dai^6 get^7 lei^6 si^6/, which means "you are very lucky or very auspicious."

A variety of special foods and pastries are prepared especially for the celebration of the Lunar Chinese New Year, and they have a symbolic meaning related to good luck. The phonetic translation of fish, oysters, lettuce, tangerines, kumquats, and other foods possess the same or similar sounds as certain Chinese words that symbolize attributes of good luck. For example, "fish is symbolically employed as the emblem of wealth or abundance, on account of the similarity in the pronunciation of the word /yu/ (meaning superfluity) and also because fish are extremely plentiful in Chinese waters" (Williams 1976, 185). Using the international phonetic system, fish is /jy/.^{2} A similar sound, /jy/,^{4} means surplus, abundance, or excess.

Another example is *oyster*, pronounced in Cantonese as /hou^4 si/.^{2} A similar pronunciation, is /hou^2 si/,^{6} which means good things or good business. A dessert called /nin/^{4} /gou/ ^{1} has the same pronunciation, but it can also mean "to grow every year." The word *tangerine* is pronounced the same as *gold* or /gem/.^{1}

Jingles and rhymes also ring in the Chinese New Year, adding to a lighthearted atmosphere. One popular food rhyme, related to fish as a favorite and meaningful New Year's dish, is as follows:

/yau/^{3} /jy/,^{4} /yau/^{3} /jy/,^{4}

Having fishes, having fishes,

/nin/^{4} /nin/^{4} /yau/^{3} /jy/.^{4}

Every year, there is excess.

My annual experience of this holiday has enlightened me to the many examples of how spoken and unspoken communicative rituals and their cultural meanings are intertwined with the belief in luck. As a young girl new to the "foreign" world of Chinatown in Los Angeles, I discovered various ways of communicating during the Chinese New Year to avoid bad luck and to increase my good luck. Even today I avoid washing my hair, cleaning the house, sweeping the floor, or taking out the trash on New Year's Day.

Note

1. The international phonetic system is used instead of the transliteration or romanization of Cantonese words. The numbers refer to the nine various tones in the Cantonese language. I would like to thank Ho Shun Yee who provided the phonetic translation of the Cantonese characters. Ms. Ho is presently a doctoral candidate in Chinese language and literature.

References

Fong, M. (1999, December). 'Luck Talk' in celebrating the Chinese New Year. *Journal of Pragmatics*, (31).

Gong, G. (1994). When Mississippi Chinese Talk. In González, A., Houston, M. and Chen, V., (Eds.), *Our voices* (92–99). Los Angeles: Roxbury.

Lau, T. (1979). *The handbook of chinese horoscopes*. New York: Harper and Row.

Williams, C.A.S. (1976). *Outlines of Chinese symbolism and art motives* (3rd rev. ed.). New York: Dover. ✦

20

Hybrid Revivals

Defining Asian Indian Ethnicity Through Celebration

Radha S. Hegde
Rutgers University

Dancers swirl into the night as the music soars high with its rhythmic beat. The scene is the Edison District of Central New Jersey and the dancers in their colorful clothes are Asian Indians[1] celebrating *Navaratri*, the Hindu festival that signifies the cosmic victory of good over evil. To immigrants from the Indian subcontinent, the months of October and November are a special time of togetherness, the time for a community to renew its commitment to the traditions of the past. Every year the number of people who gather here to participate in this traditional folk dance grows dramatically. According to the organizers, the event is "the largest *Navaratri* celebration outside of India" (Goodnough 1995).

In contrast to the popularity of the event among Asian Indian immigrants, its celebration and music has met sharp resistance elsewhere. To other residents in the Edison area, the sounds of *Navaratri* are nothing more than a nuisance and perhaps more so a reminder of the intrusion of new immigrants who are redefining the locale. Each year, almost in sync with the music, there is a matching tempo of complaints registered to the police about the event from local residents. The ethnic organizers argue that the festival is in an area separated from the residential neighborhood by a highway. When they applied for a permit for their celebration in 1995, the Town Council of Edison clamped down with a list of restrictions, primarily that the festival should end promptly at two a.m. and take place only on Friday and Saturday nights. The council pushed for another provision that would allow it to shut down the event if the noise levels exceeded the limit three times, though this was dismissed by a federal judge in Newark. The celebration finally did take place amidst an atmosphere of tension and increased surveillance. The struggle and its conflicting interpretations continue from both sides of the ethnic divide.

This episode from New Jersey exemplifies some of the ways in which ethnic groups must negotiate their identity in the face of the external resentment of their presence. Migrants, says Rushdie (1991), must of necessity make a new, imaginative relationship with the world because of the loss of familiar habitats. Celebrations like *Navaratri* provide this connection and a sense of affirmation to immigrants, playing an important part in the process of redefining selfhood and establishing a sense of community in a new environment. The vivid display of the celebration is generally an active reconstruction of significant symbols from the past. Many of these events are centered around religious festivals.[2] Ethnic celebrations can also be interpreted as a way of asserting a cultural distinctiveness. To immigrants like myself, these are opportunities to enjoy being Indian and to savor the colors, clothes, tastes, and sounds of a home left behind.

The Asian Indian Experience

Traveling between cultural worlds constitutes the lived reality of the migrant experience (Lugones 1990). Questions of identity, home, and community emerge prominently in the experience of relocation and its ensuing displacement. In a world where one is painfully aware of being different, there is a constant sense among Asian Indian immigrants of having severed their connections, left marooned without roots. "Neither here nor there" is a typical refrain I hear from Asian Indians irrespective of how long they have stayed in this country. A persistent ambivalence surrounds this awareness of inhabiting the borderlands or the realm in between. Conflict and contradiction seem inevitable in the process of moving in and out of multiple cultural frames. As I talk to my friends in the Asian Indian community, I notice how our social locations are marked not only by the sudden loss of familiarity but by continuous reminders of one's status as the foreigner, the outsider, or the "other." Hence ethnic groups provide the space and opportunity to enact familiar scripts of interactions, prompting a spontaneity that contrasts one's self-conscious posturing in the world outside.

Immigrants from the Indian subcontinent are one of the fastest-growing Asian immigrant groups in the United States. Their major influx began after 1960 when changes in the immigration law permitted the entry of professionally trained people. This wave of Asian Indians was characterized by their high levels of education and professional attainments in scientific and technological fields.[3] Today the community has grown far beyond this small homogenous elite, their numbers now concentrated on the west and east coasts of the United States.

Asian Indians, like other ethnic groups, tend to be very conscious of their cultural heritage (Fisher 1980). Coming from a traditional culture which places great emphasis on communal links and kinship structures, these immigrants form tightly organized ethnic social bonds. Networks formed around commonalities such as language, place of origin, religion, and music have recaptured the social nuances experienced in the past. The proliferation of ethnic organizations is directly related to the diversity within the Indian community. Some of these organizations are attempting to create a unified Indian identity in the United States and provide a political voice for Asian Indians. More recently several Asian Indian feminist and gay groups with a strong activist agenda have become highly visible in major American cities. But clearly the main thrust of ethnic organizations has been the reinvention of traditional culture.

Religion and the presence of Hindu temples have become a central point to this process of cultural reproduction. These temples are the sites for the ritual participation of communal life, evoking connections to an ancient religiosity. Often old church buildings are renovated and redecorated on the inside to double as Hindu temples; other temples are constructed more lavishly to replicate the ancient ones of India. Asian Indian groups go to great lengths to raise money, commissioning artists and artisans from India to create sculptures and artwork for the new Hindu temples. Weekends often bristle with events and festivals in most Hindu temples across the United States. In addition to the regular religious rituals and ceremonies, temples provide the space and the focus for cultural activities, religion classes (even Hindu Sunday school), and musical events. The whole culture that develops around Hindu temples far transcends the mystical mantras chanted for the spiritual sustenance of immigrants in their new environment. The temples represent a space for the ethnic group to collectively reconnect with the celebratory symbols that bring India and Indianness to life.

The Inside/Outside View of Ethnic Celebration

Though separated from community, country and time,

A continuity exists,

Because of the imprints of experience brought forth by memory.

—Patanjali (Fourth Century AD)

The process of cultural relocation involves the complex negotiations of claiming a position in the present and reclaiming versions of the past. Memory plays an important role in the negotiation between past and present. As Ganguly (1992) writes, the past provides a crucial discursive terrain for reconsolidating selfhood and identity, especially for those whose present world has been rendered unpredictable as a consequence of the displacement caused by migration. The migrant experience is characterized by a sense of interruption and historical discontinuity. The isolation and alienation experienced by Asian Indians in the outside world intensify the disjuncture in the narrative of self that has already been created by cultural relocation. Ethnicity provides the essential thread to establish experiential and historical continuity in migrant lives.

However, it represents far more than a nostalgic preoccupation with the past. As Hall (1990) states, cultural identity is a matter of "becoming" as well as "being" and belongs to the future as much as to the past. Cultural identities, although grounded in history, are also constantly transforming and reproducing themselves. The narratives of identity have to move forward from the past to an anticipated and projected future. Asian Indian immigrants frequently articulate their anxieties about the future—will our children know about India and maintain their Indianness? The need to perpetuate tradition and carry significant cultural symbols into the future is the driving force behind the energy and zeal of ethnic celebrations.

The active production of ethnic culture can be seen as the process of shaping the discourse of ethnicity. This enterprise gains its momentum from the many ways by which the difference and dichotomy between "us" and "them" plays a significant role in the everyday lives of immigrants. As Rutherford (1990) writes, "Our struggles for identity and a sense of personal coherence and intelligibility are centered on this threshold between interior and exterior, between self and other" (24). The term *inside/outside* metaphorically captures the tensions and ambivalence of trying to establish one's presence as a minority group.

The dichotomy between the inner and the outer, one's home and the world at large, played an important role in the construction of nationalist identity in the wake of colonialism in India. Today these terms have a special resonance that helps to situate the meaning of celebration and ritual in an immigrant context from both a spatial and a philosophical perspective. The world represents the external, the domain of the material; the home is a symbolic extension of one's spiritual self (Chatterjee 1989). In the immigrant context the outside world represents an adaptation to Western norms and the pressures to assimilate. In contrast, the home represents a cultural oasis, a space for Asian Indians to practice and instill their own versions of proper "Indianness."

"I have always had a small shrine in my house where I pray," says my friend Mira. She tells me it is important that her son remember what it means to be an Indian. For example, on *Ganesh Chathurti*, the festival to celebrate the God of auspicious beginnings, the family shrine flourishes with flowers, lights, and incense, and the house comes alive with the sounds of Indian music and the chanting of Sanskrit prayers. Asian Indian parents are eager to teach these chants to their children, often driven by the passionate need to instill in their children the values that underlie these celebrations. Stories are told of ancient heroes and their virtues, of Hindu gods and goddesses. Tales are recounted of the celebration back home: "Do you know how many types of sweet delicacies your grandmother used to serve? 21, and each one was a specialty." The past appears as a mirage and dissolves into the fragrance that spirals up from the burning incense.

Deepavali, the festival of lights, occurs in late autumn. An Indian friend who lives in New Jersey tells me, "Ours is the only house all lit up at this time of the year." In India, the lamps are lit and the sounds of fireworks crackle in the air. Here the festival assumes a different public form. At South Street Seaport in New York City Asian Indian groups have orchestrated the event as an urban, ethnic spectacle. There are booths and stalls set up to display Indian handicrafts, folk art, dance, puppet shows, and, of course, food from all parts of India. Every year the event culminates in a public display of fireworks against the city skyline in honor of an epic hero from another time and another place altogether.

August brings another important day in the lives and histories of Asian Indians—the day India gained independence from Britain. Following other ethnic groups in New York City, Asian Indians have also established a tradition of floats and parades to celebrate the occasion during which various groups and ethnic businesses march with their displays. This public celebration assumes the grandeur of spectacle and pageantry, usually with an Indian movie star or celebrity acting as the Grand Marshall. Asian Indians are given the chance to experience their homeland as a simulacrum, a floating image, a collage of past and present, inside and outside. A veil of Indianness covers the city and at least momentarily the spectacle blends into the mosaic.

The Authentic Hybrid?

Celebration in the ethnic context involves an accurate recreation of the original event, so authenticity of representation becomes central to the production of this spectacle. To transplant a cultural aura, painstaking efforts are taken to create the perfect ambiance, capture the exact flavor, and acquire the right elements. Even as ethnic groups continue in their romanticization of the past, transatlantic productions assume a material form and identity of their own. In the process of imitating the original culture, Asian Indians translate and transform it, which involves an innovative mutation of both form and content. Their reinvention creates an interesting pastiche of symbols—a hybridization of cultural forms.

In 1994 a musical event in New York City's Central Park captured the magic of this blending of cultural forms. It was the first public performance of *Bhangra*, a hybrid Asian Indian musical form that is the current rage in Britain and is fast catching on among ethnic circles in the United States. *Bhangra* is a traditional rhythm from Punjab, a northern Indian state. Young Asian Indians have recreated *Bhangra* by fusing the traditional beat with a cosmopolitan flavor, resulting in the production of a vibrant new musical statement. In the world of migrants this hybrid blending is perhaps the only one that can truly claim any type of authenticity.

The celebration of weddings in the Asian Indian community is another interesting example of hybrid authenticity. I recently attended a wedding that took place in an elite hotel. As the guests arrived, there was a rustling pageantry of saris (the traditional dress worn by Indian women) in pure silk of many colors and hues. The wedding room was decorated with Indian motifs, Hindu priests chanted the marriage rites on a decorative stage reminiscent of those used by the maharajas of India, and the strains of classical Indian music wafted through the room. During the reception, however, the cultural pendulum swung in a different direction. A wedding cake is an ethnic variation that certainly does not exist in Hindu weddings in India. Dancing is not normally part of Indian wedding celebrations, but among the diaspora the *Bhangra* beat and Indian rock were vibrantly present. For the immigrants, the new aesthetic standard in planning these events lies in the right blend of East and West, the right *masala*.[4]

In the multicultural market, difference sells. Commodifying authenticity and marketing otherness for ethnic consumers is a thriving business. If you take a stroll down the Little Indias springing up in almost all major American cities, you will witness the spectacle of Indian ethnicity, the sensuous feel of a different space-time configuration. There are restaurants serving Indian delicacies from various parts of the country, sari shops, and ethnic video rental houses carrying every single film ever produced in Bombay. More recently there has been a visible growth in services that provide festival and celebration paraphernalia to the immigrant population. One-stop services for authentic celebrations are becoming very popular business ventures in the Little Indias. The packaging of culture includes everything from Indian-style floral decorations, traditional clothes and bridal make-up, and complete arrangements for Hindu weddings to vegetarian cakes for religious occasions and DJs offering the right combination of popular Indian music and Western rhythms. Often at Indian festivals I hear the statement, "You can be more of an Indian in America." Such a baffling pronouncement attests to the fact that to immigrants India represents an unchanging essence. The costumes and the staging serve as props for an eclectic production of the past.

Behind the Spectacle

Rushdie (1991) writes of a photograph of his family home in Bombay, a city he had left behind years ago. "The photograph had naturally been taken in black and white; and my memory, feeding on images as this, had begun to see my childhood in the same way monochromatically. The colors of my history had seeped out of my mind's eye. . . . " Rushdie continues poignantly, describing how much he desired to restore the past "not in the faded greys of family-album snapshots but whole, in Cinemascope and glorious Technicolor" (10).

To immigrants the evocation of the past provides an imaginary coherence to the experience of displacement and isolation. Celebrations become an awe-inspiring reproduction with displays that try to capture a distilled image of Indianness. To the individual immigrant and the ethnic group as a whole these celebrations are communicative statements to announce the presence and cementing of ethnic bonds. The experience of seeing oneself represented as the "other" makes immigrants feel highly speculative and anxious to construct narratives that connect their relationship to that "otherness." Celebrations are the illustrations that accompany this narrative.

Yet bicultural living is fraught with emotional stress, and celebrations that jumble up symbols can also spell shame, particularly to second-generation Asian Indians to whom India is often only a construct. Sheela Bhatt (1993) recalls some of those awkward moments of celebrations and ethnic realities:

> I have memories of doing strange things when my friends' families seemed to be following the normal American etiquette. For example, on Thanksgiving, we would eat Indian food, along with vegetarian stuffing, mashed potatoes and cranberry sauce. (Of course, we kids would have liked to have had a more traditional meal on Thanksgiving like all of our friends!) Or even worse, my brothers, with my father, once had to change their Brahmin sacred thread (in front of onlookers) on a beach in Santa Cruz. Every year they would change their thread on a certain day near a body of water—whether it was an ocean, lake, pond or even a stream. Unfortunately, that year the closest body of water was one of the biggest tourist beaches in California. It was a totally humiliating sit-

uation for my brothers and me, but my father didn't even notice. (317)

The gaze from the outside that demarcates differences as weird, strange, and deviant takes a wrenching toll on the construction of immigrant subjectivity. The intergenerational dynamics of this issue are even more complex. In this culturally varied and relational constellation, Asian Indians (like most migrants) engage in frequent questions about their transplanted locations. The experience of cultural displacement from relocation destabilizes one's sense of belonging and community, the basic structures of subjectivity. Ethnicity provides the antidote. For Asian Indians weekends crammed with ethnic social events and celebrations provide a significant thematic coherence in their otherwise fragmented experiences of cultural change.

As we return to the scene of the *Navaratri* celebration, the dancers are still swirling away but it is now two a.m. and the festivities have to stop. With an almost Cindarella-esque urgency they leave and speed away down the New Jersey highways back to reality.

Notes

1. *Asian Indian* is the term created by the U.S. census in 1985 to refer to Asian immigrants from South Asia: India, Pakistan, Sri Lanka, Bangla Desh, Nepal, and Bhutan.

2. The religious festivals described here are Hindu traditions. Although the majority of Indians are Hindus, India is a land of many religions.

3. For studies on the acculturation patterns of Asian Indians in the United States, see Helweg and Helweg, 1990; Saran and Eames, 1985.

4. *Masala* is a term used in Indian cooking to denote an aromatic mixture of spices.

References

Bhatt, S. (1993). To Motiba and grandma. In women of South Asian collective (Eds.), *Our feet walk the sky: Women of the South Asian diaspora* (315–319). San Francisco: Aunt Lute Books.

Chatterjee, P. (1989). Colonialism, nationalism and colonialized women: The contest in India. *American Ethnologist*, 16(4), 622–633.

Fisher, M.P. (1980). *The Indians of New York City: A study of immigrants from India*. New Delhi: Heritage.

Ganguly, K. (1992). Migrant identities: Personal memory and the construction of selfhood. *Cultural Studies*, 6(1), 27–50.

Goodnough, A. (1995, October 1). Indian celebration draws happy throngs and complaints. *New York Times*, Section 13, 6.

Hall, S. (1990). Cultural identity and diaspora. In Rutherford J., (Ed.), *Identity, community, culture, difference* (222–237). London: Wishart.

Helweg, A.W. and Helweg, U.M. (1990). *An immigrant success story: East Indians in America*. Philadelphia: University of Pennsylvania Press.

Lugones, M. (1990). Playfulness, "world"-traveling and loving perception. In Anzaldúa, G., (Ed.), *Making face, making soul: Creative and critical perspectives by feminists of color* (390–402). San Francisco: Aunt Lute.

Patanajali. (Fourth Century AD). The yoga sutras. In Prasada, R. (1924), *Sacred books of the Hindus*. Allahabad: Panini Office.

Rushdie, S. (1991). *Imaginary homelands*. New York: Penguin.

Rutherford, J. (1990). A place called home: Identity and the cultural politics of difference. In Rutherford, J., (Ed.), *Identity, community, culture, difference?* (9–27). London: Lawrence and Wishart.

Saran, P. and Eames, E. (Eds.) (1985). *The new ethnics: Asian Indians in the United States*. New York: Praeger. ✦

Part V

Valuing and Contesting Languages

21

Identity and Struggle in Jamaican Talk

Dexter B. Gordon
University of Alabama, Tuscaloosa

And so Ashanti, Congo, Yoruba, all that mighty coast of western Africa was imported into the Caribbean. And we had the arrival in our area of a new language structure. . . . [O]fficially the conquering peoples—the Spaniards, the English, the French, and the Dutch—insisted that the language of public discourse and conversation, of obedience, command and conception should be English, French, Spanish or Dutch. They did not wish to hear people speaking Ashanti or any of the Congolese languages.

—Brathwaite (1984, 7)

Talk is central to Caribbean life. In the above epigram Edward Kamu Brathwaite (1984) captured not only the centrality of talk to Caribbean life but the historical locus of its contentiousness as well. Brathwaite contended that Caribbean people value orality because we live in the open air often in conditions of poverty, and because we come from a historical experience that has forced us to rely on our very *breath* rather than on paraphernalia like books and museums and machines (19). Jamaicans can be readily distinguishable by their talk. Like many other nationalities, they share common cadences, intonations, and accentuations unique to their country. In both what they say and how they say it, Jamaicans demonstrate their consciousness of orality and of its important role in their sense of being in the world.

A cursory look at Jamaicans and their talk can provide insights into the people of this largest English-speaking Caribbean nation, who number just over 2.5 million and who live on 4,411 square miles of what Columbus discovered in 1494 to be "the fairest island eyes have beheld."[1] Over one million other Jamaicans live outside Jamaica, primarily in the United States. Regardless of where they reside, Jamaicans' identity and experiences are revealed through their talk, as we shall explore.

Background

In *Beyond a Boundary,* C.L.R. James (1976) aptly described Caribbean people as living at the intersection of Europe and Africa in the new world. We are a people born in the cultural cross-current created when the marauding presence of the white supremacist spirit of Europe met the enslaved yet stubborn, unyielding spirit of Africa.[2] Consequently, we have always negotiated a multiplicity of cultures, including the dominating cultures of our European enslavers and colonizers as well as the dominated cultures of our African ancestors.

Such a scenario makes for a Caribbean history that includes "degradation, mimicry, violence, and blocked possibilities." Even so, Caribbean people are "rebellious, syncretic, and creative" (Clifford 1988, 15).[3] We are constantly manipulating "vitality, elan, and creativity into a viable sense of identity" (Lowenthal 1972, xiii).

As a people we have had to establish for ourselves survival mechanisms, including thriving with less than adequate resources, or in Jamaican terms, you *tun yu han an mek fashion.* This is in the face of a colonial culture, in Jamaica, which declared inferior what was local while coupling blackness with subordination and whiteness with supremacy. For colonial Jamaica, and in many instances also for post-colonial Jamaica, what Rex Nettleford (1989, 293) called "the imperial metropole" has been the center of culture, "high culture." Mimicry of things English, and later things American, and degradation of indigenous products and practices have been commonplace.

141

Still, it is important to note that as early as 1938, Jamaica sought to guide the development of its people's creative energies. And, as Nettleford (1989) did point out, Jamaica has been outstanding for its support of cultural development. Yet, as Richard Small contended in 1969, advancement in Jamaica was "determined by how non-black the blackest" of us could be (8). As a result, many Jamaicans rebelled against the degradation of everything black and local and adopted a creative mode of struggle for survival for their own sense of selfhood and dignity.

This creativity is evident in Jamaica's eclectic cultural practices including religion, entertainment, and other practices of socialization such as storytelling (Cooper 1993). In entertainment, for example, Jamaica's creativity was demonstrated in early, local cultural productions like Mento and Ska, the precursors of Rock Steady and Reggae music. Mento and Ska gained government support and international acceptance only after disinherited black Jamaicans embraced them and showed that there was an audience, in Britain as well, for this music (Small 1969). In this regard, Michael de Certeau's celebration of the inventiveness of North Africans living in France, in *The Practice of Everyday Life* (1984), is equally applicable to Caribbean people in general and Jamaicans in particular, that is, in the practice of their daily survival "art of making do" (30). Our focus is Jamaican talk.

Jamaicans are known for telling elaborate tales among themselves about themselves. The well-documented Anancy stories are the preeminent forms employed by Jamaican raconteurs to weave their particular vision of the epic struggles of Jamaican life. These anecdotes often reflect the ancient practice valorized and identified by the Sophists as *metis*, practical and cunning intelligence deployed as part of the effort to survive in the borderlands—the terrain between the legitimized and the delegitimized (Conquergood 1992). This domain includes issues of race, identity, and local culture, all highly contested in both colonial and post-colonial Jamaica. Here Jamaicans employed day-to-day tactics to contest the strategies employed by the dominant pow-

ers from the white supremacist slave powers to the present. I use the terms *tactics* and *strategies* here, following de Certeau (1984), to point to the daily survival feats of Jamaicans as based on their acting at the opportune time in each given situation in contrast to the colonial regime's strategy: the assumption of "a place that can be circumscribed as *proper* (xix)." Surviving in this realm of instability and uncertainty, under the panoptic gaze of a dominant colonial regime and among its locally appointed vassals, required special skills. Jamaicans developed such skills and survived slavery and colonialism by their wits and their rhetorical skills as evidenced in their talk. Surviving and thriving in this environment is no easy task, for as Carolyn Cooper inveighs, "social mobility in Jamaica requires the shedding of the old skin of early socialization: mother tongue, mother culture, mother wit—the feminised discourse of voice, identity and native knowledge" (Cooper 1992, 2–3).

Struggle and Identity in Jamaican Talk

Talk is an area in which Jamaicans demonstrate their particular brand of struggle and survival through creative energy and a sense of independence mixed with syncretic tendencies. Jamaica's official language is English. However, this description is like the eye of a Caribbean hurricane revealing nothing of the swirling winds of linguistic fury that remains Jamaica's battle over language. Jamaicans' use of English reflects both a clash of cultures and linguistic traditions and an awareness that English is an imposed language. As a result, there are various types of English spoken in Jamaica and throughout the Caribbean. Brathwaite (1984) identified standard English, Creole English (a Caribbean adaptation involving a mixing of English and other imported languages), and "nation language" or Jamaican (before that referred to as *Patois* "the language of slaves and labourers") (5–6). We will discuss each of these with a focus on Jamaican.

The way a Jamaican uses or "mis-uses" standard English is a common indicator of class.[4] Educated Jamaicans, often from the middle and upper class, take great pride in their mastery of standard English and often contend to be the best speakers of the language. George Lamming, of Barbados, for example, spoke for many Caribbean people when he claimed, "I can read verse much better than most English poets alive. That is a fact. And I read it [in London] exactly as I would have done in the West Indies" (Lamming 1960, 62).[5] Such a position provides a useful corrective to notions of superiority in anglocentric thought. Unfortunately, however, it also represents in many instances a flight from the local, the "low class," and a reaching for one of the markers of English pedigree—the mastery of English. People living in the Caribbean who embrace this practice are often like the early C.L.R. James (1976); "intellectually [they] live[d] abroad, chiefly in England (65)." This effort to demonstrate a mastery of the "Queen's English" is also fraught with perils, as failed attempts result in embarrassment and sometimes in a loss of social standing.

Creole English results in part from the mixing of English with other imported languages. However, a failed attempt at standard English also typically results in Creole English or what is referred to as broken English with its odd mixtures.[6] To a Jamaican ear the result is often hilarious with such linguistic slippage as *the* changed to *de, this* changed to *dis,* and several word endings lost in the shuffle. The tourist guides who meet visitors at the Donald Sangster International airport in Montego Bay or at Norman Manley in Kingston are using a funny mix of English and Jamaican when they say "welcome to Jamaica, falla backa wi."

Many Jamaicans have an aspirate problem which often emerges in our effort to speak English. The result is random disappearances and random appearances of *h*s in our talk, with *he* becoming *e, every* becoming *hevery,* and *always, halways.* Such slippages happen especially when we are trying to be, in Jamaican terms, "speaky spokey," i.e., to speak the English language with a flair beyond our abilities. Such performances often evoke snickers in public gatherings and hilarious laughter in their retelling in private settings.

While English is Jamaica's official language, an overwhelming majority of Jamaicans talk Jamaican. This is variously referred to as the language of the streets, the language of the people, Jamaican folk language, or just Jamaican. This speech has been documented by Frederic Gomes Cassidy (1961) in *Jamaica Talk;* its vocabulary has been catalogued, if not legitimized, for the literary community by Cassidy and R.B. Le Page (1980) in the *Dictionary of Jamaican English;* and it has been popularized by Jamaican poets and musicians. Cassidy and Le Page described this folk speech as Jamaican English, a creole language; "an amalgam of some features of English with others drawn from a variety of African languages" (xiii). However, despite Cassidy and Le Page's substantial orthography, it was through Bob Marley's Reggae music that the language gained popular international exposure. And, at home, in Jamaica, the chief proponent of Jamaican speech and the person perhaps most responsible for popularizing this language is leading Jamaican poet Louise Bennett. In her use of the Jamaican language, Louise Bennett is nonpareil.[7]

Bennett has written (*Jamaican Dialect Poems* 1947) of "the free expression of the people," a mode of utterance which is "unhampered by the rules of (Standard English) grammar" (Bennett [1966] 1975, 9). She consciously eschews and even undermines such rules. Jamaican poet Dennis Scott contends that Bennett is the "only poet who has hit the truth about the society in its own language" (9). Nettleford described her as a poet of utterance who uses "the normally *spoken* language, not the normally *written* tongue" (11). He noted further that she lives "in an oral tradition where people talked and listened, cross-talked and reported and posses [*sic*], almost to a fault, a high propensity for words—'bad' words, new words, archaic words, 'big,' long, and sonorous words" (11). Jamaican language, then, reflects Jamaicans' love for talk and their desire and willingness to throw off and often mock the official language. The development and usage of Jamaican language is being increasingly recognized for what it is, a protracted resistance and survival effort dating back to the arrival of the Ashanti. Cooper, for example, describes the writings of Bennett and other popular Jamaican poets Jean Breeze and Mikey Smith as "cultural resistance to the hegemony of anglocentricism" (Cooper 1993, 9).

Jamaica has a black majority which has long been marginalized. In this regard the country is more like South Africa than like the United States. As Nettleford notes, "the class structure underlined in colour, continue(d)[s] to appear immutable" (Nettleford 1989, 3). That is, the Jamaican language is usually associated with the lowest economic class. Further, the Jamaican body politic is marked by a "high/low-euro/afrocentric cultural divide" (Cooper 1993, 8). Indeed, if one is able to use only Jamaican with no efficacy in standard English, this is usually a clear marker of a lack of formal education. (However, following the radical effects of Rastafarian influences on Jamaican talk, individual Jamaicans are declaring in their talk a conscious rejection of standard English.) On the other hand, any Jamaican who uses standard English exclusively and is unable or unwilling to use Jamaican is seen as disrespecting Jamaica. Such a person would be identified in Jamaica as culturally deficient and lacking a practical language skill necessary for survival. The ability to perform with competence in both standard English and Jamaican is a highly valued educational achievement in Jamaican life.

A competent Jamaican speaker is not only bilingual, but must also be able to move dextrously between the planes of standard English and Jamaican. The emphasis here is on vocal performance, with orthography being perhaps the most difficult aspect of the development of the Jamaican language. Nettleford contends that "the rhythms and sounds [of the spoken language] are obscured by problems of orthography" (Bennett [1966] 1975, 12). And, Brathwaite (1984) argues that "when it is written, you lose the sound or the noise, and therefore you lose part of the meaning" (17). Thus Jamaican, a spoken language, is seldom read or written by Jamaicans. (This does not reveal with certainty whether they are not able or rather have chosen not to.)

Speech and phonality, then, are critical to the Jamaican identity.[8] Similarly, the use of Jamaican is not just a function of the lack of a formal education. It is a political act, an act of resistance against a cultural imperialism that constructed a Caribbean educational system reflecting the language and heritage of the English and rejecting the various African and Amerindian languages that were part of the region's culture (Brathwaite 1984). For example, focusing on Rastafari talk, Malika Lee Whitney (Hussey and Whitney 1984) notes, and Carolyn Cooper (1993) endorses, that, the "Rastafari way of speaking or 'reasoning' is not illiteracy as some would have you believe, but the tailoring of the European language for most identifiable self-expression" (115; 121). Rastafarian poet Bongo Jerry, (1970/71), like other Jamaican artists, intentionally misuses what he would call Babylonian English to contend,

Save the YOUNG

from the language that MEN teach,

the doctrine Pope preach

skin bleach. . .

MAN must use MEN language

to carry dis message:

SILENCE BABEL TONGUES:
recall and

recollect BLACK SPEECH.

  —Bongo Jerry (13–15)

And Louise Bennett ([1966] 1975) is polemical in her "Bans O' Killing."

So yuh a de man, me hear bout!

Ah yuh dem sey dah-teck

Whole heap o? English oat sey dat

Yuh gwine kill dialect

Meck me get it straight Mass Charlie

For me noh quite understan,

Yuh gwine kill all English dialect

Or just Jamaica one?

Ef yuh dah-equal up wid English

Language, den wha meck

Yuh gwine go feel inferior, wen

It come to dialect?

   —(218–219)

And, perhaps most pointed is the contention of a Jamaican mail carrier who sought to affirm Cooper in her work on the Jamaican language by noting that this language "ful de speis of our rial Afrikan langgwij": "It fills the space of our real African language" (Cooper 1993, 13). Cooper's *Noises in the Blood*, which builds on the works of Bennett, Mervyn Morris, Mervyn C. Alleyne, Brathwaite, Nettleford, and others, should go a long way in putting to rest notions of Jamaican folk talk as being the result of ignorance.[9] If, for example, you find any of the above impenetrable, interpret this as an invitation to learn this new language and join Jamaicans in a mutually liberating act of struggle for liberation and self-identity (Cooper 1993).

Jamaica Talk and Jamaican-American Relationships

Because the United States is the leading place of abode for Jamaicans outside Jamaica, it is important to consider how Jamaican talk affects Jamaican-American interpersonal relationships in the United States. In Jamaica, Jamaican speech is interpreted as a marker of class and education, distinguishing Jamaicans from other Jamaicans and from the English. But in the United States, this speech further demarcates Jamaicans from all others becoming even more significant in issues of race, class, and ethnic identity. Outside of Jamaica, sheer necessity forces Jamaicans to use the more internationally known English language, as compared to Jamaican, which is recognized but not known internationally. Nonetheless, the English spoken by Jamaicans is an English with a Jamaican sound. In the context of the United States, then, the Jamaican sound and accent produce salient markers, and they are easily distinguishable from other

U.S. speech sounds and accents. Consequently, for Jamaicans in the United States, their accent is like a Spanish machete—it cuts both ways.

Claude McKay (1937; Watkins-Owens 1996) revealed that a Jamaican identity can have advantages for black Jamaicans wishing to advance in the race conscious United States. The "native accent" is one sure way to establish a special identity (8–9). And James Weldon Johnson's experience confirmed that to be foreign-born, or even to be mistaken as being foreign-born, could result in blacks being spared the harsh discriminatory practices reserved for U.S.-born blacks (Johnson 1969, 65). This is also chronicled in Booker T. Washington's 1900 classic *Up From Slavery*.

However, for the most part, race and foreign-born status, with its attendant issue of accent, remain the double jeopardy faced by black Jamaicans who emigrate to the United States (Watkins-Owens 1996). This situation can be illustrated through the experience of my two daughters. Between 1990 and 1992 they were in public schools in the Midwest. One attended elementary school and the other, middle school. My older daughter experienced the double jeopardy of racial and ethnic discrimination. She faced racial discrimination from white schoolmates, and both blacks and whites teased her because of her Jamaican accent. Both daughters faced discrimination because of their accent when, on the premise of "deficiency in their [English] language skills," school authorities tried to place our children in ESL programs. We objected. And, as we were to find out later, these ESL proposals were made on the basis of the children's accent. The proposals became moot after both children easily passed their English comprehension tests.

The case of our younger daughter was particularly interesting for, as it turns out, her educational challenge was not her own accent but the accent of her Euro-pean-American teacher. When she heard the teacher say *binana*, my 7-year-old daughter spelled *banana* accordingly and insisted, against all our efforts to the contrary, that the word was *binana* because that was what the teacher had said. The case of *binana v. banana* has become a family joke. In preparing this essay, I asked my daughter (now age 15) to verify my account of the ESL issue. She recalled that the word *water* caused similar confusion. To her ears, the teacher kept referring to *wader*. It was left to us at home to clarify that this was just how the teacher talked, but that the word should be spelled *w-a-t-e-r*.

It is important to note that Jamaicans are forced to reckon with the dominant U.S. accent at every turn.[10] First, there were U.S. Armed Forces radio broadcasts, and, until the end of the 1980s, radio was the major source of news in the English-speaking Caribbean. The British Broadcasting Corporation (BBC), nevertheless, was the primary source of international news information. With an increasing number of households getting television sets and with the proliferation of the satellite dish, however, American television and CNN became the primary news sources.

The double jeopardy of discrimination has long been a scourge for Caribbean immigrants to the United States, often resulting in tentative and awkward relationships with Americans, both black and white. As Irma Watkins-Owens (1996) tells us, Viola Scott Thomas, who arrived as a child in 1920 from Barbados, remembered being mocked by African Americans because of her accent. *Monkey chaser* was the derisive term used by blacks in Harlem to taunt Garvey and his followers and generally to describe black immigrants from the Caribbean (Bontemps and Conroy 1966). The derisive Harlem ditty rhymed, "When a monkey chaser dies, he don't need no undertaker. Just throw him in the Harlem river. He'll float back to Jamaica" (Cronon 1955, 168).

As we know from Paule Marshall's ([1959] 1981) *Brown Girl, Brownstones,* white American women who employ Caribbean women as household workers are known to speak of their efficiency, reliability, and honesty. In my own encounter with white men and women who employed Caribbean women, they often speak in glowing terms about the competence and reliability of these women. Such compe-

tence and reliability, of course, are in contrast to unidentified others. As Marshall has noted, such expressions by these whites are often part of an "insidious divide and rule encouragement" (Bryce-Laporte 1981, 7; Watkins-Owens 1996, 51). And Marsha Houston (1994) picked up on this tactic, demonstrating that it is also used by white women to divide African American women into categories of "acceptable" and "unacceptable" (137). *Brown Girl, Brownstones* deals with Caribbean immigrants in the first half of the twentieth century; however, the practice, by white Americans, of declaring to Caribbean immigrants that they are "different" continues as a common contemporary phenomenon. I heard declarations of my "difference" before I knew that this difference was as compared to those considered as the problem in American society—African Americans. These comments were often accompanied by references to my ability to "speak so well."

Here, my ability to speak standard English becomes that which marks me as better than whites expected of a "black Jamaican" and different from (read superior to) U.S.-born blacks. Troublingly, these expressions are tendered as sincere compliments, often with a lack of consciousness of their racist undertones. The perspectives of difference and superiority embraced by many Caribbean people evidence the success of such divide and rule strategies—albeit often unconscious ones. As Marshall informs us, Caribbean women often see themselves as "different," "superior," "more ambitious," and "more hard working" than African Americans (Bryce-Laporte 1981, 7; Watkins-Owens 1996, 51–52).

African Americans, too, have imbibed the notion that black people from the Caribbean are "different." Some African Americans join those white Americans who focus on the foreign-born status of Caribbean immigrants, labeling them as intrusive outsiders. The way that Caribbean people talk is often featured and derided when this "difference" is high-lighted. Marcus Garvey is the most notable example from the early twentieth century; however, C.L.R. James and later

Kwame Toure (Stokely Carmichael) are other examples of leading Caribbean immigrants whose foreign-born status became the focus of their American detractors (*New York Age* 1920; Watkins-Owens 1996, 81). Developments such as these, with their focus on difference, used ethnicity to destabilize the racial solidarity shared by blacks from the Caribbean as well as those from the United States. The problem is both longstanding and divisive.

In 1923, W.A. Domingo, a Jamaican migrant who became well known as a Harlem radical, editor, and businessman, as contributing editor to the *Messenger*, chided the newspaper for its nativism and ethnic bias expressed against Marcus Garvey and other black people from the Caribbean living in the United States (Hill 1983). Domingo (1823; Watkins-Owens 1996) contended that the *Messenger*'s hostility would eventually "make the life of West Indians among American Negroes as unsafe or unpleasant as the life of American Negroes among their white countrymen (640; 122).

Yet, whether it is Robert Campbell, Grace P. Campbell, Claude McKay, Amy Jacques-Garvey, Marcus Garvey, J.A. Rogers, Bob Marley, Shabba Ranks, Orlando Patterson, or Colin Powell, Jamaican migrants continue to have a significant impact on U.S. culture with their unique brand of activism and social consciousness, articulating black struggle with international class struggle and specifically connecting American black interests to Caribbean interests (Watkins-Owens 1996; Delany and Campbell 1969). Such articulation often incorporates all the flair of the Jamaican language with its distinctive accent, adding to the rich mix of speech patterns already practiced in the United States.

Conclusion

Jamaican language provides its speakers a sense of identity, comfort, and shared solidarity. It bestows a feeling of uniqueness, especially in the face of the alienating function of the dominant, main- stream Euro-American culture. Jamaicans living in the United States conduct their private conver-

sations, with family or with Jamaican friends, in their local language and sometimes in a mixture of Jamaican and standard English.

In their language Jamaicans find contact with a shared world and ready access to important aspects of that world. The word *irie*, for example, is understood by Jamaicans as a greeting of goodwill, a commentary on the state of one's being, and a cultural celebration of the inventiveness of the marginalized. *Irie* emerged out of the Jamaican Rastafarian subculture. To describe everything as *kosher* comes closest to the idea of everything *irie*.

The use of this nation language is a collective tactic. The tactic is employed to survive external domination while creating a world of integrity and relevance through language. This is a language that functions for the Jamaican today similar to the way it functioned for the Ashanti brought to the Caribbean in slaveships. It disguises the personalities of the users as it conserves aspects of their (Jamaican) culture. In the face of crises or difficult situations, Jamaicans in the United Staes abandon standard English and communicate in their nation language or their mother tongue, if you will. Also at gatherings where we feel the need for a sense of solidarity, we speak to each other exclusively in Jamaican. This usage excludes those who do not share our cultural marker. We do this because we know that the language is inscrutable to outsiders. And, of course, we know that "one culture's 'knowledge' is another's 'noise'" (Cooper 1993, 4).

My amateur soccer team is made up of players from several different countries, including players from several African countries. Sometimes when tempers flare, the Africans communicate with each other in French or a select African language. That is usually a signal for my Jamaican teammate and me to begin talking to each other in Jamaican, abandoning English, the language shared in common by the entire group. At such times, I take on a new personality and my children often gasp, "Dad, is that you?" This is a sure sign that I continue to live in the Caribbean cross-current. I am a product of English (and now

American), African, neither, yet both—a new being.

Notes

1. A. Bernaldez, a Spanish historian, tells us that in 1494 Columbus saw Jamaica and declared, "It is the fairest island eyes have beheld," cited in "Geography and History of Jamaica," Gleaner, 25 June 1999 (http://www.discover jamaica.com/gleaner/discover/geography/geography.htm).

2. *Beyond a Boundary* is James' treatise on the cultural influences of cricket on Britain and its colonies in the West Indies. This text explores the various elements of race, class, and education as just some of the socio-cultural problematics involved in the acculturation of Caribbean people to this most British of games, cricket. In more direct terms, C.L. Springfield (1990) cites her interview with James where he makes the explicit argument that Caribbean people function on the cusp of this intersectionality between Europe and Africa (85).

3. It should be noted that a Jamaican identity focused on its more than 95 percent black population has not been without contention. Despite gaining independence from Britain in 1962, until the mid-1970s, Jamaica was still a place where there was "official hostility to the consciousness of being black" (Rodney 1975, 8). Such hostility, though no longer official, still lingers. And the claims of some black Jamaicans today that "a black man [sic] time now" points to an awareness that the vestiges of slavery, colonialism, and racism are yet to be overcome.

4. All this must be read with the awareness that the evolution of the English language itself is largely an arbitrary process. As R. Williams ([1953] 1983) notes: "The dialect which is normally equated with standard English has no necessary superiority over other dialects" (322). And the conversion of arbitrary sounds and uses into a category of "'good' or 'correct' or 'pure' English is merely a subterfuge" (322).

5. Brathwaite (1984) describes Lamming as "our Milton of the Caribbean" (22).

6. Here I take some liberties with Brathwaite's depiction of Creole English. He might see the mixing of English with other imported languages as being more intentional than my depiction (Brathwaite 1984, 5).

7. Louise Bennett's work extends more than fifty years and is chronicled in Bennett 1947; Bennett 1957; and Bennett [1966] 1975 as well as various anthologies.

8. There is an ongoing debate concerning the role of language in the Caribbean and the place of "dialect," "creole," and "nation languages." See the bibliography in Brathwaite (1984, 51–68). I note G. Rohlehr's caution against demonizing or sentimentalizing this form of speech, as part of this debate (Brown, Morris, and Rohlehr 1989, i). Like Brathwaite, I prefer the term *language* to *dialect* because *dialect* carries "pejorative overtones. Dialect is thought of as 'bad English.' Dialect is 'inferior English'" (Brathwaite, 13).

9. It is worth noting that M.K. Asanti ([1987] 1998) attempts similarly to highlight the integrity of Ebonics.

10. I do not wish to suggest here that there is a single U.S. accent. I am referring to the speech that dominates American media.

References

Alleyne, M.C. (1980). *Comparative Afro-American: An historical-comparative study of English-based Afro-American dialects of the new world*. With a Foreword by I. Hancock. Ann Arbor: Karoma.

Asante, M.K., [1987] 1998. *The Afrocentric idea*. Revised and Expanded Edition. Philadelphia: Temple University Press.

Bennett, L. (1947). *Jamaican dialect poems: Miss Lou Sez*. Kingston, Jamaica.

——. (1957). *Anancy stories and dialect verse*. Kingston, Jamaica: Pioneer.

——. [1966](1975). *Jamaica labrish: Jamaican dialect poems*. With Notes and Introduction by R. Nettleford. Reprint Kingston, Jamaica: Sangsters.

Bontemps, A. and Conroy, J. (1966). *Anyplace but here*. New York: Hill and Wang.

Brathwaite, E.K. (1984). *History of the voice: the development of nation language in Anglophone Caribbean poetry*. London; Port of Spain: New Beacon.

Brown, S., Morris, M. and Rohlehr, G., (Eds.) (1989). *Voiceprint: An anthology of oral and related poetry from the Caribbean*. Kingston, Jamaica: Longman.

Bryce-Laporte, R. (Ed.) (1981). *Female immigrants to the United States: Caribbean, Latin American, and African experiences*. Washington, DC: Smithsonian Research Institute on Immigration and Ethnic Studies.

Cassidy, F.G. (1961). *Jamaica talk*. London: Macmillan.

Cassidy, F.G. and Le Page, R.B., (Eds.) (1980). *Dictionary of Jamaican English*. Cambridge; New York: Cambridge University Press.

Clifford, J. (1988). *Predicament of culture*. Cambridge, MA: Harvard University Press.

Conquergood, D. (1992). Ethnography, rhetoric, and performance. *Quarterly Journal of Speech* 78, 80–97.

Cooper, C. (1993). *Noises in the blood: Orality, gender, and the 'vulgar' body of Jamaican popular culture*. London: Macmillan.

Cronon, E.D. (1955). *Black Moses: The story of Marcus Garvey and the Universal Negro Improvement Association*. Madison: University of Wisconsin Press.

de Certeau, M. (1984). *The practice of everyday life*. Translated by S. Rendall. Berkeley: University of California Press.

Delany, M.R. and Campbell, R. (1969). *Search for a place: Black separatism and Africa, 1860*. Ann Arbor: University of Michigan Press.

Domingo, W.A. (1823, March). Open forum: The policy of the *messenger* on West Indian Negroes. *Messenger*, 640.

Geography and History of Jamaica (1999, June 25). *Gleaner*. (http://www.discoverjamaica.com/gleaner/discover/geography.htm).

Hill, R.A. (Ed.). (1983). Domingo, W.A. In *The Marcus Garvey and Universal Negro Improvement Association Papers*. (Appendix L, vol. 1). Berkeley: University of California Press.

Houston, M. (1994). When black women talk with white women: Why dialogues are difficult. In González, A., Houston, M. and Chen, V., (Eds.), *Our voices: essays in culture,ethnicity, and communication (An intercultural anthology)*. 3rd Edition, 133–139. Los Angeles: Roxbury.

James, C.L.R. (1976). *Beyond a boundary*. London: Hutchinson.

Jerry, Bongo (Dec 1970/March 1971). *Savacou*, 3/4, 13–15.

Jonson, J.W. (1969). *Along this way*. New York: Viking.

Lamming, G. (1960). *The pleasures of exile*. London: Michael Joseph.

Lopez-Springfield, C. Through the people's eyes: C.L.R. James's rhetoric of history. (1990). *Caribbean Quarterly*, 36, 85–97.

Lowenthal, D. (1972). *West Indian societies*. New York: Oxford University Press.

Marshall, P. [1959](1981). *Brown girl, brownstones*. Reprint New York: Feminist Press.

Mckay, C. (1937). *A long way from home*. New York: Lee Furman.

Nettleford, R. (Ed.) (1989). *Jamaica in independence: Essays on the early years*. Kingston: Heinemann Caribbean; London: James Currey.

New York age. (1920, Aug. 28).

Rodney, W. (1975). *Groundings with my brothers*. London: Bogle-l'ouverture.

Washington, B.T. [1900] (1965). *Up from slavery*. Reprinted in Franklin, J.H., (Ed.), *Three Negro Classics*. New York: Avon.

Watkins-Owens, I. (1996). *Blood relations: Caribbean immigrants and the Harlem community, 1900–1930*. Bloomington and Indianapolis: Indiana University Press.

Williams, R. [1953](1983). *Culture and society: 1780–1950*. Reprinted with a new introduction by the Author. New York: Columbia University Press. ◆

22

The Power of *Wastah* in Lebanese Speech

Mahboub Hashem
Fort Hays State University

"**D**o you have any *wastah?*" This was the only question that many of my Lebanese friends and relatives asked me when I applied for one of the Chair of Administrative Affairs positions at the Lebanese University in 1972. I replied that I ranked among the top five in the competency exam and they needed to hire at least ten people, so why would I need a *wastah?* They simply shrugged and warned, "Wait and you'll see."

To make the story short, I was passed over and more than 10 other people were hired. Every one of those who were hired had some type of *wastah*. I was hired three years later only after I had acquired strong *wastah*, which included several influential individuals, among them Suleiman Frangieh, the President of Lebanon at that time.

Much of the research by political theorists and international journalists with regard to the Middle East has focused on the study of Islam, media representations of Arabs, the oil and mineral resources of the Gulf region, and the Arab-Israeli conflict. All these topics have been of great interest to the West. Yet, readers remain in the dark as to the significance of the Middle Eastern hierarchy of values and patterns of communication at the heart of any issue in that part of the world.

The complex region of the Middle East is far from a quick study. Its interlocking class, cultural, ethnic, linguistic, and family and religious distinctions pose challenges to the researcher who wishes to generalize research findings. However, by examining the *wastah* phenomenon in Lebanon and how it is practiced, one may be able to shed some light on this very important communicative behavior not only in Lebanon but also in the rest of the Middle East. This essay addresses the power of *wastah* (i.e., mediation), considered to be one of the most important communication patterns in the Lebanese cultural system. First, the meaning of *wastah* and its usage in various contexts is explained. Second, major factors influencing the use of *wastah* are discussed. Third, the process of how *wastah* works is described.

Meaning and Usage of *Wastah*

Wastah has been the way of life in Lebanon since before it became a republic. The term *wastah* means many things to many Lebanese people, including clout, connections, networking, recommendations, a "go-between" for two parties with different interests, and a type of contraception to prevent pregnancy.

Wastah can be used within various contexts, such as family, clan, government organizations, neighbors, villages, and nations. It is usually necessary to get a job, a wife, a date, a passport, a visa, a car, or any other commodity. It can also resolve conflicts, facilitate government decisions, or solve bureaucratic problems. For instance, I once had to wait three hours until I could find an influential person to help me pay the annual tag fee for my car. The common perception in the Arab world, particularly in Lebanon, is that "one does not do for oneself what might better be done by a friend or a friend's friend" (Ayoub, cited in Huxley 1978, 5). One example of *wastah* concerns a student who graduated with a Bachelor of Arts degree in history and sought to continue his education in France. At that time the Lebanese University only offered scholarships to graduates with BA degrees in agriculture. However, because the student's uncle was a dean at that university, the student managed to procure the full scholarship he needed.

150

Major Factors Influencing the Use of *Wastah*

Religion, kinship, *zaimship* (political leadership), and *musayara* (a communication style emphasizing commonalities) are the most interdependent factors that influence the process of *wastah* in Lebanon. Competency is a factor that may be considered only in special situations where kin are not involved.

Religion. In Lebanon, no one exists without a religion. "Religion is not a preference but is a most necessary social identity, regardless of the individual's beliefs" (Farsoun 1970, 294). Unlike Western nations where the separation of religion and state is the norm, Lebanon has incorporated religion as a legitimate structure into its political system and organizations.

Lebanese people must have their religion stated on their national IDs. For instance, my ID card states that I am a Maronite Christian (a sect of the Catholic faith). My religious affiliation has been a major factor in my getting jobs, as well as a scholarship for Ph.D. study in the United States.

All forms issued by the Lebanese government require a declaration of religion. Because religion is a major factor in employment and political appointments, especially at the highest levels of government, the Lebanese system has been labeled as confessionalism or sectarianism (whereby positions are given primarily on the basis of religious quotas and secondarily on the basis of qualifications). For example, the National Pact (an agreement among various religious sects) states that the Lebanese President must be a Maronite Christian, the Speaker of the Parliament a Shiah Muslim, the Prime Minister a Sunni Muslim, and so on. A religious balance in the number of appointees must always be maintained for national security and better relationships among various sects.

The influence of religion on families can be felt in every aspect of their lives, such as birth, death, baptism, confirmation, circumcision, education, courtship, marriage, divorce, the use of contraception, and inheritance. That influence may be more evident in the realm of education, which has always been a private endeavor of the religious communities. Thus, religious sects generally open their own schools to educate their own people. Such practices contribute to closer relations among people of the same sect and stronger feelings of identification with their religions and families.

Although Lebanon established criminal and civil codes modeled after the French legal system, the Lebanese constitution and legal codes delegated family law (known as "personal status" law) to the traditional religious law courts. Marriage, divorce, inheritance, and adoption all fall in the domain of religious courts. These courts are autonomous and separate from the civil court system. For example, until recently no civil marriage was accepted in Lebanon—only religious marriage. Such a legal system has reinforced confessionalism, traditions, the extended family structure, and *wastah*-making.

Lebanon's civil war has been characterized as sectarian partly because of the differences between Christians and Muslims in education, marriage, household patterns, and lifestyles. Because interaction between confessional factions has not taken place within the Lebanese educational systems, people from different religious beliefs have grown farther apart. This has allowed religion to become a powerful influence on the *wastah* process, rendering it even more difficult to hire someone from a religious sect other than one's own.

Kinship. Kinship consists of the extended family structure, which is part and parcel of the overall structure of the nation. The rate of face-to-face interaction among kinpersons amounts to daily contacts with parents and significant kin members. This fact reinforces *wastah*-making and the solidarity of the extended family.

Research findings suggest that the extended family has been the most economically productive unit. Retail and commercial enterprises are always family owned and run by siblings, cousins, and other extended kin. Owners maintain tight control over their business by staffing them with direct relatives, such as brothers, brothers-in-law, and nephews (Fuller 1961; Sayigh 1962; Khalaf and Shwairi 1966; Williams and Williams 1965; Farsoun 1970; Huxley 1978). Thus, ownership and control patterns remain largely patrimonial and nepotistic, leaving much room for *wastah*.

Males are usually preferred over females, especially in key positions. From birth, boys and girls receive different treatment. Boys are favored because they are considered to be capital investments for the future and excellent contributions to the social and cultural prestige of the family. A man with many sons can speak with great authority. The birth of a girl, on the other hand, is considered reprehensible, burdensome, and a potential source of shame to the family. Although women enjoy as much of Lebanese culture as men, social customs always preserve the domination of the male. For instance, a single woman may find it difficult to move away from her family to live by herself and work before marriage, an action that may endanger the reputation of the family. Today many Lebanese women work in teaching, banking, and other professions. However, most of them are pressured to stay home and manage their domestic affairs. Consequently, females need much stronger *wastah*s than males in procuring employment.

Zaimship. Zaimship refers to political leadership which is more often inherited than earned. Today's *zuama* (political leaders) are usually the sons, nephews, or cousins of previous *zuama* from the same extended families. Such families are the structures wherein political functions generally take place.

A Lebanese *zaim* is the descendent of an old feudal lord whose extended family has had a good reputation throughout Lebanese history and whose power is based on inherited estates, extensive businesses, and an important government post. The *zaim* is usually a male member of the parliament who holds a ministry position. He plays a key role as a *wasit* between the government and his constituency. On the one hand, he tries to preserve his followers' rights and interests in return for political loyalty and support. On the other hand, he represents the government in certain matters related to his constituency. Thus, the *zaim* is an essential *wastah*-maker, a focal point of relations between the government and kinship structures in the nation.

The many different political parties in Lebanon are self-styled factions and alliances of various *zuama* with the most powerful *zaim* at the top. The *zaim*, as Lazerfeld and his colleagues found in the 1940s, does not have direct contact with every person in the extended family structure. He uses informal channels of communication with opinion leaders or heads of extended families for reasons of trust and loyalty purposes. Because the *zaim* functions as a landlord, an employer, a provider, and a dual representative for both the government and his constituency, he relies heavily on certain members of his extended family to accomplish some of these various functions. Thus, he and family members serve as communication conduits from the government to opinion leaders to each individual. The *zaim*, along with influential family elders, become important *wastah*-makers in hiring kin members as well as solving conflicts between individuals, factions, and subfactions. This fact contributes to the maintenance of a society which remains somewhat dependent on deep-rooted traditions and values that constitute the essence of security for the Lebanese people.

Musayara. Musayara is a communication pattern emphasizing commonalities and relieving differences. More specifically, it is an other-oriented style of interaction aimed to conciliate and maintain harmony in social relations, a "behavior designed to enhance commonalities rather than differences, cooperation rather than conflict, and mutuality rather than self-assertion" (Griefat and Katriel 1989, 123). Griefat and Katriel discuss four dimensions of *musayara*. First, the *musayara* of respect is extended to those who are higher in social status, such as the elderly population, the clergy, and those occupying high government positions. Second, the *musayara* of magnanimity is used when the addressee is in a weaker position, such as in the cases of an elder interacting with a sick person or a teacher refraining from punishing an insubordinate student. Third, the *musayara* of politics involves the equality or inequality of the interactants and may be associated with the pursuit of one's interests, such as situations where students go out of their way to act with *musayara* toward their teacher to delay a test. Fourth, the *musayara* of conciliation is used in conflict situations. However, performing *musayara* in these situations involves a third party, usually a *wasit*, rather than the disputants themselves. During *musayara* in such a context, the *wasit* tries to appease disputants and thus prevents a conflict from escalating and reaching the government.

Although *musayara* is a preferred style of communication among the elderly, it is not usually favored by young, Western-influenced Lebanese. Though they hold high respect toward their elders, they prefer to be more direct in the way they communicate. This is a major reason why a *wasit* is usually a senior citizen who considers *musayara* an important communication vehicle in conflict situations and negotiations. Each party in the conflict is expected to act with *musayara* toward the *wasit* who in turn invites them to act with *musayara* toward each other after he works out some type of conciliation. For Arabs, "life demands *musayara*" (Griefat and Katriel 1989) and the *wasit* must understand its principles.

How Does the Process of *Wastah* Work?

Wastah is mostly used to find jobs for relatives or close friends and to solve conflicts. The extended family acts as an employment agency by searching for a *wasit* to help get a job, preferably one with high social status in the family. The *wasit* is supposed to be well "wired up," an insider who can make things happen (Hall 1984). He must also be able to use the language of persuasion (appropriate and effective *musayara*) with the elite of the religious and political groups of the nation.

In conflict situations, the *wasit*'s job is to conciliate rather than to judge. Conciliation is intended to lead disputants toward a compromise through mutual concessions, as well as to re-establish their relationship on the basis of mutual respect. The *wasit* tries to talk to each disputant separately, then brings them together to reach a possible compromise that presumes to save face for everyone involved and their extended families.

Lebanese people prefer mediators from the same family or business, depending on the type and context of the conflict. As Patai (1983) notes, the role of a *wasit* is to create a supportive climate of communication wherein conflicting parties can modify their behaviors. When a conflict is between members from two different clans, however, a *wasit* on each side tries to prevail over his or her own clan members. These mediators then come together to conciliate.

For instance, when a conflict occurred between my father and a man named Tony Ayoub, one elderly person from the Hashem clan and another one from the Ayoub clan came together to mediate and negotiate a possible settlement. Then each of the two met with their clan member to discuss the results of their meeting(s) and what the two believed to be a fair solution. After several private meetings between the two mediators, my father and Tony were asked to personally participate in the final one to announce the settlement of the problem. The common ground among mediators of different families is the mutual desire to keep the government out of the clans' affairs as much as possible. Hence, mediators seem better qualified than government agencies to resolve certain conflicts (Huxley 1978).

Conclusion

Even though Lebanon has been greatly influenced by the West, most Lebanese people's lives are still organized around their religion, extended family, *zuama*, and extensive *musayara*. The extended family remains the basic economic, political, and social unit through which individuals inherit their religion, honor, respect, social class, and cultural identity. Finally, *wastah* has been and will always be a powerful communication tool and a way of life in Lebanon.

The process of *wastah* and how it is practiced does not differ much from the same practice in other Middle Eastern nations or even some Western countries. The world's global village demands a broadly based cultural knowledge about one's own culture and other cultures as well. The Western style of direct communication and the emphasis on status symbol and professional affiliations are beneficial in many situations. However, they can be even more effective when combined with *musayara* and *wastah*. Likewise, the indirect style of interaction and the emphasis on *musayara* for *wastah*-searching and *wastah*-making in the Middle East, especially in Lebanon, does not always or necessarily thrive at the expense of individualism. The knowledge of these styles and how they are used in various cultures promotes more awareness and understanding of ourselves and others and can consequently lead to more effective intercultural relationships.

References

Ayoub, V. (1965, Spring). Conflict resolution and social reorganization in a Lebanese village. *Human Organization*, 24, 1–20.

Beeman, W. (1986). Language, status, and power in Iran. Bloomington: Indiana University Press.

Farsoun, S.K. (1970). Family structure and society in modern Lebanon. In Louise, E., (Ed.), *Peoples and cultures of the Middle East: An anthropological reader, Vol. II: Life in the cities, towns, and countryside.* New York: The National History Press.

Fuller, A. (1961). *Buarij, portrait of a Lebanese Muslim village.* Cambridge, MA: Harvard University Press.

Griefat, Y. and Katriel, T. (1989). Life demands *musayara*: Communication and culture among Arabs in Israel. In Ting-Toomey, S. and Korzenny, S., (Eds.), *Language, communication, and culture: Current directions* (121–137). Newbury Park, CA: Sage.

Hall, E.T. (1984). *The dance of life: The other dimension of time.* New York: Anchor.

Huxley, F.C. (1978). *Wasit* in a Lebanese context, social exchange among villagers and outsiders. Anthropological papers. Museum of Anthropology, University of Michigan, Ann Arbor.

Khalaf, S., and Shwayri, E. (19666, October). Family firms and industrial development: The Lebanese case. *Economic development and cultural change*, 15, 59–69.

Landall, J. (1961). Elections in Lebanon. *Western Political Quarterly*, 14, 120–147.

Patai, R. (1983). *The Arab mind.* New York: Charles Scribner's Sons.

Raschka, M. (1991, May/June). Survey shows students reject sectarianism, love Lebanon. *The Washington Report on Middle East Affairs*, X(1), 46.

Sayigh, Y.A. (1962). *Entrepreneurs of Lebanon.* Cambridge, MA: Harvard University Press.

Williams, H.H. and Williams, J.R. (1965). The extended family as a vehicle of cultural change. *Human Organization*, 24, 59–64. ✦

23

Wa-Zha-Zhe I-E

Notions on a Dying Ancestral Language

Steven B. Pratt
University of Central Oklahoma

Merry C. Buchanan
University of Oklahoma

> *Indian languages, like all languages, are vital expressions of the people who speak them. They carry within them the culture, spirit, history, and philosophy of a tribe.*
>
> —Bauman (1980, vii)

> *Language is the very essence of identity, self-worth and dignity. When language is lost, a part of a people's humanity is forever lost.*
>
> —IPOLA (1996)

Whenever I am "called upon" or asked by one of my Osage people to "speak for them" or talk in a ceremonial occasion such as a naming ceremony, ceremonial dance, feast, or our Osage way of worship, or if I am asked to pray before such an occasion, I always try to speak or pray in my Osage language. I make an effort to express myself in the appropriate Osage manner by including what is traditionally to be expressed on a particular occasion. I also try to make sure that my pronunciation is near perfect and that I have remembered all the required parts of an Osage speech or prayer. Even though I am painfully aware of what needs to be said and how to say it, my words usually fall upon non-comprehending ears, for only a handful of Osage Indians can speak or understand our tribal language. And, after each such occasion, I often silently lament that this may be the last time the Osage language is publicly spoken and that within a mere 10 years it might not ever be heard again. Indeed, most of my Osage relatives, friends, and acquaintances as well as the other ten thousand tribal members have not shown any desire to learn and perpetuate our ancestral language—the tongue of our "old people."

> Today, we are not punished by whites for speaking our language as our ancestors were, nor are our rations from the government cut off if we are caught speaking to one another in our Osage tongue. Rather, we do not speak our language because of a sanctioning force more powerful than the Bureau of Indian Affairs: apathy. Most contemporary Osages simply have no desire to learn their language and subsequently, they do not learn their heritage—the teachings of our "old people." (Pratt, *Personal Communication*, March 27, 1999)

Members of the Osage Nation are not alone in their reluctance to maintain and preserve their ancestral language. Many American Indian[1] tribes now face cultural extinction because of this fact. Although there are considerable differences among these native peoples—geographical area, family units, dwelling structures, and governmental structure—the one way they are similar is in the deterioration and subsequent loss of tribal language. Krauss (1996) notes that out of a total of more than three hundred original indigenous languages, only 175 are currently spoken in the United States. How long these languages will survive is in question.

A tribal culture is not merely an aggregate of people united by a degree of blood, but also an entity distinguished by unique characteristics such as tribal values, beliefs, patterns of thought, worldview, and most importantly, language. It is through language, both verbal and nonverbal, that members of a group communicate their thoughts, feelings, and emotions to each other. Thus, appropriate rules of conduct are exhibited and shared through ancestral language so that a tribal culture can be maintained and passed on.

Obviously, when their language ceases to exist, the cultural or tribal group, as it is known, ceases to exist. That which was, dies, and in its place something new and different arises. Too, culture is learned; it is not something that is inherent (Hall 1981). Therefore, when a culture is not taught, it will die. "Today many Indian groups are forced to consider whether they can maintain their social integrity and self-identity if they do not speak their ancestral language" (Bauman 1980, vii).

The following describes the approaching demise of the ancestral language of the Osage nation. Specifically, it addresses (a) the Osage Nation, (b) the challenge facing tribal language, (c) the state of health of Indian languages, (d) the Osage language, and (e) the Osage language restoration program.

The Osage Nation

Located in Osage County in northeastern Oklahoma, this nation consists of three districts (*Zon-zo-li*, *Wa-xa-xo-li*, *Pa-tso-li*), each affiliated with a distinct tribal band and each being centered around a few square miles of reservation land adjacent to the small towns of Hominy, Pawhuska, and Fairfax. A district is referred to (in the context of establishing tribal-familial identity) by most tribal members according to the name of a nearby town rather than by its Osage reference. For example, those in the *Zon-zo-li* district say: "I am from Hominy," "My folks are from Hominy," or "I have relatives in Hominy."

Approximately 600 members of the Osage Nation reside on or within 10 miles of their reservation, and approximately 12,000 more are dispersed throughout the country. The centers of the districts are within 20 miles of each other—a distance that facilitates the assembly of both small and large gatherings among those residing within the perimeters of the three districts. Members of the three districts are united by familial and quasi-familial relationships (cf. Pratt 1985).

Ceremonial and social events are frequently held in each district with attendees from all three districts often invited to attend. On each parcel of reservation land is a permanent physical structure utilized primarily for the *I-lon-shka* (a ceremonial war dance). Located close by are community buildings and other structures where dinners, dances, and specific forms of traditional game playing take place. Each parcel also houses a limited number of families from that district. In the Hominy district, for instance, the residences of 15 families exist on the reservation itself while many more Osage families live in the surrounding area. One housing tract within several miles of the reservation accommodates 50 Osage families and is locally called "Indian Homes."

Statement of the Challenge

The Quintessence of Tribal Language

Language and culture are intricately tied (Fishman 1996; Salzmann 1993). Language is related to culture in three significant ways: "language itself is a *part* of culture, every language provides an *index* of the culture with which it is most intimately associated, and every language becomes *symbolic* of the culture with which it is most intimately associated" (Fishman 1985, xi). Because the link between language and ethnicity is powerful, indigenous languages should be recognized as important national resources (McCarty 1994). Fishman (1977) contends that language is more than merely a means of communication because "by its very nature language is the quintessential symbol, the symbol par excellence" of a culture; that is, it is "the symbol of ethnicity" (25). Concern for indigenous language attrition is an issue of ethnolinguistic vitality wherein "the more vitality a linguistic group has, the more likely it will survive and thrive as a collective entity" (Giles, Bourhis, and Taylor 1977, 308).

Currently, many tribes are attempting to revive and restore their languages. The Osage Indians, like many others, are in a state of cultural crisis because of the possible loss of their tribal language. For example, many classes have been started on the Osage reservation in attempt to teach the language, but not any have proved successful and the number of Osage speakers continues to decline. A common challenge of all tribes is that adequate language programs have not yet been developed. Tribal governments are often lacking in concern for language preservation primarily because economic development seems more important. Simply put, leaders are more concerned with bringing in federal money for other types of projects. As a result, when no funding is available, cultural preservation goes on the back burner.

Moreover, tribal members themselves often do not express an interest in language restoration. For example, when Osage tribal members are asked why they do not speak the language and why they have no interest in learning the language, no concrete answers are given. Responses such as "I don't have the time to learn," "They never have any classes around here," "I am going to start taking some classes," and "I would but everyone would probably make fun of me" are the most common reasons given.

It appears that tribal members are typically reluctant to try to learn their own language—taking classes would diminish their tribal "cultural competency." That is, language students would be viewed by other tribal members and members of other tribes as not being as "Indian" as the persons who can speak their language. Consequently, many Osages profess to being able to speak Osage even though their vocabulary consists of only a handful of words.

Problematic Nature of Teaching a Tribal Language

Tribal languages, as a composite of the culture they represent, need to be treated as an integral part of everyday life. For example, the Osages have an elaborate system of kinship with relatives being designated on both maternal and paternal sides. Kinship is also established by the age of the speaker. These factors determine the mode in which conversation will take place. However, most outside teachers of Osage do not address this idea of kinship (i.e., noting how conversational patterns and subsequent behavioral patterns are affected by a specific kinship term). Rather, words taught are based upon a literal English translation (e.g., "mother" is i-no^{n2} and "father" is i^n-da-tsi—with no fur-

ther explanation of the Osage concept of mother and father).

In the Osage language, the word for a "mother's sister" (aunt) is the same as "mother," with a distinction noted only if the sister is older (i-no^n-do^n) or younger (i-no^n-zhi) than the mother. The word is the same because the parental obligations are the same for both a mother and her sister(s). That is, the mother functions as a parent for her nephews and nieces as well as for her own children. The same name (i^n-da-do^n, i^n-da-zhi) and the same obligations also hold true for a father's brother(s). Historically, Indians have always had a high mortality rate whether as a result of European diseases, warfare with other tribes, or the United States Cavalry. Because of this fact, the Osages made sure that all children would have a mother and a father and that there would be no orphans—hence, the role of a mother or father could be fulfilled by a brother or sister. Moreover, there is no Osage word for "cousin," but that is a story for another time.

One problem associated with creating, implementing, and maintaining tribal language programs is the necessity for linguists and other outside sources who are not knowledgeable about tribal culture. In his discussion on language and culture, Hall (1981) notes how critical it is to understand and learn language in its "context, which carries varying proportions of the meaning" (45). He further shows that "without context, the code is incomplete since it encompasses only part of the message" (1981, 45). Thus, the meaning of a word is dependent upon the environment or situation in which the symbol is spoken and as such, computers and linguists cannot provide contextual or "complete" meanings. To illustrate, Hall recounts that in the late 1950s, the U.S. government spent millions of dollars developing systems for machine translation of Russian and other languages. After years of effort on the part of some of the most talented linguists in the country, it was finally concluded that the only reliable, and ulti- mately the fastest, translator is a human being deeply conversant not only with language but with the subject as well (Hall 1981, 45).

As an exemplar, consider the Osage word for "fire," *pe-tse*. However, when "fire" is referred to in an Osage church service, it is termed *wi-tsi-ko*, which is also the word for "grandfather." The church service is held in either a "meeting house" (an octagonal structure built specifically as an Osage church) or in a *tipi*, with a ceremonial fire built in the center. The fire, although ceremonial in one sense, is also functional in that it provides light as well as warmth. Because the fire thus serves the church members throughout the night, it is regarded with respect and given the term *Wi-tsi-ko* or "grandfather." In their traditional worldview, the Osage see themselves as a part of the environment and not separate from it. Therefore, they honor water, fire, and the sun, acknowledging that without these and other natural elements life would not exist. Their respect is reflected by using the same terminology for each element as for a familial caregiver. And so, the concept of "fire" is dependent upon context.

American Indian Languages Today

American Indian tribal groups are currently in a state of crisis because there are so few members who are fluent in their languages. In fact, many tribes have already lost their language soon to be followed by many more. Bauman (1980) delineates the health status of tribal languages according to five classifications: Flourishing, Enduring, Declining, Obsolescent, and Extinct. In tribes identified as Flourishing, such as the Navajo, the language is spoken by adults and children, is spoken in the household, adapts to meet the needs of the people, and enpowers speakers to become increasingly more literate. A tribe with an Enduring language has speakers of all ages, although English tends to be used exclusively in most situations and there is little or no language literacy in the community. Tribes categorized as Declining have more older speakers than younger, younger speakers who are not fluent, and a population that is essentially illiterate in the language. An Obsolescent language is one that has an age gradient of speakers terminating with the adult population, is not taught to children in the home, has a rapidly declining number of speakers, prefers English in all situations, and exhibits no literacy. The Osage language falls into the Obsolescent category and is next to being extinct. At the end of the scale are Extinct languages, in which there no tribal speakers—such as the Chumash (Bauman 1980).

Krauss (1996) delineates a five-part typology categorizing threatened American Indian languages. Category A, with 20 languages (11 percent), represents languages learned from elders and parents in the traditional way. Category B has 30 languages (17 percent), in which languages are still spoken by the parental generation. The 70 languages (44 percent) in category C are spoken only by the middle-aged or grandparental generation and up. Category D has 40 languages (32 percent), spoken only by the very oldest people.

Wa-zha-zhe I-e, the Osage language with only four fluent elder speakers, falls into the second largest category of threatened languages. Krauss (1996) asserts that if a language is not spoken by individuals under the age of 50, its chances of survival are not any better than a language spoken by 100 people. Thus, the viability of *Wa-zha-zhe I-e* is bleak and being considered "endangered" because there are no children speakers (Wurm 1996) and "moribund" because it is not learned by children as the mother-tongue (Krauss 1992). *Ethnologue*, a comprehensive guide to languages of the world, specifically classifies the Osage language as "nearly extinct" (Grimes 1996). In order to safeguard native wisdom and culture, it is imperative to restore indigenous languages that are "irreplaceable treasures known only through oral traditions which are in the hands of tribal elders. When they pass on, a wealth of knowledge goes with them" (Hess 1997, 2).

Osage Language State of Health

There are approximately 12,000 Osage Indians identified and, of this number, nearly 2000 reside in and around the Oklahoma reservation area. Of the total number of identified Osages, there are approximately four speakers, all octogenarians, who are fluent in the Osage language (Lottie Pratt, Preston Morrell, Lucille Rubideaux, Harry Red Eagle, Jr.). Below the age of 70, there are approximately six who are able to speak briefly in Osage, yet they are not able to converse. Below the age of 40, there are no known speakers of the Osage language.

In the Osage communities of Hominy, Pawhuska, and Grayhorse, the Osage language is not spoken in any households, in any tribal offices (almost all council members speak little, if any, Osage), nor in the school systems (although some words and phrases are taught in the Head Start programs by teachers who do not speak or understand the Osage language). English is preferred in all situations, including traditional activities, and there is no literacy. Neither is language visible in the communities except for the names of a few streets, a golf course, a hotel, and a bar. At the Osage Indian agency, no signs are written in Osage nor is evidence of the language readily visible on the tribal grounds. A visitor to the agency would hear no tribal members conversing in their own language, nor would any recordings of the language be heard playing in the museum or other agency buildings. An attempt was once made to label the agency restrooms with the Osage words for "man" and "woman." However, employees complained—they did not know which restroom to enter because they did not know the Osage word for "man" or "woman."

Cultural Arenas for Language Activity

Although the Osage language is virtually unspoken by tribal members, the enactment of tribal-specific activities still occurs. The most encompassing activity is the *I-lo^n-shka*, a four-day, quasi-religious ceremonial dance hosted by each of the reservations' districts. Held annually in June, the *I-lo^n-shka* involves more than 500 participants (i.e., dancers and spectators). This celebration is the primary activity in which tribal members exhibit their "Osage-ness." For the most part, the people tend to conduct their day-to-day affairs in a contemporary, white American manner. All students attend public schools that utilize a contemporary, white American cognitive style (as opposed to a traditional Osage cognitive style), do not teach accurate Osage history, do not teach the Osage language, and do not participate in traditional religious activities. The equivalent of this situation holds true for Osage adults. Therefore, the only time that many of the Osages actively exhibit their cultural identity ("Osage-ness") is during the four days in which the *I-lo^n-shka* is held. At this time, tribal members purposefully seek out and participate in an Osage cultural milieu. By simply attending and observing this event, one's "Osage-ness" is displayed and is a focus of talk (e.g., "Did you go to the dances?", "Are you going to the dances this year?").

Another practice in which cultural identity is displayed is the Osage "naming ritual," whereby a clan name is bestowed upon one's children by an elder. Contemporary culturally-competent Osages continue to observe this centuries-old tradition in a manner similar to that of their ancestors. Naming was once a necessity because an Osage child received a name as soon after birth as possible (i.e., Osages did not have English names). The clan name, among other things, readily identifies one's family background (lineage) and birth order, such as eldest son or daughter. In the ritual prayer, the elder also seeks blessings for the child's life—to be healthy, grow to maturity, reach old age, be blessed with children and grandchildren, and to learn and teach the "Osage ways."

Contemporarily, many adult Osages are not socialized in the traditional folkways, such as being taught the Osage cognitive style of learning by silently observing an event for an extended period of time; repeating oral history that focuses upon lineage, or learning the meaning and enactment of symbolic ceremonial activities as the embodiment of traditional culture. In essence, most Osages, both young and old, are not taught Osage values, beliefs, worldview, and patterns of thought.

By not being able to speak Osage, members often enjoy alternative symbolic rituals. For example, those who were not socialized in a traditional manner and who do not speak the language will seek out a tribal member to conduct a quasi-naming ritual in which they receive their "Indian name." Many of those asking for this naming are well beyond the appropriate age for this ritual to take place. In fact, it is becoming quite common for non-traditional Osages in their late 50s and 60s to engage in this type of quasi-ceremonial activity. A ritual that was exclusively for an infant is now commonly, albeit improperly, enacted even for entire families (fathers, mothers, and children). Furthermore, the significance of the ritual has changed because the contemporary participants do not know how to speak the language. Consequently, they are unable to pronounce their names, do not understand the meaning of their names, and in many cases, cannot remember the Osage name.

The Osage Native American Church is another available tribal activity, but one that does not attract very many participants. Although this is the recognized tribal religion, the church meetings are held infrequently throughout the year. They commence at sundown, continue until noon of the next day, and usually attract between five to thirty participants.

Quasi-Osage funerals in conjunction with Protestant or Catholic services are still conducted in a ceremonial nature. Usually, when an Osage dies, two funeral services are held: the Osage service is held in the early morning, is followed by a church service, and concludes with a traditional feast. The Osage way does not fear or ignore death, but views it as a part of the life cycle in which the tribal member's passage and the concomitant mourning by family members are acknowledged by all. Preparatory activities involve most of the members who reside on or near the reservation and generally last for three days, with the actual funeral service occuring on the fourth day after the death. During this period, there are many occasions in which the Osage language could be appropriately spoken.

Motivation and Osage Language Acquisition

There is no reason why the Osage language should not be utilized on a daily basis in the Osage community. Tribal members are located close enough to be able to converse with one another and share in resource materials, there are enough social and traditional occasions that would warrant the language being spoken, and there are enough members and situations in which Osage could be used daily. Yet, the tribal language is seldom heard and, given the aforementioned variables, one would have to speculate why.

The primary deterrent to tribal members' speaking their language is due to the lack of motivation. Research confirms that learning will never occur where motivation is absent. Currently, no motivation exists for anyone to learn *Wa-zha-zhe I-e*. It is not spoken publicly, it is not used in tribal ceremonies, there are no occasions in which a person would be the only non-speaker or where Osage was the only language spoken, there are no visible signs, and ultimately, it is not crucial for the management of one's day-to-day affairs. That is, a person can function perfectly in the Osage community without speaking a word of Osage.

Recognizing that the Osage language was on the brink of extinction, a group of concerned elder, full-blood Osages met in September, 1994, to establish the Osage Elders' Council. The primary purpose of the group was to oversee the development and implementation of a language program. Rather than relying upon a non-Osage to assist them in this project, the council mandated that a culturally-competent tribal member be charged with the task. Steven Pratt, a tribal member and traditional leader, was asked to develop a culturally-sensitive language program to be utilized in both classroom and community contexts.

The Elders' Council accepted and endorsed the Osage Language Restoration Program (OLRP) developed by Pratt, passed a resolution supporting the implementation of the program, and mandated this program to be the only language program utilized by the tribe. On February 24, 1995, Pratt presented the OLRP to the Osage National Council (ONC) during their monthly meeting. The OLRP was unanimously accepted by ONC and plans were made for the implementation of the OLRP.

Osage Language Restoration Program

The objective of the OLRP was to teach both the language and the culture of the Osage, concurrently. The language program adapted to specific contextual events or aspects of the Osage culture, ignoring those parts that did not have a contemporary function. For example, certain rituals, such as tattooing, are no longer enacted and to speak of them would be inappropriate. The intent of the program was to restore the language in everyday situations by introducing vocabulary focusing upon specific events, such as the *I-lo^n-shka*, and then teach the appropriate communicative behavior associated with each context. The students were not only to learn vocabulary, but also how to properly converse. For example, students might be taught the vocabulary associated with the *I-lo^n-shka*, then taught how to appropriately engage in communicative behaviors associated with this context, such as "speaking for someone" or how to "pray for the rituals."

Language Program Implementation

Specifically, this program would (a) teach children and adults how to converse in Osage and (b) teach them about Osage culture. The OLRP was to be implemented in two areas or contexts: classroom and community. Classroom instruction was to provide a background for the language (vocabulary, orthography, and pronunciation). However, in order to obtain fluency, the Osage language would also be taught in more natural communicative situations, such as social and ceremonial settings. Obviously, home activities (eating, speaking with parents, and school activities) were to be included in classroom instruction. Community teaching on the other hand was to focus upon specific contexts such as ceremonial activities (*I-lo^n-shka* and religious activities such as *Ki-kon-zeh*). Social activities (handgame or Indian dice) would also provide useful contexts for instruction. Finally, existing language materials (tapes of speeches, written materials, and

songs) were to be compiled and made available. In addition to designing a language restoration program, a supplementary program was to be developed to motivate tribal members to learn the Osage language.

The program was also to rely upon the tribe's four fluent speakers because without their participation, language restoration could not be successful. These four speakers were not only to assist the teachers with pronunciation, grammar, and vocabulary, but more importantly, they were to teach how to appropriately engage in Osage communicative behavior. That is, they would demonstrate how to properly comport oneself as an Osage Indian, for without knowledge of Osage culture, the language cannot be taught.

Current State of the Osage Language Restoration Program

Unfortunately, the OLRP was never implemented by the Osage tribe. Even though curriculum, teaching materials (audio tapes, booklets), orthography, and assessment tools for teachers and students were developed, the program never went beyond the council chambers. Furthermore, no reason was ever provided as to why this program for a rapidly dying language has not been implemented. When the ONC members were queried by the Elders' Council and others about when the language program might be implemented, the standard response was "We're looking into it."

To date, no effort has been made to implement this or any other language restoration program by the tribal government—even though the language is on the brink of obsolescence. In September 1997, a member of the Osage Mineral Council was contacted about the approaching demise of the Osage language. The council member was sent a copy of the OLRP and was asked for help in implementing the program. The councilperson stated that it was a concern, but there was nothing that could be done. The reality is that the governing body of the Osage Nation is aware of the approaching demise of their ancestral language and a language program has been developed which could be implemented immediately, yet they choose to sit idly and do nothing while the language teeters on the edge of extinction.

Conclusion

This article describes the approaching demise of the ancestral language of the Osage Nation. Although language programs and restoration and maintenance efforts have been initiated, many indigenous languages, such as the Osage language, continue to be in peril.

Learning and utilizing one's native language has much greater ramifications than merely cultivating an appreciation for the language itself. Language performs an extensive role in the procurement, continuance, and transference of cultural knowledge. The loss of language denotes the loss of culture. While nationwide concern for mother tongue language revitalization is beginning to develop, the predicament remains of how to effectively relate this concern to those most affected by its demise— native members of a culture.

Efforts to rekindle interest in preserving American Indian languages have achieved varying degrees of success. Nonetheless, the number of language revitalization attempts is disproportionately fewer than the number of threatened indigenous languages. What remains inherently problematic for language program planners extends beyond the design or even implementation of a program. Promoting awareness among group members and employing culturally appropriate motivational methods appear to be the primary challenges in protecting the questionable future of endangered Indian languages. The Osages and their ill-fated language exemplify this complex dilemma.

> Whenever I speak my language I feel I am truly an Osage. Sometimes it is hard to maintain my identity as an Osage Indian when I am surrounded by non-Indians and have no other Osages to talk to. But all I have to do is quietly sing an Osage prayer song as I walk across campus in the morning on the way to my office and I am reminded of who I am. When I speak my language I understand what my old people were talking about, and I come to understand who I am and how I fit into the grand scheme of things better when I can explain them to myself in Osage. Sometimes I get angry at my Osage relatives and friends for not wanting to learn our language. At other times I get sad thinking about how my Osage language is dying. But there is hope for my *Wa-zhazhe I-e.* Whenever I speak Osage to my 4-year-old son, Joseph Shunkamolah, and he understands me or when he admonishes me for not speaking Osage ("Say it in Osage, Dad"), or when he sings an Osage prayer song with me, I feel that somehow, someway, our Osage language and our Osage way of life will survive. That's what the "old people" told me would happen (Pratt, personal communication, March 27, 1999).

Notes

1. "Although it is considered 'politically correct' to use the label *Native American*, I prefer the term *American Indian.* The term *Native American* is a label that is generally used, and ascribed to, by many researchers when referring to Indian people—'dominant groups can exercise power in naming others. . . it is often difficult for the less powerful groups to control their own labels' (Martin 1997, 60)—and in many situations if an Indian fails to use this term in conducting research or in referring to his or her culture he or she will find himself or herself corrected for not using this term. On many occasions at SCA, ICA, and so forth, I find I am corrected by my colleagues for not using the appropriate term. Furthermore, in the course of my research, the term *Indian* is the label that is almost always used by tribal elders and the indigenous people that I observed, and interacted with, interviewed, and not Native American" (Pratt 1998, 77).

2. Because no standard orthography exists for the Osage language, italics are used for Osage words according to the Osage orthography developed by Pratt (cf. Pratt and Wieder 1993, 357).

References

Bauman, J. (1980). *A guide to issues in Indian language retention.* Washington, DC: Center for Applied Linguistics.

Fishman, J. (1977). Language and ethnicity. In Giles, H., (Ed.), *Language, ethnicity, and intergroup relations* (15–57). London: Academic.

Fishman, J. (1985). Language and culture: The ethnic revival and the sociolinguistic enterprise. In Fishman, J., (Ed.), *The rise and fall of the ethnic revival: Perspectives on language and ethnicity* (xi–xiv). Berlin: Mouton.

Fishman, J. (1996). What do you lose when you lose your language? In Cantoni, G., (Ed.), *Stabilizing indigenous languages* (80–91). Flagstaff: Northern Arizona University Center for Excellence.

Giles, H.R., Bourhis, Y. and Taylor, D.M. (1977). Towards a theory of language in ethnic group relations. In Giles, H., (Ed.), *Language, ethnicity, and intergroup relations* (307–348). New York: Academic.

Grimes, B.F. (Ed.). (1996). *Ethnologue: languages of the world* (13th ed.). Dallas, TX: Summer Linguistics Institute.

Hall, E.T. (1981). *Beyond culture.* New York: Doubleday.

Hess, J. (1997). Language preservation: Crucial to building vital communities. In *Native language network* (vol. 2). Santa Fe, NM: Institute for the Preservation of Original Languages of the Americas.

Krauss, M. (1992). The world's languages in crisis. *Language*, 68, 4–10.

Krauss, M. (1996). Status of Native American language endangerment. In Cantoni, G., (Ed.), *Stabilizing indigenous languages* (16–21). Flagstaff: Northern Arizona University Center for Excellence.

Martin, J.N. (1997). Understanding whiteness in the United States. In Samovar, L. and Porter, R., (Eds.), *Intercultural communication: A reader* (54–62). Belmont, CA: Wadsworth.

McCarty, T.L. (1994). Bilingual education policy and the empowerment of American Indian communities. *Journal of Educational Issues of Language Minority Students*, 14, 23–42.

Pratt, S. and Wieder, D.L. (1993). The case of *Saying a few words* and *Talking for another* among the Osage people: "Public speaking" as an object of ethnography. *Research on Language and Social Interaction*, 26, 353–408.

Pratt, S.B. (1985). Being an Indian among Indians. Unpublished doctoral dissertation, University of Oklahoma, Norman.

Pratt, S.B. (1998). Razzing: Ritualized uses of humor as a form of identification among American Indians. In Tanno, D.V. and González, A., (Eds.), *Communication and Identity Across Cultures* (56–79). Thousand Oaks, CA: Sage.

Salzmann, Z. (1993). *Language, culture, and society.* Boulder, CO: Westview.

Wurm, S.A. (1996). Endangered languages and language disappearance. In Wurm, S.A., (Ed.), *Atlas of the world's languages in danger of disappearing* (1–16). Paris: UNESCO. ✦

24

Broadening the View of Black Language Use

Toward a Better Understanding of Words and Worlds

Karla D. Scott
Saint Louis University

One morning while driving to the airport in heavy traffic, I tuned in to the local "urban hip hop" radio station and happened upon a contest referred to (quite seriously) by the two disc jockeys as "Jeopardonics." The game was played by two contestants who were given the same word and challenged to use it in a sentence. The word in use as I tuned in was orientated. The first contestant used the word in the following sentence, "I orientated a meeting this morning." After acknowledgments from the DJs she was given five points. The second contestant also used the word "correctly" in a sentence referring to a man who was "not orientated before starting his new job." She was also given five points.

In the next round, both contestants were given a word that sounded to me to be *ovahur*. It was then used in the following ways by the contestants: "Tell yo baby mama to get ovahur" and "Boy you better get yo butt ovahur." After much laughter from the DJs, it was decided both contestants had done such an outstanding job they would both win free tickets to an upcoming concert. The DJs then invited us to tune in the next day for another round of "Jeopardonics."

As one who studies the role of language and identity, I was slightly intrigued by the game, which combined the title of a popular TV game show with the word *Ebonics,* a term often used in reference to language of black Americans. While this radio game was obviously developed in the name of humor and the quest for morning drive-time ratings, I see "Jeopardonics" as an example of the rampant misunderstanding that surrounds language use in the black community. Though designed to be entertainment to brighten the morning commute, this game was played on the air to a large audience of listeners (both black and white) and as such served to reinforce the perception that black language use also indicates stupidity on the part of the user. Such a widely held belief continues to both interest me and anger me, not only because I am a communication scholar but also because, as a black woman, I at various points in my daily life might find occasion to speak in a way some would define as black English. I take offense at being perceived as deficient or deviant because I occasionally express myself in the way of those who reared me from childhood to adulthood.

My goal here is not to discuss the controversy surrounding the use of black English in schools or clarify the validity of Ebonics; both issues have been taken up other places (Williams 1997; Smitherman and Cunningham 1997). Rather, I briefly discuss how understanding language use in the black community has been restricted to and constricted by the recent focus on *Ebonics* as both term and concept, and offer instead an expanded view of language use that focuses attention on the ways in which one's language is a result of living, moving, and having being in multiple communities. In addition, I suggest that this expanded view include the concept of language as a means of "marking identity" in the various worlds in which we daily participate. Such a view of language can increase the understanding of both black language use and the experiences of those who speak it.

A Brief Look at Ebonics and Black English

The term *Ebonics* as used to describe language use among black Americans, has become far too overused and misunderstood since the late 1996 controversy with the Oakland School District brought the word out of academic writings and into the mainstream press. Unfortunately, the media did the concept and the black community a disservice when it tried to condense a complex concept to catchy sound bites for the evening newscast. In many cases, the idea of *Ebonics* as the language of black America is interpreted disparagingly like the way the radio game used it—a clear demonstration that many blacks continue to suffer from a deficiency in language use that no amount of education or social programs or both can overcome.

While it may appear to have come out of nowhere, the term *Ebonics* was actually coined in the early 1970s after language in the black community had become a focus of study for both black and white scholars. In a historical account given by Robert Williams, he notes that black scholars were not satisfied with white scholars' descriptions of language in the black community and decided to name the experiences themselves, being members of the very communities in question. The words *Ebony* and *phonics* were combined to "name and define black pronunciation, vocabulary, syntax, structure and the whole ball of wax" (Williams 1997, 210). However, the term did not capture the attention of mainstream audiences at that time despite the prolific research and writing of black scholars.

In her groundbreaking work on language in the black community, Geneva Smitherman identified the uniqueness of what she terms both *black English* or *African American English* as evident in three areas:

1. Patterns of grammar and pronunciation, many of which reflect the patterns that operate in West African languages.

2. Verbal rituals from the Oral tradition and the continued importance of the Word as in African cultures.

3. Lexicon, or vocabulary, usually developed by giving special meanings to regular English words, a practice that goes back to enslavement and the need for a system of communication that only those in the enslaved community could understand. (Smitherman 1994, 5)

Each of these features of language use is discussed fully in Smitherman's *Talkin' and Testifyin': The Language of Black America*, first published in 1977 and again in 1986. More recently, in 1994, she authored *Black Talk: Words and Phrases From the Hood to the Amen Corner*, a dictionary that "captures just a slice of the dynamic, colorful span of language in the African American community" (1994, 1). Her argument that black English is a legitimate form of speech with a distinct history and origins forms the basis for perceiving language use in the black community as indeed different (as is the case with many racial and ethnic groups), but not deficient or deviant as it has often been perceived. However, despite research such as Smitherman's which legitimizes the need for, and use of, black English, the stereotype remains of blacks being ill-equipped to speak "correct" English and doomed to a life of failure because of this deficiency.

In my observations of perceptions of black language use, I have noticed that, along with deficient and deviant, what also endures in mainstream thought are perceptions in these three distinct areas: black English connotes stupidity on the part of the user(s); black English is slang; and black English use is static. I would like to briefly discuss each of these constricting notions more fully before moving on to ways to expand our understanding of black language use.

Black + English = Stupidity

The misuse, or incorrect use, of words by people of African descent in this country has been a perception perpetuated by images in popular culture dating back to the era of minstrel shows, the most popular form of nineteenth-century entertainment. In her book, *Ceramic Uncles and Celluloid Mammies*, noted African American Studies scholar Patricia Turner discusses historical depictions of blacks that include awkward speech, butchered English, and an inability to pronounce correctly multisyllabic words

(Turner 1994). More recent images have included comedic renderings of the Buckwheat character from the early twentieth-century children's show, *The Little Rascals* (which demonstrates the continued source of humor of the subject), as well as caricatures of incarcerated black men incorrectly using polysyllabic words. These depictions and many more like them reinforce long held stereotypes of black language and the deficient capacities—both mental and verbal—of the speakers.[1]

Black English as Mere Slang

The word *slang* is typically used to refer to a special vocabulary used only by a certain group of people. A popular stereotype is that teenagers adapt slang terms, using words and phrases understood only by other teens and not understood by adults. To reduce black language use to mere slang is an obvious oversimplification, but a common perception because blacks (as a distinctly different group from mainstream English speakers) appear to use words with meanings not understood by those who are not black. If one has not grown up in a community where words and phrases are commonly used by its many members, to those ears this speech does sound like slang in the same way words such as *cool, hip, happening, down, phat,* and *tight* have all been used over the past several decades to signal approval.

The difference, however, is that many words and phrases in the black community have endured and, as Geneva Smitherman illustrates in *Black Talk* (1994), many have historical implications. Unlike slang terms, many words used among speakers of black English emerged out of the experience of slavery such as *playing the dozens*, a term used for the verbal dueling game that insults family members and more recently called *snaps* in popular culture. Other words have semantic rooting in West African words such as the use of the word *bad* for something really good. In the Mandingo language, this use of *bad* translates as "it is bad goodly."

Even the word *rap*, now used to refer to a musical style, has a long history of use though the meaning has changed somewhat.

For example, my memory of early teen years and basement parties with black lights includes young black men approaching young black women asking, "Say, baby, can I rap to you?" If my memory is doubtful, Smitherman confirms this use with her definition of *rap:* "originally referred only to romantic conversation from a man to a woman to win her affection. . . the term then crossed over to mean any kind of strong aggressive powerful talk" (1994, 190). This crossover is evident by today's "rappers" who typically boast powerfully in rhythm as they describe the plight and conditions of what is the reality for many black people. This verbal prowess is an excellent point at which to note that the very act of "rapping," whether to win the affection of a woman or to voice opposition to injustice, illustrates yet another example of African language retention—the concept of *nommo* (Asante 1987), which describes the power of the word and values the proficient use of the word.

You Don't Sound Black

Perceptions of black language use seem to indicate that if black English is the language of black America then *all* blacks should use it in the same way, at *all* times, and those who don't use it are the exception. This seems to be another way of constricting the concept of language use in the black community, believing that there is only *one way* to speak black (or for that matter be black, but that is another topic). If one's skin tone or phenotype denotes black or African American but the person speaks in a way considered "more standard," the speaker is often said to be "so articulate." For those of us who have heard this phrase, it implies that we are not like "other blacks" who speak the non-standard, incorrect, butchered version of English of "real blacks."

However, despite clear articulation and the use of correct grammar, my language can still reflect my roots in a black community. The issue is not grammar when I refer to *Mother's Day* as the reason grocery stores, currency exchanges, and banks are crowded near the first of the month (*Mother's Day* has been used historically in the many black communities to refer to the day women on welfare receive checks). My pronunciation is not a factor when I joke about an event with *a boojee crowd*, meaning a function attended by only those blacks considered elite, the privileged few or bourgeoisie (Smitherman 1994). Though lacking the obvious markers of grammar and pronunciation, both of these phrases connect language use and identity in that they have roots in black communities and their use in many ways is a reflection of understanding and moving in those worlds.

As with other communities of speakers, black community speakers change language use depending on who uses it and how. What is most important to note here is that there is not one essentialist, monolithic black community; we are diverse. What features and forms of black English are used can depend on issues such as education, geography, and socio-economic status as well as the circumstances under which it is spoken. Nevertheless, the perception remains that black English as it is used and spoken by *some* at *one* time is to remain as such for *everyone* for *all* times. In other words, if you are black it is believed by many (both blacks and those who aren't) that you've *got* to speak a certain way—a way somehow sanctioned as the one and only way blacks talk. But here, again, is where I take exception to that rule and to use a phrase often heard in many black homes in heated discussions: "I aint' *got* to do nothin' but stay black and die!"

Exploring Language, Culture, and Identity

Geneva Smitherman's discussion of black English is a good starting point for expanding the discussion on the language use of many blacks living in America because, as she notes,

> Black talk crosses the boundaries—of sex, age, region, religion, social class— because the language comes from the same source: the African American Experience and the Oral Tradition embedded in that experience. On one level there is great diversity among African Americans today, but on a deeper level, race contin-

ues to be the defining core of the Black experience. (1994, 2)

I would like to add here that it is this core black experience which creates a culture shaping one's sense of self and place in both that culture and the larger world. When moving between those worlds, language is a primary means of maintaining and negotiating identity.

As theories of linguistic relativity illustrate, language influences thought and perception. When a person grows up in a world with experiences that create a particular culture (as in ways of being, doing, knowing), moving into another cultural world creates challenges for both language use and identity. For instance, the university where I teach has a large student body from Spain, where we have a campus in Madrid. Students are required to attend the Madrid campus for two years before coming to the United States to complete undergraduate study. In classes, I have often witnessed the Spanish students, like many others who speak English as a second language, mentally search for an English word only to shrug helplessly as they say, "There is no word in English to say this." The Spanish students on our campus also provide a clear illustration of how language use connects and connotes identity. It is commonly known among all our students that on certain evenings, a bar near campus is frequented by Spanish students who speak only Spanish as they gather on one particular side of the bar.

While it may be easy to understand why students who are thousands of miles and an ocean away from home would want to be with others like themselves and speak the language with which they grew up, it is harder for some to understand why black students who grew up in the United States would prefer to sit together in the cafeteria and engage in lively, emotional, and sometimes colorful conversation. This behavior is often interpreted as isolation and a rejection of other races or individuals who favor integration of all. But for the black students in such settings, the language often spoken at those tables is the language of "home" and provides a sense of comfort and connection with others who understand it. As is the case with the native Spanish speaking students, there is no need to translate or explain the meaning of things or respond to value judgments about ways of talking.

As mentioned earlier in this essay, the experience of blacks in the United States includes centuries of perceptions and stereotypes, which often influence our interactions with others as we move through our daily lives. The reality of life for those of us who grew up in black homes and communities where the language used is commonly defined as non-standard is much the same as for those who speak English as a second language; one is expected to develop some proficiency in standard English in order to move successfully between cultural worlds. The conscious choice of using one language over another, referred to as code switching (Romaine 1994), then becomes a means for "marking" identity or membership in certain groups or cultural worlds. Research on code switching among speakers of black English indicates that this "skill" is recognized by its users as a means of connecting with those who are of similar cultural or racial identity and distancing from those who are not (Hecht, Collier, and Ribeau 1993).

My own research on the language use of a group of young black women in college further illustrates this point. In their descriptions of ways of talking in settings that were predominantly white (such as classrooms or meetings), the young women indicated they avoided using "black woman's talk"—a strategy enacted in order to be perceived as intelligent and more than tokens. However, there were times when they felt they "had" to speak *as* a black woman, *like* a black woman, such as when white classmates were operating under misconceptions about the black community. As one young woman explained, "I have to go into my blackness and break it down to them, Look, in the black community. . . . " She, along with the other women, said there were times when the language they heard used from their earliest years was the only way in which they could express themselves. In this instance, the young women, who could be categorized generally as college students and quite often on the

receiving end of a well-meaning compliment, such as "You're not like other blacks," were deliberately distancing themselves from their white classmates in order to point out that their race, and experiences by virtue of it, had made a difference in their life (Scott 1996).

In the same way, these young women also connected with other young black women through language, such as in the use of *girl* as a marker of solidarity (Scott, in press). By retaining the use of their language and the experiences that had shaped it, they maintained a connection with their identity and others who were like them, rather than rejecting that identity because they had moved into another cultural world, the world of the predominantly white university. The use of standard English—or "talking proper" in settings where black English or a vernacular, informal style is the norm—is often seen as rejecting one's identity as black and an indication that one has internalized negative connotations of being black and wishes to distance from that identity.

Distancing from one's identity through the rejection of language is an issue in other communities as well, where the effort to lose one's native language as a means of assimilating may have once been valued but is now also criticized. In the anthology *This Bridge Called My Back: Radical Writings by Women of Color* (Moraga and Anzaldúa 1983), women of Asian descent, Latinas, Native American, and black women discuss the role language has played in shaping their identities and connections to the reality of those who share their experiences.

To illuminate this further, I use an example from my own life and an experience I had while on a research trip to a community along the U.S. and Mexico border, where the population is obviously very heavily Mexican American. Because of my complexion and hair texture, I am often told by those meeting me for the first time I appear to be Latina. Often when traveling, I am approached by Spanish speakers whom I can only respond to in the awkward Spanish I learned in required high school and college courses. Normally my reaction in these instances only serves to strengthen my resolve to refresh my knowledge of the language. However, in this border community, my reaction to not being able to "connect" through language was different because I was involved with women health educators working among people who have been marginalized and disenfranchised. Though many of the women I met during my stay spoke English, I found myself wanting to speak *their* language as *they* did to demonstrate solidarity with both work I share a passion for and with an identity as a woman of color though not Latina. My pidgin Spanish, however, left me feeling very inept and distant; there was not the intimacy I feel among black women with whom I share a vocabulary and the nuance of words that reflect our shared world.

Connecting Words and Worlds

My research in the area of language and identity was motivated by my own experiences in growing up black and female and finding myself moving in and out of various cultural worlds where language was a marker of identity. As light "skinned-ded,"[2] my complexion, also referred to as "high yellow" (Smitherman 1994), often caused me to be suspect in my own community. At some point in my life, I discovered language or my way of talking was a means of marking my identity as black and connecting with others who identified as black. Because I was educated in predominantly white schools, I also developed proficiency in what is commonly referred to as standard English, which serves me well today in my professional capacities. However, I will admit there are times when I bring my native way of speaking into the classroom because "there is just no other way for me to say it," and it is at these times that I try to give students a broader view of language use in the black community. It is also a chance to emphasize that black English, Ebonics, or whatever term is preferred does not equal stupidity because it is doubtful that one who is considered deficient by design could obtain a doctorate and obtain a faculty position at a university.

When talking about language and code switching in class, I often refer to Oprah Winfrey's ability to move effortlessly between talk show host style and her more informal vernacular speech complete with voice inflections and phrases tinged with her Southern upbringing, such as when she utters a "Y'all know what I mean" as she looks at the audience then turns back to her guest and proceeds to converse in her professional style. When I imitate this in class, students often laugh, perhaps because they didn't know I, a professor, could talk black "like that." When this occurs, it then opens up the discussion that Oprah's and my language proficiency in two ways of speaking is perceived as the exception rather than the rule.

I doubt that I will ever lecture exclusively in black English; as is the case for most speakers, I use a variety of language styles and forms depending on the situation and the audience. More importantly, if I were to use my native way of talking, I doubt it would consist solely of grammatical errors, mispronounced polysyllabic words, and terms from the latest hip hop artists. This is not language I use to mark myself as who I am as a black woman. I have discovered that when I do bring into my class certain words and phrases reflecting my experiences of living black in this country, the black students give me the smile of solidarity and are of great assistance as we try to explain the meaning to those who do not share understanding.

In such instances in the classroom, I do what I have tried to do in this essay, illuminate the area of language use in the black community by challenging us to think about language in broader terms. More specifically, I suggest that students of human communication look more closely at the historical roots of language in the black community, the ways in which the black experience in this country influenced language use and how the reality of the various worlds in which we interact daily require us to negotiate identity through language use.

A limited understanding of black English as equaling stupidity, slang, deficiency, or, even worse, deviancy is only a surface look at a complex matter. Furthermore, it ignores the history that continues to influence race relations today. By expanding the look at language use in the black community, we get a broader, better look at a language, a people, and the experiences that made them who and how they are today.

Notes

1. For a more thorough and compelling look at the origins of black stereotypes and how they have influenced perceptions of blacks in the United States, I encourage you to view the documentaries *Ethnic Notions* and *Color Adjustment*. Directed and produced by the late filmmaker Marlon Roggs, both provide a context for understanding how images of blacks since slavery have influenced race relations in the United States.

2. The adjective *light skinned* is often pronounced *light skinned-ded* in many black communities. Smitherman (1977) discusses this and other forms of hypercorrection as possibly the result of African slaves trying to appropriate white English without any knowledge of specified grammatical rules.

References

Asante, M.K. (1987). *The Afrocentric idea*. Philadelphia: Temple University Press.

Hecht, M.L., Collier, M.J. and Ribeau, S. (1993). *African American communication: Ethnic identity and cultural interpretation*. Newbury Park, CA: Sage.

Moraga, C. and Anzaldúa, G. (1983). *This bridge called my back: Writings by radical women of color*. New York: Kitchen Table Women of Color Press.

Scott, K.D. (1996). When I'm with my girls: Identity and ideology in black women's talk about language and cultural borders. Unpublished dissertation. University of Illinois at Urbana-Champaign.

Scott, K.D. (In press). Crossing cultural borders: "Girl" and "look" as markers of identity in black women's language use. *Discourse and Society*, 11, 2.

Smitherman, G. (1977). *Talkin' and testifyin': The language of black America*. Detroit, MI: Wayne State University Press.

Smitherman, G. (1994). *Black talk: Words and phrases from the hood to the Amen corner*. Boston: Houghton Mifflin.

Smitherman, G. and Cunningham, S. (1997). Moving beyond resistance: Ebonics and African American youth. *Journal of Black Psychology*, 23(3), 227–232.

Turner, P.A. (1994). *Ceramic uncles and celluloid mammies*. New York: Anchor.

Williams, R. (1997). *The ebonics controversy*. Journal of black psychology, 23(3), 208–214. ✦

25

Confessions of a Thirty-Something Hip-Hop (Old) Head

Eric King Watts
Wake Forest University

Confessions are by their very character and function difficult to make. They require strength and conviction on the part of the confessor as well as a sense of faith that the recorder of the confession (that is you) will be charitable. Despite the potential for insult and injury, the confessor must ask for open mindedness and serious thought on the part of the audience. Inspired as I nearly always am by the legacy of W.E.B. Du Bois, I ask, like he did a century ago, that you study "my words with me, forgiving mistake and foible for sake of the faith and passion that is in me, and seeking the grain of truth hidden there," (Du Bois [1990] 1993, 3). Unlike Du Bois, however, I know I am *not* prophetic; I merely wish to tell you of my love and of my pain. I wish to tell you of my insideness and of my outsideness. Like the boom from an 808 programmed by my coming up in hip-hop culture, I want to share with you the rhythm of my life's beat. I also want you to understand how, as an African American male, hip-hop culture has endowed me with voice. I desire you to hear how I resonate with its wicked vibe and how as an old head I am distanced from it. To the young brothers, I say please *feel* my words; learn how my confessions can teach you about your own identification with hip-hop culture and with each other. And I want to

suggest how to think critically and ethically about your own voices.

I have two confessions to make here; the first one is fairly trivial, the second one is more significant and leads me toward the heart of my joy and pain regarding hip-hop culture. But, first things first: I like the TV show *Frazier*. It bugs me out and, in some ways, makes me think about friendships and family like the show *Seinfield* used to (is this a third confession?). As a pompous, pretentious, lily-white, and self-proclaimed "Anglo-phile," Dr. Frazier Crane tortures and tickles me in a mad way. I find it particularly ironic that Frazier never quite gets his way; he never ends up with the woman of his dreams; he never wins an argument with his father; he cannot keep the dog, Eddie, off his imported leather sofa. As a man of impeccable credentials and "breeding," however, Frazier has his way already. The Seattle skyline twinkling off the edge of his balcony constantly reminds us that Frazier is "on top of the world."

Although Frazier's brother, Niles, loves him dearly, he is just as egoistic as his older brother and, thus, wants Frazier's shine. In an episode I saw recently, Niles schemes for admission into an exclusive all-male club appropriately called "The Empire." Frazier is overwhelmed when he steps into the club. He reverently whispers to himself that the club smells like "power." Frazier and Niles end up competing for the slot that is, in the end, mistakenly awarded to Frazier. Deciding to be the good sibling, Frazier asks the club president to give his slot to Niles. Stoked by the condescension suggested by Frazier's previous gesture and not knowing that the slot is really his, Niles angrily rushes down to the club to denounce its "elitism." Upon learning that it is he who was actually admitted, Niles tries to recant his rant. But it is too late. While being ejected from "The Empire," Niles begs for reconsideration crying, "I am one of you! I belong here!"

It may seem odd to you that I was reminded of my identification with and belonging to hip-hop culture as Niles' screams were muffled by the audience's laughter. I did not laugh because I know what it's like to feel a little homeless... to feel as though the folks with whom you share a language, customs, and ways of living are somehow kept at a distance. Now, don't get me wrong, I do not feel sorry for Niles. Indeed, we would all be better off without "The Empire." But, I understand his loss. I know why his sense of self is threatened by a separation from a valued public identity and consciousness. In the aftermath of this psychic trauma, Niles is forced to make do with where he is in the world; yet, he is still able to cherish the point of contact he had with "The Empire." Membership in the club represents for folks like Niles and Frazier a cultural treasure and a point of view. The premises that guide their thinking and behavior become concrete and justifiable in "The Empire." Acceptance as an "authentic" member allows one to speak as an Imperialist. And so, Niles is not only bemoaning the loss of a rich and powerful white boys' club that serves port wine nearly as old as the United States Constitution, his scream enunciates the hurt that occasions an erosion of public voice.

Despite the allusions to white supremacy, I confess that I dig Frazier. I can relate to the moments when Frazier can no longer talk to his father because it seems as though they do not speak the other's language. I can sense a degree of kinship with him when he expresses pride in his academic accomplishments and pedigree. I can relate to his impatience with some of the stuffiest characters that make periodic appearances on the show. But even now as I reflect on family, friendship, and professional activities, I relive the moment that I, like Niles, felt ejected from a prized dimension of myself, a moment that is the subject of my second confession and that brings to light a tension within the black community about language, history, and hip-hop culture.

"Nigga" What? "Nigga" Who?

Picture this: on a warm Spring day two friends are standing in the parking lot of a reception hall preparing to watch one of their best lifelong boys get married. As cars roll in and latecomers hurry into the hall, the one with the cigarette turns to the one in the blue suit. "Man, I never thought I'd live to see this day. Girlfriend must be blackmailing his ass to get him down the aisle."

"Well," blue suit replies, "that nigga ain't here. So let's not call this a done deal yet."

The groom finally pulls up and bounces out of his rental. "What y'all niggas doin' out here?"

"Waitin' on yo' silly ass," cigarette says.

"Well, my nigga," blue suit asks, giving the groom a pound of love, "you ready to do this shit here?"

"Yeah," the groom smiles, "let's go get me linked up."

Putting myself in the scene above is easy. I was there. Because I do not smoke and I am already married, I was the guy in the blue suit that had the honor of toasting the newlyweds at the reception. And it was among the elders and the children and the champagne that I was jarred outside of myself. Jay-Z's latest joint, "Nigga What, Nigga Who," was setting the dance floor ablaze when I suffered (and enjoyed) a sort of epiphany. Jay-Z was barking, about how no one can "fuck with" him and his crew; a spunky chorus of women punched up the back beat, echoing the rhetorical question (Nigga what? Nigga who?) Jay-Z scripted as a boost to his ego, for the answer each and every time is that the "nigga" Jigga must be recognized (Carter 1998). I had been mouthing the words and hadn't realized it. Jay-Z's bravado about not getting played like a fool and commanding respect (and fear) from "wannabe playas" hyped me. Jay-Z's track represents, like other public anthems resonating in hip-hop, the ever-present need to "campaign for respect" (Anderson 1994, 3). I felt like Frazier, on top of the world. But only for a moment because suddenly the world flipped upside down and I didn't know what Jay-Z was talking about. I heard my wife's voice in my head lamenting what she sees as excessive "nastiness" in rap music, and I saw a circle of kids holding hands and swinging to this "nasty" beat. Time was telescoped forward and I envisioned my son, "pimpin'," "mackin'," and "flossin'." The image was laughably surreal and all too real. Jay-Z's words were now crashing onto the floor like bricks, breaking up at the feet of those children and my elders. And I needed to get some air.

In a way, I still need some air. And so, I confess that my (infrequent) use of the "N-word" had never really bothered me before that night. When I was coming up, the word was sprayed in the air like the mist from our neighborhood water gun fights, playfully and competitively. While in college, I trimmed its usage due to changing contexts, relationships, and social expectations. As a university professor, it's an even more highly guarded utterance. Ice Cube has summed up my feelings; it has been a symbol of my "ghetto pass," denoting membership in the 'hood—a membership that can always be revoked (Ice Cube 1991). But lounging in the parking lot with one of my boys from around the way, it seemed all good. And yet, the anxiety I experienced tells me that it is not all good.

My anxiety about the word *nigga* (*nigger*—traditional usage) is animated by current debate that centers on the character of black American history and the status of language. It seems as though popular culture in the 1990s has taken the "N-word" from private in-house dialogues between the "fellas," and has mass-produced, marketed, and distributed it in easy-to-open packages of hip.[1] As early as 1993, major media outlets were asking why rap music in particular was "embracing" what was referred to as hate speech.[2] We need to note how my anxiety can be dealt with on two intersecting planes: First, as a part of "private" discourse, the "N-word" splits the black community along class and generational lines. C. Delores Tucker, for example, has consistently argued that kids today have forgotten the lessons of the civil rights era and, thus, have no real sense of the pain of the "N-word" as a racial slur (Hampton 1993, 64). As a part of "the lexicon of the cool" (Varner and Kugiya 1998) however, *nigga* signifies close friendship, cultural awareness, or fearlessness (Smitherman 1994). I attended the March on Washington as a 2-month-old infant, and I look up to Chuck D. of Public Enemy and KRS-One like big brothers. Therefore, I feel as though I straddle the line between those who share Martin Luther King, Jr.'s, dream and those who mourned the deaths of Tupac Shakur and Biggie Smalls. I also feel that

through me the two planes interpenetrate one another and can be made to dialogue about history and language.

Speaking for the legacy of the civil rights generation, the "N-word" must be understood in terms of its status as a sign of a horrific cultural history. In fact, if Frantz Fanon is correct, *nigger* (despite altered spellings) designates a specific psychology that is rooted in white people's incapacity to cope with the fact of my blackness (Fanon 1967). Focusing on the linguistic and the historic, being called a *nigger* means being subjected to white supremacist hatred and violence. I want to be clear here, for this is important: From this point of view, *nigger* has only *one* meaning—it means "worthlessness." According to Ray Winbush, director of the Race Relations Institute at Fisk University, ". . . there is no socially redeeming use of the word *nigger*. None at all" (DeYampert 1999). It is also important for us to think about what this definition entails for language and history in general. For Winbush and Tucker, the "N-word" has a stable and unchanging meaning. This notion relies on two things: first, on a particular idea of how language works and, second, on a particular perspective on history. The linguistic aspect of this perspective reminds me of my Aunt Mary's shelf of fruit and pepper preserves; each jar is sealed tightly, what it contains can neither leak out nor can its environment alter it. Likewise, *nigger* is sealed firmly; it always contains a racial slur. But, in terms of theories of language the *word* itself contains *no* meaning. There is nothing in the jar. We understand that meanings are actually created and held by people (Bakhtin 1981). And so, the second form this stable and unified definition takes is historical. We can perceive history as a record of the past. Or, we can comprehend it as something that is present with us. Concurring with Hannah Arendt, members of the civil rights era think of history as living memory (Arendt 1994). The communal act of remembrance reanimates history. If we see the matter in this way, *nigger* refers to people, places, and events that not only document white supremacy, but also stimulate collective emotions regarding our being-in-time.

Contrary to this understanding, hip-hop culture makes liberal use of the word *nigga*. Rap and hip-hop artists as diverse as Busta Rhymes, Erika Badu, Outkast, and Wyclef Jean use the term *nigga* in recordings and performances. Linguistically, hip-hop artists assert that they have flipped the term and that, depending on the context, its meaning can be positive or negative. Indeed, if one is defined as "in" the community, the use of *nigga* can even transgress racial lines. I am reminded of an event involving a former white student who, interestingly, converted from Judaism to Islam. Anyway, he was in my office one day telling me the story of a beef between roommates that he mediated. In the telling, he admitted that he was really pulling for "my nigga" because the other roommate was lame. He must have heard himself say it as clearly as I had because he paused to consider the relational and contextual dynamics present in the room. He knew that in some cases, his speech could be seen as a serious violation of racial territory and could get his "grill" crushed. I simply sat there calmly waiting for him to finish his story; he smiled, recognizing that he was safe here, and continued.

In general, hip-hop vernacular acts like a flat, smooth rock hurled sideways at the surface of a lake. It skips dozens of times across the fluid surface of conversations and locations. The meaning of any particular word or phrase depends on its "velocity" (tone) and where it touches the water (the situation in which people are involved). In terms of language theory, *nigga* is virtually a free-floating signifier obtaining its significance from contexts and usages. I say *virtually* here because everyone knows that *nigga* is a special case. *Wiggers* (the very awkward term for whites who "act black"—"white niggers") use the term carefully and most hip-hop young heads still don't play that. There is a tension here that is helpful for us. As a part of the hip-hop vernacular, *nigga* is lifted out of history. And yet, history re-asserts itself in talk about the term. If *nigga* is the flip side of racist oppression, civil rights history is not erased, but kept intact as the underbelly. This is precisely why white kids approach the term like it's a live hand grenade.

Years ago, the original "Niggas With Attitude" (N.W.A.) contemplated the serious question of "why do I call myself a nigga?" on the album *Niggaz4Life*. On the title track, "Niggaz4Life," the group explored the tension that I identify above. Dr. Dre, Ice Cube, MC Ren, Easy-E, and Yella used the term *nigga* as a "synonym for 'oppression'" (Kelly 1992, 794). and, perhaps, unwittingly demonstrated how being a "nigga" for life is both powerful and problematic (Watts 1994). For example, two years before the Rodney King beating, N.W.A. (1991) depicted the L.A.P.D. as a brutal arm of government oppression directed at public enemy number one—the African American male. N.W.A. used the term venomously and hedonistically to call attention to what black males in particular endure in this society simply by virtue of being black (Ruffhouse/Priority Records 1991). To be a "nigga" is to be profiled by police and subjected to other forms of civil rights violations. N.W.A. also understood that "yo, nigga say nigga, we cool/ But cracka say nigga," and there will be trouble. The organization of community around issues of oppression is a powerful first step toward empowerment; it is also crucial for the cultivation of a public voice. Membership in this community is in part dictated by society, but what one does as a result of racism and discrimination is constituted by the norms and values created by black folk. To speak as a hip-hop head, as N.W.A. pointed out, is to provide an account of one's own encounters with perilous situations. Membership enables the telling of one's own story about love and loss, about thrills and threats. Rap music is, thus, understood as a voicing mechanism for many urban youth (See Rose 1998). This is no small accomplishment. Speaking (and being heard) provides fundamental human agency in society (Gusdorf 1965).

Knowing what to say and knowing how to say it are different matters altogether. Many African American elders gain knowledge from lives steeped in living history. To my grandfather, history was never simply behind him; it walked beside him and, once in awhile, raced out in front to alert him about what may lurk around the next bend in the road. When I was attentive to him on visits to the Mississippi Delta, he would school me on how to hear the wisdom of my ancestors whistling through the winds of time. This communion takes a kind of quiet interest in living history. I have asserted elsewhere that the old heads and young guns have too often parted company in our communities. The current generation of hip-hop enthusiasts has its back turned away from the source of living history and has trained its face on spectacular paper chases all around (Watts 1997). For many hip-hop heads, history, quite frankly, is "dead."

Perhaps the vitality of the moment in hip-hop culture helps to explain the potency of language. There are several web sites and dictionaries that furiously attempt to keep apace of the vigor of rap vernacular (McCormick 1996). The meaning of any word or phrase can literally change shape and color in the throes of one conversation as someone goes "loco," gets "bagged" and is "put down" to "marinate." This conversational rhythm is frenetic; and so, to talk to someone, you got to know how to dance. This kind of word play is, of course, not new to the black community (Garner 1983). But, hip-hop culture has taken it to a new level because it at once samples diverse kinds of cultural knowledge and splices them into linguistic forms that are, in turn, reanimated by the next speaker, and so on. Hip-hop culture has broken down semantic barriers that previously circumscribed other kinds of word games. In short, in hip-hop culture, history may be "dead," but the word (*nommo*) is "live."

This cultural predicament, however, is precisely what troubles folks when they hear rap artists use the "N-word." To someone who chaffs at my utterance of *nigga* in even a truly loving manner, the world is occupied by "dead" languages and "living" histories. To many "ballers" and "around-the-way girls," however, language carries the spirit of the moment and history gathers dust. The problem with nearly every discussion I have heard of either the need to rehabilitate the "N-word" (McClellan-Copeland 1998). or the need to erase it from the English language

(Ager 1998). centers not on anyone's passion or commitment. Rather, I have a problem with conceptual myopia, with the tendency to see this matter one way or the other. The "N-word" is either a racial slur or it represents artists' attempts at subversion. I am not going to suggest a resolution to this issue in terms of saying that one party is right and the other is wrong. I would not presume to be so bold. Nor am I going to say that both parties are right in a particular way and that both are wrong in a particular way. I do not wish to be so ambiguous. But, I do want to assert an idea, a way to perceive this controversy.

The controversy over the "N-word" is normal and necessary. We should not be surprised by its existence, wondering where we went wrong. This mentality suggests that we should be in total control of the currents of history and that a community's strengths reside in its single-mindedness. Cornel West tells us that black survival strategies are "improvised." In a truly powerful jazz jam session, there is as much discord in the mix as there is harmony (West 1994). And as "Old Heads" (hip-hop or not) we cannot place the blame for its frequent usage at the feet of our youngsters as if they did not come from us. History lives within us and so does the "N-word." It is an ugly history to be sure. Its presence is not pathological, however, simply because it refers to a racist notion. Its presence is humanistic in the essential sense of characterizing the troubles of living in community with (white and black) others. We must convert the terror and anger we experience when confronted with the "N-word" into a passion for confronting and comforting its speaker.

To the young brothers (my "niggas"), hear me as an echo of yourselves. You need not be a "nigga for life." Silkk the Shocker is right when he declares that it "ain't my fault." But he is wrong if he thinks that means he's not responsible for his words and deeds. Hip-hop culture has endowed you with voice. You speak a language and share a fluid world of events and ideas with other "playas" and "gamers." The kinds of lives you construct in your universe of discourse are significant to those coming up behind you. You have an obligation to them to think critically and ethically about your choices. Your "now" will be their history. Consider walking beside them along the road in the decades to come, to alert them to what the next bend has in store for them. History does not have to be "dead"; it is not as N.W.A. claimed, "the way shit has to be." The vitality of your words is a key source of the agency for change. But you need to to know what you should say and how to say it. And so, you must do one thing first: turn around and greet your elders.

Notes

1. See L.K. Varner and H. Kugiya, "What's in a Name?—A Hated Racial Slur Finds New Currency—and Controversy—in Popular Culture," *The Seattle Times* 6 July 1998: E1.
2. See "Sacred Cows; commentary," *The Washington Times* 30 May 1993: 8A.; Michael Marriott, "Rap's Embrace of 'Nigger' Fires Bitter Debate," *New York Times* 24 January 1993: I, 1–2.

References

Ager, S. "Word fight: Crusader asks dictionary to turn over new page, eliminate racial slur," *Houston Chronicle*, 19 April 1998: 4.

Anderson, E. "The code of the streets," *Atlantic Monthly* 24 (1994): 86.

Arendt, H. *Essays in understanding*, 1930–1954 ed. Jerome Kohn New York: HarcourtBrace & Co., 1994.

Bakhtin, M.M. *The dialogic imagination* 1981 259–300. Austin: University of Texas.

Carter, Sean/Jay-Z. "Nigga what, Nigga who," vol. 2 *Hardknock Life* (New York: Roc-A-Fella/Def Jam Records, 1998).

De Yampert, R. (1999, Feb. 28). "The n-word; Once just a racist weapon, now a hip-hop icon, and that stirs worry among some blacks," *The Tennessean* 1D.

Dream Hampton. "G-down," *The Source* 48 (1993): 64.

Du Bois, W.E.B. *The souls of black folk.* c1903(3), 1990. New York: Vintage.

Fanon, F. *Black skin, white masks.* 109–140, 1967. New York: Grove.

Garner, T. "Playing the dozens: Folklore as strategies for living," *Quarterly Journal of Speech*, 47–57, 1983(6).

Gusdorf, G. *Speaking (La Parole)*, 3–11, 1965, UP. Evanston, IL: Northwestern.

Ice Cube. *Death certificate* (Los Angeles, *Priority Records*, 1991).

Kelley, Robin D.J. "Straight from underground," *The Nation* 64 1992: 794.

McClellan-Copeland, April. (1998, Jan. 30). "The 'n-word': Growing use of the racial slur–in films, music and even as a term of endearment–has fired debate in and out of the black community," *The Plain Dealer*, 1A.

McCormick, Neil. (1996, Dec. 12). "A white man's guide to the language of hip-hop," *The Daily Telegraph*, 17.

N.W.A., "Niggaz4Life," *Niggaz4Life* Los Angeles: Ruffhouse/Priority Records, 1991.

Rose, T. *Black noise: Rap music and black culture in contemporary America*, Hanover, MA: Wesleyan University P, 1994; Nelson George, *Hip Hop America* New York: Viking, 1998.

Smitherman, G. *Black talk: Words and phrases from the 'hood to the Amen corner* New York: Houghton Mifflin, 1994.

Varner and Kugiya, E1.

Watts, E.K. "The 'nigga' dialectic in rap artistry: Subversive weapon or consumer sellout?" *Ohio Speech Journal* 31, 1994: 98–113.

Watts, E.K. "An exploration of spectacular consumption: Gangsta rap as cultural commodity," *Communication Studies*, 48 (1997): 42–58.

West, C. *Race matters*, New York: 1994, 149–151. NY: Vintage. ✦

Part VI

Living in Bicultural Relationships

26

Sapphire and Sappho

Allies in Authenticity

Brenda J. Allen
University of Colorado, Boulder

I expected to like Anna even before I met her. She had applied for an instructor position in the Department of Communication where I had recently been hired as an assistant professor. A graduate student, one of her former students who really admired her, asked me to be sure to consider Anna's application. Based on that recommendation and Anna's clear qualifications for the job, I voted along with my colleagues to hire her. Since that time over six years ago, Anna and I have evolved from colleagues to best friends. From the beginning Anna seemed to be a pleasant person and we would exchange cordial greetings as we passed one another in the university halls. Students liked and respected her and I heard many comments about her excellence in teaching. Because I enjoy a similar reputation as a teacher, I felt a sort of kinship with Anna. In addition, she dressed with a certain flair that I appreciated because in the public housing development (a.k.a. "the projects") where I grew up, we black people took a special pride in how we looked. I admired how Anna, a white woman, knew how to coordinate her clothes and jewelry. After we grew friendlier she introduced me to her mother, and I then understood Anna's care with her appearance. To use a phrase from my childhood, her mother was "as clean as the Board of Health." The apple doesn't fall far from the tree, they say.

Anna and I didn't really get to know one another until after our department was relocated to less than desirable quarters. The faculty was cramped together in an open space separated only by partitions. As luck would have it, Anna and I were assigned adjacent desks. As a result of such proximity, I couldn't help but hear how she interacted with her students. I often teased her about her den-mother approach to their problems. She began to do the same with me and we would laugh at ourselves but feel good about our mutual concerns for students' welfare. Anna and I also discussed plans to teach a critical thinking course and found that we had similar ideas about issues, activities, and improvements on our own critical thinking skills in the classroom.

We soon discovered that we had much more in common than our teaching philosophies. We were both baby boomers from the Midwest, only months apart in age. We also came from lower-class families, and religion played a strong role in our childhoods. Anna's father was a Fundamentalist Evangelist preacher so she was not allowed to listen to music or dance. My mother, on the other hand, allowed me to explore many religious faiths and I grew to be very independent, free to dance my way through the whole Motown era. Despite the differences in how we experienced religion, we were both spiritually grounded and sometimes prayed together.

I was raised in Youngstown, Ohio, the eldest of three children in a single-parent home in the projects. Fortunately I grew up in a stimulating, warm community and my life was richly textured. Anna, as a beloved only child and a preacher's daughter, experienced a much more reserved upbringing. But we were both raised to be caring and nurturing. As a result, we often suffer from giving too much and overextending ourselves to others. Early in our relationship, I began to appreciate the strong sense of reciprocity that I felt with Anna because she often gave me what I would usually give to others yet rarely receive in return.

About a year into our friendship, a major turning point occurred in our relationship. Anna invited me to lunch offcampus, and when I met her at the restaurant she seemed somber. "I have something that I must tell you because our friendship is important to me."

She took a deep breath and told me that she was a lesbian.[1] After my initial surprise I thanked her for sharing something so personal and assured her that it would never negatively affect our friendship.

To the contrary we have grown closer. As a heterosexual I had never before given much thought to sexual orientation or gays "coming out of the closet." Thanks to Anna, I have become far more sensitive and enlightened. When she first invited me to her home, she showed me the room that had become her bedroom when family members visited because only a few people knew that she and her "roommate" were partners. I was amazed by the extent of the masquerade that she felt compelled to perform to maintain a facade of being straight. Anna has since related many stories about the effort that she and other members of her gay community have to exert to maintain a heterosexual image. For instance, she described a communication move that she terms "sanitizing," in which a person uses a noun or pronoun to reflect either gender neutrality or a heterosexual connotation. For example, while discussing her weekend a lesbian might say to a coworker, "my friend and I went dancing" or even "my boyfriend and I went dancing," when in fact she had really gone out with her lesbian partner. Anna also told me about "gaydar," the ability to spot another gay or lesbian person in a social environment: If the other person also has gaydar, the two of them might discreetly acknowledge one another with a simple nod or a smile. Anna noted that this should not be construed as flirting behavior but rather as a validating message that says "you're not the only one."[2]

The idea of passing as heterosexual intrigued me. Certainly I had heard about light-skinned blacks masquerading as whites but I had never considered that members of other traditionally oppressed groups would pretend to be like people in mainstream society. Anna and I have talked about how she has the option to hide this aspect of her identity to avoid discrimination, while I do not.

Once after we had gone to see a movie, Anna told me how angry she was about a scene that ridiculed homosexuals. I had not even noticed it. Now I am more alert and sometimes consult Anna for her impression of certain media depictions of gays, lesbians, and bisexuals. Because of Anna I also feel more responsible regarding sexuality issues in the classroom. During a course in critical thinking, I asked students to read an article with the author's name removed and speculate about the writer's identity. One student snickered and said, "It was probably some lesbian." In the past I probably would have breezed past the remark to avoid conflict. This time I responded to it without demeaning my student and managed to open up a discussion on the matter.

I tend to be a private person with a clear demarcation between my work and my personal life. Nonetheless, after Anna opened up to me about her personal life I began to reciprocate. We now discuss every aspect of our relationships with family, friends, significant others, colleagues, and students. Whenever I meet a prospective mate, Anna is usually the first and often the only person I will tell. Once the relationship fizzles, she is always there to help me to get back out there in my quest for a significant other. I have often been pleasantly surprised by the similarities of issues that confront us both as we try to develop and maintain positive, intimate relationships.

I have grown comfortable enough with Anna to let her in on the "black" ways of communicating that stem from my background. When I tell her that someone or something is "workin' my last nerve" (i.e., aggravating me), she knows exactly what I mean. I find myself calling her "Girl," an affectionate appellation that I normally reserve for African American sisters. I also have discussed my enjoyment of and pride in the colorful, expressive ways that many black people communicate and Anna shares my sense of wonder.

One day an African American student was talking with us about her graduation. When I made the teasing comment, "*if* you graduate," the student (who up to that moment had been speaking "proper" English) assumed a haughty stance and shot back a flippant response in an unmistakably "black" style. Anna and I marveled at this great example of "code switching," when people sometimes revert to their own cultural way of speaking during moments of high emotion.

When I moved from a predominantly white area to a racially mixed neighborhood, Anna understood why I felt more at home in my new surroundings. She has felt the same way in settings with a majority of gays and lesbians (e.g., Evangelicals Concerned[3] events, Gay Pride parades, etc.). We both seem to enjoy a similar sense of validation and contentment that differs from how we feel at work, where I am the only person of color and she is the only lesbian on the faculty.

Anna and I laugh a great deal, often at each other, as well as cry together about personal trials and tribulations and the plight of our world. We talk with each other in supportive ways regarding world events, particularly those having to do with oppression against people of color and members of gay, lesbian, and bisexual communities, and can openly discuss any sensitive topic related to race-ethnicity or sexuality. For instance, when someone in my department tried to compliment me by saying that she didn't notice my skin color, I was insulted. (This is a complicated issue that I won't attempt to explain here; see Houston (1994) for a discussion of this topic.) Fortunately, Anna was there to help me process my feelings.

At work and in our private lives each of us is actively addressing issues that concern us about the socially constructed elements of our identity, in Anna's case sexual orientation and religious background, in mine race-ethnicity and gender. We are both committed to effecting change and always resist the temptation to take on the status of "victim." We swap stories and perspectives on the socially constructed aspects of our identity for which society would condemn us, and we find beauty and awe in our differences. We collaborate with one another. We report to one another. We share challenges, victories, and failures together.

When Anna spoke at a Parents and Friends of Gays and Lesbians (PFLAG) event, I was proud to be there to give her support. Impressed by her speech, I knew that she was passionate about and committed to shedding light on gay issues, but I had no idea of the power and impact she could express. By the same token, when I was working on a community fundraiser for the Judie Davis Marrow Donor Recruitment Program (a group seeking to increase the number of persons of color registered to donate bone marrow), Anna immediately bought a ticket and attended our jazz brunch. She was the only colleague who volunteered to come without my asking, and I deeply appreciated her support.

During a faculty meeting about our department's diversity plan, I asked how we planned to evaluate our activities. Someone responded, "Well, as long as you and Anna are here, we won't have to worry." I resented the glibness of the comment and the idea that as members of "minority" groups, Anna and I were expected to carry the weight. However, my colleague was absolutely right. As long as we are part of this faculty, we will continue to address issues related to oppression and domination in its many guises at our university.

Although we are particularly concerned about women, students of color, and gays, lesbians, and bisexuals, we also care about students in general and how the "system" treats them. We do not consider ourselves either radical or passive and our alliance has made us stronger. I feel accountable to Anna, which motivates me to sometimes speak out on an issue even when I would rather not take on the burden of explaining my views to my other white colleagues. Anna feels the same way. In a sense we are both each other's back-up.

Until 1995, few of our colleagues knew that Anna was a lesbian. Our relationship reached a new turning point when I asked her to write and present a paper about passing as a heterosexual. A graduate student and I were developing a proposal for a panel on feminist standpoints on organizational communication to be presented at the national convention of the Speech Communication Association (SCA). It was suggested that I invite Anna to share her viewpoint. I knew that this was going to be a difficult request: Anna would have to "come out" to a national group of her peers. However, I firmly believed that her story would provide a critical and important perspective on organizational communication processes which probably had never been aired before and that her contribution would strengthen the panel. As Anna's friend I felt that if she did this, she would make significant progress toward liberating herself.

So I asked her. "Whew," she responded. I said, "I know." "This is major," she said. "I know," I replied. Finally she announced, "I'll do it."

Our proposal was accepted. Anna began to work on her paper[4] and I started mine.[5] In a conscientious move to negate the status of victim or stigmatized other, I focused on positive as well as negative aspects of being black and female. During this time Anna shared with me some of her fears about exposing herself to members of our field, as well as to faculty and graduate students in our department. As I wrote my paper, I occasionally hesitated to share some of my experiences and feelings because I knew that most of my colleagues would not have a clue about the pain I have endured or the pride I feel about my black womanhood. Yet whenever I thought of the monumental risks that Anna was taking, I would dismiss my reservations and press on.

We scheduled a "preview" of our SCA panel for the university community. Anna was late coming to work that day, having had a difficult night with little sleep. She was extremely anxious about doing her presentation but she came anyway. As we sat in front of a room filled with colleagues and students, Anna credited me for her being there and then she introduced her partner who was seated in the audience. The rest of the audience was visibly moved by Anna's presentation. When she concluded, they sat in stunned silence for a moment, then applauded her at length. Since that time, Anna has placed a photograph of her partner on her desk, something that heterosexuals do routinely but that often engenders great risk for some gays and lesbians.

As I review my friendship with Anna, an interracial relationship that is much more

than that, I notice that it contains many elements of the classic model of interpersonal attraction. Despite our similarities in personal style and background, Anna and I would probably not have become such good friends if she were straight. Because of her sexual orientation she can be empathetic with me in ways that my other white, straight friends cannot. Thus, I believe that our marginalized positions in society and academia have been a major factor in forming the center of our friendship.

In regard to the title of this essay, Sapphire[6] was a black female character in the old radio and television series *Amos 'n Andy*.[7] She was sassy, verbose, and intensely expressive. Sappho was a Greek poet (circa 600 B.C.) from the isle of Lesbos who wrote about romantic love between women. Each of these characters personifies one aspect of the multifaceted identities that Anna and I rarely allow others to see. Because we trust and respect one another, we are comfortable being our authentic selves—in all their complexities—with one another. We will continue to work toward helping our society become a place where members of traditionally oppressed groups can be themselves without feeling ashamed, afraid, or defensive.

Notes

1. Anna has granted me full permission to tell this story, having read and approved the essay in its entirety.

2. For a compelling discussion of examples of communication behaviors enacted in "don't ask, don't tell" environments, see Spradlin, A.L. (1998). The price of "passing:" A lesbian perspective on authenticity in organizations. *Management Communication Quarterly*, 11, 590–605.

3. A support network for gays and lesbians from Evangelical Fundamentalist church backgrounds; see Taylor, B., and Spra- dlin, A. (Eds.) (1998). *Speaking out: Faith stories of evangelical gays and lesbians*. (2nd Ed.). Denver, CO: Evangelicals Concerned Western Region.

4. Spradlin, Anna (1998), op. cit.

5. Allen, B.J. (1998). Black womanhood and feminist standpoints. *Management Communication Quarterly, 11,* 575–586.

6. Much has been written about Sapphire, a controversial fictional character. Many consider her to be an extremely negative stereotype (e.g., a shrew or "mammy") of African American women. My reference is intended to refer only to her in-your-face style of communicating. For another perspective, see Chapter 8.

7. See Ely, M.P. (1991). *The adventures of Amos 'n' Andy: A social history of an American phenomenon.* New York: Free Press.

References

Allen, B.J. (1995). 'Diversity' and organizational communication. *Journal of Applied Communication Research, 23,* 143–155.

Bell, E.L. (1992). Myths, stereotypes and realities of black women: A personal reflection. *Journal of Applied Behavioral Science, 28,* 363–376.

Hearn, J., Sheppard, D.L., Tancred-Sheriff, P. and Burrell, G. (Eds.) (1992). *The sexuality of organization.* London: Sage.

Houston, M. (1994). When black women talk with white women: Why dialogues are difficult. In González, A., Houston, M. and Chen V., (Eds.), *Our voices: Essays in culture, ethnicity, and communication (an intercultural anthology)* (133–139). Los Angeles: Roxbury.

Leonard, R. and Locke, D.C. (1993). Communication stereotypes: Is interracial communication possible? *Journal of Black Studies, 23,* 332–343.

Moses, Y.T. (1989). *Black women in academe: Issues and strategies.* Project on the status and education of women, association of American Colleges, Washington, DC. ✦

27

'I Know It Was the Blood'

Defining the Biracial Self in a Euro-American Society

Tina M. Harris
University of Georgia

As a communication researcher I have had many "defining moments" that have helped me to better understand my scholastic and research goals. It is through research projects and studies that I have become aware of how deeply embedded the issues of racial and cultural identity are in my personal life. When people ask me about the impetus behind my dissertation on interracial dating, I can not speak from the standpoint of one who has been in such a relationship. Yet my life circumstances are at a point where such a relationship *could* become a possibility, given my predominantly Euro-American environment.

Other life events have helped me to understand my interests in the areas of interracial communication, interracial romantic relationships, and biracial identity, originating with my family when we lived in Spain and continuing from recent knowledge I had acquired about my family lineage.

A short time ago I returned home to Atlanta, Georgia, for a ceremony performed at the church where my father has been the pastor for 18 years. The church was renaming the street in honor of my great-grandfather, David Franklin "Papa" Fuller. It also was dedicating a beautiful portrait of Papa to commemorate his invaluable contributions during his tenure as pastor. Although I never met Papa and only know of him through the oral history of my grandmother's and father's stories, this dedication made me

realize the richness of my family heritage through the experiences of slavery, freedom, religion, and sense of family commitment.

My great-grandfather was the product of a relationship between a prominent Euro-American man in the community and an African American woman of Native American descent. Papa's biological father never publicly acknowledged him as his son. However, he made sure that Papa's financial needs were met through gifts of land, money, clothes, and other things that symbolized an unspoken connection between them. Although his cultural identity was rarely spoken of, Papa was taught to love and value his heritage and pass that appreciation on to his children, grandchildren, and great-grandchildren. It is this part of my multicultural background—African American, Euro-American, and Native American—that forms the collective approach which I use to embrace those who are culturally, racially, and ethnically different from me. When I look at them, I see parts of myself that have yet to be discovered.

Given my family history and physical features, there is little or no hint of my multicultural identity. I am short, have medium brown skin tone with orange undertones, short kinky hair, and almond-shaped brown eyes. These distinct features have allowed me the privilege of being an African American.

American society uses a dichotomous approach to cultural diversity. On the one hand, diversity is appreciated and pro- moted; on the other, it stifles socio-economic advancement, ignites racist and prejudiced behavior, and creates instances of isolation in social situations. Such experiences often breed feelings of loneliness, anger, bitterness, resentment, and even self-loathing, all of which benefit only the dominant culture. People of the minority are alienated just for being who they are.

The concepts of *race* and *culture* are symbolically structured to create meaning. Culture involves the shared meaning of symbols, values, beliefs, and rituals within a certain group. Conversely, Europeans invented the notion of race for the sole purpose of colonizing, enslaving, and oppressing "others" of different physical characteristics, such as skin color and facial features. Because of such categorizations, individuals today are pressured by society to ascribe to various ethnic or racial groups simply to survive.

As evidenced in newspaper reports and television news stories, certain social incidents frequently contribute to the development or stagnation of one's biracial or multicultural identity. Recently, for example, an Alabama principal threatened to ban all interracial couples from attending his school's prom (Lindsay 1994; Walsh 1994). When a biracial student questioned this, Principal Humphries replied that her parents had made a mistake (by conceiving her) and that he did not want to see others do the same. In the end the principal was suspended, but this incident illustrates how those in positions of authority can cause destruction and havoc just by the words they utter—denouncing instead of celebrating diversity and biracial or bicultural identity.

As perceived by this principal and others like him, such "racial ambiguity" cannot be tolerated (Cose 1995). Because we live in a society obsessed with racial categorization, the "dilemma" of biracial and bicultural identity has angered many people. Rather than viewing biracial and bicultural identity as the fusion of two cultures with different qualities, they perceive it as an individual's choice of one race or culture over another.

The purpose of this essay is to explore two communication phenomena that aptly capture the experiences of biracial and bicultural people and their search for identity within a racially and culturally oppressive society. After conducting interviews with two self-identified bicultural individuals and evaluating research on how biracial men and women develop their racial or cultural identities (Funderburg 1994), I found evidence of two primary internal processes that may be experienced: *static cultural identity and fluid cultural identity.*

A static cultural identity may be described as a person's choice to identify with one or both cultures or races in all contexts and interactions. For example, such a person will identify himself or herself solely as African American, Euro-American, Latino, biracial, or bicultural. Throughout his or her life, that person's identity remains constant with a strong identification with a specific racial or cultural persona.

A fluid cultural identity is one whereby the person's choice of identity is context-specific and influenced by social situations and interpersonal interactions. In such instances, that person identifies with his or her cultural identity for one of two reasons: (1) to acknowledge his or her varied cultural heritage when certain concerns are central to one's being or (2) to "play the race/culture card" for unethical or manipulative purposes. Although the interviewees for this essay indicated that playing the race card was not a motivating factor in their cultural identification process, the manipulative use of one's race was noted by some subjects in Funderburg's study (1994). Unlike static cultural identity, fluid cultural identity is heavily influenced by an individual's freedom to choose the culture to which he or she most closely identifies.

This essay will explore the cultural phenomena of biracial identity as either static or fluid. Although one type of cultural identity is no more favorable than the other, each is presented as a means to understand how identity is defined by and developed within individuals from multicultural backgrounds. We will consider real-life experiences and accounts where such factors as family, friends, society, and personal experiences have greatly influenced a biracial person's decision to maintain either a static or fluid cultural identity.

Feelings of Cultural Duality

Cultural duality is a common and quite apparent phenomenon. For the thousands of people like me who come from a multiracial background but whose features do not reveal such a lineage, a search for a cultural identity can be a lifelong and tumultuous journey. Because our physical appearance sends basic information to others about who we are, certain instinctive and stereotypical behaviors are often employed that challenge one's appreciation for their culture and family history. This dilemma becomes even more difficult and complex when people who are the product of an interracial relationship must deal with a society that redefines their very being. By virtue of the fact that they are biracial and represent two or more different races or cultures, their cultural composition breeds varying emotions, opinions, and beliefs in the biracial person and in family members, friends, strangers, and society as a whole. Not only negative misperceptions and racial stereotyping from without but also personal experiences with significant others from within can have a profound impact on whether or not biracial individuals will embrace or reject one or both of their cultures.

Parents and Family

The role of a parent entails the responsibility of fulfilling the physical, emotional, spiritual, and mental needs of one's children. The biological relationship between a parent and child is unchangeable, but it is the involvement and commitment of the parent that will ensure the child's emotional well-being. Although this obligation is difficult by itself, the merging of two culturally different parents adds yet another dimension to the role of being a *true* parent. In a bicultural home it is the responsibility of one or both parents to take an active role in educating their children about the cultures and survival in a society preoccupied with categorizing race, ethnicity, and culture.

One parent who experienced a great deal of internal conflict over his obligation to his daughter and her knowledge of their Japanese ancestry was David Mura (1992). In an essay published in *Mother Jones*, Mura shares his experiences of an interracial marriage with a Euro-American and his firm desire for his daughter to possess a strong static cultural identity in both cultures. Mura believes that ultimately she will decide how to define herself—as Japanese, Japanese American, or any other label that she feels accurately defines who she is. His wife takes a more active role in educating their daughter about her biracial heritage, and Mura admits he harbors feelings of shame and guilt bred into him by his low self-esteem and lack of cultural pride as a young adult—a form of *cultural amnesia* that had

robbed him of his opportunity to discover Japanese language, culture, and history. The dominant culture has formed who he is, stripping away his multidimensional identity and creating one that is acceptable in *its* eyes only. Mura yearns for his daughter to learn about both his and his wife's cultural backgrounds and to embrace them both without placing greater importance on one over the other.

One person who shared with me the pains and joys associated with the development of identity and the significance of the parent's role was "Dana," a 22-year-old Mexican American woman who was interviewed for this essay. When asked how her divorced parents educated her about her Mexican and Irish-Catholic cultures, Dana explained that her mother, with whom she had lived in Florida until she was 13 years old, never really tried to teach her about her heritage. Instead, she instructed her to be a good person who has been extracted from all cultures. Although Dana was aware of her Mexican heritage, her environment encouraged her to present herself as a Euro-American like her school and neighborhood peers. Dana upheld a strong static cultural identity as a Euro-American female until she moved to Detroit to live with her Mexican father. There she came to really understand and appreciate all that her culture had to offer—new ways of dress, food, language, and a true sense of family. Due to her new environment, her cultural identity underwent the transition from static to fluid. Her father took an active role in educating her about her Mexican culture. As a result, Dana has now come to identify herself as fully Mexican American.

Dana's cultural identity remains static due to her desire to maintain a constant self-definition. Although her identity in her younger years was more influenced by social interactions and her peers, Dana has now made a conscious effort to claim her biracial identity despite the negative consequences. Although she has olive-colored skin, dark brown hair, and hazel eyes, her physical features are not what defines who she is—*she* defines who she is. When asked how she would educate her future biracial children, Dana said she would definitely have an active role in educating them about her and her spouse's heritages. While she does not fault her mother for failing to foster her cultural identity in her childhood, Dana is more appreciative of her father's commitment to educate her about the Mexican heritage from which she was sheltered for the first half of her life.

A similar interviewee was Jimmy, a Mexican American male whose father is Mexican and whose mother is Euro-American. Jimmy's parents were divorced as well and neither tried to educate him about his distinctly different heritages. Although his physical appearance does not reveal his dual ethnicity, Jimmy's surname quickly relays to others that he hails from an interracial household. Much like Dana, Jimmy experienced fluid cultural identity for most of his youth and had a limited knowledge of who he was or from where he had come. Not until he entered college did he begin to develop his bicultural identity.

Jimmy has tried to learn more about his Mexican heritage. He and his Euro-American wife take an active role in their daughter's life by giving her some exposure to his culture, but Jimmy believes there are other elements of her self that are just as important. From this evidence Jimmy appears to have a fluid cultural identity that embodies the many dimensions of his culture as influenced by social interactions and interpersonal relationships. Although he identifies himself as Mexican American, he only acknowledges his cultural heritage when certain concerns are central to his definition of self or when others are engaged in unethical intercultural communication. For example, Jimmy noted that in the past he has had to confront an associate or friend for using language that he deemed offensive to Mexicans. Although he is not consumed by his cultural identity, he knows there is more than one way to define oneself culturally without denying one's identity.

Dana, on the other hand, said she would go to great lengths to teach her children about their multiethnic background. Certain childhood experiences, during which her cousins called her "spic" and "wetback," crystallized her role as a future parent. She believes that her cousins must have been taught by their parents to use such derogatory words to demean those who are culturally different from them.

The experiences of Dana and Jimmy effectively illustrate how crucial the discursive role of the parent is in developing a sense of self, especially when the child is the product of a cross-cultural union. Whether parents choose to take an active or passive role in molding a child's identity, it is important that they teach their children the beauty and distinctiveness of their respective cultures and heritages. If this is not done, feelings of cultural amnesia could ultimately manifest in the hearts of many young bicultural Americans.

Another factor that contributes to the development of a static or fluid cultural identity is the role of family members other than the parents. In her personal essay, Kathleen Cross (1990) describes the emotional turmoil she experienced growing up as the product of an interracial marriage. By all appearances, Cross looks like a Euro-American female. Her features almost conceal her African American heritage, but her very being communicates a persona contrary to the naked eye. Cross is an expert on how different family members can influence how one defines oneself in a society preoccupied with race. As the title of her article—*Trapped in the Body of a White Woman*—suggests, both skin color and cultural issues are more obvious obstacles that bicultural people must overcome on a day-to-day basis.

According to Cross, she "embraces [her] African Americanness without appearing to be at odds with the European in [her]," although she has been accused of "denying [her] white heritage, being emotionally and socially confused, or being a 'wanna-be.'" Her decision to have a static cultural identity with her African American parentage is deeply rooted in the fact that she has "loved and been loved in the black community." However, she has experienced rejection by family members who have invalidated her cultural membership because of her Euro-American heritage and mannerisms. Despite this, Cross has elected to treasure the fact that "the only pigment that God saw fit to give [her] was in the freckles which He sprinkled across [her] face."

Cross married an African American man and has raised her children as African American without denying her Euro-American heritage, thereby reinforcing her preference for static cultural identity. Her case reminds us of how family, friends, and the community can alienate the ones closest to them because of their parentage or the color of their skin. In the end, however, children must reclaim their own identity through self-love and self-acceptance.

Society

As previously noted, we live in a society preoccupied with racial categorization. In her interview, Dana validated this observation by her experiences of growing up in two culturally different environments. When she lived in her Euro-American society with her mother, her peers ostracized minority children; Dana downplayed her Mexican heritage to fit in. The tables were turned when she moved to Detroit and was submerged in Mexican culture. The children in her school and neighborhood were either Mexican or African American. Because of her "white girl" features, she was treated as an outsider. It was not until she voiced her ethnic identity and said, "Hey, I am Mexican, too," that she was accepted by her peers. Having been forced to maintain a fluid cultural identity as a communication device, Dana now realizes how much society influences how we identify ourselves by these imagined and often detrimental standards.

In his personal essay in *Newsweek*, Brian Courtney (1995) personifies the internal identity struggle that biracial indi- viduals like himself must endure. He was taught by his African American father and Euro-American mother to be proud of who he is *because* of his two cultures and who he is as a person. In this case his struggle has not been between his parents' roles in his cultural education but between his two groups of African American and Euro-American friends. When he is with either one, behavioral expectations force him to reflect the race of the group whose company he keeps. His African American friends accuse him of "acting white" and thinking he is better

than they because he is "only half black." On the other hand, Brian's Euro-American friends want him to ascribe to dress codes and behaviors that are blatantly scrutinized by his African American peers. This self-described "never-ending tug of war" has only solidified Brian's belief that America must identify biracial individuals for the distinct group they are, neither one nor the other but a combination of the two. Brian's argument for a static cultural identity further exemplifies the internal duality that a biracial person experiences within interpersonal interactions.

In their qualitative study of biracial identity among children, Kerwin, Ponterotto, Jackson, and Harris (1993) found that older subjects felt that the friendships they developed were the direct result of their primary racial identification. They identified themselves as Euro-American when they associated with their Euro-American peers and vice versa with those who identified themselves as African American. Like Dana and Brian, their social networks have forced them to adopt a static cultural identity to sustain a sense of belonging. Unfortunately, such a decision is made for the sake of others rather than for one's own self-evolution.

Where Do We Go From Here?

As evidenced by the previous accounts, individuals who are culturally diverse by birth and racial or cultural identity—as we *all* are—are often pressured to choose one culture over another. They can be educated by their parents and members of their community to embrace both cultures while simultaneously identifying with their biracial community. Unfortunately, this is not always the case. So what must be done to celebrate this unique state of cultural diversity?

Journalist Bechetta Jackson (1995) argues that parents must try to educate their own children about their heritages, particularly when the issue of transracial adoption has to be addressed. How can parents from one culture educate their adopted children about *their* culture if it is not a part of their lived experience? In a case involving a Euro-American couple planning to adopt two African American boys, the parents stated that they are "committed to doing everything they can to raise the children with knowledge about who they are and where they come from. . . .They need to know who they are" (Jackson 1995). The couple attends a predominantly African American church, lives in a multiracial community, and has frequent interactions with both their African American and Euro-American friends. This would seem to be an ideal environment to foster a healthy cultural identity within the boys. Yet, however their cultural identity is shaped by their adoptive parents, they will ultimately have to construct their own identity as they mature into adulthood.

Conclusion

The issue of racial and cultural identity for biracial and bicultural people is a constant internal battle which forces them to either reject or accept certain parts of their entire being. It is through static or fluid cultural identity that a person can truly experience self-definition, understanding, and appreciation of who they are. Although neither form of self-definition is healthier than the other, it is the freedom of choice that allows individuals to determine their own cultural identity. Static cultural identity and fluid cultural identity are communication phenomena reflecting the developmental processes that biracial individuals experience in an attempt to define themselves *for* themselves. Whether their identity is constant or influenced by social situations and interpersonal interactions with family, friends, and society, it is inevitably an individual choice.

American society needs to learn to acknowledge, respect, and celebrate cultural diversity through cultural identity. Public policy has mandated integration in the workplace, classrooms, restaurants, and other public domains, but what about our interpersonal relationships? Will society as a whole *ever* look beyond the pigmentation of one's skin to deem one as worthy? Presently, the answer is a sad, resounding "no." However, the remedy must not be one of acceptance but one of determination, celebration, and jubilation.

Until this comes to pass, it is the right and responsibility of parents and biracial children, as well as children from same-race unions, to become more educated about the heritages that have produced a myriad of beautiful people who have made valuable contributions to their communities, society, and the world. If we look at the surface of their skin, we see a people with rituals, experiences, and wisdom different from our own. If we look *beneath* their skin, we will find intelligence, spirituality, beauty, soul, determination, and peace.

Come celebrate your diversity. Although we all take different paths in life, who is to say that our ancestors never shared the same road we travel? When we look at each other, do we see reflections of ourselves or what we are going to be? Whether our cultural identities are static or fluid, it is only through our cultural histories that these questions can be answered.

References

Cose, E. (1995, Feb. 13). One drop of bloody history: Americans have always defined themselves on the basis of race. *Newsweek*, 125(7), 70–72.

Courtney, B. (1995, Feb. 13). Freedom from choice: Being biracial has meant denying half of my identity. *Newsweek*, 125(7), 16.

Cross, K. (1990, Oct.). Trapped in the body of a white woman. *Ebony Magazine*, 70–74.

Funderburg, L. (1994). *Black, white, other: Biracial Americans talk about race and identity.* New York: William Morrow.

Jackson, B. (1995, May 8). Should white families adopt black children? *JET,* 87(26) 34–38.

Kerwin, C., Ponterotto, J., Jackson, B. and Harris, A. (1993). Racial identity in biracial children: A qualitative investigation. *Journal of Counseling Psychology*, 40 (2), 221–231.

Lindsay, D. (1994, Mar. 23). Alabama principal suspended in flap over mixed-race couples. *Education Week*, 13(26), 12.

Mura, D. (1992, Sept./Oct.). What should I tell Samantha, my biracial daughter, about secrets and anger? How is she going to choose an identity? *Mother Jones*, 17(5), 18–22.

Walsh, M. (1994, May 25). Justice Department seeks to out Alabama principal: At issue is alleged race discrimination. *Education Week,*13(35) 1, 13. ✦

28

Being *Hapa*

A Choice for Cultural Empowerment

Diane M. Kimoto
Grand Valley State University

> *If then, in the near future, Japanese Americans continue to be regarded as "other," the challenge for them is to identify the cultural strands that underlie this "otherness," cultivating those that produce optimal benefits.*
>
> —Okamura (1995, A16)

When I first read this quote in a recent issue of the *Pacific Citizen*, a journal produced by the Japanese American Citizens' League, I was delighted. It discussed how many people like myself had searched for their cultural identities, incorporating the perspectives of young and old alike. Younger generations of *hapas*, individuals from mixed Asian American backgrounds (e.g., Japanese, Chinese, Filipino, etc.), reveled in their multiracial heritage. Furthermore, they applauded the efforts of their parents, second (i.e., *nisei*) and third (i.e., *sansei*) generations of Asian Americans who had suffered through years of marginalization and soul searching in their efforts to lay the foundation for their cultural empowerment. It became clear to me that my own search for cultural identity lay within these intergenerational narratives.

When I first turned to my parents for an explanation of my mixed culture, I was not quite sure if I should ask my adoptive parents or my biological ones. Had I adopted the culture and heritage of my new parents along with the background I was born with?

On the one hand, some believe that children should be adopted only by those who share a similar cultural heritage so that the confusion surrounding their natural versus adoptive roots may be avoided. On the other hand, many adoptive families have successfully negotiated this challenge without any problems. In either event, the role that adoption plays in the development and negotiation of one's ethnic identity will continue to be hotly debated.

The importance of understanding the negotiation of my cultural identity and being able to recount that struggle has been heightened by the fact that I am expecting my first child. I wonder to what degree I will be able to explain to him the cultural impressions and knowledge of both my adoptive and biological parents. When I was adopted in 1956, there were no guidelines for a multiracial couple to follow to be an ideal adoptive family. Instead, my parents had to create their own means for integrating my biological (Japanese, Mexican, Spanish, and Indian) and adoptive (Japanese, Lebanese, German, Greek, Italian, etc.) backgrounds.

I was born Monica Lynn Arcinega. However, when I was adopted, my name was changed to Diane Michelle Kimoto. Although the change was a simple legality, the merging of my cultural pasts has since involved a series of conscious choices. It is the goal of this essay to describe some of these choices so that the reader may understand how adoption continues to play a role in the shaping of my cultural identity and how my present cultural identity reflects an empowerment of multiculturality. In delineating this process of ethnic empowerment, this essay addresses the following questions: What is cultural knowledge? What is power? How does cultural knowledge cultivate power?

What Is Cultural Knowledge?

Cultural knowledge is based on sensing differences. Thus, to understand where you are or what you are doing, you must learn about yourself in relation to where others live and how they behave. According to Bateson (1990),

> one of the greatest steps forward in history was learning to regard those who spoke odd-sounding languages and had different smells and habits as fully

human, as similar to oneself. The next step from this realization, the step which we have still not fully made, is the willingness to question and purposefully alter one's own conditions and habits, to learn by observing others. (57)

As this quote suggests, cultural knowledge entails a search for one's ethnic identity in relation to others.

In much the same manner my biological mother no doubt hoped that I would learn what it means to be a Japanese American and a person of color in this country. Because she was only 16 years old when I was born, it is likely that part of her early childhood was spent in an internment camp during World War II. As a consequence, not only did she and her family have to prove their loyalty to the United States, but they had to do so in light of extreme prejudice. Therefore, her request that I be reared in a more "American" fashion (e.g., Christian religion, Eurocentric education, English language, etc.) rather than according to traditional Japanese customs (e.g., an arranged marriage, Buddhist religion, attendance at a private Japanese-language school, etc.) did not appear out of place. It was simply her way of justifying my American background so that I might be better accepted within the mainstream of society.

My biological mother also asked that I be placed with a multiracial couple as opposed to a Japanese American or Anglo American one. At first I did not understand why. However, after perusing historical records, personal essays, and oral histories about the Japanese and Hispanic communities in Los Angeles during the 1950s, I began to fathom the degree to which these communities had been marginalized (e.g., restricted in segregated communities), demeaned for the color of their skin, or relegated to non-professional jobs. My mother's petition, I believe now, was an attempt to ensure that my background as a person of color would not be forgotten.

When I was young, my parents told me how a petition had been circulated in the neighborhood to keep them from purchasing our home. I turned to my adoptive father, a blind, World War II, *nisei* veteran, for an explanation as to why there was so much antagonism toward us. He explained that some people were frightened of what they did not know or understand. Instead of denigrating our biased neighbors, he spoke of the need to be patient and understanding. He felt that we could change their opinions through our actions.

I imagine that my biological parents would have said and done the same thing. They too were Americans. Through experiences such as these, my parents have reinforced for me the importance of our country's democratic ideals and foundations. They have also tempered this knowledge with the realism that people of color have been marginalized by these same ideals.

My adoptive mother also played a significant role in the development of my cultural knowledge. Through her gastronomic feasts she introduced me to an appreciation of cultural differences. For example, she never missed an opportunity to combine the food and folklore of several cultures into a meal. I would come to dinner and find a bowl of saimin (Japanese noodles in broth) next to a Mexican tamale, topped off with some kibbi (a layered Lebanese dish with meat, pine nuts, and cracked wheat). Using her Lebanese background as the catalyst for discussions on cultural rituals and customs, she emphasized the importance of my heritage.

In a sense I was a living example of the United Nations; my cultural identity developed as a composite of the multiple views held and created by myself along with those created by others. As such, cultural identity came to,

reflect the social construction and acquisition of culture where a tacit agreement determines what is real and not real in any given society. . . and communication creates meaning as opposed to merely messages and in this way aids the individual in understanding personal and social experiences. (Stoller 1985, 5)

The constraints stipulated by my biological mother for my adoption had just as much an impact on the construction of my cultural identity as my day-to-day interactions with my adoptive parents.

What Is Power?

Power has often been defined as the ability to control behaviors, gain compliance, or change the beliefs, opinions, and values of others. In each of these instances power is directed outward toward the control of others. An alternative way of considering power, particularly when addressing the issue of cultural identity, might be to focus the direction of control inward. Building upon Mead's (1934) notion that using a name or label for oneself is the foundation on which one acquires a self, power could then be defined as an individual's ability to choose or create the labels necessary for cultural self-identification. As such, cultural empowerment would be equated with choice rather than with mere emulation.

My first association with the label *hapa* came from my parents who, like other multiracial couples, wanted to convey to me the benefits of my physical and cultural blending. *Hapa* is usually interpreted to mean "mixed" or "half." As a small child I enjoyed my *hapa* status because it allowed me to mingle with various cultures. Possibly these interactions were fostered by the fact that I presented a different "look" that seemed neither Japanese nor Mexican. Instead I was mistaken as being Filipina, Portuguese, Hawaiian, Italian, Indian, or French. On the other hand, I believe that the exposure and appreciation of cultural differences cultivated by my adoptive parents was the underlying reason why being *hapa* was such a satisfying experience. Through their help I regarded the term *hapa* as the ability to get along with everyone. It was the antithesis of racism and racial hatred.

My viewpoint changed after I turned 18, however, when I allowed others to create a new interpretation of *hapa* for me, and I first experienced the powerful and negative influence of being labeled *multiracial*. I was dating a young man whose mother wanted him to date someone "more his kind." Having resided our entire lives around the corner from each other, I never suspected for a moment that my cultural heritage would present a problem. Besides, this was liberal Southern California where people were sup-posedly tolerant. Being *hapa* took on new meaning as I was labeled a "half-breed." I was so hurt that I began to rationalize my varied cultural background into distinct categories, percentages, and labels. Instead of being Japanese American, I was now only one-quarter Japanese American, one-eighth Mexican American, and so on. By buying into the mechanics of this fragmenting process, I had allowed others to control my behavior and self-identification.

Over the next 10 years I gradually realized that I had a right to identify myself differently in various situations. Just as people identify themselves differently according to their varied social roles (e.g., child, parent, lover, employee, student, etc.), multiracial people have the right— even the privilege— to identify themselves differently in response to the social demands of the situation. When I worked at a family center for Latina women, I felt comfortable with my reliance on my Mexican American heritage and identified myself as such. I did not feel like I had betrayed my Japanese American background. Therefore, it is important to recognize that this changeability is not an exercise in cultural fragmenting or parceling, but rather an attempt to reaffirm one's power to self-identify.

How Does Cultural Knowledge Provide Power?

We are not born with labels. Usually they are given to us. In turn, we associate power with the individual who directs the labeling process. Some multiracial individuals, by accepting the cultural labels given to them, relinquish their power to control how they are identified. Others exert their power by questioning these cultural labels and choosing to develop and negotiate new ones that better reflect their identities. If we are to convert our knowledge of cultural differences into power, then we must encourage our children to question cultural labels no matter how confusing, frightening, or threatening that might be. Through this process, labels that empower our cultural identities and bridge the differences between ourselves and others will continue.

However, the manner in which this perpetuation process occurs is unspecified. From research on intergenerational communication we have learned that "continuity is an adaptive response to both internal and external pressures" (Atchley 1985, 238). Internal pressures stem from an individual's need to develop and maintain a stable foundation of viewpoints from which to make future judgments and predictions. External pressures arise from an individual's need to incorporate these viewpoints into their various social roles. Associated within this balance between internal and external pressures lies an inherent sense of permanence and power in the knowledge that how one thinks, believes, and acts will continue long after one is gone.

Similarly, multiracial people are confronted with the notion of balance when considering cultural continuity. In this case, internal pressures for continuity may be interpreted as a need by multiracial individuals to select or construct labels and images that empower their cultural identities. External pressures for continuity may be interpreted as a need to use these constructions during the various roles of daily interaction. The key to transforming cultural knowledge into power seems to rest on the attainment of cultural continuity.

For me to pass on to my son the tools with which to find his own answers, I have had to re-evaluate the concept of *hapa*. Recently, however, this term has been replaced by a more empowering one: *doubling*. As mentioned earlier, *hapa* is often translated as "mixed" or "half." *Doubling* suggests that an individual's identity is an intact whole derived from complete rather than half versions of culture. The meaning and the choice of each term carries with it different constructions of reality. Personally, I prefer to employ both terms interchangeably. In my view, my *hapa* status or multiracial background has doubled my understanding and appreciation of who I am. The attainment of cultural continuity for me rests on cultivating in my son the desire to know more about himself and the courage to ask his own questions. I hope to fuel his curiosity by sharing with

him how I came to identify myself as both a *hapa* and a *double*.

Conclusion

My life has been enriched by the strength and depth of the cultures from which my families hail. The continuity and meaning of these traditions connect me more closely to that history, and I am fortunate to feel such a connection with both sets of parents. Through open discussions about my cultural identity with my adoptive parents, I have gained the reassurance and confidence to search for and create new personal links to my cultural past.

In my struggle for and development of a cultural identity, the establishment of some connection to my biological parents has been important. For example, the connection to my Japanese American heritage was enhanced as I ascertained similarities between my biological mother and my adoptive father, such as their common treatment as objects of prejudice during World War II. On the other hand, I became more tied to my Mexican American heritage as I immersed myself in the folklore, customs, and genealogy of my Arcinega background. Moreover, these feelings were bolstered during high school when I worked at an orphanage in Tecate, Mexico, and during college when I was working and learning Spanish from co-employees in a Mexican restaurant. I have taken every opportunity to write about, interview, or experience the lives of my ancestors.

As to whether or not adopted children can feel as if they have inherited the cultural roots of their adoptive parents, the answer for me is "yes." Inasmuch as I am Japanese and Mexican, I choose also to be Lebanese, Hawaiian, Italian, German, and so on. However, I realize that my decision may not be the same as my child's. He alone must choose how to identify himself. In sharing with him the reasons for my decision, I hope to nurture his ability and confidence to question who he is.

By learning the stories of other people of color, I have come to understand some of the tensions in my relationships with them as well as within myself. I believe that in finding ways to empower oneself through self-created labels, multicultural people can reclaim their culture and history. According to Hirabayashi (1995), the future of multiracial people will be ensured through the encouragement of individuals' abilities to order their own thoughts, determine their own goals, and claim responsibility or ownership for their own actions.

In general, the development of one's cultural identity is an ongoing process, and my family and I have dealt with the issues of adoption and cultural empowerment in the nourishing of that identity. But what kinds of choices remain in my future? How will I label myself tomorrow or the year after? The answers to these questions are unknown. What is known is that I will continue to freely and independently choose the labels with which I identify myself. As such, my ability to imagine myself in various cultural roles and identities carries with it the opportunity to alter the racial ignorance of myself and others.

References

Atchley, R.C. (1985). *Social forces and aging.* Belmont, CA: Wadsworth.

Bateson, M.C. (1990). *Composing a life.* New York: Plume.

Hamamoto, D.Y. (1994). *Monitored peril.* Minneapolis: University of Minnesota.

Hirabayashi, L. (1995, Dec.). Teaching as mastery and mystery. *Pacific Citizen,* B38–B39.

Mead, G.H. (1934). *Mind, self, and society.* Chicago, IL: University of Chicago.

Moraga, C. and Anzaldúa, G., (Eds.). (1983). *This bridge called my back: Writings by radical women of color.* New York: Kitchen Table Women of Color.

Okamura, L. (1995, Dec.). Who were the Japanese Americans? *Pacific Citizen,* A15–A16.

Root, M.P.P. (1992). *Racially mixed people in America.* Newbury Park, CA: Sage.

Root, M.P.P. (1994). *Racially mixed people in the new millennium.* Thousand Oaks, CA: Sage.

Stoller, P. (1985). Towards a phenomenological perspective in pidgin and Creole studies. In Hancock, I.F., (Ed.), *Diversity and development in English-created Creoles* (1–12). Ann Arbor, MI: Karoma.

Yoshimura, V. (1995, Dec.). Ethnicity: Please check one. *Pacific Citizen,* A18. ✦

29

Living In/Between

Richard Morris
Arizona State University West

> *The experiences of Indians since the 1880s have been uniform in the sense that they have been confined within the boundaries of white individualism and whenever and wherever they have attempted to recapture the old sense of community, technology and domestic American politics have combined to beat back their efforts.*
>
> —Vine Deloria, Jr.
> (1989, 265–266)

Several years ago my great aunt Orie entered the last days of her century. For decades she had been the matriarch and therefore the keeper of secrets for our family. In her last days she passed on to her successor, my mother, the well-kept secrets—the most closely guarded of which concerned our family origins. Although we had always been taught to acknowledge that there was "a little Indian blood in our family"—a confession always uttered in the muted tones of whispered conversation—the oral history of our family, now passed to my mother, revealed that my mother's parents were each three-fourths Mescalero. The details of this revelation are intriguing, but what is most significant for the purposes of this essay is what the difficulties of maintaining a cultural identity tell us about some of the key problems of intercultural communication. For through this revelation we began to glimpse brief portraits of lived experiences that help us to understand the disparate treatments of alterity, significant origins of self-hatred and hatred of the "other," the sanctification and mummification of cultural identity, the consequences of the theft of cultural identity, and among other things, why the dominance of singu-

larity over inclusive alterity threatens not only cultural identity but also the survival of the species.

We might begin by noticing that one of the great tragedies of our time is that so many for so long have been taught that they must cast off their cultural identities if they are to survive, that the only possibility of liberation and freedom lay in ceasing to be what they had always been so they might become something they could never be. At various times and in various places in the United States, at least, this imperative has been advanced and defended as the spoils of conquest, as the inexorable forward march of progress, as the needs of the many outweighing the needs of the few, as an unavoidable evolutionary outcome, as a matter of creating the singular America that is so completely envisioned by the "melting pot" metaphor, as the urgency of bringing "civilization" to the "uncivilized" (see, e.g., Allen 1989; Bataille and Silet 1980; Berkhofer 1978; Christensen and Demmert 1978; Clifton 1990; Cornell 1987; Crow Dog and Erdoes 1995; Deloria 1978; Deloria and Lytle 1984; Hirschfelder 1982; Means 1995; Stedman 1982; and Takaki 1993). The imperative's most recent incarnation is amply illustrated by efforts to make English the official language of the United States, is in the form of efficiency. Elevating English to the status of official language, some believe, will be less costly (more efficient) and will stand as an explicit sign to immigrants that they are expected to assimilate into the dominant culture as quickly as possible (more efficiently) so that the United States can maintain its supposedly singular cultural identity with as little disruption (to efficiency) as possible.

I leave for other discussions the numerous flaws in this reasoning and move directly to the main thesis of this essay that requiring "the other" to cast off cultural identity has severe consequences for personal, cultural, social, and species stability. Although I have no doubt that my observations and arguments here are in many respects applicable to other groups, I restrict my focus to the experiences of Native Americans. My thesis begins with a brief personal narrative that serves to identify some of the key problems of maintaining cultural identity within a larger society that tremendously values and requires homogeneity while at the same time claiming to value and promote diversity.[1] I then move to a consideration of these problems within a broader frame of reference.

Origins

Having been raised almost exclusively by my mother, I spent my early life learning lessons about how to get along in a world in which I did not live. Much later I would come to understand the meaning of this disparity. As a child, however, I experienced the world as being divided between the beliefs with which I was reared and the beliefs that I was required to manifest in my behaviors whenever I interacted with the world at large. I don't recall when I first came to the realization that these very different ways of living in the world were incompatible and were not to be confused without undesirable consequences. But I do recall constantly struggling to discover the limits of my two sets of beliefs, and I remember with remarkable clarity the unease with which I moved between these two disparate worlds, rarely feeling comfortable by either. The magnitude of my unease was variously attenuated or exacerbated and in many respects, I suppose, was not significantly different from what children generally experience in their struggle to fit into an identity of their own. But the quality of that unease, I was later to discover, was markedly different from the unease of my cohorts.

While my cohorts struggled for the most part with choosing which part of the dominant culture's worldview they could accept, I confronted a qualitatively different set of choices—to embrace this or that worldview, to embrace both worldviews simultaneously, to attempt to create an amalgam of clearly incompatible worldviews, to bid to remake myself according to the dictates of some other image. This language is imported, of course, at the time my experiences focused on whether to live according to my mother's rules or the rules of the dominant society. Throughout childhood, adoles-

cence, and early adulthood I labored and experimented continually: rejecting society and its rules, there rejecting my mother and her rules, there attempting to force my own internal rules on the external world, there trying to force my external self on my internal self, there trying to blend the rules of both worlds to make a coherent whole, there resigning myself to a life of duality.

Not until much later, while conducting research on a reservation, did I first adequately experience the resolution of my unease. Unexpectedly I felt "at home," where I no longer felt a tension between internal and external selves, and where I no longer confronted a qualitative choice. After considerable introspection and contemplation, and through the keen insights of others, I began to understand that my unease was fundamentally ontological rather than epistemological and that dissolving or even dissipating the unease of living "in/between" worlds hinges on the freedom to choose between those worlds.

Even now, as I write this essay, I feel the tension between these two worlds—one, advising me to take a position of "standing back," of backgrounding the "I" and foregrounding the "we" as a means of elevating my discourse beyond considerations of self to considerations of tribe, collectivity, of community; the other pressing me through long years of training and conditioning to reach further into an analysis of self as a means of exploring the unease to which I have alluded. Just as those who understand the latter understand that a parable is about the collectivity rather than the ostensible self, those who understand the former understand that stories about the collectivity are also stories about the self. Even so, to live "in/between" is to live constantly with choices between the ontological and the epistemological, between being one's self and one's other self, with every choice becoming both a rejection and an acceptance of self. To understand how such lack of freedom becomes the nexus of personal experiences that translate directly and indirectly into destructive cultural and societal tensions, I chose here to look toward the collectivity, to look more deeply into why diversity cannot dissolve into singularity. The forced acculturation and assimilation of Native Americans is illustrative.

Living In

From the beginnings of colonization to the present and into the foreseeable future, Native Americans have faced and continue to face constant pressures to acculturate and assimilate, to abandon their cultures and integrate themselves into the mainstream (Allen 1992; Armstrong 1972; Berkhofer 1978; Bruchac 1989; Buckanaga 1978; Cahn 1969; Clifton 1990; Cornell 1987; Deloria 1978; Deloria and Lytle 1984; Dippie 1982; Klien and Ackerman 1995; Korsmo 1990; McDonald 1978; Mankiller and Wallis 1993; Means 1995; Nabokov 1991; Riley 1993; Stedman 1982; Takaki 1993; Thomas 1966–1967; Todorov 1992; Washburn 1971; Wax and Buchanan 1975; and Wilkinson 1987). The means whereby this process has been, is being, and will be carried out are manifold, but there have been, are, and will continue to be at least two clearly indentifiable consequences of such efforts—first, the irreconcilable division of society into self and other; second, a divided cultural self.

The irreconcilable division of society into self and other is poignantly portrayed by my mother's experiences. Like many others from her generation, my mother was raised within the framework of a Native American worldview—while simultaneously being taught that nothing was worse than being "Indian," that passing for anything was preferable to being identified as an "Indian," that she must seek to look and act as "white" as possible, that she must marry a white man for the sake of her children, and that her children must be raised according to the dictates of the "white" world.

In some measure my mother's generation—as well as the generations before and after—lived under a caliginous cloud of extraordinarily negative stereotypes, according to which "Indians" were and are drunkards, lazy, lewd, fanatical, stoic to the point of unfeeling and uncaring, butcherers of small children, rapists, irrational, uncivilized, Godless, heathens, stupid, promiscu-

ous, uneducatable, dirty, rapacious, directionless, depraved, a doomed species, befeathered, sneaky, shameless, treacherous, immoral, unethical, criminally inclined, murderous, moribund, animals, kidnappers, an atavistic anachronism, given to torturing their victims mercilessly and without reason, the children of Satan, childlike without any of the redeeming qualities that "normal" children possess, given to uncontrollable and unfounded fits of rage, chauvinistic beyond measure, craftily dangerous, inutile, incapable of governing or of being governed, primitive, bloodthirsty, savage (Armstrong 1972; Bataille and Silet 1980; Berkhofer 1978; Christensen and Demmert 1978; Clifton 1990; Cornell 1987; Deloria 1978; Deloria 1989; Deloria and Lytle 1984; Friar 1972; Hirschfelder 1982; McDonald 1978; Means 1995; Morris and Wander 1990; O'Connor 1980; Riley 1993; Stechnan 1982; and Thomas 1966–1967). This is only a short list, to be sure, and it cannot account entirely for the fact that Native Americans have been and are yet counseled to work assiduously to hide their identities by pretending to be anything other than "Indian."

To reach a fuller understanding of this phenomenon, we must look further still.[2] The institution of the reservation system, for example, has been and continues to be enormously successful in isolating Native Americans.[3] Such isolation has had and continues to have a three-fold benefit for the dominant society. In the first place, it prevents Native Americans from assembling and mobilizing to bring about the kinds of change that would permit them to live their lives according to their own worldviews. In the second place, it prevents the general population of the United States from seeing and experiencing Native Americans as fully human, from witnessing the inhumane conditions under which they were and are forced to live, from comprehending the hatefulness behind the stereotypes. And in the third place, ghettoizing Native Americans allows the government to run and control the lives of Native Americans—to take away their religions, their sacred lands, their children, their livelihoods, their social, political, and cultural alignments, their food sources, their mobility, their sovereignty, their communities, and their dignity.

The irreconcilable division of society into self and other is further perpetuated by the little known and little understood fact that Native Americans are "wards of the state" and that many Native American tribes are independent, sovereign nations (Berkhofer 1978; Cahn 1969; Clifton 1990; Cornell 1987: Deloria 1974; Deloria and Lytle 1984; Dippie 1982; Nabokov 1991; Washburn 1971; and Wilkinson 1987). Some of the central consequences of not understanding these facts are far-reaching, as illustrated by a recent editorial, titled "Indians Need More Self-Help, Not Handouts," by Joseph Perkins (1995).

There is nothing extraordinary about Perkins' editorial. The writer's poor understanding of history, glittering generalizations, inconsistent reasoning, misperceptions of legal and political issues, and failure to grasp the special relationship that the federal government has to Native Americans as "wards of the state" and as independent, sovereign nations that have validated, legal contracts (treaties) with the United States government are hardly conspiratorial, the result of an atypical education, or any worse than the average citizen. In fact, the editorial's banality—the distinct possibility that these sentiments might be or have been uttered by nearly anyone, nearly anywhere in the United States, nearly anytime within the last 100 years—is precisely what makes it of value. For within the narrow confines of that banality, explanations abound.

For example, the writer seems quite content with the explanation that the "big difference (between Indians and non-Indians) is that most non-Indians don't believe that the government is obliged to meet those needs for them." Had the writer been better informed about history, or had he taken the time to investigate the matter (say, simply by asking Ada Deer or any one of the other eminently qualified individuals at the NCAI conference), he would have learned that the federal government does in fact have a double obligation to Native Americans that it does not have with any other group—viz, because the federal government persists in regarding Native Americans as "wards of the state,"

and because many Native American tribes are legally independent, sovereign nations, the federal government is obliged to live up to the terms of its contracts with those nations.

Having discovered this much, the writer might then have learned that, far from having "succumbed to an entitlement mentality" and further still from being in the position of taking "handouts" from the federal government, the federal government has given far, far less than it promised repeatedly in return for taking much more than it ever threatened. To put the matter in more practical terms, had the federal government simply lived up to the terms of its treaties with the Native Americans, the frightening statistics that the writer repeats in this editorial very likely would not exist. The high infant mortality rate, the short life expectancy, alcoholism brought on by years of despair, the low unemployment rate, poor nutrition, and so forth, very likely would be quite other than what they are because the treaties that the federal government made with the Native Americans would have prevented such things from occurring (i.e., we have no evidence to suggest that any of these problems existed among Native Americans prior to the arrival of Europeans).

The writer also seems quite content with the explanation that "Indians may be entitled to certain benefits from the federal government. But no more or less than other groups of U.S. citizens." The reasons for this, from the writer's perspective, are two-fold: first, Native Americans are just another interest group and, second, because the atrocities committed against Native Americans, including the theft of their lands and the butchery of their people, are now irrelevant since "most Americans had nothing to do with the taking of their land" (see, e.g., Berkhofer 1978; Cahn 1969; Clifton 1990; Cornell 1987; Deloria 1974; Deloria and Lytle 1984; Dippie 1982; Nabokov 1991; Takaki 1993; Todorov 1992: Washburn 1971; and Wilkinson 1987). These are complicated fallacies that merit further consideration.

For example, the popular view that Native Americans are just another interest group seems like nothing more than a simple historical error that could be answered by paying attention to the fact that Native Americans, unlike any other minority group, are independent, sovereign nations that have legal contracts with the federal government, which is why there is not a Bureau of African American Affairs, a Bureau of Irish American Affairs, a Bureau of Asian American Affairs, and so forth. But this is not really the crux of the matter. What seems to be underlying this point of view is the belief that history has no relevance to the present and the even more troubling belief that the root of Native American problems is their failure to acculturate and assimilate.

Suppose we personalize the first belief thus: an armed man walks into Mr. Perkins' home, demands that the occupants move themselves into the backyard, and moves his family into Mr. Perkins' home. Suppose further that the Perkins family are forced to continue to live in the backyard, are not permitted to conduct commerce, to practice their religion, or to participate in any significant way in the defining elements of their culture, and that new "owners" of the Perkins' home repeatedly decrease the amount of the backyard in which the Perkins' may "roam." Suppose the family that now occupies the Perkins' home forcibly removes their children from the backyard, puts them in a school that will not permit them to speak their own language, teaches them that being a Perkins is the worst possible thing one might be, requires them to learn a new language and way of life, and sends them home to the backyard where they can help other Perkins family members learn this new reality. Suppose finally, that this continues for 50 years. Is the home any less stolen 50 years after the fact than it was on the day when the man with the gun forced the Perkins family from their home? Does the fact that other people have subsequently moved into the neighborhood in any way alter the fact that their home was stolen? This is an oversimplification, to be sure; to get closer to the mark we would have to create treaties, make the land sacred, make the Perkins family wards, kill several of the Perkins' children, and so forth. No doubt, we would also wish to point out that the theft of

Perkins-like homes has been occurring continuously from the beginnings of "colonization" to the present (see, e.g., Berkhofer 1978; Cahn 1969; Clifton 1990; Cornell 1987; Deloria 1974; Deloria and Lytle 1984; Dippie 1982; Nabokov 1991; Takaki 1991; Todorov 1992; Washburn 1971; and Wilkinson 1987). But the point is sufficiently clear: history always matters, and it is no more legitimate to argue that people who arrived in the United States after the fact are not obligated to live up to the conditions of treaties that were made before their arrival than it would be to argue that the Bill of Rights does not apply to anyone who arrived after its ratification.

Underlying all of the writer's explanations, however, is a seemingly incontestable belief that the very best thing that Native Americans can do for themselves is acculturate and assimilate. Consider each of the writer's key points: the reason that Native Americans decry "proposals by the 'mean-spirited' Republican Congress," the reason they have "succumbed to an entitlement mentality," the reason they cannot "make a claim on all the taxpayers when most Americans had nothing to do with the taking of" Native American lands, the reason they "must be prepared to share the burden of balancing the federal budget," the reason that their dependency "has robbed them of their sovereignty and deprived them of self-determination," the reason they live in "Third World conditions," and the reason for their poverty, their joblessness, their lack of indoor toilets and telephones, their short life-span, their high rates of diabetes and tuberculosis, their high incidence of influenza and pneumonia, their high infant mortality and murder rates, and their high rate of alcohol dependency—all are the result of the failure of Native Americans to acculturate and assimilate, to shed their "outdated," "outmoded," "atavistic" view of the world and join with a more "progressive," "enlightened," and "inevitable" view of the world.

Like so many other things to which we might point, this editorial points us toward an unfortunate truth: Native Americans like my mother—and African Americans like Mr.

Perkins—were and still are being taught to use their lives as the means for destroying their cultural identities, thereby aiding in the destruction of alterity. Within this frame of reference, alterity hypothetically dissolves across two or three generations. An "Indian" marries a "white" person to create children who are half white and half "Indian" by blood and completely "white" by training, thus accomplishing in a short period of time both the goals enshrined within the melting pot metaphor and in theory, the dissolution of alterity.

Because alterity cannot be restricted to lineage or race, however, this process actually perpetuates rather than dissolves the irreconcilable division of society into self and other. Because difference, within this perspective, is "bad," it must be sought out and eradicated continually, relentlessly. Since difference cannot be eradicated so long as more than one thing exists (given the nature of identity), the division between self and other is forever irreconcilable. The searchers who are charged with creating a unity of singularity through the eradication of difference cannot reach their goal without reducing the world to a single individual, and those who follow the promise of a place within the unity of singularity cannot experience the cessation of their unease because they will always and forever be the difference that must be destroyed.

Living Between

A second significant consequence of efforts to force Native Americans to acculturate and assimilate—the creation of a culturally divided self—turns our essay in an inward direction: for in struggling to resist acculturation and assimilation, many Native Americans have constructed and continue to construct an identity indirectly derived from the irreconcilable division of society into self and other. As far back as Native American oral histories extend—to the beginning of time, according to many such histories—cultural identity has been purely a behavioral matter. So long as one behaved like a Zuni, for example, one was a Zuni. Such a distinction acknowledges self and non-self, which is

markedly different from the creation of self and other in that non-self is entitled (expected, permitted, allowed, encouraged, etc.) to be whatever non-self is—for example, Lakota. Sitting Bull articulated the matter with extraordinary clarity: "It is not necessary that eagles should become crows."

Some contemporary Native Americans, by contrast have begun to distinguish self from other on the basis of what I call "blood logic." According to this perspective, identity is determined not on the basis of behavior but on one's ability to prove one's lineage. Thus, anyone who can prove he or she is three-quarters Winnebago, for example, is more "authentically" Native American than someone only one-fourth Winnebago but is not nearly as "authentic" as someone who can establish the fact of being four-fourths Winnebago. While this construction first emerged in the nineteenth century with the government's desire to know exactly which individuals it would count as "real Indians" for purposes of living up to the contracts into which it willingly entered with various Native American nations, it now serves to determine whether any given individual will count as a self or an other, thus remanding identity into the hands of anti-alterity.

The desire to close ranks and separate out those who will contribute to the survival of the group from those who will be destructive of the group is entirely understandable. First and foremost, there can be no doubt that if Native Americans are to survive as Native Americans, we must reject acculturation and resist assimilation. To do otherwise, as more than 500 years of experience testifies, would sanction cultural genocide. Second, a great many individuals who were not four-fourths Native American historically have been destructive forces within Native American communities, and a long history of such betrayal would appear to link authenticity to blood. Third, since the end of World War II there has been a growing sense of pride among many Native Americans, a sense of pride that clearly signals a new vigor, a new hope. Finally, the intrusions of foreign religions, the persistent denigration of our religions as mere "cults," that may be outlawed because they are not "real" religions, the government's insistence that Native Americans must adopt economic and social principles that mirror the dominant society, and the legal division of Native Americans into enrolled versus unenrolled individuals and recognized versus unrecognized tribes make protecting tribal integrity significant beyond measure.

For all these reasons and more, authentication is understandable because it is necessary. Yet blood logic is both counter-intuitive and ultimately destructive of Native American identities, because collective efforts that isolate themselves from those who are empowered to alter conditions for the better by excluding all but the most fervently committed are destined to fail miserably. The fervently committed quickly fragment and begin to alienate even those who might become or are on the verge of becoming one of the chosen. Attrition becomes entropy. It is counter-intuitive and destructive because—as the Lakota eloquently demonstrated in 1973 at Wounded Knee—gaining the attention of those who can change things for the better requires a great deal more than a worthy cause and a pure heart; at a minimum, it requires a membership large enough to attract attention and coalition formalities that are capable of sustaining that attention. It is counterintuitive and destructive because blood does not in any way insure behavior—a point well proven by the fact that many enrolled and full-blooded Native Americans have been hugely destructive of cultural identity. It is counter-intuitive and destructive because cultural identity is invariably subject to modification, whereas blood logic directly and irrecoverably leads to the mummification of cultural identity. And it is counter-intuitive and destructive because, contrary to thousands of years of experience, it denies an alterity of inclusion in favor of an alterity of exclusion.

Conclusions

Let me be a free man, free to travel, free to stop, free to work, free to trade where I choose, free to choose my own teachers, free to follow the religion of my fathers, free to talk, think and act for myself—and I will obey every law or submit to the penalty.

—Chief Joseph of the Nez Perce, (as quoted in *Means*, 1995, frontpiece)

Individuals and groups who confront great difficulties in lived experience by necessity find themselves at a double juncture of intercultural communication difficulties. On the one hand, they must constantly struggle to maintain their cultural identities in a world that persistently denies, degrades, ignores, elides, transforms, exploits, confounds, and confuses those identities. On the other hand, they are perpetually in the position of defending themselves against incursions, against erroneous images, and against fragmentation. In the short run, this double juncture leads to self-doubt in a variety of forms, and in the long run it threatens the existence of the individual, the group, and perhaps even the human race.

The ceaseless struggle to maintain and pass along cultural identity is difficult under the best of circumstances. But when the conditions engulfing such efforts are hostile or even antithetical, self-doubt is inevitable. In its most obvious form, self-doubt is an introspective search for a self that does not produce feelings of alienation and discomfort, which introspection may lead the individual to move in the direction of adopting a self that is more consistent with the demands of anti-alterity. This movement typically leads to communication most notable for its conciliatory or ameliorative or self-hating texture, whereby the individual or group actually begins to participate in the destruction of cultural identity. Such was the circumstance for many Native American children throughout much of the last hundred years who were forcibly taken from their homes, placed in "Indian" boarding schools, forbidden to have contact with their parents or other members of their group, coerced into abandoning their language and into learning English, told endlessly that the ways of their ancestors were evil and that the ways of the dominant society were good, and taught to return to their homes where they could pass on this new reality to their friends and families (Berkhofer 1978; Boyer 1978; Buckanaga 1978; Cahn 1969; Christensen and Demmert 1978; Clifton 1990; Cornell 1987; Crow Dog and Erdoes 1995; Deloria 1974; Deloria 1978; Deloria and Lytle 1984; Dippie 1982; Fuchs and Havighurst 1972; Gipp 1979; Hill 1991; Kidwell 1991; Little-Soldier 1989; Locke 1978; Loretto 1989; McBeth 1983; McDonald 1978; Mankiller and Wallis 1993; Means 1995; Morris, forthcoming; Nabokov 1991; Riley 1993; Thomas 1966–1967; Thompson 1978; Tierney 1991; Trennert 1990; Washburn 1971; M. Wax and Buchanan 1975; Wax 1967; Wescott 1991; and Whiteman 1978).

But when the individual or group is certain that the problem is not with the self but with its inaccurate portrayals of or inappropriate attacks on the self, the result is a markedly different kind of self-doubt. Here, the group or individual begins to doubt whether the self can survive as they wish it to survive under the conditions in which that self is required to exist. The search for change then turns outward to the environment and the individuals and groups who have created the unacceptable conditions of existence. Self-doubt thus transforms into despair, depression, hopelessness, suspicion, distrust, disdain, anger, hatred, and destruction—all of which lend themselves to the texture of intercultural communication.

To speak from the position of the other rather than the position of the non-self invariably, inevitably perpetuates conditions under which communication is problematic if not impossible. The problematic here might be subsumed under the heading of "credibility," though I tend to think that concept may be too thin (at least in contemporary terms). The "other's" credibility, to be sure, is automatically in question (why else would the person be the "other"?) but the problem runs deeper. To live under the conditions of being the "other" calls into question not only one's voice as it seeks out those who struggle with their otherness and, paradoxically, their own self.

This is in part, a consequence of a divide-and-conquer mentality whereby "others," amalgamated as a conjunctive whole by hegemonic blocs, compete for positioning within the larger society—each struggling against "others" (rather than the hegemonic

bloc) for a place that is less "other." This leads not to liberation in any fundamental sense, but to a form of self-perpetuating non-freedom whereby "others" accomplish the goal of the divide-and-conquer mentality by keeping themselves divided. To return to the problem of "blood logic" (as but one among many possibilities), this form of non-freedom might lead, for instance, one Native American to stand in front of another, insisting that "because your parents lived at a time when concealing identity was a viable survival option, you and all subsequent generations cannot claim to be Native American; so you are forever other." This form of communicative non-freedom may well be the second most effective means for Native Americans (and others) to destroy themselves and "others."

In a larger part, to live under the conditions of being the "other" calls into question one's voice even as it seeks out one's self because the self—unless the person is extraordinary—is divided against itself. To speak to one's self under such conditions thus is to speak to the self that seeks liberation, to the self that sees liberation as an impossibility, to the self that despairs, to the self that is depressed, to the self that is mired in hopelessness, to the self that is suspicious of "others" and the "other" within, to the self that is filled with distrust and disdain and anger and hatred and destruction. This form of communicative non-freedom may well be the most effective means for · "others" to destroy themselves.

For those of us who live in/between, being required, on the one hand, to cast off our cultural selves in order to don the worldview and ethos of an alien culture, on the other hand, to cast off the influences of the alien culture as a means of purification and identification is more than a personal dilemma; it is always and most of all a condition of living in/between. Within the darkness of that limnality, I often wonder what life might have been like had my mother not found herself in an environment created by the kind of alterity that pits self against other. And I tremble to imagine what life will be like if we fail to learn to embrace alterity.

Notes

1. Because society is not a singularity, one might claim that valuing both homogeneity and diversity simultaneously is not specious, given that different groups might seek to promote one over and against the other, thus revealing the character of democracy. On the other hand, insofar as there is an identifiable national agenda, it would be erroneous to imagine that efforts by some to promote diversity as a means of counteracting a poignant history of promoting homogeneity would somehow ameliorate this contradiction. On the whole, difference typically has been and is tolerated only to the extent that those who are different can obtain and sustain concessions from those who press for homogeneity.

2. The few considerations that follow clearly are not the only means by which the irreconcilable division of society into self and other is perpetuated. The discussion is intended to be indicative rather than exhaustive.

3. I focus here on the negative dimensions and consequences of the reservation system in keeping with the main thesis of this essay. There are also positive dimensions and consequences—for example, that reservations often permit some semblance of unity, that they often allow the continuation of tribalism, that they sometimes provide tribes with a degree of privacy from peering outsider's eyes of tourists and "scholars," that they occasionally embrace sacred lands, and so forth.

References

Allen, P.G. (Ed.). (1989). *Spider woman's granddaughters: Traditional tales and contemporary writing by Native American women.* New York: Fawcett-Columbia.

Allen, P.G. (1992 [1986]). *The sacred hoop: Recovering the feminine in American Indian traditions.* Boston: Beacon.

Armstrong, V. (Ed.). (1972). *I have spoken: American history through the voices of the Indians.* New York: Pocket.

Bataille, G. and C. Silet. (1980). *The pretend Indians: images of Native Americans in the movies.* Ames: Iowa State University Press.

Berkhofer, R. (1978). *The white man's Indian: Images of the American Indian from Columbus to the present.* New York: Knopf.

Boyer, L. (1978). Growing up in E'Da how— one Idaho girlhood. In Thompson, T. (Ed.), *The schooling of Native America.* 31–35. Washington, DC: American Association of Colleges for Teacher Education.

Bruchac, J. (1989). Introduction. In Dooling, D.M. and Jordan-Smith, P. (Eds.), *I become part of it.* 1–8. New York: Parabola.

Buckanaga, J. (1978). Interracial politics: The pressure to integrate an experimental school. In Thompson, T. (Ed.), *The schooling of Native America.* 53–71. Washington, DC: American Association of Colleges for Teacher Education.

Cahn, E. (Ed.). (1969). *Our brother's keeper: The Indian in white America.* New York: New Community Press.

Christensen, R. and Demmert, W. (1978). The education of Indians and the mandate of history. In Thompson, T. (Ed.), *The schooling of Native America.* 139–152.Washington, DC: American Association of Colleges for Teacher Education.

Clifton, J. (1990). *The invented Indian: Cultural fictions and government policies.* Brunswick: Transaction.

Cornell, S. (1987). *The return of the native: American Indian political resurgence.* New York: Oxford University Press.

Crow Dog, L. and Erdoes, R. (1995). *Crow Dog: Four generations of Sioux Medicine Men.* New York: HarperCollins.

Deloria, V., Jr. (1974). *Behind the trail of broken treaties: An Indian Declaration of Independence.* New York: Dell.

Deloria, V., Jr. (1978). The Indian student amid American inconsistencies. In Thompson, T. (Ed.), *The schooling of Native America.* 2–26. Washington, DC: American Association of Colleges for Teacher Education.

Deloria, V., Jr. (1989). Out of chaos. In Dooling, D.M. and Jordan-Smith, P. (Eds.), *I become part of it.* 259–268. New York: Parabola.

Deloria, V., Jr. and Lytle, C. (1984). *The nations within: The past and future of American Indian sovereignty.* New York: Pantheon.

Dippie, B. (1982). *Vanishing American: While attitudes and U.S. Indian policy.* Middletown: Wesleyan University Press.

Friar, R. (1972). *The only good Indian: The Hollywood gospel.* New York: Drama Book Specialists.

Fuchs, E. and Havighurst, R. (1972). *To live on this earth: American Indian education.* New York: Doubleday.

Gipp, G. (1979, August/September). Help for Dana Fast Horse and friends. *American Education,* 18–21.

Hill, N. (1991, March/April). AISES: A college intervention program that works. *Change,* 24–26.

204 Part VI ◆ Living in Bicultural Relationships

Hirschfelder, A. (1982). *American Indian stereotypes in the world of children: A reader and bibliography*. Metuchen: Scarecrow.

Kidwell, C. (1991, March/April). The vanishing native reappears in the college curriculum. *Change*, 19–23.

Klien, L. and Ackerman, L. (Eds.). (1995). *Women and power in Native North America*. Norman: University of Oklahoma Press.

Korsmo, F. (1990). Problem definition and the Alaska Natives: Ethnic identity and policy formation. *Policy Studies Review*, 9(2), 100–105.

Little-Soldier, L. (1989, October). Cooperative learning and the Native American student. *Kappan*, 161–163.

Locke, P. (1978). An ideal school system for American Indians—A theoretical construct. In Thompson, T. (Ed.), *The schooling of Native America*. 119–136. Washington, DC: American Association of Colleges for Teacher Education.

Loretto, J. (1989, March/April). A Native American CDA: My personal story. *Children Today*, 26–27.

McBeth, S. (1981). *Ethnic identity and the boarding school experience of West-Central Oklahoma American Indians*. Washington, DC: University Press of America.

McDonald, A. (1978). Why do Indian students drop out of College? In Thompson, T. (Ed.), *The schooling of Native America*. 73–85. Washington, DC: American Association of Colleges for Teacher Education.

Mankiller, W. and Wallis, M. (1993). *Mankiller: A Chief and her people*. New York: St. Martin's.

Means, R. (1995). *Where white men fear to tread*. New York: St. Martin's.

Morris, R. (forthcoming). Educating savages. *Quarterly Journal of Speech*.

Morris, R. and Wander, P. (1991). Native American rhetoric: dancing in the shadows of the ghost dance. *Quarterly Journal of Speech*, 76, 164–191.

Nabokov, P., (Ed.). (1991 [1978]). *Native American testimony: A chronicle of Indian-White relations, from prophecy to the present, 492–1992*. New York: Penguin.

O'Connor, J. (1980). *The Hollywood Indian: Stereotypes of Native Americans in films*. Trenton: New Jersey State Museum.

Perkins, J. (1995, Nov. 12). Indians need more self-help, not handouts. *Rockford Register Star*, B3.

Riley, R. (Ed.). (1993). *rowing up Native American: An anthology*. New York: Morrow.

Stedman, R. (1982). *Shadows of the Indians: Stereotypes in American Culture*. Norman: University of Oklahoma Press.

Takaki, R. (1993). *A different mirror: A History of multicultural America*. Boston: Little, Brown.

Thomas, R. (1966–1967, Winter). Colonialism: Classic and internal. *New University Thought* 4, 39.

Thompson, T., (Ed.). (1978). *The schooling of Native America*. Washington, DC: American Association of Colleges for Teacher Education.

Tierney, W. (1991, March/April). Native voices in academe: strategies for empowerment. *Change*, 36–39.

Todorov, T. (1992 [1982]). *The conquest of America*. New York: HarperPerennial.

Trennert, R., Jr. (1990). *The Phoenix Indian school: Forced assimilation in Arizona, 1891–1935*. Norman: University of Oklahoma Press.

Washburn, W.E. (1971). *Red man's land—White man's law: A study of the past and present status of the American Indian*. New York: Schribner's Sons.

Wax, M.L. and Buchanan, R.W. (1975). *Solving 'the Indian problem': The white man's burdensome business*. New York: New York Times.

Wax, R. (1967, May). The warrior reports. *Transaction*, 233.

Wescott, S. (1991, March/April). Educate to Americanize: Captain Pratt and early Indian education. *change*, 45–46.

Whiteman, H. (1978). Native American studies, the University, and the Indian student. In Thompson, T. (Ed.), *The schooling of Native America*. 105–116. Washington, DC: American Association of Colleges for Teacher Education.

Wilkinson, C. (1987). Indians, time, and the law: Native societies in a modern constitutional democracy. New Haven, CT: Yale University Press. ◆

Part VII

Traversing Cultural Paths

30

Women Writing Borders, Borders Writing Women

Immigration, Assimilation, and the Politics of Speaking

Aimee M. Carrillo Rowe
University of Washington

> *La mojada, la mujer indocumentada, is doubly threatened in this country. Not only does she have to contend with sexual violence, but like all women, she is prey to a sense of physical helplessness. As a refugee, she leaves the familiar and safe homeground to venture into an unknown and possibly dangerous terrain. This is her home. This thin edge of barbwire.*
>
> —Gloria Anzaldúa (1987)

A Narrative of Immigration?

This essay addresses immigration within the genre of personal narrative, which means that as its author, I am supposed to write autobiographically about my experience of immigration. One of the editors of this volume invited me to write about immigration after she heard me present my research at a conference. The critical impulses that inform both the study of the topic (immigration) and the form of delivery (autobiography) are potentially disruptive as they become counter-hegemonic articulations and remembering and writing against the grain. Yet, this combination places me (a middle-class, English-speaking, U.S. citizen, a biracial woman, self- and politically-identified Chicana) in the uneasy position of facing my own privilege within the Western academy as I write "personally" about immigration. I do not offer an "authentic" immigrant voice, nor could I ever claim to "recover" one in an unmediated fashion.1 Why was I invited to insert my voice into this elite academic space? Why not ask "*la mojada*" to share her story?

These questions relate to issues of voice and representation. The privilege to speak, particularly within a popular medium, affords a degree of control (or agency) over the construction of one's identity. But most of the inhabitants of this planet are denied such a privilege at great material, psychological, and social cost:

> When a people has no control over public perceptions of it, when its sense of self is denied at every turn in the books, films, television, and radio shows it is forced to imbibe, it cannot help but falter. But when its image is shaped by its own people, the hope for survival can be turned into a much greater hope: it can become a hope for life, for vitality, for affirmation. (Gunn Allen in Visweswaran 1994, 32)

The systemic privileging of a few voices (those with the proper "authority") squelches this hope. The systematic silencing of "others" (those who remain exploited by the conditions created and a lack of power) contributes to the maintenance of their suffering. The voices of authority speak not only for themselves, but for "others" as well, to construct worlds of meaning in which oppression may be dismissed through attitudes of hatred, pity, and paternalism toward marginalized people.

As a leftist scholar, I constantly struggle with the dilemma of speaking for "others" whom I seek to empower. Ironically, while racist, (hetero)sexist, classist, and nationalist representations of "others" must be challenged—and that is part of what my work aims to do—my position in the academy (my pay, my power, my passion) is secured through my ability to speak for and about them. This essay, for instance, serves not only my identity interests, but also my career. I get to speak my own story; I get recognition from those of you who are reading it (perhaps): I get a line on my vitae; I get to feel good about myself, like I am making a difference. But am I really? How can I use my privileged voice in order to challenge the very system that has privileged me? Why have I been privileged? If the goal of cultural studies is not to "speak for the masses as a ventriloquist, but rather, to make a space in which the voices of the masses can be heard" (Grossberg 1996, 166), *how* can I contribute to such a task?

These questions drive this essay. I want to focus on voice—the struggle over the ability to speak and represent one's self or one's social group or both. Although increasingly spaces are becoming available in which marginalized voices may be heard, such as *Our Voices*, the mere existence of these voices within hegemonic spaces is not necessarily evidence of systemic change. In fact, the inclusion of our marginalized voices risks our becoming tokenized as proof that a given "we" (the academy, communication studies, U.S. society) are "beyond" racist, sexist, homophobic elitism. I do not wish to dispute the fact that contributors to this and similar alternative, oppositional collections experience various forms of violent discrimination. Nor do I wish to compare oppressions. However, I do want to point to the way in which my own privilege as author of this text functions, to explore the implications of my speech act, and to explore some possible ways of addressing inequality in the realm of representation.

The systematic silencing of most of the world's inhabitants is a necessary component of the authoritative capacity to speak. Authority is lost if just *anyone's* voice counts. The authoritative voice of an author "allows a limitation of the cancerous and dangerous proliferation of significations within a world where one is thrifty not only with one's resources and riches, but also with one's discourses and their significations. The author is the principle of thrift in the proliferation of meaning" (Foucault 1984, 118). Representation of "others" is in and of itself a form of exploitation and, perhaps more importantly, it is the ideological foundation that ultimately sustains systematic material exploitation. As long as "illegal immigrants," for instance, lack control over their representa-

tion, they have very little leverage for sustained resistance against an exploitative work environment, daily encounters with racism and nationalism, and a political system that despises (even as it fetishizes) them.

There exists a dialectical relationship, then, between representation and exploitation. A social group with no power to control the social forces that construct its identity is vulnerable to various forms of exploitation, while the conditions of poverty arising out of such material exploitation often prohibit that group's ability to seize control over the ways in which it is represented. This dialectical relationship creates and maintains the conditions of possibility in which systemic poverty and privilege become naturalized.

Typically, few people are allowed to "rise above" their exploitative conditions and speak their stories. These stories are expected to provide proof that the myths of meritocracy, equality, and democracy are, in fact, true. In exchange for the opportunity to speak, the privileged are expected to "talk the talk" and "walk the walk" of the white man's game, a game at which they are already disadvantaged and do not threaten to really win. In my case, for instance, I am asked to speak because I am a product of assimilation. My foreparents have successfully crossed many borders—those of nation, race, and class—in order that I may speak. How many "others" will be allowed to follow in my footsteps and be asked to speak? Certainly not all of them.

The first section of this essay explores the context in which my family assimilated as well as the social benefits (such as my privileged speech) and emotional and political costs that accompany this process. Next, I examine the contemporary cultural climate surrounding Latino immigration to the United States to argue that a systemic and necessary relationship exists between the inability of *la mojada* to represent herself and her exploitation. Finally, I theorize about connections between white, First World privilege and the condition of "subalternity" (a social position lacking the power of self-representation), to mark the explicit and implicit connections between privileged voices and material exploitation.

My Home and Assimilation

I am a white girl gone brown to the blood color of my mother speaking for her through the unnamed part of the mouth the wide-arched muzzle of brown women.

—Cherríe Morraga (1981)

I am Joaquín

Lost in a world of confusion,

Caught up in a whirl of gringo society. . . .

—Rodolfo Gonzalez (1967)

My home in southern California is the evolution of cultural mixing, colonization, and shifting borders. It is a place that is at once cozy and safe for me, while at the same time violently exclusionary. My parents raised us (my brother, sister, and, the youngest, me) in this home as good liberals, which meant being color-blind with regard to race. Looking back, I see how ineffective this strategy is because I distinctly remember wishing for blond hair and blue eyes. Although we saw ourselves as white,[2] for some reason I was insecure about my whiteness. I always suspected that I was not white enough. I wished to be like all the girls on *The Brady Bunch*, like women considered beautiful and powerful such as the "bionic woman" and Christy Brinkley. To this day, I do not understand all of the complexities of how I came to internalize racism and see myself as lacking when I was never told that I was "not quite white," but it does suggest that racism functions in subtle ways that are not necessarily literal. How, for instance, has my mother's internalized racism modeled femininity for me? How have my father's white paternalism toward my mother and his rejection of my working-class Chicano relatives disciplined and contained my possibility of forging an oppositional identity?

In my work as a young scholar, race is one of my primary interests. This interest in and focus on race clashes with my parents' hegemonic strategy of turning a color-blind eye to race, which makes for some tension in our relationship. They cannot seem to hear what I have to say about race, especially when I implicate our own family (although I recognize my work as an ongoing process and that they are not necessarily stuck here). They think I'm going through a phase, like my sister did when she was studying anticolonial environmentalism at the University of California, Santa Cruz. This construction poses my work as less threatening, as more of a fleeting phase that "kids go through" than a commitment to a life of struggle and resistance. I believe my parents really just want me to be "happy," but this seemingly benign impulse begs the larger question of who gets to choose such ignorant bliss? Only the privileged few. I know too much now, I am too committed to a certain politics to return to some nascent phase of multicultural plurality. Nor do I think such a possibility exists without political and personal consequences, not only for those who lack this choice, but also for those privileged enough to turn a blind eye.

I know so many people who are left empty and deadened by dominant U.S. culture with its precepts of isolation and indulgence. For instance, I cannot help wondering why no one wants to consider the relationship between high school kids who are shooting each other and myopic white masculinity, the pressures of capitalism and wealth production, or the lack of connection among people when everyone works overtime within the belly of the beast. There are "no guarantees" that all our theories of power and resistance will effect social change (Hall 1996), but I choose the struggle over the certain and slow death of blind complicity. However, this choice necessarily implicates my parents because it involves deconstructing my privilege, which means deconstructing my home. This home is a product of both their lives and of ideological formations of domination-racism, classism, heterosexism. These two creative forces cannot be separated.

I am trying to develop a language to speak to them of negotiating the contradictory space between responsibility and blame. My parents are so proud that I'm a doctoral student, but what this *means* they seem unable to fully grasp. Part of what this means for me is re-thinking and re-imagining *home*—factoring in what I know about power, colonialism, globalization, racism, heterosexism—into the places closest to me, the spaces that have produced me. This is threatening to them because I seem to be questioning all of the "truths" they brought us up to believe.

It is scary work to speak the unspoken and the unspeakable. Nevertheless, the work I am undertaking compels me to speak of my own complicity and privilege within these structures, which means tracing my history, thus implicating my parents as agents of both complicity and resistance in my analysis. This is an uneasy place in which to place them, and I do not mean to single them out as anomalous. In fact, they are not. It is really their *commonness* I wish to foreground and ask my reader to identify with.

With this struggle in mind, I will try to convey some historical information productive of my home. My white, upwardly mobile, previously working-class father met my biracial (Hispanic), middle-class mother when they were both living in San Francisco. He was an Air Force pilot; she was an airline stewardess. Although their union involved the blurring of racial and class lines, they were really not so far apart socially or economically. He had pulled himself up from his working-class roots through the repressive state apparatus of the military. She was raised to consider herself as Spanish, a cultural marker of successful assimilation (achieved through upward class mobility and the acquisition of bourgeois sensibilities) into an Anglo-dominated society. Her assimilation functions through the erasure of the traces of her Mexican heritage, including her surname, Carrillo, which she shed through marital union with my father. I wish to focus on my maternal heritage, because this provided a site of racial assimilation that has produced my ability to speak as a white woman, as Chicana, as neither, and as both. By tracing this history, I hope to come to terms with the history with which my mother has negotiated, to understand the context out of which the chasm over racial identity that separates us has emerged.

It is not uncommon for Mexicanos who "make it" to construct their identities as Hispanic. This theme is played out in the film *Lone Star,* in which the maternal figure raises her daughter as Spanish and takes a tough stand against Latino immigration, but we later find that the mother herself was an illegal immigrant to the United States, who had succeeded economically and socially. The Spanish identity foregrounds family's blood linkages to colonial Spain, as if that fact alone could justify our right to mobility within Anglo society. In the face of the violence of the colonial history upon which "America" and "Mexico" were both founded, however, it seems counter-intuitive to identify with a heritage of domination through brutal violence. This contradiction renders transparent the extent to which colonization and racism have become naturalized socially and internalized personally. Why would we desire to align ourselves with the brute colonizer? Why is it necessary to identify as a white colonial subject to justify one's existence within the violent spaces of the U.S. nation? Does one woman's freedom necessitate another's exploitation? Then there are the personal questions, the most pressing of which is: Who am I to speak for my mother? In doing so, I reproduce the violence of her assimilation, but I do so in an effort to remember the conditions of erasure of the Mexicana.

My act of "betrayal" speaks against the possibility of "pure" feminist alliances. "Feminist innocence is betrayed by relations of power; betrayal signals the loss of innocence" (Visweswaran 1994, 40). Betrayal within feminism is a site of negotiated resistance and consent, over-determined by relations of power that preclude the possibility of "universal sisterhood." Such alliances are not possible without "attending to the divides that separated women" (Viseswaran 1994, 40). We are all involved in betrayals; there is no innocent space from which to theorize oppositional resistance. *My betrayal of my own mother is not "intentional," nor is it escapable, as I speak within against the hegemony that has produced her complicity and her limited means of seizing power. In some ways, I am not ready to write this essay. I realize it cannot be done without betrayal. It almost cannot be done. It is too painful to rip these words out that would hurt (do hurt to) my mom. When I gave her Anzaldúa's book, she never read it. I thought she'd identify, it would liberate her fiery heart as it did mine. But she could not hear Gloria's words. They were too sharp for my mom's heart, and it scared her that I could hear. How does one just heal from the tearing between mother and daughter when she realizes that the tearing is necessary for the baby to fly? I have not healed, so I am not ready to write. But if I do not write, I will never heal.*

My mother's side of the family migrated from what is now California in 1839. At that time, my ancestor, Francisco Marquez, received a Mexican land grant in the Santa Monica area in exchange for his military service (Pacific Palisades Historical Society 1980). It was a historical moment marked by increasing Anglo migration to California, creating a predominantly white population by 1849, which qualified that territory for statehood (Acuñu 1988, 111). Elite *Californios* played into the hands of the Anglo moves to take California from Mexico because they figured that supporting the transfer would promote their own interests. This racial treachery begins to hint at the complexity and the lack of guarantees that criss-cross power relations. Mexican blood has no *necessary* meaning, but it is a racial signifier to which political forces struggle to give meaning.

Under the U.S. government, *Californios* were systematically forced from their land through a variety of measures, such as the Land Act of 1851, the "foreign miner's tax." Such measures encouraged violence against Mexicans who were ultimately "driven off their land by gross violations of the Treaty of Guadeloupe Hidalgo" (designed to ensure the civil and property rights of Mexicans). "As Mexicans were alienated from their land, equality under the law became a sham" (Acuña 1988, 108). My family suffered under these conditions, although the stories of how this happened are not entirely clear. It seems the U.S. government "bought" their land in return for back taxes they supposedly owed on it but could not pay. Ultimately, they lost their land, and the small amounts of money they received were insufficient to start over.

My grandfather ("Billy" Carrillo) was orphaned as a young boy. Both of his parents died quite young due to the dangerous work and living conditions created by his family's poverty: his father in an accident at the end of the Santa Monica pier where he was a laborer, his mother in a plague that took many lives. Because of their death, Billy was raised by his aunt yet was never fully accepted by her or her family. He was referred to as "the little bird who fell out of the nest," a continuous reminder that he was not quite part of the family. In an effort to prove his loyalty to his extended family, he quit school in sixth grade to sell vegetables from a cart to make money to support the family. This business was ultimately quite lucrative. When he met Alice, my white and college-educated grandmother, he fell instantly in love with her. With her help, he was eventually quite "successful" in his vegetable business.

My mom (Alicia, "little Alice") was sent to boarding school, because both Alice and Billy were working. She was not exposed to Chicano culture and she spent her formative years in a Catholic boarding school, trying to be a "good girl"—Pollyanna was her favorite story character. My mother's assimilation is largely a function of a historical moment prior to organized forms of resistance for Chicanos. Anzaldúa reminds us that "Chicanos did not know we were a people until 1965 when Céasar Chávez and the farmworkers united and *I Am Joaquín* was published and *la Raza Unida* party was formed in Texas" (1987, 63). By this time, my parents were already married and my mother simply was relieved to have shed her Latino surname.

While the Chicano movement rearticulated the national spatial terrain upon which Chicano social mobility could take place, the movement did not necessarily open up spaces for Chicana liberation (García 1997). Alicia's "choices" to Anglicize are overdetermined by the relational configuration of her gender, her race, and her class positioning. This does not mean that she had *no* choice, or that her negotiations along these axes of power have been merely responsive to these exclusionary conditions. Chandra Mohanty rightly points out that relations of power are "not reducible to binary oppositions or oppressor/oppressed relation" (1991, 13). Instead, she argues for the possibility of retaining "the idea of multiple, fluid structures of domination" which situate women differently, while still "insisting on the dynamic oppositional agency of individuals and collectives and their engagement in 'daily life'" (1991, 13). Under the conditions in which Alicia grew up, there was very little option for her to "claim" a Chicana identity in resistance. Because she carried all of the markers of her middle-class position, she did not feel the need to resist the violent process of assimilation. This class position was articulated to whiteness, while poverty meant Mexican. So she felt different from other Mexicans. She did not feel Mexican. She was raised to think of herself as Spanish, as a signifier of both racial and class privilege, which set her apart from Mexicans.

My mother's assimilation has produced contradictory effects. On one hand, it *has* contributed to the conditions under which she can move and travel "as a citizen" within and outside of the United States. I am the privileged product of her "choice" to marry a white man and live safely within the parameters of Anglo culture. As this privilege relates to the issue of voice, my ability to write this essay and succeed in the academy is influenced by my middle-class upbringing. Education was always emphasized. I have and have always had quiet and private spaces in which to do my work, and my parents had leisure time to help me with my homework as I was growing up. Also, my freedom to speak out against the oppression I saw all around, my indignation at this oppression, have been byproducts of my privilege. I was raised to believe that U.S.- American society is just, so I am shocked and outraged when I see injustice. But this middle-class, white response is often amusing, and at times offensive, to those for whom systemic injustice is part of their daily experience. My whiteness has insulated me. I was raised to have faith in the myth of free speech with no regard for *who* was speaking.

If I had spent my childhood bent over strawberry patches and grapevines, inhaling toxic chemicals, being subjected to sexual harassment, if there were no time for school, no space or time to study because the whole family had to work or we would starve—if *this* were my childhood—it is rather unlikely that I would be writing this essay today. Most people's lives are simply not set up in ways in which they learn "proper" grammar, read lots of theory and criticism, spend hours discussing ideas. The skills I have acquired that sustain my voice require leisure time and leisure time requires someone else to do the grunt work (at least in a capitalistic society). *Who* does this work? *How* does labor get systematically divided along lines of race, class, gender, and nationality?

My mother's "choices"—and the daily "choices" people of color make in the face of violent U.S. racism and that women make as they are continually inflicted with sexism—*do* function to maintain the exclusionary conditions that overdetermined her choice in the first place. This is not to exonerate people of color who are doing what they can to survive Anglo culture, but to point to the ways in which whiteness remains hegemonic. This occurs primarily through divisions among people of color that are produced when we become effectively white. There is also the personal pain of "passing" as white when you know that you are "not quite" white. If we never question the standards by which we measure ourselves, they become so naturalized that we blindly assume we must adhere. I am suggesting that we take a critical stance toward whiteness as a universal standard of attainment for personhood.

Immigration Within a Postcolonial Context

Immigration is an effect of late capitalism and the desolate poverty of the so-called Third World as a function of continual First World exploitation. Under the ideology of neo-liberalism (the effort to globally institute laissez-faire economics under the banner of democracy), Northern nations have systematically sucked resources and labor power from the South, creating living conditions and the distribution of wealth within and between both regions to become increasingly polarized. Because "one-fourth of all Mexicans work at *maquiladoras*" under such conditions of unmanageable exploitation, they are forced to leave their homelands, *cruzando la frontera al norte* (Anzaldúa 1987, 10). Arriving in the United States, the "land of opportunity," they are paradoxically situated as an integral part of the economic system (unprotected surplus labor) even as they are despised for invading "our" clean living spaces. This paradox is a *function* of the systematic justification of their exploitation. If they are continually terrorized, that is, they are less likely to demand humane treatment.

In Washington State, for instance, apple workers are organizing as a labor force to demand protection, rights, and adequate working conditions. I recently attended a United Farm Workers' meeting in which two migrant workers, a man and a woman, spoke of their unlivable circumstances that could be changed through organized resistance. The woman started out by describing the hours she worked, how there were no bathrooms in the fields, and the "living" conditions of the apple workers. A few minutes later, after she had finished, she asked to speak again. She addressed the women at the meeting. She spoke as a woman to the women present, as the translator spoke for her. "How would you like it if men grabbed you as you worked?" her voice was rising and trembling. She stood up and enacted picking, then suddenly crouched to illustrate her reaction to a predator grabbing her from behind. She cried as she spoke of the humiliating sexual harassment she endured, the daily practices of being fondled by supervisors who hold total power within the circumscribed space of the fields.[3]

While very few people would argue that such conditions should not or could not be altered, the Washington State apple workers voted *against* the union support that would facilitate such changes. In the weeks approaching the day they were to vote, business owners intimidated "their" workers through a variety of strategies, which ranged from hiring labor attorneys to, I assume, unspeakable means of persuasion. In this and multiple other instances, migrant workers are both needed and despised. They are despised *because* they are needed. Despising them already circumvents the possibility of resistance with fair treatment.

The tragic ironies of the process of Latino immigration should not be lost. The "we" who create, maintain, and benefit from the rich-poor gap responsible for immigration in the first place are the same "we" who are being "victimized" by the "immigrant invasion" (described by right-wing author, Pete Brimelow, 1995). The "we" who benefit from "their" dirt-cheap labor on either side of the U.S.-Mexican border are the same "we" who vote "yes" on Proposition 187 and support the English- Only movement (California Proposition 227), blaming "them" for destroying our schools, filling our prisons, killing our citizens, outbreeding us, and turning the United States into an "alien nation" (Brimelow 1995).

This historical moment in the United States is dominated by "anti-immigrant hysteria," in which "stories of homelessness, violence, and suffering are falling on ears that no longer bear to listen" (Behar in Saldívar 1997, x). The vendeta against immigration is gearing up, as the space of the U.S.-Mexican border is transformed into a battle zone under the violent gaze and control of the U.S. military, the National Guard, and local police at the cost of $2.6 million monthly (Saldívar 1997, x). The site of this border is a microcosm for U.S. imperialism through a form of "low-intensity conflict" that has endured three different presidential administrations and both political parties (Dunn in Saldívar 1997, xi). Saldívar contextualizes the implications of the militarization of this border so concretely that I quote him at length here:

> What is significant about this intensive militarization of the U.S.-Mexico border is the extent to which it led not only to a "loosening" of the Posse Comitatus Statute (which outlawed the use of the military in the domestic sphere) but also to new alliances between the civilian police and the military to enforce drug and immigration policies. . . . Further, it extended Reagan's and Bush's undeclared wars in Central America, 'sig-

nal[ling] and subject[ing] to especially punitive immigration enforcement measurements' [Dunn 1996, 163] refugees and immigrants from El Salvador and Guatemala. (1997, xi)

The hegemony of U.S. imperialism shows its weak underbelly through such repressive mobilization of state apparatuses. Here is where the hegemony of the "most democratic nation" belies its foundations through systematic outbursts of terror and violence. This exposure must be ceased, brought out into the light. Self-righteousness is no consolation to those who lose their lives, either literally or figuratively, in the crossing.

The policing of this external border is matched only by the harsh surveillance on the inside. The popular support for Proposition 187 in California, Operation Hold the Line in Texas, and the anti-immigration measures contained within the Contract With America all signal a moment marked by an increasing drive to demarcate the "enemies within"

> —those who might transgress the 'interior frontiers' of the nation-state, who were the same but not quite, potentially more brazen in making their claims to an equality of rights with 'true' [Americans]
>
> —Stoler (1997, 52).

Proposition 187, for instance, institutionalizes this internal surveillance by demanding that social workers confirm citizenship of anyone seeking social services who *looks* Latino or has a Latino surname. Under such conditions, it should not be surprising that Latino populations become divided between those with established residency and the new arrivals. Each group is scratching to survive in a system that succeeds through division. The process of assimilation demands that the newly arrived "citizen" *prove* patriotic loyalty to the racist system.

The proliferation of discourse that accompanies the current national focus on immigration, particularly Latino immigration, reveals the dialectical relationship between representation and exploitation. Because Latino immigrants lack citizenship, in every sense of the term, they remain powerless to control their own representation

and to *speak back* to the racist and nationalist hegemony that constructs them as violently other. In turn, this powerlessness translates into the painfully ironic system of exploitation from which they remain predominantly unable to escape. One source of hope for resistance for such groups, I think, lies in social movements such as the United Farm Workers (UFW). The UFW, mobilized under the leadership of human rights advocate César Chávez, has struggled to raise consciousness around migrant exploitation since the 1970s (Acuña 1988, 368–370). The point I wish to make is that representation is *contral* to struggles for social change, which highlights the importance of working to create the conditions in which marginalized groups may gain control over their own representation.

Reversal and the Question of Subalternity

A woman named Douloti illustrates the concept of subalternity. Douloti is a subaltern woman in one of Indian writer/activist Mahasweta Devi's (1995) stories. *Subalternity* refers to a social location lacking a political voice that may be heard by those who hold social power. For example, members of subaltern groups lack the social currency to represent their group within hegemonic discourse. As a result, any exploitation—particularly the ways in which that exploitation is related to hegemonic social relations—of the subaltern remains outside the purview of dominant ideologies and thus is virtually invisible. As the daughter of a bonded laborer, Douloti is sold into prostitution to secure her family's debt. It is the transformation of her body that insures the continuance of global capitalism into an economic resource. The owner of that debt will make his money back hundreds of times over through the sale of Douloti's body. As Spivak notes, the subaltern woman's body is "the last instance" of global capitalism "in a system whose general regulator is still the loan: usurer's capital, imbricated, level by level, in national industrial and transnational global capital" (1993, 82). It is these linkages through complex layers of capital-driven geopolitics—and the history of colonialism that has provided the economic and social frameworks for contemporary forms of neo-imperialism that connect us in the West to Douloti in India. But here I want to assert a more affective linkage in an effort to articulate an oppositional politics.

People in the West who are committed to alternative visions and liberating voices, such as the contributors to and readers of this volume, must not forget subaltern women in our struggles for justice. I want to mark the parallels between the decolonization of India and the decolonization of our classrooms within the academy that is the aim of *Our Voices*—not to undermine, but to extend this political project. Although the anticolonial struggle in India was (and continues to be) an important site of resistance and rearticulation of a nation for certain groups, "for the subaltern, and especially the subaltern woman, 'Empire' and 'Nation' are interchangeable names" (Spivak 1993, 78). Thus, the regime of power that creates Douloti's suffering remains intact. Whether or not India is liberated from its colonial ties to England, Douloti's circumstances will not be changed. Decolonization of the nation, then, is not sufficient to liberate Douloti because global capitalism increasingly penetrates her subaltern spaces and reconfigures her life by incorporating her into a system of exploitation in which *her* voice remains unspoken and unspeakable. In a similar way, even as "our voices" are raised to a status of social recognition, the system that allows this speech necessarily functions through her silence and her ultimate death. During hegemonic shifts, there is no *guaranteed* fundamental shift to lessen the hold of ideologies of domination and exploitation. This lack of guarantee means that constant critique is necessary.

Douloti's death and her story do not represent isolated events. Gayatri Spivak brilliantly reminds us that *douloti* means "traffic in wealth" and that when Devi writes, "Douloti's body is all over India," she points to the double meaning that douloti is "all over the globe" (1993, 95).[4] Transnational capital is increasingly "fluid" and multinational corporations are increasingly "frag-

menting" production so that contemporary capitalism takes on a form of "flexible accumulation"[5] (Harvey 1990). We are living in a historical moment of late capitalism marked by rapid change and uncertainty (for many in the West who have been displaced by economic shifts, and for many in power who are insecure about losing control) brought about by radical shifts within systems of production, exchange, communication, and marketing.

Benjamin Lee captures this moment when he writes:

> Consumer products are assembled in one country from parts and raw materials produced in many others, and then marketed internationally; global capital and investment move through transnational corporations capable of coordinating massive amounts of information about new sites of production. Networks of coordinated production are now competitive alternatives to more traditional, 'vertically' organized, hierarchical corporations. (1996, 217)

These shifts, of course, affect different people and social groups in different ways. Feminist geographer, Doreen Massy, conceptualizes the unevenness through which such shifts are experienced in her notion of "power geometry," which addresses not only the issue of "who moves and who doesn't," but also the play of "power in relation *to* the flows and movement" (1994, 149). These radical economic shifts are enabled by new forms of technology and communication that seem to render obsolete (for the privileged, at least) traditional territorial boundaries, while these borders remain entirely "real" for those who are beaten for crossing in an effort to try to gain a better life for themselves and their families.

Exploitation, in many ways, is facilitated by the shift to flexible accumulation because this form of capitalism is increasingly far-reaching and difficult to resist. For instance, localized resistance often results in corporate relocation rather than labor rights or local control over resources (Alexander and Mohanty 1997; Dirlik 1996). Consider that *los gringos* do not stop at the Mexican border; and that by the turn of the twentieth century, "powerful landowners in Mexico, in partnership with U.S. colonizing companies, had dispossessed millions of Indians of their land" (Anzaldúa 1987, 10). Indeed, neo-imperialistic expansion continues, even while many in the United States perceive themselves as being overrun by illegal immigrants. We must remember that "one-fourth of all Mexicans work as *maquiladoras*; most are young women" (Anzaldúa 1987, 10). We must not forget these facts when we struggle to rearticulate the spaces that exclude us, and vigilantly work to expand the "us" who demand inclusion. As we insert "our voices" into the academy, it is important to be mindful of those (like Douloti) for whom this book makes no difference and continue to fight for and alongside her.

Conclusion: Memory, Voice, and Resistance

Resistance inheres in the very gaps, fissures, and silences of hegemonic narratives. Resistance is encoded in the practices of remembering, and of writing.

—Chandra Mohanty (*Cartographies of Struggle*, 38)

Memory serves a vital function in the articulation of any space. In his discussion of the "imagined community" of the nation, for instance, Benedict Anderson (1983)[6] demonstrates that what is selectively remembered or forgotten are formative moments of violence, which undergird the nation's founding. Thus, *members* of the community are unified by what they each particularly re-*member*. That which remains unspoken, like the subaltern experience, remains forgotten. As an example, while the events of violence that forged U.S-American history as well as its contemporary presence and global positioning exist in the national collective memory, social subjects "agree" to forget the specifics of such events. The "imagined community" is bound by an agreement, based on both strategic *memory* and forgetting, in which the specificities of dominant memories are articulated through hegemonic narratives that conveniently con-

stitute the community's history as heroic and justified.

Because remembering, writing, and speaking "against the grain" comprise central moments and strategies of resistance (Mohanty 1991), *Our Voices* is a vital site of agency for those of us who feel embattled by the academy as a microcosm of white, Western, capitalist society at large. But there is more. As we forget resistant communities, we must also remember the too-easily-forgotten phenomenon of *forgetting* and the oppressive function that dominant ways of remembering serve. Hegemonic discourses continually interpellate us into systems of forgetting because hegemony functions through the erasure and naturalization of the violent exclusions that contradict the stated values of such systems (democracy alongside capitalism; justice based on imperialism; diversity from forced assimilation).

The "we" who are privileged to write here enact resistance through raising "our voices" even as we are invited to consent to a circumscribed form of power as token "radical" intellectuals. In return for that power, and as a by-product of our investments in the exclusionary system through which we may speak, our radical edge becomes contained, the potential damage of our anger minimized. We are invited to forget the subaltern woman whose body functions as the "last instance" of transnational capitalism, a system that benefits that same resistant "we" working in and speaking against the First-World academy.

This is not to say that our oppositional voices within the academy have no political effect. The oppositional struggles of radical women of color (Anzaldúa, Morraga, Mohanty, Shome, Spivak, to name a few, all cited here) have opened up spaces for me to critique the cultural processes that have shaped me. The voices of radical white women (Frankenberg 1993; Lazarre 1996, to name a few) have marked my own whiteness and the ways in which whiteness functions as a hegemonic social formation defining the terrain of cultural politics through its ever-outward gaze. Through the work of these women, I have gained some powerful insights into my own life and into the complex set of exclusionary arrangements within contemporary geopolitics. These voices have reconfigured the terrain that shapes my "choices" and the ways in which I may negotiate between resistance and consent. By seeing my personalized and localized struggles, confusions, and internalized oppressions within the larger social fields that give them meaning, I am able to make some sense of "the personal" *in context* and increasingly muster the courage to resist. I find that a relative degree of freedom can be carved out through marking and denaturalizing the seeming naturalness and inevitability of the mandates of dominant culture. From this space I, who am privileged to write and speak, can contribute to a larger struggle that would rearticulate the ideological terrain to be more inclusive and less exploitative. As I contextualize my own experiences within larger systems of power, I reread and rewrite not only my experiences, but also begin to disrupt the systems that produce them.

Rather, I suggest that as we forge oppositional spaces within the elite sphere of the academy, we must remember the academy is just that—an elite space. It is too easy to forget, as we present research by day and party by night at conventions, the backs of those whose blood and sweat built every square foot of the bourgeois hotels that "host" us. The homeless beg from us at the door, people of color wait on us, while we pontificate about their oppression.

We must remember that our voices have already been co-opted to some extent through the very act of their being included in the academy. We must also remember the conditions of exploitation in which most people of this planet are forced to live. Remember, "others" who lack voice, the systematic ways in which they are silenced, the concrete connections between this silence and their material exploitation, and that the hope for change lies in *their* voices, not just *ours*. Justice has not been served until the subaltern can speak and be heard.

Notes

1. Spivak's critique of Foucault's effort to "recover" the voice of the oppressed reveals how such projects re-center the intellectual as the necessary figure to recover the "concrete experience" of the subaltern (1988, 275). It is precisely this project of "knowing" the "other" that has placed academia (anthropology, ethnography, intercultural studies by First-World researchers on Third-World subjects) as central to colonial projects, historically and today. Spivak notes that the imperial researcher (in this case, Foucault and Deleuze) seems unaware that "the intellectual within socialized capital, brandishing concrete experience, can help consolidate the international division of labor" (1988, 275).

2. Our Mexican heritage was constructed as "Spanish" in the footsteps of Mother's parents, who constructed their identity as "Spanish." Since those early days, my Uncle Eddie, a committed Chicano, has researched my maternal family's genealogy (some of that work I draw on here). Now I know that our heritage is Mexican and proudly, although tenuously, I embrace a Chicana identity to ally myself with Chicanos/as and other people of color. I am tenuous only because of my own privilege that results from my constructed whiteness has insulated me from experiencing overt racism and placed me in a powerful position socially. My Chicano friends have mixed reactions to my adoption, or appropriation, of this identity. They tend to waver between embracing this move, supporting it, understanding my motivations, and remaining skeptical of it. Am I merely "trying on" identities? Am I trying to escape the disease of my own whiteness? These are questions I take seriously and critiques that I must consider. The question for me is, How can I be of most political service? Chicana feminist Aída Hurtado argues for the relevance to feminism while "growing numbers of offspring of intermarriage who can potentially pass as white *refuse* their inherited white privilege and join subordinate groups to sabotage existing arrangements" (1996, 12). Although this notion of "refusal" may be problematic (whether or not I participate in actively maintaining white privilege, I still am the recipient of its benefits), I strategically forge a Chicana identity (by foregrounding my Latino heritage in conversations and in writing, by taking my mother's name, by actively working *against* white privilege) in a continual attempt to "refuse" my white privilege. If,

as Hurtado notes, white privilege requires white solidarity, I seek to actively betray the white race.

3. Here is an example of her double-erasure. The nation despises her and fears her. Right-wing politicians make their careers through vehement rejection of her. They fear the white nation will be replaced by brown, the brown mother will replace the white mother. Pete Wilson decries the fact that "two-thirds of all babies born in Los Angeles County" hospitals are born to illegal immigrant women (1994) and wins the gubernatorial election, in spite of the fact that he was trailing by 27 points prior to his anti-immigrant campaign. She is also despised in the field, where those with limited power in outside spaces cease on their unrestrained power within the contained space of the work place. She is denied control over her body in each case.

4. Douloti dies on Independence Day, her body no longer able to withstand the exploitation that permeates her life. She lays her body over a map of India, which is etched into a clay courtyard and used for teaching school children about nationalism. Spivak explains Devi's final critique as "the space *displaced* from the Empire-Nation negotiation [that] now comes to inhabit and appropriate the national map, and makes the agenda of nationalism impossible" (1993, 94). Devi's poetic statement that Douloti is "all over India" (1995, 93) suggests the prevalence of Douloti's circumstance, critiquing the promise of nationalism through her death.

5. Flexible accumulation, in many ways, helps to explain current phenomena such as the low unemployment rate in this country coupled with the increasing gap between rich and poor within the United States and globally. Current figures show that the wealthiest 20 percent of the global population "earn" 80 percent of the income, while the poorest 60 percent "earn" only *six* percent. These figures take shape in the United States, where many people are currently "employed" in temporary work without benefits or security. This raises the question, What do we mean by "employment"? At the same time, welfare recipients have to work for their checks, displacing city and state employees. On a global scale, the United States (through the IMF and World Bank) continue to force "lesser developed" economies open at the expense of those countries, to produce for export and not for themselves, which drives up the prices for staples so that the people of those countries

cannot afford to eat (Bello 1994). The U.S. and other First-World countries directly benefit from the extraction of cheap labor and resources from the Third World. The imperialist relations, out of contemporary global relations emerge, have so thoroughly structured not only First and Third World economies, but also the geopolitical relations *among* nations, that neoimperial modes of exploitation flow almost seamlessly from our imperialist past. Multi- and trans-national corporations, coupled with neoliberal monetary policies, are the modern equivalent to (and the natural outgrowth of) a history of violent imperialism.

6. Although Anderson's work has been appropriately critiqued for homogenizing "the imagined community" and the "nation" based on "the Western nation" (Chatterjee 1993, 19–222), his discussion of the *function* of selective memory remains important for constructing oppositional forms of agency.

References

Acuña, R. (1988). *Occupied America: A history of Chicanos*. New York: Harper Collins.

Alexander, M.J. and Mohanty, C.T. (1997). Introduction: genealogies, legacies, movements. In Alexander, M.J. and Mohanty, C.T., *Feminist genealogies, colonial legacies, democratic futures*. New York: Routlege.

Anderson, B. (1983). *Imagined Communities*. London and New York: Verso.

Anzaldúa, G. (1987). *Borderlands/la Frontera: The new Mestiza*. San Francisco: Aunt Lute Books.

Brimelow, P. (1995). *Alien nation: Common sense about America's Immigration Disaster*. New York: HarperCollins.

Chatterjee, P. (1993). *Nationalist thought and the colonial world: A derivative discourse*. Minneapolis: University of Minnesota Press.

Devi, M. (1995). Trans. by Spivak, G. C. *Imaginary maps*. New York and London: Routledge.

Frankenberg, R. (1993). *White women, race matters: The social construction of whiteness*. Minneapolis: University of Minnesota Press.

Foucault, M. (1984). What is an author? In Rabinow, P., (Ed.) *The Foucault Reader*. New York: Pantheon.

Grossberg, L. (1997). *Bringing it all back home*. Durham, NC, and London: Duke University Press.

Grossberg, L. (1996). History, politics and postmodernism: Stuart Hall and cultural studies. In Morley, D. and Chen, K.H., (Eds.),

Stuart Hall: Critical dialogues in cultural studies. New York: Routlege.

Hall, S. (1996). Gramsci's relevance for the study of race and ethnicity. In Morley, D. and Chen, K.H., (Eds.), *Stuart Hall: Critical dialogues in cultural studies.* New York: Routlege.

Harvey, D. (1990). *The condition of postmodernity.* Cambridge, MA: Blackwell.

Lazarre, J. (1996). *Beyond the whiteness of whiteness: Memoir of a white mother of black sons.* Durham, NC, and London: Duke University Press.

Lee, B. (1996). Between nations and disciplines. In Nelson, C. and Gaonkar, D.P., (Eds.), *Disciplinarily and dissent in cultural studies.* New York and London: Routledge.

Massey, D. (1994). *Space, place, and gender.* Minneapolis: University of Minnesota Press.

Mohanty, C.T. (1991). Cartographies of struggle: Third world women and the politics of feminism. In Mohanty, C.T., Russo, A., and Torres, L., (Eds.), *Third world women and the politics of feminism.* Bloomington and Indianapolis: Indiana University Press.

Morraga, C. (1981). For the color of my mother. In Morraga, C. and Anzaldúa, G., *This bridge called my back: Writings by radical women of color.* New York: Kitchen Table/Women of Color.

Pacific Palisades Historical Society. (1980). *Rancho Boca de Santa Monica.* California: Marquez Land Marking Program.

Saldívar, J.D. (1997). *Border matters: Remapping American cultural studies.* Berkeley: University of California Press.

Shome, R. (1998). Space matters. *Western Journal of Communication, 62,* 1.

Spivak, G.C. (1988). Can the subaltern speak? In Nelson, C. and Grossberg, L., *Marxism and the interpretation of culture.* Urbana and Chicago: University of Illinois Press.

Spivak, G.C. (1992). *Thinking academic freedom in gendered post-coloniality.* Cape Town: University of Cape Town.

Spivak, G.C. (1993). Woman in difference. *Outside in the teaching machine.* New York and London: Routledge.

Stoler, A. (1997). *Race and the education of desire: Foucault's history of sexuality and the colonial order of things.* Durham, NC, and London: Duke University Press.

Visweswaran, K. (1994). *Fictions of feminist ethnography.* Minneapolis and London: University of Minnesota Press.

Wilson, P. (1994, June 15). Securing our nation's borders: Illegal immigration. *Vital Speeches, 60,* 17. 534–536 ✦

31

How We Know What We Know About Americans

Chinese Sojourners Account for Their Experiences

Ling Chen
Hong Kong Baptist University

In the last decade or so there has been a steady influx of mainland Chinese visitors into the United States: students and scholars who have come to study, teach, or do research for an extended period of time. Unlike early Chinese immigrants who typically settled in Chinese communities, this group of sojourners are scattered all over the country in academic institutions. As adults fully socialized by their native culture, these people are competent communicators in Chinese culture. Like sojourners everywhere, they engage in intercultural interactions on a daily basis.

From the day they arrive, these Chinese find themselves on new terrain in more ways than one. The rules they are brought up with and are accustomed to follow do not apply anymore, though this comes as no real shock. Psychologically, these people are prepared for a big change in their lives. Aside from the academic and professional achievements to which they aspire, most of them are eager to learn first-hand about America, a world different from China in almost every aspect—political, economic, historical, and cultural. Generally, their first perception of the United States is that of a highly industrialized, efficient, fast-paced, materialistic, and individualistic society. For many Chinese with fresh memories of the spiritually

and materially impoverishing "Cultural Revolution," America represents what China is striving for: a democracy, a thriving economy, and a high living and educational standard. Based on information from media and hearsay, these sojourners feel they know what to expect in the United States.

However, to know is never the same as to experience (Merleau-Ponty 1959). Phenomenologically, these Chinese are removed from the familiar, in terms of time as well as space, as their routine is upset by the change of environment. They now share both time and space with the unfamiliar, where little can be taken for granted. It is a situation that calls for ingenuity, resourcefulness, and problem solving with heightened awareness.

The purpose of this essay is to explore the process of active sense-making among Chinese sojourners in the U.S. and the paradoxical imbalance between familiarity and reality. By definition, sense-making is activated by social interactions, either by direct experience or as reflection in hindsight (Blumer 1969). The central question here is, "How do these Chinese interpret interactions they have with Americans, whether singly or as a group?" Throughout their stay in this country as foreign visitors, even if they decide to become residents, they are constantly confronted with the question "What should I make of this situation?"

From a cultural perspective, how these Chinese cope with living in America provides a specific example of the way in which people experience the phenomenon of intercultural communication. Though I have observed this phenomenon first-hand as a participant, the following accounts are related by selected Chinese friends and acquaintances who describe their experiences since arriving in this country. Specific attention will be focused on cases in which the participants become aware of their own sense-making efforts. These accounts were obtained through interviews with Chinese students in their mid-20s and early 30s at two mid-Western universities. These interviews were spoken in Chinese, except where remarks were quoted, and then translated by this author. Each translation was verified by each interviewee to ensure accuracy. These accounts will demonstrate the conscious sense-making process: how the experience is triggered and brought into awareness, how it operates, and how it ends with tentative knowledge. Each stage will be discussed in three sections in that order.

Taking for Granted and Surprise

Chinese as cultural strangers in the United States face a situation in which little can be taken for granted. Though they may anticipate this and feel prepared for the unfamiliar, in practice true awareness only surfaces when something unexpected occurs. Until then, sojourners move about as if they knew the ropes, going about their business as if they were still in their native culture. They deal with matters in ways they always do, until that moment when they find themselves in a problematic situation. Only then are they surprised, realizing that too much has been taken for granted; only then do they begin trying to understand the situation, particularly the American with whom they interacted at the time. This process is reactivated every time a taken-for-granted situation results in a surprise. A student (Mr. An)[1] told me the following story about his first contact with an American on his way to the United States:

> *Mr. An:* I was so excited about the trip and the opportunity to study here that I took the first flight available to the city where my school is. The flight would arrive at night which didn't bother me, as I figured I would find a way to get to school, although *I hadn't really thought about it.* I was sitting next to a woman named Alice, and we got into a conversation. I told her this was my first time visiting the U.S., and I was so excited about going to this school, etc. She asked me where I would be staying. I said I would probably be living in a student dormitory. She asked if I had made arrangements for the lodging and informed the school of my arrival. I said no, but the school must have places. I would find out about it. She asked what I would do tonight. Offices would not be open until tomorrow. It was then I started to vaguely sense the situation I might be in. I said there must be a night guard post on campus where I could get directions to

a school guest house or something. At this Alice said she could put me up for the night, that I could live in her house until I found a place, that I could use her son's room who was away. I was surprised but also very grateful. I now realized the seriousness of my mistake in not making any arrangements beforehand. . . .

This is a typical story among Chinese sojourners. As revealed by Mr. An's excitement, he anticipated a new and different life. The anticipation, however, was about life as a whole and about something different in general without a clear notion of what specifically would be different. His mode of thinking did not entirely incorporate this anticipation and his unacknowledged expectation of mundane daily routines still remained the same. When questioned, he justified his decision for not making housing arrangements with Chinese common sense: (1) schools in China have an obligation to allocate living quarters to students, be it in the guest house or a dormitory, and (2) there is always a security guard at the campus gate. He had no doubt that he could expect the same when arriving on a campus in the United States. Mr. An's story continues:

> *Mr. An:* The next day I visited the International Students' Office, assuming I would find a place to stay. A foreign student advisor who talked to me was very nice and tried to be helpful. She gave me a lot of information about a lot of things, one of which was housing. Instead of a place, I was given a list of rental offices and a local map. But I didn't know what to do with them. . . .

Obviously, Mr. An had not quite learned his lesson yet. His visit to the school was guided by the belief that he would find lodgings without a problem, again based on his past experience at home. So he was disappointed at the kind of help he got. Looking back, he now understands that the advisor had made an effort to be helpful in the American way, which was not taken as much help at all at the time.

Similarly, a Ms. Bian remembered her surprise upon landing in the U.S.:

> *Ms. Bian:* I walked off the plane and followed the signs to the baggage claim.

"This is really *convenient*," I remember thinking. I had two extra- large suitcases and a big carry-on bag. After picking up the bags, I started to look around, trying to find someone to help me carry them. But not many people were around, and everyone had luggage of their own—only they all had wheels. I walked around and noticed there was a line of luggage trolleys on the far side of the hall. I was so relieved, thinking, "After all, it is America. Nothing is neglected." I walked over and immediately saw a sign: "Deposit One Dollar." My good mood was quickly replaced by a self-mocking thought: "You should have known better. This is America, after all." Somehow this first impression always stuck in my mind. Sometime later, I picked up an American saying, "No free lunch." It very vividly sums up my first experience in America. . . . It is now one of my favorite phrases.

Ms. Bian seemed to be more aware of the change of environment than Mr. An. She was impressed by the convenient signs in the airport, which apparently were new to her. She was soon applying this new knowledge to the luggage carts, only to be disappointed by another surprise. Her self-mocking attitude indicated her aware- ness of her own unrealistic assumption: in China, a (free) helping hand is usually available in crowded places like airports and train stations.

Reliance on familiar cultural schemes of behavior is also highlighted in the following two examples: (1) Mr. Cong's experience with marijuana, and (2) Ms. Dai's experience with her landlady.

Mr. Cong: The other day I came across Rod, a fellow student, outside the library. We started chatting. Somehow we brought up the topic of marijuana, and I said I knew about it but had never seen it. On this, Rod took out a pouch from a pocket and told me it was marijuana. He showed it to me, then put a pinch into a pipe and smoked it. I watched curiously. "You want to try it?" he asked as he demonstrated, offering me his pipe. I didn't expect such an offer, letting me share his pipe. I felt obliged to take the pipe and briefly tried it before handing it back to Rod, although I had no real interest. I guess I might have appeared to be too interested in it. Still, this was a novel experience. A couple of days later in the GTA office, several of us were around during the lunch hour, and naturally there was small talk. I remembered my experience with marijuana and told them about what happened without thinking about it. To my surprise, my story was met with an unusual reception. It seemed that these people were surprised by my telling this story and didn't know how to respond. Nobody commented on it or said anything about it. . . .

Ms. Dai: I rented a room from Mrs. Robinson the first year I was here. The Robinsons also lived in the same house. The house had a back yard with laundry lines. Whenever I did laundry, I would hang my washing outside in the morning, and it would be dry by the time I returned from the school at the end of day. On one of those days, it rained shortly after lunch time. When I got home, I found the washing I had put out that morning sitting on the floor near the stairs. Everything was dry. I realized someone had brought it in before the rain. It had to be Mrs. Robinson, I realized, since she was at home all day. That was *really very kind of her*, I thought, and I was glad not to have to worry about wet clothes. Just then, Mrs. Robinson came out and, to my amazement, she started apologizing for removing my washing from the lines before I could thank her. For a while, I didn't know what to say. I assured her that she did just what I would have wanted her to do, that I must thank her for her kindness. I couldn't understand why she apologized for bringing in the wash for me. . . .

Both Mr. Cong and Ms. Dai had been in the United States for some time when these encounters occurred. Still they lived mostly by their cultural intuition. Mr. Cong Was content with knowing what marijuana looked like and was surprised, not by the act of the offer but by the nature of the offer: the sharing of a pipe with a casual acquaintance, usually a sign of intimacy for a Chinese. What was more interesting was his response. In spite of a lack of interest, and not without some reluctance, he accepted the offer. His sense of obligation to humor an offered kindness is reflective of the deeply rooted Asian tradition of "face-giving" (Goffman

1967). Another surprise was in store for Mr. Cong when he casually shared his experience with other Americans "without thinking," another common practice among Chinese acquaintances. The unexpected reaction from his audience alerted him that something was wrong. He sensed that it might be the telling of the story but could not figure out the complete meaning of the reaction to his friendly sharing of information.

As for Ms. Dai, she simply assumed Mrs. Robinson's kindness based on the fact that she was the only one home. Naturally she was prepared to offer her thanks. But never would she have imagined that her landlady would apologize for her own act of kindness. Though Ms. Dai was left momentarily speechless, she quickly recovered and reciprocated with an assurance of no ill feelings. She instinctively enacted what seemed to be an appropriate response to an unexpected apology. Still, she couldn't understand what was wrong. From her Chinese perspective, it was a kind favor to keep her washing from being spoiled by rain. In China it is common for roommates to move around each others' possessions, an act no Chinese would normally consider unusual or imprudent, as there is usually a reason for it. When the reason is for the benefit of another, it is considered a favor.

So far, our analysis has posed the theoretical premise of the cultural stranger "who has to question nearly everything that seems to be unquestionable to the members of the native cultural group" (Schutz 1964, 96), as illustrated by the true stories of these Chinese sojourners. Yet by and large, they still rely heavily on a knowledge of dealing with the world that they acquired in their home cultures.

The constant surprises in these people's new cultural environment no doubt reminded them that their old frame of reference was no longer valid here. This alone, however, was not sufficient to reorient their outlook. Their problem is rooted in a contradictory state associated with the status of being strangers—the paradox alluded to earlier—that prevents them from identifying potential problems before they are experienced. The change in physical location does not axiomatically bring about a corresponding change in their social or cultural perspective. As a product of cultural development in a particular environment, one's social perspective constitutes one's reserve of knowledge, accumulated over time, that provides a frame of reference to make sense of the empirical world. Consequently, such a perspective cannot be replaced overnight without prior empirical knowledge, as there is nothing yet there to take its place. Inconsistency of position and viewpoint, therefore, is the dilemma facing all sojourners, which cannot be alleviated by simply acknowledging it. One may be fully aware of this dilemma but still be unable to question anything one encounters in a foreign environment, despite subjective intent, because one cannot know the unknown or what to question. Questions can be asked only after situations are experienced as different from the expected.

Making Sense

Once unexpected surprises have brought the foreign environment to immediate attention, the sense-making process is activated. At this point, one does not automatically "know" just by being directly involved and must make efforts to figure out and actively seek further explanation under the circumstances. From Mr. An's account, not only did he not consider any possible lodging problems, he also gave no thought to his casual interaction with a helpful American. Once the conversation awakened him to his false assumptions, he could no longer take things for granted. Mr. An's account continues:

Mr. An: I now realized the seriousness of my mistake by not having made any arrangements beforehand. It was very kind of Alice to ask, but what her offer also told me was that I might not be able to move into the dorm right away, which I was soon to find out. I was even more grateful to Alice. It turned out that, not only was there no guest house on campus, but the student dorms had to be booked beforehand. There was no place on campus that could have solved my immediate problem that night—nor even during the day. I felt fortunate to have met such a warm-hearted friend and was also glad to have someone to visit with later. . . .

Mr. An was wiser now. Alice's offer was interpreted not just as kindness, the most common assessment the Chinese make in similar situations. It was taken also as a warning that there was likely to be a serious problem under the circumstances. Reality was beginning to sink in and other possibilities were emerging. He realized that she would not have invited him, a stranger, to her home if there had not been a real need on his part. Further, he took Alice's kindness as an offer of friendship. This type of situation is often the beginning of a friendship in China. The assumption that both persons will stay in touch is made without question, especially when they live in the same town. Once again Mr. An took a situation for granted, and his assumption later also proved to be wrong.

In the International Students' Office, an unexpected situation triggered a series of analytical questions to search for an explanation on the part of Mr. An.

Mr. An: From what my advisor Mrs. Hugh explained to me, I understood that I was to call people on the list and make arrangements. But how? I didn't have the faintest idea. On the map the city looked huge; even the campus area was too big to cross. I didn't know what to say when calling, because I had never done anything like this before. And I didn't know whom to call first; there were so many of them. I was painfully aware of being on my own. I had always been independent, but this was nothing like the independence I knew. I felt so alone, so much in the hands of the unknown. I had to try to do the best I could without knowing what would come out of it. On the other hand, I started to better understand the meaning of independence. I felt I really understood America now and was overjoyed when Mrs. Hugh told me there was a Chinese Student Association on campus. This meant that maybe I could get help from them. And I did. . . .

Confronted with this new problem of apartment hunting, Mr. An neatly assessed the situation. The city was big, and he had no transportation. He understood that he was facing a challenge, that he had to figure out a way to take it on. What had once been hearsay about being individualistic and independent in the United States was now a living experience for Mr. An; independence had taken on a new meaning. It meant not only his will to act, but also his responsibility and initiative, as well as the possibility of failure and its ramifications. Mr. An had come to grips with the reality he was facing.

Analogous to Mr. An's progress was Ms. Bian's experience, in which she had made a connection between what she knew indirectly about American materialism and what she had experienced first-hand—a charge for use of a luggage cart. In the world of business, she had realized, convenience and services are provided as a business consideration rather than out of kindness. Here is how she came to that realization in a second interaction:

Ms. Bian: I was looking around in the lady's dress section of a department store, when a salesperson approached me. She appeared so *sincere* in wanting to help, so I told her what I wanted. She showed me a couple of items, but none of them appealed to me. So I thanked her and wandered into another area. Then at some other racks, she came up to me again, trying to help. Again I declined. As I didn't really have a particular thing in mind, I felt more efficient searching on my own. However, she was not discouraged. I felt maybe I *should* buy something. As soon as I found a sweater I liked, I bought it from her before continuing to look around. Sure enough, the lady didn't approach me again after that. "No free lunch." How very true. . . .

The first interpretation Ms. Bian made of the saleswoman's offer to assist was due to her sincerity, believing she wanted to help as one would help a fellow human being. Of course she realized the woman's role as a salesperson but felt she was only trying to help—a natural reflection of Ms. Bian's cultural intuition. Chinese culture emphasizes human relations as an integral part of human interactions. Thus, Ms. Bian acknowledged what she saw as good will from the salesperson by accepting the help and expressing her thanks, which was socially appropriate. We can see that Ms. Bian's initial understanding of the interaction was basically a social gesture, as opposed to business motive in the world of sales. What constituted the end of a social transaction to Ms. Bian was not regarded as such by the salesperson, who considered it the beginning of a possible financial transaction. Thus, she continued to interact with Ms. Bian until something was sold. Her persistence prompted Ms. Bian to reconsider their relationship and correctly reassess the offered assistance as a "Can I help you?" sales pitch.

Ms. Bian was in a similar situation as Ms. Dai: the immediate context of the situation provided each of them with informational cues to make an alternative sense of the interaction; they then adjusted their own behaviors to accommodate the situation and take on the expected role. However, while Ms. Bian managed to grasp the situation for what it was, Ms. Dai was induced to make a seemingly appropriate response without understanding why.

Likewise, Mr. Cong, puzzled by the unexpected response he received from his story about marijuana, consciously tried to find an answer.

Mr. Cong. It could be that some people might not have attended to what I said. But the man I was talking to couldn't have missed it. Yet, his reaction was to just took at me with an expression' that made me wonder what I had done wrong. . . .

Mr. Cong considered circumstantial explanations of the others' unresponsiveness during this interaction. He immediately ruled out that people had missed what he said—their facial expressions indicated otherwise. Moreover, the man's expression was unusual and odd under the circumstances. This assessment led Mr. Cong to suspect that he probably had done something he should not have, but still he could not figure out what that might be.

Sense-making is a process by which strangers reorient themselves. The change of environment brings about a two-fold separation of the sojourner's personal history, physically from that of the home culture and per-

ceptually from that of the host culture. The surprise and the ensuing state of confusion are instrumental in solidifying the mismatch between physical standpoint and perceptual viewpoint. The abstract knowledge of differences has been activated by direct experience. In the struggle to come to grips with the here and now, the stranger is forced to cut ties to the past—slowly, a little at a time—and look for unfamiliar input from the immediate context to use in place of the old. As soon as old assumptions lose their relevance, the stranger stops taking things for granted and seeks new input. The questioning process initiates the perceptual, experiential, and psychological transition of the stranger into the new society.

Amidst all these questions, something fundamental remains unchallenged for these Chinese: the presumption of rationality and logic in the behavior of their American interactants. When confronted with the unfamiliar these Chinese did not doubt for a moment the Americans' reasonableness in their search for alternative interpretations.

Coming to Understand

The above interpretations of various accounts have demonstrated how these Chinese came to realize their own misconstrued perceptions of an interaction as different from that of the Americans, and how they constructed alternative readings of the situation from contextual cues. This new interpretation is certainly not taken as a complete understanding of the new cultural environment. Nevertheless, it is one step toward solving an immediate problem, though of course the process of sense-making does not end when the triggering episode is over. This new information is not treated as part of their reserve of intuitive knowledge (Schutz 1964), but as subject to further verification the next time a similar situation is encountered. This information is indexical and reflexive by nature, being given shape by the social context and help to make of that context as an integral part (Garfinkel 1967). It remains incomplete and unfinished: earlier and later versions are mutual elaboration and refinement of one and the other (Wieder and Pratt 1990). In the case of Ms. Dai, she was puzzled by Mrs. Robinson's apology. She accepted the apology, but a question mark remained in her mind. She continued to search for an explanation:

> *Ms. Dai:* Later I learned that people here don't usually touch things that belong to others. I noticed in our office that my American colleagues would borrow each other's stationery only when the owner was present and after they had asked for permission. A student once told me that she and her roommate had a big fight, because the roommate had moved something that belonged to her without asking. Although she claimed that it was no big deal, I was impressed by the fact that it had caused such a quarrel. Now I know why my landlady apologized about the laundry: she didn't feel comfortable about moving my things while I was away, even for a good reason.

Ms. Dai considered various observations of what transpires when someone moves someone else's things, until she uncovered a recurring pattern that revealed an underlying cultural rule. This observation was then applied to her earlier experience for interpretation.

Mr. Cong's account of his story about marijuana also provided an explanation:

> *Mr. Cong:* I didn't know what to make of it at the time, but later I learned that marijuana was an illegal drug. I probably shouldn't have told those people about my experience with an illegal substance, especially when it involved a third party, whom I referred to by name. I am glad that I didn't get anybody into trouble.

The knowledge of the legal complication of marijuana use solved the puzzle for him. Rightly or wrongly, it also shed a different light on the episode. Mr. Cong felt the weight of his fellow student's trust and his own carelessness.

Ms. Bian's understanding of American materialism was also achieved gradually. The first encounter in the airport gave her first-hand knowledge, which was verified by her later encounter in the department store. Accumulation of first-hand experience and verification finally led to understanding, as

summarized by her repetition of the saying "No free lunch." For her, these words had acquired the status of a theory. On several occasions I have witnessed her using it at the conclusion of other stories and as a piece of advice for others.

Mr. An's account of his friendship with Alice is also of interest. It follows as such:

> *Mr. An:* I stayed in Alice's house for four days until I found an apartment. For over half a year, I kept in touch with her, calling her a couple of times a month and visiting her. She came to visit me once after I just moved. Then I was too busy and called her less and less often. One day I realized I had not called Alice in a long time, then it occurred to me that she rarely called me; I was the one who usually made the calls. Since then, we haven't been in touch for about two years now. I just didn't get around to calling her again, but now I don't feel guilty about it. She didn't seem to mind one way or the other. I've learned that many Americans are ready to help others but never see them again afterwards. I have been helped several times by strangers when my car broke down. I also have seen it happen to others. People will jump-start your car or call for help, often before being asked. Sometimes, especially when there is snow, several people will stop and push your car, not even minding getting exhausted and dirty. Americans are really great.

Here Mr. An finally learns about American culture's emphasis on basic humanism. The revelation came as a result of repeated observations of strangers helping strangers. Understanding this phenomenon helped him to reassess the friendship he thought he had with Alice: in actuality it was a momentary helping relationship built on a humanistic base, which is common in American society. Once the help was no longer needed, there was no reason to keep up the relationship. Mr. An reinterpreted Alice's friendliness as an appropriate gesture to help a stranger and not as an intended offer to become friends, contrary to what he originally thought was expected of him. His experience with his stalled car again showed him that people were ready to help when others were in trouble, which brought him greater understanding of his experience with Alice and reinforced this new understanding. Now he no longer feels guilty for not being concerned about a "friendship" that is not mutual. Instead, he has acquired a new frame of reference.

Coming to a tentative understanding is the last stage in a cycle of sense-making. At this stage, the sojourner has solved the problem of a misplaced perspective and temporarily regained some balance. One can now see eye to eye with the American interactant and know how to deal with each situation. In the long run, however, this new perspective will never be completely fulfilled by one's accumulation of knowledge about various different situations within the host culture; hence, there is always the likelihood of further such learning cycles for the sojourner.

Conclusion

The sense-making process discussed in this essay is one whereby we begin to understand a new cultural environment by uncovering its implicit cultural rules. It is a process by which certain adjustments must be made to bring about a unity between physical proximity and perceptual familiarity. This is a slow and gradual process, barely noticeable at first, just like children growing up. Unlike growing children, however, the Chinese adults described above are more conscious and ready to make associations and inferences. They do so with the assumption that what they are learning must be reasonable, as it is part of the native common sense. It also becomes knowledge for these Chinese sojourners. Once verified, the knowledge they acquired will add to their own stockpile of information and be applied without question, until the next surprise comes around. The cycle of taking things for granted, surprises, and searching for and discovering meaning will be repeated often in the process of sense-making. Over time, there will be fewer surprises as the sojourners come to better understand and are assimilated into their environment. When this happens, they will no longer be strangers.

Note

1. The names used are not real names.

References

Blumer, H. (1969). *Symbolic interactionism.* Englewood Cliffs, NJ: Prentice Hall.

Garfinkel, H. (1967). *Studies in ethnomethodology.* Englewood Cliffs, NJ: Prentice Hall.

Goffman, E. (1967). *Interaction ritual.* New York: Anchor.

Merleau-Ponty, M. (1959). *Phenomenology of perception.* London: Routledge.

Schutz, A. (1964). *Collected papers II: Studies in social theory.* The Hague: Martinus Nijhoff.

Wieder, D.L. and Pratt, S. (1990). On being a recognizable Indian among Indians. In Carbough, D., (Ed.), *Cultural communication and intercultural contact* (45–64). Hillsdale, NJ: Erlbaum. ✦

32

The Cultural Experience of Space and Body

A Reading of Latin American and Anglo American Comportment in Public

Elizabeth Lozano
Loyola University of Chicago

This essay describes the cultural patterns of Latin American and Anglo American comportment in public space. It is grounded on my experience as a *Latinoamericana* (Latin American woman) who lives in the United States and as a researcher who studies matters of intercultural communication.

The essay is the result of a structural ethnography, an investigation that is based on lived experience, participant observation, interviewing, and extended descriptions of social settings and interactions. It focuses on the ways in which the body is understood and treated by Latin Americans and Anglo Americans, and the cultural differences that become apparent when these two cultural groups find themselves sharing a common space. It is also an opportunity to study the transformation and recreation of social rules that take place when one becomes part of a new social setting, as is the case for the Latin Americans who now live in the United States.[1]

The need to address and understand the Latin American culture appears now more urgent than ever. The influence of this cultural heritage, which has been present in the United States for more than a century, is going to have an ever growing influence in the next few decades on the Anglo American scene, as Hispanics become the largest ethnic and linguistic minority in the United States. The more knowledge we gain from that which makes us culturally diverse, the more we will be able to appreciate what unifies us through the mixing and mutual exchanges of our cultures. Processes of transformation and adaptation are as important as tradition, historical roots, and language in understanding the nature of contemporary society.

The Territory of Cultural Differences

It has been argued that under the ethnic category "Hispanic" (which occasionally is used synonymously with "Latino"), a variety of cultural differences are disguised and overlooked (Bean and Tienda 1987). "Hispanic" refers to any resident of the United States whose origin can be traced to a Spanish-speaking country. Such description is seen as both too general and too restrictive, for it bases ethnicity on the sole consideration of language. On one hand, the category seems to refer to a cultural tradition, the Latin American, but it excludes some of the Latin American countries (e.g., Brazil) whose language is not Spanish. On the other hand, the category includes Spain, a country whose cultural tradition, although very influential in Latin America, is distinctively *European*. Finally, not all Hispanic Americans speak Spanish. Some Chicanos (i.e., Mexican Americans) have been in the United States for over a century, and although they have ties with Mexico, they do not necessarily speak Spanish.

There are, in turn, important differences among the Latin American countries, from Brazil and Mexico, to Bolivia and Guatemala, to Cuba and the Dominican Republic. And yet, in spite of social and historical differences, there is a sense of cultural commonality among the societies of Central and South America, Mexico, and the Caribbean (see, for example, Neruda 1991). The latter can be seen in aspects of social life as diverse as literature, music, television, political rhetoric, and oral storytelling (Martin-Barbero 1988). In every case, the Latin

American culture appears to be the common ground from which it is possible to examine national or regional differences (Lozano and Mickunas 1992). In spite of social differences, in the realm of cultural practice Latin Americans recognize themselves as such.

A similar tension or ambiguity between commonality and difference can be seen in the case of the United States. Traditionally it has been assumed that the United States is a single culture. But recent critical reflections question the existence of this unified "American culture" in which everybody's cultural background "melts" into a mainstream that erases differences and makes us all equal. After all, ask the critics, what is *American* about the American culture? A nation formed by immigrants, the United States is a collection of differences. What is there in common among an African American, an Appalachian, a Midwesterner, or a Native American? What about the Germans, Irish, Scottish, Polish, Lithuanians, or Japanese that call themselves Americans? Where do we draw the line between similarity-in-difference and differences that assimilate?

The "melting pot" is not an adequate metaphor for a country that is comprised of a multiplicity of cultural backgrounds and traditions that affect one another and contribute to the creation of a distinctive, yet multifaceted "American culture." Instead, suggests Reed (1991), we might better think of the United States in terms of a "cultural bouillabaisse" in which all ingredients conserve their unique flavor, while also transforming and being transformed by the adjacent textures and scents.

This does not imply, by any means, that the United States is a land in which diverse traditions have an equal share of power or influence. The white, Anglo-Saxon Protestant tradition constitutes the norm, the standard and the referent by which the United States defines its social mainstream and its "average" citizen. Nevertheless, such a standard and posited mainstream is continuously challenged by the presence of other cultural traditions (e.g., the African American, the Latin American, the Chinese, or the Japanese) that are neither dissolved within an Anglo mainstream nor relegated to the status of curiosity or extravaganza. Instead, cultural traditions survive within the United States as *transformed cultural practices*. Thus, the Latin American community of the United States is no longer purely Latin American or Anglo American, but an integration and transformation of both.[2] In fact, cultural traditions within the United States could be thought of as voices in a polyphonic chorus which is always struggling between dissonance and harmony, attraction and contradiction. To better understand the United States, one should examine the particular tensions and differences that appear when the "standard" voice—the Anglo-Saxon American—confronts a "marginal" voice—e.g., the Latino.

Although it is impossible to determine the limits or boundaries of a culture, we can recognize our own when we experience something that is shocking, unnatural, and alien to us, but unnoticeable, normal, and routine to others. Cultural shock can have a double edge: being alien to the familiar and finding the familiar alienating and out of place. Features, styles, voices, and cultural signatures appear that allow us to speak of an American culture as compared to that of the French, the Japanese, the Indian, or the English. The volatile features of the American culture—or of any culture, for that matter—which seem to defy definition and escape delimitations, become apparent in the contrasting light of another culture. That which is Latin American becomes apparent in the surprise and wonder that the Anglo American social space provokes in the Latin American newcomer. For the latter, the Anglo American social space and customs might seem as exotic, uncertain, or unnatural as Central or South America would appear to the Anglo American visitor.[3]

Contact with another culture is a form of *activating* one's own culture, of reflecting on it, making it visible and, therefore, "unnatural." It also allows one to understand the social and cultural ways in which diverse cultures intersect, overlap, and transform one another. Thus, what is Latin American will appear to be articulated differently, depending on whether the contrasting culture is Anglo-Saxon, Arabic, East European, or Japanese. Differences and similarities are held in simultaneous relief.[4]

Although Latin America is a mosaic of accents, racial mixtures, political traditions, and social customs, it remains *mosaic*—that is, a common pattern, a distinguishable design, a complex but characteristic texture. A common culture does not suppose the same accent or history, but a sense of recognition and understanding that is based on aesthetic grounds, myths, rituals, and social expressivity. In the same way that to speak of a Western culture does not deny or contradict the idea of a French or a German culture, a Latin American culture exists and coexists with differences and similarities among countries, regions, classes, and ethnicities.

The U.S. Public Space

It is 6:00 p.m. The Bayfront, a shopping mall near the Miami marina, reverberates with the noise and movement of people coming and going, contemplating the lights of the bay, sampling exotic juice blends, savoring the not-so-exotic foods from Cuba, Nicaragua, or Mexico, and listening to the bands that here and there intone rock songs, blues, ballads, and, once in a while, something with a Hispanic flavor—"La Bamba," most likely, or "Guantanamera." The Bayfront is at once an outdoor and indoor space. It is a mall of homogenous halls, predictable stores, and casual window-shopping. It extends into a plaza that faces the sea and sky and invites one to contemplate the spectacle of people, sunsets, and boats.

The Bayfront provides an environment for the exercise of two different rituals: the Anglo American visit to the mall and the Latin American *paseo*, the visit to the outdoor spaces of the city—the plaza, the streets of the barrio, and the open cafes. The Bayfront is simultaneously a place for window shoppers and a place to see and be seen, where display and consumption include the display of oneself and the consumption of others. It is a place where one goes if one wants the company of Latinos and the sight of others.

Some of the people sitting in the plaza look insistently at me, making comments, laughing, whispering. Instead of feeling uneasy or surprised, I find myself looking back at them, entering this inquisitive game and asking myself some of the same questions they might be asking. Who are they, where are they from, what are they up to? I follow their gaze and I see it extend to other groups, the couples holding hands and kissing, the young women who have started dancing to the band, the children playing on the stairs. The gaze is returned by some in the crowd, so that a play of silent dialogue seems to grow amidst the anonymity of the crowd.

The crowd that participates in this complicity of wandering looks is not Anglo American. English is the language spoken; Anglo American, the architecture, the bands, the dress code, and the social rules. But the play of looks described above has a different "accent," a Hispanic accent, which reveals a different understanding of the plaza and its public space.

The Bicultural Dialogue

The Miami Bayfront is a place in which two cultural styles of body expressivity can be seen enacted simultaneously, interacting and overlapping. Although the Hispanic passers-by are strangers to one another, there is a sense of interaction among them. If I were to be addressed by anyone in this crowd, I would not be surprised, nor would I feel threatened. It would be no different from being addressed by someone in a crowded room. When I am walking by myself along the halls of a "Hispanic" mall, I am not *alone*. I do not expect, therefore, to be treated by others as if they were suddenly confronting me in a dark alley. I am in a crowd, with the crowd, and anyone there has access to my attention.

The Anglo American passers-by understand their vital space, their relationship with strangers, and their public interaction in a different manner. If I address them in the street, I better assume that I am confronting them in an alley. Pragmatically speaking, Anglo Americans are alone (even in the middle of the crowd) if they choose to be, for they have a guaranteed cultural right to be "left alone" on their private way to and from anywhere.

To approach or touch someone without that person's consent is a violation of a fundamental right within the Anglo-Saxon, Protestant cultural tradition. This is the right to one's own body as private property. Within this tradition, touching is understood as an excursion into someone else's territory. It requires, as such, an explicit permission to "trespass" the spatial barriers that protect the perimeter of that physical property. The American remains in a private niche, the personal bubble, even when being in a public space.

It is understandable that, to the surprise of the Latin American newcomer, Anglo Americans excuse themselves not only when they accidentally touch someone, but even when there is the imminence of a touch. To accidentally penetrate someone else's boundary (especially if that person is a stranger) demands an apology and a willingness to repair the damage—by stepping back from the violated territory. This supposes an allegiance to the fundamental principles that the law dictates and protects (i.e., private property, autonomy, equality), as well as acceptance of the law as a universal mediator that guarantees the exercise of basic social rights. To excuse oneself, therefore, is to assure the other person that one recognizes and believes in the law and that no harm is intended.[5]

One can see how rude a Latin American might appear to an Anglo American when the former distractingly touches another person without apologizing or showing concern. Within the Latino and Mediterranean traditions (which are predominantly Catholic), the body is not understood as property. There is no formal distance between self and body, so that it is not possible to say "*I* own my body," as if it were something "I" have acquired somewhere. That is, the body is not understood as *belonging* to its owner. It does not belong to me or anyone else; it is, in principle, *public*. It is an expressive and sensual region open to the scrutiny, discipline, and sanction of the community; not to be regulated by universal law as property, but by the contextual rules of interaction.

It is, therefore, quite impossible to be "left alone" on the Latin American street. As long as one is there, one is a visible and accessible cipher, an enigma subject to interrogation. This implies that it is not possible to be neutral in the public space; it is sensually and erotically charged, a territory of mutual flirting and *seducción* that is expressed bodily in the ways of walking, moving, looking, smiling and—in the case of men—direct interpellation.[6]

In the United States, street flirting is understood basically as a form of harassment. In Latin America, street flirting has more ambiguous significations. Public forms of flirting (such as the *piropo*) are not only socially sanctioned but also welcomed—and expected—as expressions of a man's gallantry or *caballerosidad* regarding a woman's appeal or charm.[7] Piropos are *frases galantes*, courtly phrases that are meant to be celebrating, flattering, and appreciative of a woman's "graces." Piropos range from exclamations such as "adiós mamita," (hi/bye, mama), *"qué buena que está"* (how good/delicious you look), or *"adiós cuñado"* (hi/bye, brother-in-law, said to the man who accompanies a woman), to statements such as *"si cocina como camina, me como hasta el pegado"* (if you cook like you walk, I'll eat the left-overs), *"bendita la madre que la trajo al mundo"* (blessed be the mother who brought you to the world), or *"benditos los ojos que la ven"* (blessed be the eyes that can see you. But the distance between flattery and abuse grows very thin when a piropo progresses from "gallant" salutation to an appraisal of beauty to an explicit comment about somebody's anatomy. It may be that the only one flattered by the flattery is the one who volunteers it. Street flirting in Latin America can be play or provocation, cordiality or aggression, salutation or harassment.

While interrogating and examining others within the Latino public space are not gender-exclusive privileges (i.e., both men and women participate), such activity is, nonetheless, *gendered*. That is, the forms of such public interpellation are defined along gender lines, their direct and most explicit forms being the male prerogative. Although women might use *piropos* with men, men will "celebrate" women in the street, regardless of the latter's acknowledgement or approval. Both the Latin American and the Anglo American public spaces demand different attitudes by men and women—although this is more openly and clearly the case in Latin America.

Civility and Politeness

The U.S. public space is a homogeneous territory in which there is little ambiguity and options are clear and well-articulated. The struggle for non-ambiguity can be seen in the very architectural logic of the mall, a space in which everything is clearly identified, named, and defined in terms of purpose and function. It can also be seen in the logic of the fast-food purchase. When buying a hamburger at McDonald's™, one knows precisely how the food is going to taste, how much it is going to cost, how long it is going to take before the order is ready, and how many options are offered. Every number corresponds to a different option, every name to a mass-produced, identical item. The space has been designed so that no time or energy is wasted, and no extra gestures, conversation, or interactions are required.

Walking the street in the United States is very much an anonymous activity to be performed in a field of unobstructive and invisible bodies. Since one is essentially carrying one's own space into the public sphere, no one is actually ever *in public*, exposed to the simultaneous and pervasive accessibility of others—unless that is one's specific function, as in the case of a public performer. Given that the public is private, no intimacy is granted in the public space, for its compartmentalization prevents any contact that lacks a specific and sanctioned function. Thus, while the Latin American public look is round, inquisitive, and wandering, the Anglo American is straight, non-obstructive, and neutral.

For Latin Americans, the access to others in a public space is not restricted by the "privacy" of their bodies. Thus, the Latin American does not find casual contact a form of property trespassing or a violation of rights. Civility requires the Anglo American to restrict looks, de-limit gestures, and orient movement; civility requires the Latin American to acknowledge looks, gestures, and movement and actively engage with them. For example, the Anglo American will respect the sorrow of another by remaining distant. He or she will likely intervene only if the other explicitly asks for help or consolation. On the other hand, the Latin American will approach the sorrowed one and offer consolation, even if it is not requested. For the Latin American, the unavoidable nature of a shared space is always a demand for attention and a request to participate.

An Anglo American considers "mind your own business" to be fair and civil. A Latin American might find this an ungranted restriction. What takes place in the public space is everybody's business by the very fact that it is taking place *in public*.

One can understand, in light of the above, the possible cultural misunderstandings between Anglo Americans and Latin Americans. If Anglo Americans protest the "impertinence" of Latin Americans as nosy and curious, Latin Americans protest the indifference and lack of concern of Anglo Americans. Anglo Americans would defend their privacy above all, and Latin Americans would take for granted their right to access in a communal space.

Conclusion

The scene in the Miami mall could happen just as easily in Los Angeles, Chicago, Philadelphia, or New York, cities in which Latin Americans comprise an important segment of the population. Latin Americans will not use the Anglo American public space as they would their own, but in the presence of other Latin Americans, they may choose to engage in the play of looks that transforms the anonymous crowd into a "community of strangers," so to speak. Although one might choose to remain a stranger and avoid personal contact, one cannot be anonymous, for one is recognized, addressed, and visually interpellated.

Alternately, one can make oneself more or less visible in a bicultural setting by changing the way of addressing and looking at others. Indeed, if I "look" like an American (in both senses of the word), I will be looked at in a similar way. I can use my "bilingual" knowledge as a Latin American in the United States to shift to a more Anglo American body language. I know, for example, that politeness and good manners require me to behave as if the Anglo American passers-by were not there. I also change my manners and bodily accent when I converse with American strangers. I will not look frantically at an Anglo American, and I will excuse myself if I accidentally touch her or him, avoiding any sign of intimacy that has not been explicitly called for.

Survival within a new cultural setting requires, as much as the acquisition of the language, an ability to perform according to the local rules of public interaction and to recognize patterns and rituals in daily encounters with others. This adaptation, however, is never a complete substitution of one style for another, but rather an interpretation and integration of two different languages which acquire its own, new features. Another style, a cultural, bilingual language, emerges from those who cannot consider themselves as Latin Americans any longer but are now Hispanic Americans: Hispanic citizens of the United States.

Notes

1. Estimates on the number of Latin Americans living in the United States vary greatly from source to source (some say 10 million, others suggest 15 or 20 million). This is due, in part, to the fact that Latin Americans are usually considered a subgroup of a wider category, the "Hispanic." Thus, it is hard to find data that refer specifically to the Latin American. In this essay I focus on the Latin American, contrasting the Anglo and Latino traditions from which the Hispanic American emerges.

2. I use the term *Hispanic* (in the absence of a better term) to name this new cultural practice that takes place "between" Latin American and Anglo American traditions and that, in turn, influences its two originating cultures. This term is not without its problems, for communities such as Chicanos (i.e., Mexican Americans) and Nuyoricans (i.e., Puerto Ricans born in the continental U.S.) resent its official use as a term that groups together anyone whose origin can be traced to a Spanish-speaking country.

3. See, for example, the reflections of Paz (1987).

4. For an interesting look at this cross-cultural dialogue and plurality, see Hall 1982, Verburg 1991.

5. A gender difference still pervades what is supposed to be a gender-blind right to privacy. Although nobody has access to a man's or a woman's body without their consent in the Anglo American tradition, women find this right often violated in subtle (and not so subtle) ways. In spite of an equal right to privacy, the culture still assigns a higher value to the respect of "his" right. "No trespassing" penalties are much higher for the violation of a man's territory. Historically speaking, "her" rights are not as clearly defined or socially grounded as are "his."

6. I am using the Spanish word, *seducción*, instead of its English translation, *seduction;* although they might appear to mean the same thing, they have very different implications. Indeed, the meaning here is closer to the French *seduisant* than to the English *seduction*. It does not imply a malicious abuse of an innocent, but a mix of personal atractiveness, sensuous appeal, and coquettish behavior.

7. This does not mean, though, that women like *piropos*, but that it is very gentlemanly to speak in courteous and embellishing ways to women. Most forms of gallantry and deference to women are well accepted and indeed expected from men.

References

Bean, F.D. and Tienda, M. (1987). *The Hispanic population of the United States*. New York: Russell Sage Foundation.

Hall, E.T. (1982). *The hidden dimension*. New York: Doubleday.

Lozano, E. and Mickunas, A. (1992). Pedagogy as integral difference. In E.M. Kramer (Ed.), *Consciousness and culture: An introduction to the thought of Jean Gebser* (179–199). Westport, CT. Greenwood.

Martin-Barbero, J. (1988). Communication from culture: The crisis of the national and the emergence of the popular. *Media, Culture, and Society*, 10, 447–465.

Neruda, P. (1991). The word. In Verburg, C., (Ed.), *Ourselves among others. Cross culural readings for writers* (478–479). Boston: Bedford. (Reprinted from Memoirs 1977).

Paz, O. (1987). *Convergences: Essays on art and literature*. New York: HarcourtBrace Jovanovich.

Reed, I. (1991). What's American about America? In Verburg, C., (Ed.), *Ourselves among others. Cross-cultural readings for writers* (4–8). Boston: Bedford.

Verburg, C. (Ed.). (1991). *Ourselves among others. Cross-cultural readings for writers*. Boston: Bedford. ✦

33

Regionalism and Communication

Exploring Chinese Immigrant Perspectives

Casey Man Kong Lum
William Paterson University

A Cantonese immigrant in New York City once told me that getting lost in Midtown Manhattan is an inconvenient and embarrassing experience. To him, however, the inconvenience does not stem from the fact that he cannot speak English. After all, it would never occur to him to ask an English-speaking person for directions. Finding a fellow Chinese in Midtown Manhattan in the late twentieth century is by no means a difficult task. Ironically, the source of his difficulty emerges when he *does* find another Chinese person. As he approaches his prospective rescuer, he always experiences anxiety: Will this person turn out to be a Chinese who speaks Cantonese, one with whom he can converse and feel at ease?

The experience of this Cantonese immigrant is not an uncommon one for Chinese immigrants in New York City. Immigrants have to adjust to all aspects of life in their host country, but facing uncertainties while interacting with their compatriots is not something they expect when they leave their homeland.

For example, Chinese immigrants from Hong Kong are members of an ethnic and social majority in the British colony. Although many Hong Kong natives acquire a unique perspective about their ethnic identity, because of the colonial influences there, they are raised in Chinese families that speak Cantonese, most of whom relate to themselves as definitively Chinese.

However, their sense of "Chineseness" is challenged when they immigrate to large overseas Chinese communities where they are no longer a clear majority, even within the Chinese population, and where they are constantly confronted by the different cultural sensitivities of Chinese from other regional backgrounds. Although Hong Kong immigrants represent a large percentage of the Chinese community in New York City, Chinese from other regions, such as various parts of the People's Republic of China, Taiwan, and Southeast Asia, are also represented economically, politically, and culturally. Many of these people do not speak or understand Cantonese, just as many Hong Kong Cantonese do not speak or understand Fujianese, Taiwanese, or Toishanese, or the many other regional dialects from Southern China. Because of the language barriers, many overseas Chinese tend to socialize only with people of regional backgrounds similar to their own.

Indeed, regionalism has long been an important element in facilitating and maintaining diversity in Chinese culture. In this essay, I will explore (1) the regional origins of Chinese immigrants in New York City and (2) the role that regionalism plays in the maintenance of these immigrants' culture, ethnicity, and communication. I will focus my exploration on the experience of the three dominant groups of contemporary Chinese immigrants in New York City: those from China, Hong Kong, and Taiwan.

Regional Origins of Chinese Immigrants in New York City

The region from which one originates is an important criterion in judging one's ethnicity (Isajiw 1974; Keyes 1976; Subervi-Velez 1986). To acknowledge region as a basis of ethnicity, in turn, is to accept the assumption that the environment in which people are nurtured has a certain degree of influence on their cultural development and identification. China, Hong Kong, and Taiwan encompass a great variety of regions, which are defined by varying social, economic, and political arrangements as well as diverse language compositions.

Indigenous social, economic, and political arrangements play an important role in defining the regional characters of these immigrants. As a British colony for more than a century and a half, for instance, Hong Kong has evolved from a tranquil fishing village in the Qing Dynasty (1644–1911) to one of the most vibrant financial centers in the world. As a result, many people in or from Hong Kong have long acquired the skills necessary to survive in a cosmopolitan world.

Although China lived under a rigidly centralized economic and political system since 1949, people in the country are very diverse in their regional outlooks. China's geography encompasses a complex typography and climate system that fosters a great variety of economic activities and lifestyles (Ginsburg 1958, 155–273; Sivin 1988, 36–37). Both this physical diversity and the uneven distribution of natural as well as social and political resources have affected the growth of China's various regions, resulting in varying degrees of economic sufficiency and modernization. As a result, people from the cities, such as Canton, Beijing, and Shanghai, tend to be more adaptive than those from the farming villages in Gansu Province or the western loess highlands to the pace of life in such modern urban centers as New York City.

Taiwan returned to the Republic of China in 1945 after 51 years of Japanese occupation.[1] In 1949, the Nationalist government regained complete political control over Taiwan, much to the dismay of many native Taiwanese.[2] However, with tremendous self-determination, a fierce, anti-Communist policy, and support from the United States, Taiwan has prospered and become a remarkable economic force. Because of their affluence and increasing contact with the West, people in Taiwan today, especially those from the urban areas such as Taipei or Kaohsiung, have acquired a cosmopolitan outlook; people from outside the cities still maintain a certain degree of provincialism.

The diversity of Chinese languages is another key contributing factor to the perpetuation of regionalism among many Chinese. There are seven major dialect groups in China, each with its own subgroups (Sivin 1988, 126; see also Sun, 1990, 276–281). People in the northern regions of China generally speak *putonghua* ("common speech"), or what is known in Taiwan and the West as Mandarin. In regions south of the Yangtze River, the major dialect groups are Wu, Xiang, Gan, Hakka, Min, and Yue, under which there are numerous subgroups.[3] Cantonese is but one subgroup of Yue spoken in and around the Canton area in southern Guangdong Province as well as in Hong Kong. In Taiwan, the two major languages are Mandarin and Taiwanese, although many other Chinese dialects are also spoken in families with ancestral links to the mainland.

Speakers of these regional dialects are generally incomprehensible to one another, not because their accent is too thick, but because the dialects they use employ different sounding systems and idiomatic usages.[4] Linguistically, these dialects are in fact distinct languages (Sivin 1988, 126). A Mandarin-speaking graduate student from China told me that he and his Cantonese-speaking classmates from Hong Kong had to converse in English because they could not understand each other's dialect. Although many Chinese are bilingual,[5] they remain divided into hundreds of language communities in which their regional identities are constantly reinforced by their respective dialects.

Regionalism and Social Interaction Among Chinese Immigrants in New York City

Not only is regionalism a key element in the diversity of Chinese culture, it also plays a vital role in helping many Chinese maintain their sense of cultural continuity when they resettle as immigrants. In a study of Chinese immigrants in Southeast Asia between 1850 and 1940, for example, Hamilton (1977) examined how these early Chinese immigrants adapted among themselves and to indigenous people in host countries. He concluded that the ethnic identities of these Chinese immigrants were highly adaptive to their adopted societies, especially to conditions that "favored the continuation and even intensification of subethnic distinctions patterned after those made in China" (Hamilton 1977, 347–348). As Crissman (1967, 185) observed, the organizational patterns of overseas Chinese communities "derived from patterns indigenous to China itself" (cited in Hamilton 1977, 338; see also Mark and Chih 1982, 45–59).

Many early Chinese immigrants living in Southeast Asia organized among themselves strictly along regional lines, such as in the form of same-countryside or same-name associations modeled after similar organizations in their indigenous regions. Moreover, these overseas Chinese tended to maintain a double identity, i.e., an ethnic Chinese identification and a regional identification. That is to say, while it was essential for them to be acknowledged as being ethnically Chinese, it was equally important for them to retain their respective subethnic, regional origins for the maintenance of their social, economic, and cultural well-being.

Indeed, this "double ethnic identity" of early Chinese immigrants in Southeast Asia still persists and is manifested in many other Chinese immigrant communities today. While all Chinese immigrants in such communities acknowledge their ancestral origins in China (i.e., their ethnic roots), many would tend to associate with people from similar indigenous regions (i.e., their subethnic identification and affiliation). At the level of language affiliation, for instance, the two Chinatowns in New York City provide an interesting illustration of this phenomenon of regional affiliation (or "separation").

New York's first Chinatown, located in the Manhattan's Lower East Side, is an established community with a history that goes back to the mid-1800s (Kwok 1985; Kwong 1987; Lum 1991, 1996a; Wong 1982; Zhou and Logan 1991). The majority of Chinese residents in this neighborhood—most of whom came from Hong Kong and South China—speak Cantonese, Toishanese,[6] and increasingly Fujianese (from the Fujian Province). As all native Hong Kong Chinese are educated in both Chinese (Cantonese) and English, it is not uncommon for them to mix Cantonese and English in their daily speech. For example, one may say *Keui hou handsome*, which means "He is very handsome." Hong Kong Chinese have also transliterated certain English words or expressions and have employed them as part of their daily vocabulary. For example, *salum* is used in the same way as the English *salute* from which it is derived. (One may say *Ogo yiu heung keui salum*, which means "I have to *salute* that person.") By comparison, this linguistic habit is less apparent among Chinese immigrants from China or Taiwan.

The second Chinatown in the Flushing area of Queens evolved into being over the past two decades.[7] Many Chinese immigrants in this area are Mandarin- and Taiwanese-speaking Chinese from Taiwan. This Chinatown is also referred to by some as "New York's Taiwantown" (*Hsiang Hsun* 1992, 2).

Although economic opportunities have brought Chinese from diverse regional backgrounds together in the Chinatown marketplaces at large (Zhou 1992; Zhou and Logan 1991), close regional affiliation still plays an important role in securing social and economic success among many Chinese immigrants in the area.[8] Most "old overseas Chinese" who came from Guangdong Province to New York City before 1965 (Wong 1982, 74–78) built very tight personal and business networks and close regional associations, because (1) they were ethnocentric and faithful to their indigenous culture; (2) they lacked the language skills to interact with the larger social environment; (3) the ethnic community offered more convenient economic opportunities; and (4) restrictive immigration laws did not allow most males to maintain a normal family life with a spouse and children, especially during the period of 1882 through 1943 (Wong 1985, 234). These networks are exemplified by such organizations as same-surname associations and same-countryside clubs, or *tongs*, that are similar in their social nature to those organizations in Crissman's (1967) study of early Chinese immigrants in Southeast Asia cited above. They provide their members with a variety of services: job referrals, the adjudication of disputes, financial assistance, and a context for leisurely social interaction. Of course, these organizations are also sources of regional or subethnic rivalries in business, politics, and crime.

Similarly, thousands of illegal immigrants from Hong Kong, China, Taiwan, and Southeast Asia who stay away from the social mainstream for obvious legal reasons, also have played a part in maintaining regionalism in the Chinese population of New York City. They often feel unwelcome by the larger society (Wong 1982, 83), particularly at times when anti-immigrant sentiments are high,[9] and they therefore are forced to remain in their subethnic groups for support and survival. I have observed how an interpretive community of illegal Malaysian Chinese immigrants was formed in the working-class neighborhoods of Flushing, Queens (Lum 1996a). While they shared a similar passion and need for karaoke singing as a form of personal expression and communal experience, these people were also bound as a group by a common subethnic, regional background.

The regionalism of Chinese immigrants in New York City is also manifest in their cultural customs and practices. Although Chinese immigrants in New York City celebrate important festive occasions or Chinese holidays, such as the Lunar New Year, Dragon Boat Festival, and Mid-Autumn Festival, they differ along regional lines in how they celebrate.[10] While people from Hong Kong and the Canton area celebrate Mid-Autumn Festival with homemade or commercially available paper lanterns, people from Taiwan celebrate the occasion without lanterns. Food that people serve at home as part of any festive or significant celebration also differs according to regional culinary habits. During the Chinese New Year, for instance, pig's feet are popular food items among Hong Kong Cantonese because the Cantonese pronunciation of pig's feet (*chusau*) resembles the pronunciation of another term (*jausau*), which means "easy" or "effortless." Put in the proper context, eating pig's feet during the New Year is part of a ritual to bring in easy wealth all year round. During the Chinese New Year, the act of serving a friend pig's feet is an offering of good luck used to win friendship or make a good impression. Among Taiwanese, on the other hand, pig's feet are served with noodles to symbolize longevity at a birthday celebration rather than at the Chinese New Year.

Chinese immigrant media are another cultural arena where regionalism is evident. For example, Chinese-language newspapers published in the United States tend to put more emphasis on events or issues that are perceived to have more relevance to people coming from their respective backers' places of origin.[11] On the other hand, in an informal survey I came to realize that many Chinese immigrants feel more comfortable with papers produced by their "own people" (e.g., Hong Kong Chinese identify with *Sing Tao Jih Pao*, a Hong Kong-affiliated paper; Taiwanese Chinese identify with *World Journal*, a paper published by people from Taiwan). This is not to say, however, that the newspapers are entirely "regionalized." They have made conscious efforts to include news from a good variety of areas in China, Hong Kong, Macau, and Taiwan and areas with a substantial Chinese immigrant population, such as Great Britain, Southeast Asia, and Canada to help diversify the regional profiles of their readership. The broadening of regional coverage, and the fact that written Chinese has long been standardized, have brought about a mixed readership. But that does not necessarily entail a cross-identification among Chinese from the various regions, social and economic strata, or political groups.

Regionalism is even more pronounced in the Chinese immigrant electronic media. These media are mostly targeted at audiences representing specific regional language groups. For example, radio programs *Chinese American Voice* and *Chinese Radio* of New York are designed specifically for Mandarin and Taiwanese listeners, whereas Chung Hwa Commercial Broadcasting and Sinocast Radio Broadcasts Corporation serve only Cantonese listeners (Lum 1996b). In the television field, World Television is an all-Mandarin program on UHF produced by *World Journal's* parent corporation, a media company from Taiwan (Cheng 1990). On the other hand, the now-defunct Chinese Cable

Television was an all Cantonese cable television program serving subscribers in the Chinatown area (Lum 1996c). In order to capture a larger share in the Chinese-language television markets in the United States, however, companies with strong substantial financial backings (e.g., TVB Satellite, North American Television, and Sino Vision) have begun to carry a mixture of Mandarin and Cantonese news and entertainment segments in their programming. These services capture a sizable immigrant audience, especially among those who lack the English skill to enjoy mainstream media for information and entertainment. More importantly, they offer all Chinese immigrants in New York City familiar media content relating to their cultural life before they were uprooted. In short, these media, along with social organizations and personal networks, furnish Chinese immigrants in New York City with a means to help maintain their ethnic and regional culture and identification.

Nevertheless, it is obvious that this regional culture cannot exist without any influence from the new social environment. After all, these immigrants and their offspring must adapt to the larger American social and cultural environment. Culture evolves through its interactions with external forces. A U.S. Chinatown is the result of cultural evolution in a North American context, which produces new practices that may look deceptively "Chinese" at first glance. Eating rice from a plate with chopsticks instead of from a bowl or receiving enigmatic advice from a fortune cookie[12] have become common practice in American Chinese restaurants, even though these customs seem awkward to new Chinese immigrants. New vocabulary also comes into being. For example, many long-time Toishanese and Cantonese in Chinatown use the Cantonese word *paa man* for the English word "apartment," as opposed to *lau* (as an apartment is called by Chinese from Hong Kong) or *kung yu* (the word used by Chinese from Taiwan). "*Paa man,*" in its written version (with two characters that are phonetically close to two of "apartment's" syllables), is often used as an accepted term in the rental section of Chinese newspapers published in New York City,

including those published by Taiwanese. New immigrants from China, Hong Kong, and Taiwan would certainly find this term unusual.

Conclusion

Chinese immigrants in New York City come from a great diversity of linguistic, social, economic, and political regions. As a result, regionalism has become a key component in defining the ethnic and subethnic or regional identity and affiliation of these immigrants. It also plays an important role in helping Chinese immigrants in New York City maintain a sense of cultural continuity. The regionalism among Chinese immigrants is manifested in how they interact among themselves, including social and economic associations, the maintenance of cultural customs or practices, media consumptions and the dialects or languages they use.

However, although the Cantonese immigrants who are afraid of getting lost in Midtown Manhattan, like many other Chinese immigrants, would hold dear his or her indigenous regional culture and identity, others may have different attitudes. Chinese immigrants who have higher levels of academic, professional, social, or economic achievement have much less difficulty in becoming an active part of the larger American social and cultural environment. Similarly, because foreign-born children of Chinese immigrants are better prepared to assimilate into American society, they may have less desire and very little need to cling to their parents' ethnic or regional networks. The same could be said even more emphatically for immigrants' children who are born in the United States as Chinese Americans. After all, the United States is their country now, even though they may be confronted by racism and discrimination as well as questions surrounding their blend of "double identity."

Notes

1. Japan gained cession of Taiwan in 1895 after its military victory over China (Qing Dynasty)—despite strong resistance from the local populace. Many of the parents, grandparents, and great grandparents of the post-

World War II generation of native Taiwanese were educated by the Japanese.

2. There was a long period of mutual suspicion between native Taiwanese and Chinese from the Mainland, although the social tension between them (especially between those who were born after World War II) has subsided considerably. Intermarriage between Mainland Chinese and native Taiwanese, for example, is not uncommon today. However, the tension between native Taiwanese politicians or political parties and the Nationalist-controlled government remains intense.

3. In addition, there are 52 officially recognized minority languages in China (Sivin 1988, 100), including Mongolian, Manchurian, and a variety of other dialects of Indo-European origins.

4. Although there are many regional dialects in China, there is only one official writing system in the country that every school child is taught to use. However, a number of regional dialects still maintain their localized writings. For example, in New York City, one has the choice to take a Cantonese version of the written test for a driver's license. Parts of many Chinese newspapers in New York's Chinatown, such as entertainment news from Hong Kong, are written partially in Cantonese (i.e., Cantonese writing or *Kwongdung man*, as it is called by some Chinese immigrants in New York).

5. Although the governments of China and Taiwan have promoted Mandarin as the official language, many people who were born and raised in families with a regional dialect still use their own regional dialect whenever necessary.

6. Toishanese (or Toysanese) was the lingua franca for the New York Chinese community in the pre-1965 period because the majority of Chinese immigrants in the area then originated from Toishan in Guangdong Province. Now, the standard Cantonese spoken in Canton in Guangdong and its vicinities (including Hong Kong and Macau) has taken the place of Toishanese as the predominant dialect in New York's Chinatown (Wong 1985, 232).

7. Chen (1992) argued that the characterization of Flushing as a new Chinatown is inappropriate. He contended that Chinatown is normally referred to as "a compact homogeneous Chinese settlement, with a core of Chinese businesses" and that this traditional conception of a Chinatown does not fit the characteristics of "the Queens Chinese communities in the mixed neighborhood of Flushing and Elmhurst" (x). Whatever the Chinese community in Flushing is called, the fact that this community is prominently represented by Chinese immigrants from Taiwan, a fact that is amply examined by Chen (1992) himself, illustrates the subethnic, regional distinction between the Chinese immigrant communities in Manhattan's Lower East Side and Flushing.

8. Building personal networks consisting of people with family or regional ties in order to achieve social and economic success is a common practice among Chinese. See Chang and Holt (1991) for a study of how certain Chinese in Taiwan construct and maintain their social networks.

9. Many of these illegal immigrants are discriminated against by both the larger society and the more established Chinese businesses to the extent that they cannot enjoy any social benefit and, because of their illegal status, they often have to take jobs with substandard financial returns or protection.

10. Because all Chinese holidays or festivals are based on the Chinese lunar calendar, it becomes unlikely that many Chinese immigrants will participate in U.S. public celebrations, such as joining the New Year's parade with firecrackers and dragon and lion dances in Chinatown. After work, however, many of these immigrants often celebrate privately at home.

11. Historically, Chinese newspapers have tended to be more openly partisan than their counterparts in the United States. It is not uncommon for newspapers in China, Hong Kong, Taiwan, and overseas Chinese immigrant communities to have an overt editorial identification with a given political party, cause, or government (see Chan and Lee 1988; Mertill 1991, 224–230).

12. See Kwok (1985, 188–189) for a brief account of the origins of fortune cookies.

References

Chan, J.M. and Lee, C.C. (Spring, 1988). Journalistic paradigms in flux: Editorial stance and political transition in Hong Kong. *The China Quarterly* (UK), 117, 98–117.

Chang, H.C. and Holt, G.R. (1991). More than relationship: Chinese interaction and the principle of Kuan-Hsi. *Communication Quarterly*, 39 (3), 251–271.

Chen, H.S. (1992). *Chinatown no more: Taiwan immigrants in contemporary New York.* Ithaca, NY: Cornell University Press.

Cheng, H.Y (1990, December 8–14). Uncovering the history of New York's Chinese-language television [in Chinese]. *China Times Weekly,* American ed., 73–74.

Crissman, L.W. (1967). The segmentary structure of urban overseas Chinese communities. *Man,* 2, 185–204.

Ginsburg, N., (Ed.). (1958). *The pattern of Asia.* Englewood Cliffs, NJ: Prentice Hall.

Hamilton, G.G. (1977). Ethnicity and regionalism: Some factors influencing Chinese identities in Southeast Asia. *Ethnicity,* 4, 337–351.

Hsiang Hsun [in Chinese]. (1992, March). Taiwanese Association of America Greater New York Chapter.

Isajiw, W.W. (1974). Definitions of ethnicity. *Ethnicity,* 1, 111–124.

Keyes, C.F. (1976). Towards a new formulation of the concept of ethnic group. *Ethnicity,* 3, 202–223.

Kwok, J.C. (1985). *Changes of Chinatown: Historical anecdotes of New York's Chinatown* [in Chinese]. Hong Kong: Po I Publishing.

Kwong, P. (1987). *The new Chinatown.* New York: Hill and Wang.

Lum, C.M.K. (1991). Communication and cultural insularity: The Chinese immigrant experience. *Critical Studies in Mass Communication,* 8 (1), 91–101.

Lum, C.M.K. (1996a). *In search of a voice: Karaoke and the construction of identity in Chinese America.* Mahwah, NJ: Erlbaum.

Lum, C.M.K. (1996b, May 23–27). An intimate voice from afar: A brief history of New York's Chinese-language radio. Paper presented at the annual meeting of the International Communication Association, Chicago, Illinois.

Lum, C.M.K. (1996c). Chinese cable television: Social activism, community service, and non-profit media in New York's Chinatown. In G. Gumpert and S. Drucker (Eds.), *Communication and Immigration.* Cresskill, NJ: Hampton.

Mark, D.M.L. and Chih, G. (1993). *A place called Chinese America.* Dubuque, IA: Kendall/Hunt.

Merrill, J.C. (1991). *Global journalism: Survey of international communication* (2nd ed.). New York: Longman.

Sivin, N. (Consulting Ed.). (1988). *The contemporary atlas of China.* Boston: Houghton Mifflin.

Subervi-Velez, F.A. (1986). The mass media and ethnic assimilation and pluralism: A review and research proposal with special focus on Hispanics. *Communication Research,* 13 (1), 71–96.

Sun, R.F. (Ed.-in-Chief). (1990). *Zhongguo Shao Shuo Min Zi Jiao Yu Xue* [in Chinese] (*An Introduction to Pedagogy for Ethnic Minorities in China*). Beijing: China Labor Publishing.

Won, B.P. (1982). *Chinatown: Economic adaptation and ethnic identity of the Chinese.* New York: Holt, Rinehart and Winston.

Wong, B. (1985). Family, kinship, and ethnic identity of the Chinese in New York City, with comparative remarks on the Chinese in Lima, Peru, and Manila, Philippines. *Journal of Comparative Family Studies,* 16 (2), 231–254.

Zhou, M. (1992). *Chinatown: The socioeconomic potential of an urban enclave.* Philadelphia, PA: Temple University Press.

Zhou, M. and Logan, J.R. (1991). In and out of Chinatown: Residential mobility and segregation of New York City's Chinese. *Social Forces,* 70 (2), 387–407. ✦

34

Traversing Disparate Cultures in a Transnational World

A Bicultural/Hybrid Experience[1]

Maria Rogers-Pascual
San Francisco State University

For as long as I can remember, I have been living within at least two clearly disparate cultures. At times, one is clearly juxtaposed over the other in accordance to its position of power (in a nationalistic sense): My *birth culture*, U.S. American or *Norteamericana,* sits firmly on top of what I often think of as my *spirit culture*—my Mexican childhood. At other times, the two appear to co-exist side by side, not necessarily equal but separate. Most of the time, however (and certainly more often than I am capable of recognizing), these two cultures intermingle to the point of becoming almost one—that is, something entirely new—inextricably entangled and mutually reflecting each other's contradictions.

I have yet to discover a way to separate or untangle these two cultures that live inside me and together shape the way I see, understand, and experience the world. Before I learned legitimate alternatives to belonging to, or becoming part of, one dominant national culture, I used to feel that I had a split personality; that I had to go through some kind of process that would make me part of one culture or the other, like (I assumed) everybody else was. I used to (and

often still do) respond to the seemingly simple and recurring question "Where are you from?" with ambivalence and trepidation.

Responding to this question, which I interpret to mean "Who are you?" or better yet, "Who's side are you on?" has certainly been an empowering process of discovering and asserting my unique and complex cultural identity. But I have found it is the question, more than the answer itself, that can guide to a deeper understanding of identity formation and transformation in complex intercultural communication processes. Rather than attempt to unravel and separate the cultural threads that often combine into a web of contradictions, it is worthwhile exploring and paying attention to some of the gaps generated by the experience. It is worth asking how continual intercultural interactions, in particular those involving cultures with a long history of marked unequal power relations (as is the case with my experience living in both the United States and Mexico), shape bicultural identity. Further, what can such experience tell us about the process of intercultural communication?

There is a plethora of research addressing the "predicament" of individuals caught between the cracks of two cultures (for a thorough review see La Framboise et al. 1993). As these authors argue, it has long been established that the phenomenon of life on the border between cultures is not only beneficial to the individual but also to society. The study of marginality and second culture acquisition gives life to a number of models including assimilation, acculturation, and biculturation. When I first began to explore these models to better understand my experiences, I adopted the last one. The concept of biculturation enabled me to consider my ongoing experience of two cultures as a legitimate process rather than as a process of necessarily becoming part of the dominant culture and thereby shedding some "original" culture (assimilation), or as a process of learning the dominant culture while maintaining my roots firmly in the "original" and now "marginal" culture (acculturation).

Biculturalism can be generally defined as "the ability to operate within at least two worldviews, whereby one represents a dominant culture and the other represents a marginal culture. Following this definition, bicultural peoples include gays and lesbians operating in a heterosexual world (e.g., Brown 1989), women living in a patriarchal society, ethnic and racial minorities living in a white Western European society, et cetera. This definition assumes that power relations are inherent in intercultural interactions; thus, bicultural peoples are always in one way or another confronting issues of power and dominance. How one approaches identity, culture, and power, therefore, is key to interpreting one's own personal, social, and political experience.

Identity is "one's theory of oneself. . . . It gives one a sense of one's own ontological status and serves as an interpretive frame for experience" (Cupach and Imahori 1993, 113). And because identities are also inherently a communicative process (Hecht 1993), intercultural encounters are central to the way I see myself in the world. While the notion of biculturalism has shaped my worldview significantly, more recently I have begun to explore the idea of hybridization (see Featherstone 1995; Canclini 1996). This model provides a more complex understanding of how my individual experience is framed within a broader social and transnational context. It also gives some tools to understand the mobility and fluidity of my identity as I move in and out of both dominant and marginal positions. What follows is a discussion of how I see my bicultural identity forming and transforming when framed within three different models. First, I discuss models that stress the psychological aspects of being bicultural. Second, I discuss the bicultural experience as a form of resistance to dominant ideology. And third, I explore hybridization processes as experienced by what is sometimes referred to as fourth world peoples.[2] Each set of models, I argue, is based on different assumptions about the notion of culture and power, and each provides insights as well as raises new issues with regard to the role of ideology in intercultural communication processes.

The Psychological Benefits of Biculturalism: A Socio-Psychological Approach

I remember feeling "different" for the first time at age 9, when my family moved "back"[2] to the United States from Mexico. I was placed in a predominantly white public school in Lafayette, Louisiana. While I spoke English fluently (even though I had to relearn it at age 7), and after all this was my *birth culture*, I knew in a very fundamental way that I did not belong there (neither with the 29 white kids in my class nor with the one or two black kids in the school). Clearly (or so it appeared), my immediate happiness or just my sense of stability was dependent upon being able to adapt to the norms of the dominant group. I have vivid memories of this learning process, which includes a furious paddling by my fourth grade teacher for failing to produce the correct results on an assignment, as well as ostracism by other children because I did not dress appropriately. But I learned quickly and adapted my behavior accordingly. I made several friends and six months later I even struggled when my parents informed me that our move back to the States had been a mistake, and that we were returning to Mexico.

It was this short, intense experience in the United States that alerted me to my "difference" likewise in Mexico. I was now clearly in my mind an *American* in a foreign country, even though for the first 9 years of my life I had no conception of what that meant. I began to notice, for instance, that I had access to friendships with some of the wealthiest Mexican kids even though I was not from a wealthy family per se. And my relationship with *los de enfrente* (the family of car mechanics across the street)—an association that prior to my visit to the states, had seemed "normal" and "natural"— became awkward and uncomfortable at times. I began to wonder why I would always spend the night with my girlfriend although she never stayed with me. It was during these moments that my *birth culture* overshadowed my *spirit culture*. Eventually, as my relationship to this family matured and I gained some distance from the United States, I was able once again to experience fully my Mexican identity.

These two sets of experiences can be understood, at least partially, as a process of second culture acquisition. In their discussion on the psychological impacts of biculturalism, La Framboise et al. (1993) argue in favor of the alternation model of second culture acquisition (as opposed to either acculturation or assimilation), which posits that people can learn to "alternate their behavior to fit into the cultures [in] which they are involved [and as a result, they] will be less stressed and less anxious than those who are undergoing either the process of acculturation or assimilation" (400). Further, the authors argue that the alternation model allows one to consider two important aspects of intercultural contact: a) that the individual has an active role (agency) in the relationship and can thus choose how to interact and b) that intercultural contact is a two-way street. That is, by applying the alternation model, we can consider the impact of intercultural interaction on both cultural groups.

Indeed, learning how to operate in both cultural systems was key to my emotional survival at such a young age. This model allows me to look back to those difficult moments and rather than focus on what I had to discard, tap into a sense of empowerment that comes from a unique way of knowing. I can pay attention, for instance, to the curiosity expressed by others about this foreign land that I'd come from; I can acknowledge the awe inspired by the fact that, because of my Mexican education, I was the only one who could do long division in an American fourth grade. I can also acknowledge that perhaps I had the choice to re-claim my Mexican identity and that my Mexican and American friends at the time were part of that process.

But what might be some of the social benefits or impacts of my experience? By presenting the construct of bicultural competence, LaFramboise et al. (1993) suggest that being able to operate within two cultural systems allows one to view both cultures from a positive and equal footing. This implies that

by so doing, intercultural conflict can be minimized, at least in relation to the bicultural individual's life within two specific cultural systems. Similarly, Blechman (1992) applies this concept of bicultural communicative competence to minority youth mentoring. She contends that bicultural mentors can model this as an alternative for "group members who cannot fully assimilate into the powerful majority because they look different (i.e., have black skin or oriental [*sic*] features, are female or have physical deformity). . . to overcome their disadvantage" (164). From this perspective, bicultural competence becomes a way of coping with the dominant culture, rather than a means to assert one's difference, and as a result contributes something unique to society. Unfortunately, this model provides no other alternative for becoming empowered than to play by the specific rules of the game, whether it be the rules of the dominant or of the minority culture.

One of the fundamental drawbacks of this model is the assumption that it is from the individual's own perspective and not in relation to the group, that the ability is acquired to succeed and play by the rules of the dominant culture, while also maintaining a sense of belonging to the culture of origin. While this genre of model gives insight into some of the positive psychological aspects of being bicultural (e.g., LaFramboise et al. 1993), and attempts, albeit with serious difficulty, to point to ways that disempowered individuals can overcome certain obstacles (e.g., Blechman 1992), it is impossible from this position to discern the individual's cultural experience in relation to broader sociopolitical processes that generate such conditions in the first place. This is in part due to the fact that these models have been framed within the traditional paradigm, which views both culture and the self as relatively static (Banks and Banks 1995). Further, this approach is based on an individualistic ideology, informing much of today's intercultural communication literature, which tends to focus on "ethnicity as an aspect of an 'individual's background. . . not as dynamic organizing collectivities of structuring social relations" (Olnec 1990, 154–

155). That is, the process of acquiring a bicultural identity, and the resulting bicultural competence, is seen as an individual process of acquiring skills and developing positive attitudes rather than as a means of gaining insight into the self as an integral part of a much larger social process.

I cannot, however, overlook some of the individual psychological benefits that this model highlights. I did, in fact, gain a level of bicultural competence from my first set of experiences that helped me cope later with a second and more permanent move back to the United States at age 13. But what does one do with such experiences besides learning from them or teaching others to cope? And how can I make sense of this process as something that isn't just about me or only a few other individuals? It is crucial, I believe, to consider an approach to biculturalism that recognizes some of the political aspects of one's experience; and how, for instance, being bicultural, and claiming that experience, is an empowering process, which shapes one's approach to life in general and to social change in particular.

Biculturalism as Resistance to Dominant Ideology

Efforts to articulate a conclusive politics of biculturalism is a highly complex and messy endeavor. Yet it is significant to note that even the naming of such a phenomenon clearly is linked to an experience of listening to 'the whisper within' and giving voice to an unspoken, yet ever present memory of difference.

—Darder (1995, 1)

If something or someone is neither nor, but kind of both, not quite either. . . if it threatens by its very ambiguity the orderliness of the system, of schematized reality, if given [that] its ambiguity in the univocal ordering of it is anomalous, deviant, can it be tamed through separation? Should it separate as to avoid taming? Should it resist separation? Separate as in the separation of the white from the yolk?

—Lugones (1994, 459)

The second time I moved back to the States (to Austin, Texas, this time) at age 13, I became once again conscious of my difference in a country that was supposedly mine. Yet this time, I became aware that it was an experience not unique to my particular family. Identifying with marginal ethnic groups somehow became more natural for me than attempting to assimilate into the white dominant culture. I found that my mixed identity seemed to influence the color of my skin: My "olive" complexion was "white" to some and "brown" to others. And this, among other factors, gave me certain choices and limitations that were difficult to discern.

It was ironic, in a sense, that we happened to move to an all-white street in the middle of a historic black neighborhood. Coming from Mexico, in the eyes of the neighbors from our street, we were simply Mexican or Chicanos. To our African American neighbors, however, we were clearly white, benefiting from the same privileges as any other white person. In school, judging by the classes I was placed in, I was identified as part of a minority group by the administration. My first instinct, due to my strong sense of Mexican identity, was to associate with the Chicano group living across town in East Austin, even though they were clearly inclined to reject me. To them, I was merely a *mojada*, a wetback from the other side of the border.

In her discussion on the politics of the bicultural experience in the United States, Darder (1995) notes that "biculturalism must be understood as a contested terrain of difference [that] acknowledges openly and engages forthrightly the significance of power relations in structuring and prescribing societal definitions of truth, rules of normalcy, and notions of legitimacy which often denigrate the cultural existence and lived experience of subordinate groups" (2). This approach, according to the author, requires a rethinking of the concept of identity formation in terms of its function as a liberatory process, a means to challenge the status quo.

Various scholars have written about this experience. In his essay on multicultural identities, Yep (1998) discusses identity negotiation as an empowering strategy that allows one to re-assign meaning to labels and resist having one's identity "frozen" into place. Moreover, "negotiating from the cultural margins can allow us to see things both from the center and the margins—a perspective that those who attempt to prescribe labels to us simply do not have" (83). Lugones (1994) engages in a metaphorical disclosure, which compares her identity as *mestiza* to the separation of the egg from the white. She argues that *mestizage* comes from a process of curdling (like the curdling of the egg) that requires resisting the logic of purity, one which forces one to either separate completely or become unified with dominant culture. According to this author, the invisible and oppressive logic of purity creates a dichotomy between the pure and the impure, and between unity and fragmentation.

Understanding Rosaldo's (1993) notion of invisible and visible cultures is central to understanding the complexity of both Yep's (1998) and Lugones' (1994) insights. Rosaldo argues that traditional anthropology, which informs much of our understanding of culture today, considers that to be seen and understood culture must be static and fixed. Those "blurred zones within a culture and the zones between cultures are endowed by the norms with a curious kind of hybrid invisibility" (199). Within this framework, biculturalism becomes a form of active resistance to a dominant logic that either a) renders one invisible through the process (and illusion) of assimilation; b) makes one visible by identifying one's culture as nothing more than an authentic ornament; or c) allows one to maintain both cultures, which are of necessity fragmented or split (Lugones, 1994). Thus, as the author notes, new conceptualizations are needed that would give "solution to the problem of walking from one of one's groups to another, being mistreated, misunderstood, [and] engaging in self-abuse and self-betrayal for the sake of the group that only distorts our needs, because they erase our complexity" (473). From this perspective, the concept of biculturalism, also referred to as "marginality" by Yep (1997) or *mestizage* by Lugones (1994), is associated with a process that constantly defies any attempt to structure people and groups. This is logic that conceptualizes communication as an "act of creative social defiance" (Lugones 1994, 479).

The political approach discussed here takes me beyond my immediate experience of arriving to the United States from Mexico, to a more pro-active sense of self: a way to claim my cultural experience as legitimate and put it to use. Nonetheless, because it is framed within a national context centered on U.S. cultural politics—which, according to Darder (1995), defines biculturalism as experienced primarily by people of color—I often find it difficult to interpret some of my bicultural and transnational experiences from within this framework. Interpreting my more recent travels to Mexico as well as many other Latin American countries has become quite a challenge. How, for instance, might I begin to understand my experience as a *gringa* in Mexico after being identified as or identifying myself as white, Hispanic, and Latina in the United States? How can I begin to discern my role in my previous job as a liaison between Latin Americans, Western Europeans, and U.S. Americans? These are some of the questions that have driven me to explore the concept of hybridization.

Hybrid Identities and Fourth World Peoples[3]

The increase in processes of hybridization makes it evident that we understand very little about power. . . . Hybridization would not function if it were exercises only by bourgeoisie over proletarians, whites over indigenous people, parents over children. . . . Since all of these relations are interwoven with each other, each one achieves an effectiveness that it would never be able to by itself. But it is not simply a question of some forms of domination being superimposed on others and thereby being strengthened. What gives them their efficacy is the obliqueness that is established in the fabric. How can we discern where ethnic power ends and family power begins. . . . ? What is most important is the shrewdness with which the cables are mixed, and secret orders passed and responded to affirmatively. (Garcia Canclini 1996, 259)

At about the time that I finally started to acknowledge my bicultural experience as a unique and powerful place to be, and became comfortable with my identity for the first time in my life, I both was placed in and placed myself in a position that would once again disrupt my apple cart. My experience working in a non-profit international organization became key to further inquiry about the role of power in intercultural communication. It was evident from my previous experiences that, on some level, issues of power and dominance colored my view of my place in the world. But now, the complexity involved in intercultural power relations was blaring in my ears on a consistent basis. In many ways, my role as development director for the newly formed Latin American division was one of power broker. My job entailed building programs to ensure financial self-sufficiency for five offices concurrently dependent on the organization's U.S. American and Western European programs. Central to this strategy was creating a funding base that would allow the new Latin American offices to have a say, not just in determining their own course of action but also in the strategies to be implemented in the interest of the organization as a whole.

Much of what is considered when looking at intercultural communication processes within any given society today, is the role of economic and political globalization. When developing strategies to improve intercultural relations, one must take into account that the very same structures that oppress are often those also providing benefits, particularly if we understand economic and political globalization as a continuation of modernization and colonization processes (Featherstone 1995). In the case of the environmental organization where I worked, these were the very forces that had brought individuals from various cultures together, with different perspectives and ways of tackling problems. When I look back on my role in the coming together of diverse cultures, in this case with the specific task of crafting effective fundraising strategies in Latin America, I must also consider my identity in relation to these social forces.

Hybridization is a social process best understood in relation to the effects of globalization. Featherstone (1995) describes this process as two simultaneous images of culture. The first image is that of one dominant culture extending itself outward, homogenizing the diverse cultures with which it comes into contact. The second image is one of compression, whereby diverse cultures are brought together in no coherent fashion, resulting in a more complex interactive dynamic. Featherstone (1995) and Garcia Canclini (1996) also suggest that as a result of the process of modernization, traditionally associated with colonial and imperialistic social and economic processes, cultural goods that were originally controlled by the elite are now also accessed by diverse cultural groups and social classes. This dynamic is generated by increased border crossings both geographically and conceptually, and it creates a certain level of disarray resulting in "the shifting global balance of power away from the West, with more voices talking back to the West" (Featherstone 1995, 10). In other words, the power dynamics once so clearly delineated by assimilationist strategies are no longer feasible. More and more people are of mixed identities living in a social context whereby the notion of nation and culture can no longer provide the steady reign it once did.

In a sense, those with experience living in undefined spaces—usually relegated to the margins—eventually gain an upper hand. This is not to suggest that the power imbalance is not still severely skewed, with most resources in the hands of a few elite groups. It does, however, point to certain overlapping spaces that emerge, ironically, as a result of colonizing and modernizing efforts. In his satirical attempt to articulate a borderless utopia, Gómez-Peña (1996) describes "Fourth World" peoples as those who live within this hybrid reality and resist the "Third World/First World dichotomy" (7). It is a borderless space where immigrants and indigenous peoples come together to compose the dominant culture, making those who resist hybridity part of a new minority. Further "there is little space for static identities, fixed nationalities, 'pure' languages, or sacred cultural traditions" (7).

The contradictions that emerge from a mingling of Featherstone's (1995) two images of culture homogenization and unorganized juxtaposition. . . represent a tension between cultural maintenance and cultural change on a number of levels. From the perspective of the dominant group, assimilation is necessary in order to maintain certain norms that ensure stability and as a result maintain this group's original place in the power structure. It reflects a resistance to any change—good or bad—that new and "different" cultures bring with them. In my previous job, the incorporation of Latin Americans into the organization, as well as efforts to diversify the U.S. organization, was experienced by many Europeans and European Americans as a serious threat to the maintenance of the organization's original strategies. In fact, though it was often acknowledged that "good ideas" came from new perspectives (new to the Eurocentric organization, that is), these were often discussed as threatening the maintenance of the organization's "core values." For many Latin Americans, adopting strategies that had come from Europe and the United States was often seen as a cultural imposition, or as part of becoming modern and acquiring certain privilege, or as both.

If we were to consider the organization I worked with as a microcosm of a broader social dynamic, as expressed by the notion of hybridization, then we must conceptualize power as something that is continually being reorganized and constantly shifting (Featherstone 1995; Canclini 1996). As one of the supervisory staff for the Latin American division, funded by monies controlled largely by its Western European offices, I was in a situation that often involved a conflict of interests. I was responsible for obtaining funds from the European-based international organization in order to disburse them to the Latin American offices. From this position, and as a member of both groups, I was able to observe constant power plays that emerged from both places. Although dominance was exercised most often by my European counterparts (both

blatantly and invisibly), I also observed how power was wielded quite often and sometimes much more effectively by the Latin American staff. The capacity to develop sophisticated strategies in response to complex social dynamics presented by globalization processes typically gave my Latin American counterparts an edge over the European group. It is here that Gómez-Peña's (1996) imaginary world becomes real, if only for a few moments. In fact, from my experience, it was precisely when the Latin American staff conceived of themselves as part of a hybrid, Fourth World reality that they were able to situate themselves firmly as an integral part of the international organization. Unfortunately, in times of crisis, usually involving funding or territorial decisions, both groups tended to fall into what Gómez-Peña refers to as the old "Third World/ First World dichotomy."

How I managed my own position of power in relation to both groups was a source of significant tension, which I had to come to terms with on a regular basis. My interests were strongly with the Latin American division, primarily because I thought this perspective represented the best interests of the entire organization. However, there were times when my Latin American counterparts associated me instead with the dominant power structure (the Europeans) because I was capable of working also within that particular logic, and thus I was often called upon to represent the region in various functions. On the one hand, I was often seen as part of the problem by my European counterparts, particularly when we challenged some of their assumptions that stemmed from a logic outside of their realm of understanding, or simply because they did not agree. At other times, in the height of tension, particularly when it came time to make difficult funding decisions, I was caught right in the middle of the power struggle and became a scapegoat for both groups.

Rather than viewing intercultural communication as either a process of assimilation with, or resistance to the dominant culture, the hybrid model considers that both processes are actually intertwined. This approach allows us to consider our individual involvement in the daily struggle for power and social change. That is, we cannot get away from using the dominant logic even when our aim is to resist it. For instance, just because I cannot come to terms with belonging to one single national culture does not mean that I don't end up presenting myself as a member of one particular group. I often wonder whether accepting a monocultural label isn't simply a lazy alternative to stumbling around to find language that can express my complex and often ambiguous cultural identity. But the fact that I often fall prey to these confining conceptual frameworks is illustrative of just how intermingled the process of assimilation and resistance have become. For example, identifying myself as an *American, a Norte Americano,* or a *Gringa,* even though I don't necessarily agree with what these labels represent, often means I must acknowledge and be mindful of the privileges that come with that label. Not challenging the label *Mexican, wetback, Chicana,* or *Latina,* even though I cannot "legitimately" claim either by birth-right or by blood line, sometimes means experiencing a minority status and other times means claiming a unique way of knowing that might not otherwise be acknowledged. My ability to operate in these undefined spaces is both powerful and dangerous. While I am often confronted with the problem of not belonging to any group at all, I have at the same time, the "legitimacy" to speak within or for more than one group. And, as Alcoff (1995) notes, this is a tremendous responsibility that entails understanding the nature of my location and positionality every time I engage in discourse.

Conclusion

The three perspectives of the bicultural experience discussed here differ significantly in terms of the way they conceptualize identity, culture, and power. The first, the socio-psychological approach, tends to describe culture and identity as relatively static and clearly definable spaces. This approach implicitly assumes that minority cultures are necessarily in a disadvantaged position of power. The concept of biculturalism becomes a means to equalize that power imbalance while maintaining a certain loyalty to one's original roots. The second genre, the resistance approach, describes power as being wielded invisibly by the norms of the dominant system. New strategies entail changing the rules of the game in order that oppressed groups may become empowered. The third approach, or hybridization, is similar to the second approach in that it acknowledges the incomplete and fluid nature of culture. It differs in that it calls for a more ambiguous and multidirectional understanding of power. It acknowledges the coming together of two systems that operate with contradictory logic.

These perspectives are all important and essential in transforming intercultural processes. Peoples' lives and situations are in different places and thus warrant a variety of strategies. In certain cases, coping might well be very much of one's reality. In other cases, taking risks to reconfigure the game is possible. As a bicultural person who experiences being in both privileged and subordinate positions of power (as white, *gringa,* Hispanic, Latina, woman, etc.), I am concerned with understanding the multidirectional aspects of power in relation to intercultural communication. In particular, as someone who often carries the privileges (and in many respects the disadvantages) of being associated as white or *Norte-americana,* I must ask how some of the responsibility can be transferred over to the "invisible oppressors." We must continue to ask: What are the conditions in today's intercultural world that make this possible? And in what ways is this not possible?

So, what is the significance of a bicultural/hybrid perspective for the study of intercultural communication in general? First, it suggests that all communication is on some level intercultural. Second, individual identities and thus interpersonal relationships cannot be separated from socio-cultural processes. Third, as a central process in the creation and negotiation of social meaning, communication, regardless of its motive, cannot be isolated from issues of power. From this perspective, intercultural communication is not necessarily about adapting to given sets of norms within specific cultures or contexts, armed with appropriate communicative behavior. Rather, it is about becoming aware of one's dynamic position of power within a larger and more complex transnational social structure. Intercultural communication is intertwined with seriously conflicting ideologies that stem from entirely different experiences and conceptualizations of reality.

We need to acknowledge the need for improvisation, which requires an ability to understand and inquire into the historical power relations between and among cultures as well as to discern the impact of our actions in relation to a rapidly changing transnational world. We need to constantly rethink the relationship between self and other, not necessarily as unified but as complex beings inseparable from the social context (Alcoff 1995; Lugones 1995). And finally, we need to let go of the assumption that oppressed groups will always be either resisting dominant ideology or going along with it (Alcoff 1995; Canclini 1996). Instead, we need to look at how they are instrumental in transforming dominant ideology (Yep 1998).

A bicultural/hybrid perspective allows us to consider the complex, political nature of identities in relation to intercultural communication. From this perspective, culture is no longer just a control device that regulates society (Rosaldo 1993). It is a fluid socio-political space where individuals struggle to make sense out of their own positions of power. Moreover, biculturalism/hybridity is not just experienced by an individual with mixed ethnic, racial, sexual, or gender identities. It is part of a social condition that affects everyone, regardless of their position in the social structure. Intercultural communication is a daily part of our lives, and we must learn to live within the changing social dynamics this represents.

Notes

1. This is an edited version of a paper presented to the La Raza Caucus for the 83rd annual meeting of the National Communication Association in Chicago, Illinois, in November 1997. The original title, *Bridging Disparate Realities: Understanding Intercultural Communication From a Bicultural/Hybrid Perspective,* has been modified to reflect the changes made to this essay which emphasize personal experience. I have chosen to present the concepts *bicultural* and *hybrid* together as they reflect my process of exploring the possibilities of both. I thank two individuals in particular who contributed deeply to the thinking and the writing involved in this essay. Tani Adams, a dear friend and mentor, first brought the concept of biculturalism to my attention and helped me "see" the power of such an experience. Gust Yep, my professor and mentor at San Francisco State University, inspired me to explore these experiences further. He has guided me to place them within a theoretical framework. He also encouraged me to submit this paper to the 1997 NCA competitive papers panel. I also thank Jennifer Willis for her helpful feedback and support.

2. The concept of *Fourth World* is used to refer to indigenous peoples; to minority groups living in developed countries under Third World conditions; and more generally, to members who live between and across various cultures, communities, and countries. In my discussion, I adopt the latter meaning.

3. I moved from the United States to Mexico with my family at age 3. While that may seem like going back to my home country, for me it was like visiting a foreign country.

References

Alcoff, L. (1995). The problem of speaking for others. In Roof, J. and Wiegman, R., (Eds.), *Who can speak? Authority and critical identity* (97–119). Chicago: University of Illinois Press.

Banks, A. and Banks, S.P. (1995). Cultural identity, resistance and "good theory:" Implications for intercultural communication theory from Gypsy culture. *The Howard Journal of Communications*, 6(39), 146–163.

Blechman, E.A. (1992). Mentors for high-risk youth: From effective communication to bicultural competence. *Journal of Clinical Child Psychology*, 21(2), 160–169.

Brown, L.S. (1989). New voices, new visions: Toward a lesbian/gay paradigm for psychology. *Psychology of Women Quarterly*, 13, 445–458.

Cupach, W.R. and Imahori, T.T. (1993). Identity management theory: Communication competence in intercultural episodes and relationships. In Wiseman, R.L. and Koester, J.,

(Eds.), *Intercultural Communication Competence* (113–247). Newbury Park, CA: Sage.

Darder, A. (1995). The politics of biculturalism: Culture and difference in the formation of warriors of Gringostroika and the new Mestizas. In Darder, A., (Ed.), Culture and difference: Critical perspectives on the bicultural experience in the United States. Westport, CT: Bergin and Garvey.

Featherstone, M. (1995). *Undoing culture: Globalization, postmodernity, and identity.* Thousand Oaks, CA: Sage.

Garcia Canclini, N. (1996). *Hybrid cultures: Strategies for entering and leaving modernity.* Minneapolis: University of Minnesota Press.

Gómez-Peña, G. (1996). *The new world border: Prophesies, poems and loqueras for the end of the century.* San Francisco: City Lights.

Hecht, M.L. (1993). 2002. A research odyssey: Toward the development of a communication theory of identity. *Communication Monographs,* 60(1), 76–82.

LaFramboise, T., Hardin, L.K., Coleman and Gerton, J. (1993). Psychological impact of biculturalism: Evidence and theory. *Psychological Bulletin,* 114(3), 395–412.

Lugones, M. (1994). Purity, impurity, and separation. *signs: Journal of women in culture and society,* 19(21), 458–479.

Olnek, M.R. (1990). The recurring dream: Symbolism and ideology in intercultural and multicultural education. *American Journal of Education,* 147–175.

Rosaldo, R. (1993). *Culture and truth: The remaking of social analysis.* Boston: Beacon.

Yep, G.A. (1998). My three cultures: Navigating the multicultural identity landscape. In Martin, J.N., Nakayama, T.K. and Flores, L., (Eds.), *Readings in Cultural Contexts* (79–85). Mountain View, CA: Mayfield. ✦

Appendices

Suggested Questions for Discussion

Part I: Naming Ourselves

1. In what ways is naming and defining one's ethnicity a political activity?

2. In the U.S., what institutions have the authority to name ethnic populations?

3. What are some arguments for cultural participants/communities naming themselves?

4. What are some characteristics that you associate with the term *American?*

5. What are some arguments for and against populations using the generic term *American?*

6. Rent and view the film *White Man's Burden* (starring John Travolta and Harry Belafonte). How does this film challenge white and black identity?

7. What are some strengths and weaknesses of cultural distinctiveness and cultural uniformity? How does each belief affect the process of communication?

Part II: Negotiating Sexuality and Gender

1. Identify prescriptions for "proper" male communication in cultures with which you are familiar.

2. Identify prescriptions for "proper" female communication in these same cultures.

3. In what ways has Eurocentric patriarchy shaped our view toward men and women of color in the U.S.?

4. What cultural beliefs underlie opposition to women flying combat missions in the U.S. military?

5. What cultural beliefs underlie opposition to ending the ban on gays in the U.S. military?

6. What cultural assumptions about men and women lie behind actions in the Navy Tailhook scandal?

7. Is talk between any male and any female an intercultural interaction?

Part III: Representing Cultural Knowledge in Interpersonal and Mass Media Contexts

1. Some students have described their cultural origins as so distant or forgotten that they are essentially "without a culture." Support or counter this statement.

2. How does your way of speaking reflect a distinct cultural community?

3. How can a mass media outlet, such as radio or TV, maintain and recreate cultural knowledge?

4. Identify a joke or humorous narrative from a cultural community other than your own, and provide a cultural explanation for the (understood) premise of this humor.

5. Rent and view the film *My Family/Mi Familia* (starring Jimmy Smits and Edward James Olmos) and writer-director Li An's *Eat, Drink, Man, Woman.* How do these films present cultural knowledge?

6. What are some salient cultural themes in American media?

7. Cultural values and practices can be self-contradictory. Discuss some contradictions that you have observed in U.S. society.

Part IV: Celebrating Cultures

1. Describe several community celebrations. How do your community celebrations reflect ethnic heritage?

2. How do community celebrations sometimes mask ethnicity and ethnic difference?

3. Talk to members of an ethnic group from two different generations and describe variations in their valuing of ethnic celebrations.

4. Describe an ethnic celebration you have experienced from the point of view of either an "insider" or an "outsider." What difference does this relationship make to the understanding of the celebration?

5. Describe how ordinary objects become special symbols in celebrations.

6. How are celebrations regulated or constrained in society?

7. How does a "national" celebration like the Fourth of July differ from an ethnic celebration like *Kwanzaa?*

Part V: Valuing and Contesting Languages

1. How do ways of speaking connect you to social, professional, ethnic, and other communities?

2. How does language reveal an orientation, or a way of thinking about the world?

3. Select a metaphor or phrase that you commonly use. What knowledge does a person need in order to understand this metaphor or phrase?

4. Think of the terms that you choose to name various ethnic and racial communities. Where do these terms come from? What do your choices say about your knowledge and feelings toward these communities?

5. How is language used to create new ways of thinking about cultural groups?

6. Rent and view the films *Smoke Signals* or *Selena.* What are some examples of cultural expressions that you share or do not share with characters in these films?

7. Should nations or communities have "official" languages?

Part VI: Living in Bicultural Relationships

1. Many times we hear people objecting to interracial friendships and romance. According to them, what is threatened or in danger in these relationships?

2. Rent and view Spike Lee's film *Jungle Fever.* How are you like or unlike the characters in the film? What choices would you make if you were in their situations?

3. How do courses in interpersonal communication prepare students for interracial relationships?

4. Agree or disagree with the following assertion: Business is business, so it doesn't matter how interculturally sensitive or insensitive you are. Make the sale and close the deal.

5. Should social service agencies permit interracial adoptions? Why or why not?

6. If you became the guardian of a child from an ethnic or racial group other than your own, what impact would this have on how you cared for the child?

7. What went through your mind when you assumed that a new friend had a particular sexual orientation and your assumption was wrong?

Part VII: Traversing Cultural Paths

1. In what contexts are the following terms used in ordinary conversation: *foreigner, alien, immigrant, naturalized citizen?* What are some assumptions associated with each term?

2. What expectations do you have when speaking to someone of a different race or culture? Where do these expectations come from?

3. Describe an interaction you have had with someone of a different race or culture.

4. Interpret and discuss the notion of "cultural differences."

5. Define the term tourist. What is the relationship between the tourist and the cultural native?

6. Research the following topic: Exactly what information was given to U.S. military personnel about the Middle East during the Gulf War? How did this in-

formation facilitate or hinder intercultural communication?

7. Research the information given to U.S. military personnel about Somalia dur-
ing recent relief efforts there. Compare this information with that given about the Middle East. Account for the differences in approach. ✦

Supplementary Readings

Part I: Naming Ourselves

Altorki, S. and El-Solh, C.F. (Eds.). (1988). *Arab women in the field: Studying your own society.* Syracuse, NY: Syracuse University Press.

Anderson, M.L., and Collins, P.H. (Eds.). (1995). *Race, class, and gender: An anthology.* (2nd Ed.). Belmont, CA: Wadsworth.

Anzaldúa, G. (1987). *Borderlands/La Frontera: The new Mestiza.* San Francisco, CA: Spinsters/Aunt Lute.

Bammer, A. (1994). *Displacements: Cultural identities in question.* Bloomington: Indiana University Press.

Beck, P.V., and Walters, A.L. (1988). *The sacred: Ways of knowledge, sources of life.* Tsalie, AZ: Navajo Community College Press.

Chan, A.B. (1984). Born again Asian: The making of a new literature. *Journal of Ethnic Studies, 11,* 57–73.

Chan, S. (1991). *Asian Americans: An interpretive history.* Boston, MA: Twayne.

Chow, R. (1991). *Woman and Chinese modernity.* Minneapolis: University of Minnesota Press.

Collins, C.A., and Clark, J.E. (1992). A structural narrative analysis of *Nightline's* 'This Week in the Holy Land.' *Critical Studies in Mass Communication, 9,* 25–43.

Daniels, R. (1988). *Asian America.* Seattle: University of Washington Press.

Fessler, L. W. (1985). *Chinese in America: Stereotyped past, changing present.* New York: Vantage.

Flores, J. and Yudice, G. (1990). Living borders/*buscando* America: Languages of Latino self-formation. *Social Text, 8,* 57–84.

González, A. (1990). Mexican 'otherness' in the rhetoric of Mexican Americans. *Southern Communication Journal, 55,* 276–291.

Hammerback, J.C., and Jensen, R.J. (1994). Ethnic heritage as rhetorical legacy: The plan of Delano. *Quarterly Journal of Speech, 80,* 53–70.

Hobson, G. (Ed.). (1979). *The remembered earth: An anthology of contemporary Native American literature.* Albuquerque, NM: Red Earth.

Hoskins, L.A. (1992). Eurocentrism vs. Afrocentrism: Age of political linkage analysis. *Journal of Black Studies, 23,* 247–257.

Hourani, A.H. (1991). A history of the Arab peoples. Cambridge, MA: Harvard University Press.

Keefe, S.E., and Padilla, A.M. (1987). *Chicano ethnicity.* Albuquerque: University of New Mexico Press.

Lincoln, K. (1983). *Native American renaissance.* Berkeley: University of California Press.

Ling, A. (1990). *Between worlds: Women writers of Chinese ancestry.* New York: Pergamon.

Mails, T. (1992). *The Cherokee people: The story of the Cherokees from earliest origins to contemporary times.* Tulsa, OK: Council Oaks.

Momaday, N.S. (1976). *The names: A memoir.* Tucson: University of Arizona Press.

Oboler, S. (1995). *Ethnic labels, Latino lives: Identity and the politics of (re)presentation in the United States.* Minneapolis: University of Minnesota Press.

Ogawa, D. (1971). *From Japs to Japanese: The evolution of Japanese-American stereotypes.* Berkeley, CA: McCutchan.

Omi, M. and Winant, H. (1986). *Racial formation in the United States.* New York: Routledge and Kegan Paul.

Padilla, F.M. (1985). *Latino ethnic consciousness.* South Bend, IN: University of Notre Dame Press.

Riley, P. (1993). *Growing up Native American: An anthology.* New York: Morrow.

Rotberg, R.I. (Ed.). (1978). *The mixing of peoples: Problems of identification and ethnicity.* New York: Greylock.

Sedano, M.V. (1980). Chicanismo: *A rhetorical analysis of themes and images of selected poetry from the Chicano movement. Western Journal of Speech Communication, 44,* 170–190.

Shorris, E. (1992). *Latinos: A biography of the people.* New York: Norton.

Takaki, R. (1989). *Strangers from a different shore.* Boston, MA: Little, Brown.

Trinh, T.M. (1989). *Woman, native, other.* Bloomington: Indiana University Press.

Tsai, S.H. (1986). *The Chinese experience in America.* Bloomington: Indiana University Press.

West, B.A. (1992). Women's diaries as ethnographic resources. *Journal of Narrative and Life History, 2,* 333–354.

Part II: Negotiating Sexuality and Gender

Allen, P.G. (1986). *The sacred hoop: Recovering the feminine in American Indian traditions.* Boston, MA: Beacon.

Anzaldúa, G. (Ed.). (1990). Making face, making soul. In Haciendo Caras: *Creative and critical perspectives by women of color.* San Francisco, CA: Aunt Lute.

Belenky, M.F., Clinchy, B.M., Goldberger, N.R. and Tarule, J.M. (1986). *Women's ways of knowing: The development of self, voice, and mind.* New York: Basic.

Bell-Scott, P., Guy-Sheftall, B., Jones-Royster, J., Sims-Wood, J., DeCosta-Willis, M. and Fultz, L. (1991). *Double stitch: Black women write about mothers and daughters.* Boston, MA: Beacon.

Carter, K. (1992). Disrupting identity: Feminist reflections on women and difference(s). *World Communication, 21,* 13–21.

Carter, K., and Spitzack, C. (1990). Formation and empowerment in gender and communication courses. *Women's Studies in Communication, 13,* 92–110.

Cisneros, S. (1991). *Woman Hollering Creek and other stories.* New York: Random House.

Christian, B. (1985). *Black feminist criticism.* New York: Pergamon.

Doucet, S.A. (1989). Cajun music: Songs and psyche. *Journal of Popular Culture, 23,* 89–99.

Fitch, K.L. (1991). The interplay of linguistic universals and cultural knowledge in personal address: Colombian *madre* terms. *Communication Monographs, 58,* 254–272.

Foss, K.A. and Foss, S.J. (1991). *Women speak: The eloquence of women's lives.* Prospect Heights, IL: Waveland.

Frankenberg, R. (1993). *White women, race matters: The social construction of whiteness.* Mnneapolis: University of Minnesota Press.

Gay Men's Oral History Group (1989). *Walking after midnight: Gay men's life stories.* London: Routledge.

hooks, b. (1981). *Ain't I a woman: Black women and feminism.* Boston, MA: South End.

hooks, b. (1990). *Yearning: Race, gender, and cultural politics.* Boston, MA: South End.

Houston Stanback, M. (1985). Language and black women's place: Evidence from the black middle class. In Treichler, P.A., Kramarae, C. and Stafford, B. (Eds.), *For alma mater: Theory and practice in feminist scholarship (177–193).* Urbana: University of Illinois Press.

Johnson, F.L. (1989). Women's culture and communication: An analytical perspective. In

Lont, C.M. and Friedley, S.A. (Eds.), *Beyond boundaries: Sex and gender diversity in communication (301–316).* Fairfax, VA: George Mason University Press.

Lesbian Oral History Group. (1989). *Inventing ourselves: Lesbian life stories.* London: Routledge.

Lim, S.G. and Tsutakawa, M. (Eds.). (1989). *The forbidden stitch: An Asian American women's anthology.* Corvallis, OR: Calyx.

Martin, E. (1987). *The woman in the body.* Boston, MA: Beacon.

Perlmutter Bowen, S. and Wyatt, N. (1993). *Transforming visions: Feminist critiques in communication studies.* Cresskill, NJ: Hampton.

Pharr, S. (1988). *Homophobia: A weapon of sexism.* Little Rock, AR: The Women's Project.

Rao, S. (1993). Nature and oral women in India: Reconstituting social knowledge. *Howard Journal of Communications, 4,* 329–341.

Reese, D. (1996). Covering and communication: The symbolism of dress among Muslim women. *Howard Journal of Communications, 7,* 35–52.

Steihm, E. (Ed.). (1984). *Women's views of the political world of men.* Dobbs Ferry, NY: Transnational.

Trujillo, N. (1991). Hegemonic masculinity on the mound: Media representations of Nolan Ryan and American sports culture. *Critical Studies in Mass Communication, 8,* 290–308.

Valdivia, A.N. (Ed.). (1995). *Feminism, multiculturalism, and the media: Global diversities.* Thousand Oaks, CA: Sage.

Part III: Representing Cultural Knowledge in Interpersonal and Mass Media Contexts

Allen, P.G. (Ed.). (1983). *Studies in American Indian literatures: Critical essays and course designs.* New York: Modern Language Association of America.

Asante, M.K. (1990). The tradition of advocacy in the Yoruba courts. *Southern Communication Journal, 55,* 250–259.

Balsamo, A. (1996). *Technologies of the gendered body: Reading cyborg women.* Durham, NC: Duke University Press.

Basso, K.H. (1979). *Portraits of 'the whiteman': Linguistic play and cultural symbols among the Western Apache.* Cambridge, MA: Cambridge University Press.

Chen, V. (1990/1991). *Mien Tze* at the Chinese dinner table: A study of the interactional accomplishment of 'face.' *Research on Language and Social Interaction, 24,* 109–140.

Conquergood, D. (1992). Life in big red: Struggles and accommodations in a Chicago polyethnic tenement. In Lamphere, L. (Ed.), *Structuring diversity: Ethnographic perspectives on the new immigration (95–144).* Chicago, IL: University of Chicago Press.

Conquergood, D. (1994). Homeboys and hoods: Gang communication and cultural space. In Frey, L.R. (Ed.), *Group communication in context: Studies of natural groups (23–55).* Hillsdale, NJ: Erlbaum.

Engen, D.E. (1995). The making of a people's champion: An analysis of media representations of George Foreman. *Southern Communication Journal,* 60, 141–151.

Garfield, E.P. (1985). *Women's voices from Latin America: Interviews with six contemporary authors.* Detroit, MI: Wayne State University Press.

González, A. and Bradley, C. (1990). Breaking into silence: Technology transfer and mythical knowledge among the Acomas of Nuevo Mexico. In Medhurst, M.J., González, A. and Peterson, T.R. (Eds.), *Communication and the culture of technology (63–76).* Pullman: Washington State University Press.

Gray, H. (1989). Television, Black Americans, and the American dream. *Critical Studies in Mass Communication,* 6, 376–386.

Haraway, D.J. (1991). *Simians, cyborgs, and women: The reinvention of nature.* New York: Routledge.

Katriel, T. (1986). *Talking straight: Dugri speech in Israeli Sabra culture.* Cambridge, MA: Cambridge University Press.

Katriel, T. (1987). Rhetoric in flames: Fire inscriptions in Israeli youth movement ceremonials. *Quarterly Journal of Speech,* 73, 444–459.

Kim, M.S. (1992). A comparative analysis of nonverbal expressions as portrayed by Korean and American print-media advertising. *Howard Journal of Communications,* 3, 317–339.

Kroker, A. and Kroker M. (Eds.). (1997). *Digital delirium.* New York: St. Martin's.

Lake, R.A. (1991). Between myth and history: Enacting time in Native American protest rhetoric. *Quarterly Journal of Speech,* 77, 123–151.

Larson, J.F., McAnany, E.G. and Storey, J.D. (1986). News of Latin America on network television, 1972–1981: A northern perspective on the Southern Hemisphere. *Critical Studies in Mass Communication,* 3, 169–183.

Lewels, F.L., Jr. (1974). *The uses of the media by the Chicano movement: A study in minority access.* New York: Praeger.

Lopez, B. (1977). *Giving birth to Thunder, sleeping with his daughter: Coyote builds North America.* New York: Avon.

Loza, S. (1993). *Barrio rhythm: Mexican American music in Los Angeles.* Urbana: University of Illinois Press.

Mayerle, J. (1987). A dream deferred: The failed fantasy of Norman Lear's *a.k.a. Pablo. Central States Speech Journal,* 38, 223–239.

Merskin, D. (1998). Sending up signals: A survey of Native American media use and representation in the mass media. *Howard Journal of Communications,* 9, 333–345.

Morris, R., and Wander, P. (1990). Native American rhetoric: Dancing in the shadows of the ghost dance. *Quarterly Journal of Speech,* 76, 164–191.

Mulvaney, B.M. (1990). Popular art as rhetorical artifact: The case of Reggae music. In Thomas, S. (Ed.), *Communication and culture: Language performance, technology, and media (117–127).* Norwood, NJ: Ablex.

Novek, E.M. (1995). Buried treasure: The community newspaper as an empowerment strategy for African American high school students. *Howard Journal of Communications,* 6, 69–88.

Orbe, M.P. (1994). 'Remember, it's always whites' ball': Descriptions of African American male communication. *Communication Quarterly,* 42, 287–300.

Owens, L. (1992). *Other destinies: Understanding the American Indian novel.* Norman: University of Oklahoma Press.

Ruoff, A.L.B. (1990). *American Indian literatures: An introduction, bibliographic review, and selected bibliography.* New York: Modern Language Association of America.

Strate, L. (1999). The varieties of cyberspace: Problems in definition and delimitation. *Western Journal of Communication,* 63, 382–412.

Trafzer, C. (1993). *Earth song, sky spirit: An anthology of Native American fiction.* New York: Doubleday.

Tucker, L.R. and Shah, H. (1992). Race and the transformation of culture: The making of the television mini-series *Roots. Critical Studies in Mass Communication,* 9, 325–336.

Part IV: Celebrating Cultures

Beatty, J. (1974). Chinese new year and lion dance. *Papers in Anthropology,* 15, 102–116.

Bowers, D.L. (1995). A place to stand: African Americans and the First of August platform. *Southern Communication Journal*, 60, 348–361.

Copage, E.V. (1991). Kwanzaa: *A celebration of culture and cooking*. New York: Morrow.

Gravely, W.B. (1982). The dialectic of double-consciousness in black freedom celebrations, 1808–1863. *Journal of Negro History*, 67, 302–313.

Helweg, A.W., and Helweg, U.M. (1990). *An immigrant success story: East Indians in America*. Philadelphia: University of Pennsylvania Press.

Huang, S. (1991). Chinese traditional festivals. *Journal of Popular Culture*, 25, 163–180.

Karenga, M. (1989). *The African American holiday of* Kwanzaa: *A celebration of family, community and culture*. Los Angeles, CA: University of Sankore Press.

Opoku, A.A. (1970). *Festivals of Ghana*. Accra: Ghana Publishing Corporation.

Peña, M.H. (1985). *The Texas-Mexican conjunto: History of a working-class music*. Austin: University of Texas Press.

Saran, P. and Rames, E. (Eds.). (1985). *The new ethnics: Asian Indians in the United States*. New York: Praeger.

Saso, M. (1965). The Chinese new year festival. *Journal of the China Society*, 5, 37–52.

Sellman, J. (1982). From myth to festival: A structural analysis of the Chinese new year celebration. *Chinese Culture*, 23, 41–58.

Women of South Asian Collective. (Eds). (1993). *Our feet walk the sky: Women of South Asian diaspora*. San Francisco, CA: Aunt Lute.

Part V: Valuing and Contesting Languages

Cargile, A.C. (1998). Meanings and modes of friendship: Verbal descriptions by native Japanese. *Howard Journal of Communications*, 9, 347–370.

Gilroy, P. (1991). *"There ain't no black in the Union Jack": The cultural politics of race and nation*. Chicago, IL: University of Chicago Press.

Gómez-Peña, G. (1993). *Warrior for Gringostroika*. St. Paul, MN: Graywolf.

Orbe, M.P. (1998). Constructions of reality on MTV's *The Real World*: An analysis of the restrictive coding of black masculinity. *Southern Communication Journal*, 64, 32–47.

Smith, C.A. (Ed.). (1998). Race and communication in America. *Southern Communication Journal*, 63. [This special issue contains six articles that explore various historical and contemporary speeches and arguments on the U.S. racial experience.]

Sunwolf, A. (1999). The pedagogical and persuasive effects of Native American lesson stories: Sufi Wisdom Tales, and African Dilemma Tales. *Howard Journal of Communications*, 10, 47–71.

Whaley, B.B., Nicotera, A.M. and Samter, W. (1998). African American women's perception of rebuttal analogy: Judgments concerning politeness, likability, and ethics. *Southern Communication Journal*, 64, 48–58.

Willis, J.L. (1997). "Latino Night": Performances of Latino/a culture in Northwest Ohio. *Communication Quarterly*, 45, 335–354.

Part VI: Living in Bicultural Relationships

Fong-Torres, B. (1994). *The rice room: Growing up Chinese-American from number two son to rock 'n' roll*. New York: Penguin.

Hamamoto, D.Y. (1994). *Monitored peril*. Minneapolis: University of Minnesota Press.

Moraga, C. and Anzaldúa, G. (Eds.). (1983). *This bridge called my back: Writings by radical women of color*. New York: Kitchen Table/Women of Color Press.

Mura, D. (1991). *Turning Japanese: Memoirs of a sansei*. New York: Anchor.

O'Hearn, C.C. (1998). *Half and half: Writers on growing up biracial and bicultural*. New York: Pantheon.

Posadas, B.M. (1989). *Mestiza girlhood: Interracial families in Chicago's Filipino American community since 1925*. In Asian Women United of California (Ed.), *Making waves: An anthology of writings by and about Asian American women (273–282)*. Boston, MA: Beacon.

Root, M.P.P. (1992). *Racially mixed people in America*. Newbury Park, CA: Sage.

Root, M.P.P. (1994). *Racially mixed people in the new millenium*. Newbury Park, CA: Sage.

Part VII: Traversing Cultural Paths

Alexander, A.F., Cronen, V.E., Kang, K.W., Tsou, B. and Banks, J. (1986). Patterns of topic sequencing and information gain: A comparative analysis of relationship development in Chinese and American cultures. *Communication Quarterly*, 34, 66–78.

Althen, G. (1992). The Americans have to say everything. *Communication Quarterly*, 40, 413–421.

Anderson, T. (1992). Comparative experience factor among Black, Asian, and Hispanic Americans: Coalitions or conflicts? *Journal of Black Studies*, 23, 27–38

Behar, R. (1993). Translated woman: Crossing the border with Esperanza's story. Boston, MA: Beacon.

Bruner, E. (Ed.). (1984). *Text, play, and story: The construction and reconstruction of self and society.* Washington, DC: American Ethnological Society.

Chesebro, J.W. (1982). Illness as a rhetorical act: A cross-cultural perspective. *Communication Quarterly, 30,* 321–331.

Churchill, W. (1992). *Fantasies of the master race: Literature, cinema, and the colonization of American Indians.* (Jaimes, M.A., Ed.). Monroe, ME: Common Courage Press.

Clifford, J. (1997). *Routes: Travel and translation in the late twentieth century.* Cambridge, MA: Harvard University Press.

Essed, P. (1991). *Understanding everyday racism: An interdisciplinary theory.* Newbury Park, CA: Sage.

Gómez-Peña, G. (1996). *The new world border: Prophesies, poems, and loqueras for the end of the century.* San Francisco, CA: City Lights.

González, A. (1989). Participation at WMEX-FM: Interventional rhetoric of Ohio Mexican Americans. *Western Journal of Speech Communication, 53,* 398–410.

Jaimes, M.A. (Ed.). (1992). *The state of Native America: Genocide, colonization, and resistance.* Boston, MA: South End.

Kang, K.W. and Pearce, W.B. (1984). The place of transcultural concepts in communication theory and research, with a case study of reticence. *Communication, 9,* 79–96.

Kim, E.H. (1982). *Asian American literature: An introduction to the writings and their social context.* Philadelphia, PA: Temple University Press.

Leonard, R., and Locke D.C. (1993). Communication stereotypes: Is interracial communication possible? *Journal of Black Studies, 23,* 332–343.

Leroux, N. (1991). Frederick Douglass and the attention shift. *Rhetoric Society Quarterly, 21,* 36–46.

Limón, J.E. (1998). *American encounters: Greater Mexico, the United States, and erotics of culture.* Boston, MA: Beacon.

Lum, C.M.K. (1996). *In search of a voice: Karaoke and the construction of identity in Chinese America.* Mahwah, NJ: Erlbaum.

Marsella, A.J., DeVos, G. and Hsu, F.L.K. (Eds.). (1985). *Culture and self: Asian and Western perspectives.* New York: Tavistock.

Momaday, N.S. (1966). *House made of dawn.* New York: Harper and Row. (Reprint by Perennial Library, 1989)

Penfield, J., and Omstein-Garcia, J.L. (1985). *Chicano English: An ethnic contact dialect.* Philadelphia, PA: Benjamins.

Philips. S.U. (1983). *The invisible culture: Communication in classroom and community on the Warm Springs Indian Reservation.* Prospect Heights, IL: Waveland.

Philipsen, G. (1992). *Speaking culturally: Explorations in social communication.* Albany: State University of New York Press.

van Dijk, T.A. (1987). *Communicating racism: Ethnic prejudice in thought and talk.* Newbury Park, CA: Sage.

West, C. (1993). *Race matters.* Boston, MA: Beacon.

Zaharna, R.S. (1991). The ontological function of interpersonal communication: A cross-cultural analysis of Americans and Palestinians. *Howard Journal of Communications, 3,* 87–98. ✦

About the Contributors

Brenda J. Allen (Ph.D., Howard University) teaches in the Department of Communication at the University of Colorado in Boulder. Her primary area of study is organizational communication with an emphasis on computer-mediated communication technology and race, ethnicity, and gender. Her work has been published in the *Journal of Applied Communication Research*, the *Southern Journal of Communication*, and *Sex Roles*.

Sheryl Perlmutter Bowen (Ph.D., University of Massachusetts) teaches communication and women's studies at Villanova University. She has coedited *Transforming Visions: Feminist Critiques in Communication Studies* (Hampton Press 1993), and has written and worked extensively in the area of HIV/AIDS education and prevention among college students and urban African Americans. She is currently involved in research on the narratives of Holocaust survivors.

Detine L. Bowers (Ph.D., Purdue University) has served on the Communication Studies faculty of Virginia Polytechnic Institute. Her communication scholarship has focused on the speeches of African American rhetoric. She is now the founder and facilitator of Harmony Blessings, Inc., and the William A. Thomas Harmony Center Project. Harmony Center is located at 308 Chowning Place, Blacksburg, VA 24060.

Merry C. Buchanan (A.B.D., University of Oklahoma) teaches at University of Oklahoma and University of Central Oklahoma. Her interests include communication research in intercultural, relational, and instructional communication. She has conducted extensive field work on the Osage Indian reservation and is co-author of several ethnographies of Osage Indian communicative behavior.

Aimee M. Carrillo Rowe is a doctoral candidate in speech communication and part-time lecturer in Women Studies at the University of Washington. She is currently writing her dissertation on feminist alliances in the academy, based on interviews with women from a variety of institutional and cultural backgrounds. Her recent work on whiteness is published in *Communication Theory* and *International Journal of Educational Reform*.

Ling Chen (Ph.D., Ohio State University) teaches at the Hong Kong Baptist University. She has been published in *Gazette, Asian Journal of Communication, Howard Journal of Communications*, and *Speech Communication Association International and Intercultural Communication Annual*. Her major areas of interest include interpersonal communication, intercultural communication, cross-cultural communication (particularly of Chinese culture), and discourse analysis.

Victoria Chen (Ph.D., University of Massachusetts) teaches in the Department of Speech and Communication Studies at San Francisco State University. Her work has appeared in *Research on Language and Social Interaction, International and Intercultural Communication Annual*, and several anthologies. Her research interests include qualitative and systemic analyses of multicultural enmeshment with a focus on Asian American bicultural identity.

Lynda Dee Dixon (Ph.D., University of Oklahoma) is a member of the Oklahoma Cherokee Nation. She has taught at the University of Oklahoma, New Mexico, and Indiana University South Bend and is an associate professor and graduate program coordinator for the School of Communication Studies, Bowling Green. Her publications have examined issues in health communication, gerontology, organizational communication, Oklahoma Indian social problems, and rap music.

Mary Fong (Ph.D., University of Washington) teaches intercultural communication at California State University, San Bernardino. She has been published in *Intercultural Communication: A Reader* (8th edition) by L. Samovar and R. Porter. Her research interests include instructional communication, cultural and intercultural communication, ethnography of communication, and language behavior.

Radhika Gajjala (Ph.D., University of Pittsburgh) teaches in the Department of Interpersonal Communication at Bowling Green State University. She is a member of the Spoon Collective (see http://lists.village.virginia.edu) and comoderator for postcolonial E-mail discussion list. She is also founder of Third-World-Women list, Sa-cyborgs list and Women-Writing-Culture list and has been one of several moderators for SAWNET (South Asian Women's Network) since 1994. Her webpage is http://www.cyberdiva.org. She has published articles in journals such as *Gender and Development*.

Margarita Gangotena (Ph.D., University of Minnesota) teaches at Blinn College in Bryan, Texas. She also is founder and president of Gangotena Consultants and Trainers and of ELADEV, a corporation to promote entrepreneurship among the less privileged. She is a presenter in the areas of health communication, international and intercultural communication, child education, teacher training, problem-solution, and conflict management and negotiation. Dr. Gangotena has taught at the University of Minnesota, Texas A&M University, Central Michigan University, and the University of Houston-Downtown.

Gwendolyn Gong (Ph.D., Purdue University) teaches in the Department of English at the Chinese University of Hong Kong. She edits (with George Braine) the *Asian Journal of English Language Teaching*. She has authored (with Sam Dragga) *Editing: The Design of Rhetoric* (Baywood, 1989), which received the 1990 NCTE Achievement Award for the category of "Best Book of the Year;" *A Writer's Repertoire* (HarperCollins, 1995); and *A Reader's Repertoire* (HarperCollins, 1996).

Alberto González (Ph.D., Ohio State University) teaches interpersonal communication at Bowling Green State University. He has been published in the *Quarterly Journal of Speech*, *Western Journal of Communication*, *Southern Communication Journal*, and else-where. He coedited (with M.J. Medhurst and T.R. Peterson) *Communication and the Culture of Technology* (Washington State University Press, 1990).

Dexter B. Gordon (Ph.D., Indiana University) teaches at the University of Alabama, Tuscaloosa. He has been published in the *Journal of Black Studies*. His interests include rhetoric, social theory, and cultural studies. He seeks to theorize connections between Caribbean and African American communicative cultures.

Janice D. Hamlet (Ph.D., Ohio State University) teaches African American communication and rhetorical criticism in the Department of Speech and Theatre Arts at Shippensburg University and is also the founding director of the ethnic studies program. She has been published in the *Western Journal of Black Studies*, the *Black Studies Journal*, the *Speech Teacher* and several anthologies. She is the editor of *Afrocentric Visions: Studies in Culture and Communication*. Her research interests include rhetorical studies of African American experiences, womanist epistemology and methodology, and intercultural communication.

Tina M. Harris (Ph.D., University of Kentucky) teaches in the Deptartment of Speech Communication at the University of Georgia, Athens. As an assistant professor, she teaches undergraduate courses in the areas of professional communication, interracial communication, intercultural communication, advanced interpersonal communication, romantic and marriage relationships, as well as graduate courses in interracial communication, mentoring and social support, romantic and marriage relationships, and women and communication. As an extension of her teaching, her research interests include race and gender representation in the media, interracial romantic relationships, language and identity issues, and date initiation. Her most recent publications appear in *Encore* and *Women and Language* and explore portrayals of African American females in the cinema.

Mahboub Hashem (Ph.D., Florida State University) teaches communication at Fort Hays State University. He is co-editor of *Fundamentals of Oral Communication: Theory* *and Practice* (with C.B. Crawford, E.L. Krug, C.S. Strokirch, and W.M. Watt; McGraw-Hill, 1995). His research interests are in the areas of interpersonal and intercultural communication.

Radha S. Hegde (Ph.D., Ohio State University) teaches in the Department of Communication at Rutgers University. Her teaching and research interests include race and gender with a specific focus on identity issues among South Asian immigrants and Third World women. Her work has appeared in *Communication Quarterly, Women's Studies in Communication,* and *International and Intercultural Communication Annual.*

Marsha Houston (Ph.D., University of Massachusetts) is a professor and Chair of the Communication Studies Department at the University of Alabama, Tuscaloosa. Her work on African American communi- cation and culture as well as women's language and social interaction has been published in numerous journals and anthol- ogies, including the *Quarterly Journal of Speech, Women's Studies in Communication,* and *Discourse and Society.* She is coeditor of *African American Feminist* and *Womanist Studies in Communication,* a collection of essays forthcoming from Hampton Press.

Navita Cummings James (Ph.D., Ohio State University) teaches communication at the University of South Florida in Tampa and currently serves as director of African Studies. She is also president of the Southern States Communication Association and vice-chair of the Florida Commission on the Status of Women. Her teaching and research interests include cultural diversity, gender, media, technology, and communication.

Diane M. Kimoto (Ph.D., University of Southern California) teaches speech communication at Grand Valley State University. Her research focuses on social interaction (particularly in reference to HIV and AIDS), and the personal and interpersonal dynamics of cultural interactions and relationships.

Elizabeth Lozano (Ph.D., Ohio University) teaches in the Department of Communication at Loyola University in Chicago. Her articles have been published in *Commu-*nication *Theory, Dialogos de la Comunicación, Media Development, Communications,* and other journals on the topics of communication and Pan-American cultures, postmodern literature, aesthetics, and television.

Casey Man Kong Lum (Ph.D., New York University) teaches communication and media studies at William Paterson University and is the author of *In Search of a Voice: Karaoke and the Construction of Identity in Chinese America.* He is the founding Vice President of the Media Ecology Association and formally a Chair of the National Communication Association's International and Intercultural Division and President of the Association for Chinese Communication Studies. His work has also appeared in *Critical Choices in Mass Communication, Mass Communication Research* (in Chinese), *ETC: A Review of General Semantics,* the *Speech Communication Annual,* and a number of other book chapters. His research interests include media ecology, popular culture and communication, and Asian and Asian American media and cultures.

Bishetta D. Merritt (Ph.D., Ohio State University) is Chair of the Department of Radio, Television and Film School of Communications at Howard University. She has served on various committees in the Speech Communication Association. Her articles have been published in the *Journal of Black Studies, Howard Journal of Communications, Journal of Popular Crime,* and *Perspectives of Black Popular Culture.*

Richard Morris (Ph.D., University of Wisconsin-Madison) teaches in the Department of Communication at Arizona State University West. He has authored and edited books and essays concerning cultural communication problems with an emphasis on the communication difficulties that many Native Americans experience. He is Mescalero, Kiowa, and English.

Thomas Nakayama (Ph.D., University of Iowa) teaches rhetoric and public communication in the Department of Communication at Arizona State University. He is currently serving as vice-chair of the Asian/Pacific Islander caucus of the Speech Communication Association. His research interests include rhetorical studies, cultural studies, and intercultural communication.

Charles I. Nero (Ph.D., Indiana University) teaches rhetoric and serves as chair of African American Studies at Bates College. His articles have been published in *Howard Journal of Communications, Journal of Counseling and Development, Brother to Brother: New Writings by Black Gay Men,* and *Law and Sexuality: A Review of Gay and Lesbian Legal Issues.* He has received fellowships from the Ford and Rockefeller Foundations and is currently in residency at the Center for Lesbian and Gay Studies of the City University of New York.

Steven B. Pratt (Ph.D., University of Oklahoma, 1985) is a professor in the Department of Communication at the University of Central Oklahoma. His research interests focus on cultural identification, as well as language and social interaction, with an emphasis on identifying American Indian communicative behaviors. He serves as a traditional and ceremonial leader of the Osage Nation and works extensively with the revitalization of the Osage language.

Sidney A. Ribeau (Ph.D., University of Illinois) is president at Bowling Green State University. He has published numerous articles and chapters and has recently coauthored a book titled *African American Communication.* He has taught courses in intercultural communication, African American culture, and media criticism.

Diana I. Ríos (Ph.D., University of Texas) teaches in the Department of Communication Sciences and the Puerto Rican and Latino Studies Institute, at the University of Rhode Island. She is also the Associate Director of Puerto Rican and Latino Studies at the Institute. She conducts survey and field research on Chicana/o-Latina/o audience utilization of English and Spanish language television, newspapers, and radio as well as reception of domestic and Latin American cinema. Her most recent projects include Puerto Rican heritage audiences and their relationship with media, and older generation women's memories of Golden Age cinema stars. She teaches and publishes in the interdisciplinary areas of mass communication and Latino studies.

Maria Rogers-Pascual is a graduate student in the Department of Speech and Communication Studies at San Francisco State University. Her research focus is in intercultural communication from a critical perspective. Currently she is working on an ethnographic study with an immigrant rights organization, investigating the power relations amongst a culturally diverse group of first and second generation immigrants. She has extensive experience working with international non-profit organizations.

Karla D. Scott (Ph.D., University of Illinois) is a member of the Communication Department at Saint Louis University where she teaches in the area of intercultural communication with a specific focus on issues related to race and gender. In addition to her research on the identity implications of black women's language, she also studies the role of culture in HIV/AIDS prevention education in communities of color. Her articles have been published in *Linguistics and Education, Women and Language,* and *Discourse and Society.*

Charmaine Shutiva (Ph.D., Texas A&M University) is teacher and coordinator at Isleta Elementary School in Isleta Pueblo, New Mexico. She has been published in several journals and chapters on the topic of Native American gifted and talented education and multicultural education and cation and was principal writer for Project Northstar, a 1992 national study investigating the current status of Native American education for the gifted and talented.

Dolores V. Tanno (Ph.D., University of Southern California) teaches intercultural communication and rhetoric at the University of Nevada, Las Vegas. She has been published in *International Journal of Intercultural Relations, Howard Journal of Communications,* and elsewhere. She has also coedited (with A. González) *Politics, Communication and Culture* (1997, Sage), and *Communication and Identity Across Cultures* (1998, Sage).

Eric King Watts (Ph.D., Northwestern University) teaches in the Department of Communication Studies at Wake Forest University. He was trained in rhetorical theory and criticism, and his doctoral dissertation on Hip-Hop culture won an outstanding dissertation award. He has published and presented several papers relating to rap music and African American culture and rhetoric.

Jennifer L. Willis-Rivera (Ph.D., Bowling Green State University) teaches at Southern Illinois University. Her research interests include race and ethnicity, specifically focusing on issues of prejudice and racism. Her ethnography of "Latino Night" at a midwestern tavern was recognized as the 1996 Top Student Paper in the Language and Social Interaction Division of the Speech Communication Association. ✦